The urge to autobiography reveals itself every day in the stories we tell about ourselves. Literary autobiography is the most highly developed form of this universal activity of self-promotion, a kind of writing practised in the west over many centuries. In this major new study of the western tradition, John Sturrock analyses the means by which more than twenty of the greatest literary autobiographers have gone about their task. The book concentrates on the productive tension between the writer's will to singularity and the autobiographical act itself, which restores by conventional and rhetorical means the harmony between the writer and a community of readers. By attending closely and sceptically to the truth-claims made by autobiographers from Augustine through Rousseau and Darwin to Sartre and Michel Leiris, Sturrock establishes some of the deep, hidden continuities of autobiographical writing, and shows how artful and self-conscious this supposedly most sincere of literary genres can be.

THE LANGUAGE OF AUTOBIOGRAPHY

THE LANGUAGE OF AUTOBIOGRAPHY

Studies in the first person singular

JOHN STURROCK

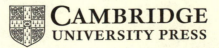

Published by the Press Syndicate of the University of Cambridge
The Pitt Building, Trumpington Street, Cambridge CB2 1RP
40 West 20th Street, New York, NY 10011-4211, USA
10 Stamford Road, Oakleigh, Victoria 3166, Australia

© Cambridge University Press

First published 1993

Printed in Great Britain at the University Press, Cambridge

A catalogue record for this book is available from the British Library

Library of Congress cataloguing in publication data

Sturrock, John.
The language of autobiography: studies in the first person singular / John Sturrock.
p.   cm.
ISBN 0-521-41290-0
1. Autobiography.   1. Title.
CT275.S898A3   1993
808'.06692 – dc20 92–29784 CIP

ISBN 0 521 41290 0 hardback

TAG

For Lucy and Oliver, by way of an epithalamium

Contents

Acknowledgments

The subject of this book has been with me for a dozen years or more, and the writing of it has involved a limited amount of what one of the autobiographers I am concerned with in it typically called 'auto-plagiarism' (this was Vladimir Nabokov). I have here re-used or adapted portions of essays published since the late 1970s in a variety of places and I am grateful for the permission to do so kindly given me by: Professor Ralph Cohen of the University of Virginia, the editor of *New Literary History*; the editors of *Scripsi*, published in the English department of the University of Melbourne; Professor Margaret McGowan and Mr George Craig of the University of Sussex, the editors of the collective volume *Moy qui me voy*; and to Professor Robert Folkenflik, of the University of California, Irvine, and the editors of the Stanford University Press, as the organizer and publishers of a conference on *The Culture of Autobiography* held at Irvine in March 1990, my invitation to speak at which was the clinching incentive to get this book written.

Introduction

But in order to make
you understand, to give
you my life, I must
tell you a story.
    Virginia Woolf, *The Waves*.

Autobiographers give their lives to be understood by others in a dangerously elaborate form. They gather us around them to hear their story confidentially out, yet tell it by a means so strikingly formal as to produce in us a critical reserve complicating if not downright destructive of the intimacy they are inviting. Consider the pathetic instance of Jean-Jacques Rousseau and the manuscript of *Rousseau juge de Jean Jacques*, the three tormented dialogues in which he set out to defend his character against the calumnies of those whom he believed were plotting his ruin. The manuscript complete, its author attempted to deposit a fair copy of it on the high altar of Notre Dame, with an appeal to Providence to keep it safe from his enemies so that it might one day be read and taken to heart by a 'better generation' than his own. But the way in to the choir of the cathedral was locked, and Rousseau confided his manuscript instead to the *abbé* de Condillac, someone whom he thought sufficiently uncorrupt to act as its trustee. Two weeks later Rousseau returned, hoping to find that Condillac had read the Dialogues and been won over by them to the side of their author and of the Truth concerning him. But Condillac was not the ideal reader whom Rousseau had been desperate to find:

Nothing of what I had foreseen occurred. He spoke to me of what I had written as he would have spoken to me about a work of literature which I had asked him to examine so as to tell me his opinion of it. He spoke of the transpositions to be made which would improve the order of the subject-

I

matter; but he said nothing to me about the effect my work had had on him nor of what he thought about its author.[1]

The experience is one which Rousseau had suffered once before, when giving public readings from his *Confessions*: the audience that should have been moved by them, in harmony with his own feelings as their author, had failed lamentably to respond, the literary medium having interposed itself as a fatal barrier to the emotional togetherness he had been craving. And so with Condillac also, the ill-chosen trustee, who receives indifferently as literature what had been offered to him as the anguished justification of a life. It is Rousseau himself who tells the story of his manuscript, and not ironically, in recognition that his actions had been perhaps unreasonable, but self-pityingly, as further evidence that he is the man of virtue and sincerity exiled in a vicious and unfeeling world.

The theorist of autobiography must take on the inhumane role of a Condillac: the autobiographers parade their lives before him one after another, as individuals asking to be understood, but instead of yielding to them passively and in sympathy, the theoretically minded reader counters self-assertion with self-assertion, and conscripts them as illustrations in a rhetorical exposé of his own. A leading question then, appropriate to this liminal moment of my own removal as an author from a social to a textual setting: should we feel bad when we theorize about autobiography? Or, supposing all literary theory to have something unsociable about it, should we feel particularly bad when theorizing about autobiography? My answer, briefly, is yes, we should, we should sense in ourselves a discomfort that is specific to theorizing about autobiography, and is brought on by responding with the wariness of the theorist to a kind of writing which, more than any other, dreams of suppressing the distance between writer and reader.

But this sense of discomfort is not a reason for giving up the theoretical study of autobiography; quite the reverse, it is a feeling around which we might one day make a successful theory of autobiography to turn. For if autobiography does not lend itself comfortably to theorization, this means that it may have something

---

[1] See the 'Histoire du précédent écrit', an addendum to the three Dialogues in which the increasingly paranoid Rousseau describes the need he had felt to preserve them for posterity, so that one day the truth about him might be known. It can be found in Jean-Jacques Rousseau, *Oeuvres complètes*, Tome 1, edited by Bernard Gagnebin, Marcel Raymond and Robert Osmont (Paris, 1959), pp. 977–89.

precious to tell us about the wider question of whether literary theory in general derives its present energy from the theorist's sense of himself as a defaulter from certain ideals of sociability. An auto-biography is a text that seeks to draw us into itself without reservations and one which we are invited to read as being sanctioned by a 'metaphysics of presence', its formal nature being belied by the intimacy and truthfulness with which it seems to address us. In autobiography, if anywhere in literature, we are expected to sense that these are texts inhabited by a living person, that an author who was peculiarly present to himself while he was writing is now present to us as we read. Autobiography is the certificate of a unique human passage through time and the theorist who comes to it full of sceptical questions about its rhetorical nature knows that he is playing an unkind game; he is not as other, more charitable readers of autobiography.

Who but a theorist after all would read one autobiography after another, read, it may be, nothing but autobiographies for months on end, in the furtherance of his specialism? In the Preface to his attractive study of *Autobiography and the Experience of Childhood*, Richard N. Coe records having read 'some six hundred' primary sources during the eight years he was working on it.[2] That is a punishing programme, unthinkable for anyone but a theorist, who must proceed towards his general conclusions about the genre by induction from individual cases. The theorist's hypothetical Other, the Common Reader, does no such thing, because his interest in autobiography is exactly opposite. The term autobiography does not for him function as a count-noun. For the Common Reader an autobiography is not just one more contribution to a genre or to a future typology of autobiographical writing, but the unique self-presentation of Author X or Author Y, some public figure already known to him in part and about whom he wants to know more. The Common Reader does not normally read the autobiographies of authors of whom previously he has never heard. The theorist on the other hand may read them indiscriminately, in search of formal or textual variety, and thus of comprehensiveness.

The theoretical need is to locate generic sameness in a kind of writing which aims at imposing difference. Autobiographical theory

---

[2] Richard N. Coe, *When the Grass was Greener: Autobiography and the Experience of Childhood* (New Haven and London, 1984), p. xiv.

has in fact to confront what the profoundly theoretical Paul de Man once declared to be the 'disreputability' of the genre, or 'its incompatibility with the monumental dignity of aesthetic values'.[3] In common with others who have reflected on the specific nature of autobiography, de Man doubts whether it constitutes a literary genre at all, given the apparent miscellaneousness and 'self-indulgence' of the forms in which the autobiographical project may be realized. But that is an issue on whose outcome rather little, practically, appears to hang; whether or not the autobiographies I have taken for my examples in the present book prove strictly congenerous, they are undeniably works of literature and sufficiently distinctive as such to be classed together. No one will deny that they are autobiographical. To a deconstructionist critic such as de Man, autobiography is an especially inviting literary kind because it purports to be so straightforwardly mimetic of life: it is charged with turning life into a Life. But the way from life to a Life lies through language and de Man argues that far from being restorative of the past as its practitioners and Common Readers would like it to be, auto-biography can but mummify the past, the effects of language being necessarily 'privative' in putting rhetoric in place of reality. De Man's is a frigid (and insufficiently explicit) argument, and one which few even among theorists could feel happy with, so far does it go in asserting the constitutional inability of autobiography to deliver genuine self-knowledge; but his essay is not to be ignored, since in warning us against any facile assumptions of the transparency of autobiographical writing as a record of the past, it redirects our attention to its troublingly rhetorical nature.

Autobiography represents an effort made by those who write it at the integration of their past lives and present selves: the autobiographer wishes to stand forth in print in the form of a *whole*. According to de Man the rhetorical figure which presides over autobiography is that of prosopopoeia, a Greek term translatable literally as a 'face-making' – the autobiographer attempts to create in words a 'face' by which we can tell him apart from others, and thus to pass from a merely verbal to a conclusively pictorial representation of himself. There is some truth in de Man's assertion, but also much tendentious-

---

[3] Paul de Man, 'Autobiography as De-Facement', in *The Rhetoric of Romanticism* (New York, 1984), p. 67.

ness. It is true in so far as autobiography does indeed aspire to delineate the 'features' of his personal history and character which its author believes are his claim to distinction, so that his text can finally take the place of his person, as the tangible evidence of his identity. The argument is tendentious in that prosopopoeia is a rhetorical figure which endows abstractions with the power of 'speech' – as Dante employs it in his autobiographical *Vita nuova*, to enable Love to address him as if Love were a person. But the autobiographer qua human being is not an abstraction, he is someone who in life has had a *real* face; so to argue without qualification that autobiography is simply an extended exercise in prosopopoeia is to banish the living and suffering author from the scene too radically, as nothing more substantial than a projection of his rhetorical endeavours. We can agree that, in writing, an autobiographer does not so much put his name to his life-story as put his life-story to his name; or, should he be more drawn to self-portraiture than to narrative, that he provides for that name a psychological identity. Whether it be story or portrait – and all autobiographical stories are in practice part portrait, just as all self-portraits are in part story – autobiography wills the unity of its subject.

In demonstration of this simple thesis, I take an autobiography which is on the face of things more self-portrait than narrative, the *Ecce Homo* of Nietzsche, which has relatively little to say about the outward events of the philosopher's life and much to say concerning the formation of his ideas and of the wholly singular, not to say superhuman being he believes himself to have become.[4] But for all Nietzsche's vatic flights and lyrical sermonizing, the narrative impulsion of his autobiography is paramount. *Ecce Homo* has the subtitle, 'How one becomes what one is', and the story which the autobiographer tells is of his own philosophical Becoming. Such a story ought logically to end in the stasis of Being, with the autobiographer shamming dead, as if any further change in himself were not to be thought of. That so many autobiographies have been written and then put aside, to be published only posthumously, suggests that autobiographers want the time that has intervened between the completion of their life-story and the completion of their life to be overlooked, it having led to no revision of the written record. Some autobiographers – of those I shall be concerned with here,

---

[4] Nietzsche did not as a philosopher believe in 'events', looking on them as constructs of discourse, artificially isolated from out of the pure continuity of the life-process.

Charles Darwin most notably – preface their text with an assurance that writing as they are in old age their course is all but run and their character is fixed; they can honestly write as if they were dead – Darwin's impersonation of a revenant perhaps conforms the closest to de Man's model of autobiography as an extended prosopopoeia.

But no such funereal anticipation would be tolerated by Nietzsche, who writes as a vitalist, with a Dionysian moral to proclaim. He has not ceased from becoming because there is nothing for him to become, no substantial self that might be assumed as the product of the narrative process. As an autobiographical subject, he seeks to merge with his text, on the ground, given elsewhere in his writings, that 'There is no "being" behind doing, effecting, becoming; "the doer" is merely a fiction added to the deed – the deed is everything ... our entire science still lies under the misleading influence of language and has not disposed of that little changeling, the "subject"'.[5] *Ecce Homo* is none the less the tale of an unfolding. Its premiss is that in the early part of the narrator's life his doings were without focus or point, his defining 'life-task' having not as yet revealed itself. There may be no fictitious 'subject' to be added a posteriori to his deeds, but these may now be seen as constitutive of the subject who writes, the 'little changeling' whose perspective on the past alters with every passing moment and who glories in accepting everything that has happened to him. The *amor fati* which Nietzsche takes for the creed of a manly, unrepining soul might at a less exalted level be taken also as the creed befitting an autobiographer, whose virtue lies in embracing in retrospect accidents that may have seemed painful and unmeaning at the time.

A precondition of autobiography is that there *is* something of the nature of a 'life-task' waiting to be revealed in the fullness of time and in the clear light of retrospection. Autobiography raises into consciousness whatever unconscious process the autobiographer accepts has brought him to his present condition. For the atheist Nietzsche, as for the Christian Augustine, confident that his conversion has been gradually effected by the secret operation of God's grace, autobiography tells a tale of suspense, as it moves presciently closer to its appointed end:

---

[5] *The Genealogy of Morals*, I,13; but it is quoted here from Alexander Nehamas, *Nietzsche: Life as Literature* (Cambridge and London, 1985), p. 127. This superlative commentary on Nietzsche should be read by anyone with a theoretical interest in autobiography: my own debt to it is enormous.

In the meantime the organizing 'idea' destined to rule grows and grows in the depths – it begins to command, it slowly leads *back* from sidepaths and wrong turnings, it prepares *individual* qualities and abilities which will one day prove themselves indispensable as means to achieving the whole – it constructs the *ancillary* capacities one after the other before it gives any hint of the dominating task, of the 'goal', 'objective', 'meaning'. (65)[6]

The 'dominating task' which Nietzsche now knows had been allotted to him is nothing less than the 'transvaluation of all values'. The bizarrely presumptuous title he found for his autobiography is explained by his bizarrely presumptuous ambition to be recognized as the Antichrist, or as the godless prophet whose teachings and example would cleanse the world of a decadent Christian morality. This is a 'life-task' of a size to exceed the capacities of any one individual to carry it out. But Nietzsche is not any one individual; like autobiographers in general, he is as a subject boldly expansive and contemptuous of the limitations of individuality. In *Ecce Homo* he dons at will the prophetic garb of his own literary creation, Zarathustra, the proud and vehement aphorist whose ample vision transcends all moral and philosophical contradictions – the desire to be seen to dwell alone in a grand independency, above all local allegiances, is one to be found expressed even in such gentlemanly and unNietzschean autobiographers as David Hume and Edward Gibbon. And like the volatile Rousseau of the *Confessions*, whose moods and actions are so erratic that he finds it hard to suppose he possesses anything as constricting as an identity, so Nietzsche celebrates the far-ranging fluctuations of his mental state, the sheer variety of which is a part of his Dionysian entitlement: 'It is my sagacity to have been many things and in many places so as to be able to become *one person* – so as to be able to attain *one thing*'(88).

Nietzsche is like Rousseau in another, and this time more vulnerable aspect also. Rousseau turned to autobiography in self-defence, and in the paranoid fancy that he was the subject of innumerable false reports; he wrote the hundreds of pages of the *Confessions*, the Dialogues and the *Rêveries d'un promeneur solitaire* meaning to swamp all these false reports by a crazy profusion of truthful ones. Autobiographers need an excuse for indulging to the extent that they do in self-advertisement and Rousseau's excuse was not new, his predecessors in the genre having all been more or less

---

[6] Quotations are from the Penguin Classics edition, *Ecce Homo*, translated by R. J. Hollingdale (Harmondsworth, 1979).

aware that they were writing in their own justification. A Nietzsche might seem not quite to fit in this tradition, no question of his right to be heard ever crossing his mind. But if his right to be heard is not in question, the readiness of the world to hear him is. In order to write *Ecce Homo* Zarathustra has had to swallow some of his pride, for the fact is that his teachings have so far gone unheeded. Despite his great vigour and productivity as an author, the despicable values of Christianity are still in place, they have not been transvalued; and his neglect by the world has naturally served to confirm him in his sense of solitude and of his uniqueness: 'But the disparity between the greatness of my task and the *smallness* of my contemporaries has found expression in the fact that I have been neither heard nor even so much as seen'(33). Yet this is as good as an admission that a book such as *Ecce Homo* should not have been needed, in order to mediate between his oeuvre and a public which is patently unfitted to have been offered it. As a corrective to the indifference with which his writings have been met, a volume of autobiography can but strike us as a desperate, even a sad expedient, for far from correcting it can only reinforce the deadly aestheticization of his redemptive message. The proud Nietzsche is in danger of descending into pathos.

Ecce Homo is autobiography with a purpose, even if the most that it might achieve would be to persuade those who read it to read others of the books that Nietzsche has written. These are themselves autobiographical 'events' whose continuity one with the next he establishes by the brief glosses he provides for them in his long third chapter, on 'Why I write such excellent books'. His books have been the principal 'deeds' of his life and Nietzsche represents his published oeuvre in narrative form, each successive volume now being given its place as a contribution to the whole, and the apparent diversity of their contents shown to be an illusion that has had to wait upon the retrospective moment to be revealed as such. (The autobiographical precedent for *Ecce Homo* in this respect is Goethe's *Poetry and Truth*, specifically written according to Goethe in answer to a friendly request to show how his bafflingly various oeuvre had come to be written.) Thus the unification of the oeuvre reflects and supports the unification of its author, in their joint coming to be what they presently are. But there unification must stop: the oneness of the author, supposing he has proved able to persuade us of it, does not entail the oneness of the person of whom the author is the agent. The textual Nietzsche is, like any other autobiographical subject, presented as a 'character', constructed with a partly conscious and partly unconscious will to consistency, and a 'character' whose inconsistencies we shall ourselves be happy to recuperate, so desirous are we of finding our own integrity as persons reflected back at us by the autobiographical text.

The theorist, however, must bring that text out from under a too close tutelage of the life of which it is the representation. His loyalty is to the genre of which he is a connoisseur and he reads autobiographies not as gratifying evidence of how it is possible – or not – textually to establish one's coherence as a living entity, but in order to integrate them successively in whatever theoretical model of the genre he has been able to build, either as confirmation of its soundness, or else as proving the need to overhaul and complicate it. If we accept that the property rights of autobiography lie inalienably with the author, then what the theorist is set upon is an act of expropriation, or of dismemberment. He assumes that we can, with profit, distinguish the dance from the dancer, or the self as impersonal performance from the self as unique and transcendent originator of the text.

The theoretical task is to relate one autobiographical performance to others and to reclassify particular examples of autobiography radically as members one of another. Autobiographers themselves have learnt how to write from their own writing and reading, of history, or fiction, or (auto)biography; they have had to acquire the rules by which alone any narrative, or essay in self-presentation, can be sustained. But if they are themselves already generically adept when they set out to write, they do not write hoping to be read generically, as unexceptional new entrants on to an already crowded stage, to be used in illustration of some literary theoretical argument. Rather, they hope that by making us intent on the story which they have to tell, we shall accept as 'natural' the conventions they have adopted in order to tell it, so that it will strike us a failure of readerly decorum and fellow-feeling if we decide to switch our attention from the tale to the technique. There has never yet been an autobiography addressed to a readership of literary theorists, though who is to say that there never will be? Writing has become so self-conscious a business at this far end of the twentieth century that there may soon be autobiographers who see their role in terms of parody, or of the humorous exploitation of a literary genre practised over the centuries with what they adjudge to be too high a solemnity. Autobiography's jaded theorist may well reflect that he has chosen to specialize in a kind of writing that were it not to be practised seriously would probably not be practised at all.

His tunnel vision faces the theorist with a serious dilemma in fixing the direction and bounds of his research: how far should he pursue the historical context of the autobiographies he reads? Autobiography does not report only on the inner life of its author, but on the commerce with the outside world by which that inner life has been conditioned. In some cases, the exchange between self and the society in which it has been formed is the writer's guiding theme: the autobiographies of Goethe and of John Stuart Mill are so constructed as to make their subject appear as the rarely capacious representative of his intellectual epoch, in all its manifold developments. Should the theorist then not try to provide himself with knowledge of that background independently of what the autobiographer has chosen to give, the better to appreciate the perspectival nature of the writer's account? Were the theorist in question swayed by the arguments of the New Historicism, then he would indeed feel obliged to take the cultural and historical context of a work such as Goethe's *Poetry and Truth* into account, in order to determine how this particular example of self-presentation compares with others that were being written at the same time, in the form of diaries, memoirs or full autobiographies, and even with current examples of self-portraiture in art. That would be a sound and rewarding method by which to formulate at least a topical theory of autobiographical writing.

It is a method, however, whose findings, like its pleasures, are more likely to be historical than theoretical. A theory so context-dependent as this scarcely deserves to be called a theory, and a theory of autobiography, if we are ever to have one, must be broad enough to account for all known examples of the genre whenever and wherever they were written. The theorist who is anxious to locate if he can the constants of autobiography has no chance of doing so if he dallies too long over any one autobiographical work. Having resisted the temptation to compromise his theoretical virtue by enrolling among the New Historicists, he must resist a second distraction, which is to be so taken with a particular autobiography as to turn aside from that to study the literary or other oeuvre of its author, and relate the one to the other. There are perhaps instances in literary history of an autobiography being the one and only book that its author published;

but they must be exceedingly few. Literary autobiography exists as I have earlier said to put a story to a name: it is written by those already known for their writings and as such it invariably forms a part of an oeuvre. Here again the theorist is in trouble, for how much if anything of that oeuvre should he take in, to act as a literary context for the autobiography itself? How many of Nabokov's novels should he read, or of Stendhal's journals, in order to confirm or modify the conclusions he has come to exclusively from reading *Speak, Memory* or *The Life of Henry Brulard*? Or if the autobiographer is a thinker rather than a writer, is it feasible to interpret his account of his intellectual development without reference to the works in which that thought has been fully worked out? Does it make sense to read Vico's brief *Life*, or Jean-Paul Sartre's *Words*, without also reading *The New Science* of the one and some at least of the prolix philosophical and political writings of the other?

The theorist has the choice: he can pass single-mindedly on from autobiography to autobiography, looking to neither right nor left, or he can pause and make a few excursions into the surrounding literary or intellectual landscape before resuming his austere itinerary. In practice, it is my assumption that the autobiographical theorist will compromise and try to learn *something* of the relevant context before proceeding. That has been my own experience, as occasional forays and footnotes in this book will testify. But rather than appeasing the theoretical conscience, such a compromise tends further to tax it, since to read a little around the subject is to make one aware of how much one might read. One can only take comfort in the thought that, however long one chose to linger over a subject as alien, as complex and as voluminously written about as St Augustine, say, the conclusions one might eventually reach concerning the structure and meaning of the *Confessions* would be no more intelligent or convincing than those reachable after a single close reading, made more or less in ignorance of that work's cultural and historical setting. A truly determined theorist would no doubt wish to exclude from his mind all that he knows about the subject of a particular autobiography learnt from sources other than the autobiography itself; I am far from wanting to be so ruthless and have preferred to read the auto-biographies studied here in the light of whatever knowledge I have of them.

The theorist discounts the documentary value of autobiography. He does not read Augustine in the idea that the *Confessions* are firsthand evidence of the *mentalité* of a late fourth-century Christian convert or provincial church dignitary, nor Edward Gibbon's *Memoirs* as an index to the mind-set of an eighteenth-century Tory intellectual. The specific inwardness of autobiography makes of it an attractive source for historians, and all the more so now that they are concerned with cultural history and with such inchoate topics as the history of 'privacy'. Autobiographers inevitably record details of contemporary life that are too small and too ordinary to have been found worth recording in any official source, as well as recording their own reactions and attitudes towards all manner of events. Hence the interest now being shown by social historians in Britain and in France for the – mainly unpublished – autobiographies of the nineteenth-century working class, as the nearest thing to be found to an oral history of those members of society who were for so long supposed to have had no history. Yet historians who go to autobiography for documentary evidence about the past are in no better case than the literary theorist, since their profession demands that they treat all such writings as typical, and certainly not as the work of resolutely idiosyncratic individuals whose experiences and responses were unlike those of anyone else. They would do well moreover to heed the warning of the theorist and question to what extent artifice and literary convention may have determined the 'historical' evidence they assume they have found. It is not literary autobiography alone that is textual and therefore often ambiguous and calling for interpretation. It would be absurd and condescending to suppose that working-class autobiographers were formed by nature alone and were therefore peculiarly reliable witnesses to the historical process in which they were implicated.

The inductive urges of the theorist run counter to the desire of the autobiographer (as that desire is posited by the theorist, be it allowed). The theorist is looking constantly to generalize, the autobiographer to gain recognition as a singular being. The itinerary of the life traced in autobiography is one of an emergence from the crowd, that faceless 'herd' of which Nietzsche is so bitingly scornful. Autobiography begins in dissociation, with the writer stepping out front on his own in order to impose himself on us as someone *sui generis*. It puts an end to anonymity: we shall never be given to read a book entitled *The Autobiography of an Anonymous Man*, or if we are, only so that we can know that one anonymous man at least has made his name by being so. In the terms that Nietzsche favours, the autobiographer is an 'entity' writing in order to proclaim his superiority over a population of nonentities. So unbridled an assertion of self is immoral, judged by the pallid principles of the Christian religion, which Nietzsche might have argued are anti-autobiographical, Gospel morality having fostered in those who follow it a despicable 'will to nonentity'. It is as the prophet of a new and contrary religion that he addresses the world in the preface to *Ecce Homo*, in the imperative mood and an italic typeface: '*Listen to me! for I am thus and thus. Do not, above all, confound me with what I am not!*'. There speaks the true voice of autobiography, if raised by Nietzsche to a pitch whose shrillness other autobiographers and most readers will recoil from, reluctant as we understandably are to acknowledge that autobiography may only be the acceptable face of megalomania.

The theorist's answer to Nietzsche's clamant declaration of his singularity is to reduce it to an autobiographical topos, and to remark the extent to which it echoes the most quoted (and resented) of all such declarations, that made by Rousseau in the preamble to his *Confessions*:

I have resolved on an enterprise which has no precedent, and which, once complete, will have no imitator. My purpose is to display to my kind a portrait in every way true to nature, and the man I shall portray will be myself. Simply myself. I know my heart and understand my fellow man. But I am made unlike anyone I have ever met; I will even venture to say that I am like no one in the whole world. I may be no better but at least I am different.[7]

Perhaps we should see this as a claim to uniqueness more extravagant still than that made by Nietzsche, since Rousseau is distinguishing himself not simply from all other human beings but from all other autobiographers, the dead, the living and the yet to be born, whose efforts will be eclipsed by his own. His claim is to a uniqueness of form as well as of content. Moreover, rather than thrusting the anonymous 'crowd' distastefully from him, as Nietzsche does, Rousseau contrives to ingest it, by taking an apodeictic self-knowledge ('I know my heart') to underwrite his knowledge of the species ('and understand my fellow-man'). He exceeds Nietzsche in implying that the

---

[7] *The Confessions of Jean-Jacques Rousseau*, translated by J. M. Cohen (Harmondsworth, 1953), p. 17. The preamble to the narrative which contains these words was one of two written by Rousseau, and that which editors of the *Confessions* invariably include; the alternative, so-called Neuchâtel preface differs from it in interesting ways, and is discussed in my chapter on Rousseau later in the book.

multitude is composed of very many versions of himself. There could be no more extreme – or deluded – statement than Rousseau's of the autobiographer's desire to be spared the mediation of literary form and to be free to present himself to others in the immediacy of his physical being. Rousseau would like, as we say, to be *himself* in the *Confessions*, a real presence. And yet he has had to resort to the language of artifice in order to tell what his deep intentions as an autobiographer are: for all his terrible sincerity he can put nothing more real before us than a self-portrait, 'in every way true to nature' it may be, but none the less only a 'face' – that very simulacrum which it is the specific task of prosopopoeia to create. Where Rousseau can not accept the fatally aesthetic nature of the autobiographical text, Nietzsche revels in it, happy as he is to appear as the subject of his narrative and as nothing more. We should be wise to the aesthetic as well as the purely biblical connotations of Nietzsche's title: an 'ecce homo' is the name given to a painting showing the figure of Christ as he stood before Pilate, crowned with thorns. The painter depicts what the writer can only say, but in giving his autobiography an ostensive title Nietzsche is asking to be 'seen' as well as read, as the unique physical whole secreted seriatim by his words.

If autobiography starts in the writer's sense of his singularity, it also singularizes as it goes: it is the story of a singularization, or of how the autobiographer came to acquire the conviction of uniqueness that has impelled him to write. Who more singular, as the thinker who introduced new, vastly influential and still not quite defunct paradigms into the philosophy of mind, than René Descartes in the seventeenth century? Descartes' epochal *Method of Discourse* has the form of an autobiographical narrative (bearing out another of Nietzsche's profound aperçus, that every great philosophy has been 'the personal confession of its author'). He begins by assuring us that the one faculty required of a philosopher is possessed by us all in equal measure: the faculty of common sense; and goes on to demonstrate the incomparable use he has himself made of this universal endowment. In developing his philosophical method he has been beholden to nobody but himself, it is perfectly original. Curiously, Descartes is recorded by his contemporary biographer, Baillet, as having striven in his life to avoid all forms of 'singularity', in his dress as in his behaviour – he was a man who chose to live apart and discreetly. But he is very prepared to have the utter singularity of his thought recognized and admired in the *Discourse*.

The process of singularization is one which is to be found narrated with a particular clarity in the autobiographers of thinkers, of philosophers like Descartes or Vico and others whose distinction has been earned by their ideas rather than their actions. The theory of autobiography has much to learn from the autobiographies of theorizers. Thinkers want us to know that the ideas they have promulgated and which have become associated with their names are *their* ideas, that they are an original addition or corrective to the ideas which were there previously, not old ideas recovered from oblivion nor fresh ones found in intimate collaboration with other thinkers. The original thinker who writes an autobiography can represent himself there as something more than a 'face', he can be the inherent genius of an integral 'body' of thought.

Autobiography is by its nature an authoritarian mode of writing, and intellectual autobiography especially so, since whatever the writer asserts concerning the rightness of his thought is now ungainsayable by others. No modern thinker has been more influential, nor deemed to have been more authoritarian, than Sigmund Freud, who in the 1920s was commissioned by a German editor to write a short autobiographical essay describing the evolution and present state of his psychoanalytical doctrines. Freud's *Autobiographical Study* thus first appeared in a collective volume, of similar accounts written by other medical scientists.[8] Such collections seem to have been something of a tradition in Germany – Darwin's autobiographical essay was also written for inclusion in one. The collective format is well suited to the ethos of science, conceived of innocently as the common endeavour of many scientists working together, and unconcerned to impose their own names in its annals. But some scientists nevertheless make their names, and an anthology of autobiographical essays recognizes that fact, while reminding its contributors that whatever the distinction they have achieved they are not alone.

Freud, however, wastes no time in marking himself off from his fellow autobiographers, whose contributions he seems to have been able to read before writing his own. They have complained of the difficulty of what the editor has asked them to do; but his difficulties

[8] I shall quote it here from the 'authorized translation' by James Strachey: *An Autobiographical Study* (London, 1935), which contains some additions and alterations to the original text and a brief postscript written by Freud covering the ten years that had elapsed between the essay appearing in Germany and its publication in London.

are the greater, 'for I have already more than once published papers upon the same lines as the present one, papers which, from the nature of the subject, have dealt more with personal considerations than is usual or than would otherwise have been necessary'(11) – he is referring to the use he had made in such books as *The Interpretation of Dreams* or *The Psychopathology of Everyday Life* of his own intimate experience. Freud does not wish either to repeat or to contradict himself, so 'I must endeavour to construct a narrative in which subjective and objective attitudes, biographical and historical interests, are combined in a new proportion'(12). In having to countenance the intrusion of subjectivity on to the objective terrain of science, Freud parts company at the start with his fellow contributors, who are presumably well able to give an account of their careers in medicine without so blatant a use of the first person singular as is incumbent on him.

His *Autobiographical Study* is like all of autobiography in being both assertive and defensive. It is the story of how psychoanalysis came first to be practised and later institutionalized, these two moments of the story representing as it were the inner and outer aspects of Freud's career. Both moments are marked equally by the narrator's will to autonomy. Freudian psychoanalysis, and the metapsychological ideas that have both derived from and been fed back in to his clinical practice, has emerged from the medical context of the time. This context is evoked by Freud principally as an agent of resistance – that same force within the psychic economy of the individual which opposes itself to the therapeutic promptings of the analyst. His narrative begins as it will go on, in conflict, when as a Jewish medical student in Vienna he is taunted by anti-semites and made aware that he can never belong to the 'compact majority' (which is a polite name for Nietzsche's 'herd'). At this stage he is himself the 'Opposition', but that will change as Freud becomes a compact majority of one and the orthodox medical world is relegated to play the part of opposition.

The *Autobiographical Study* is defensive in countering charges that Freud's theories are not altogether original, important parts of them having been appropriated from others, from the work of the French psychologist Pierre Janet, for example, active in Paris when Freud had gone there to study under Charcot. But Freud is adamant: Janet's name had not once been so much as mentioned on that visit and when later Freud reverts to Janet's theory of female hysteria it is in order to dismiss it as in any way a model for his own: 'The reader will have learned from my account that historically psycho-analysis is completely independent of Janet's discoveries, just as in its content it diverges from them and goes far beyond them'(54). The story which Freud has to tell is indeed one of a regular divergence and consequent transcendence of the theories of all those with whom he has worked. His relationship with Josef Breuer may be taken as the model of this characteristic sequence. Freud first works closely with Breuer, in a professional association that culminates in their together producing a book of studies on hysteria. He has 'always maintained' and now repeats that this was 'the product of Breuer's mind', he having contributed only a certain element of theory. But he has subsequently broken with Breuer, who had proved unable to accept the predominant role of sexuality in the theory and practice of psychoanalysis, a break which consummates their relationship in Freud's narrative. Indeed, Freudian theory might be said to have been inaugurated by Freud's percipience respecting Breuer, who broke off from analysing a female patient in embarrassment when he found she had become erotically attached to him: it required Freud to interpret this, as it turned out, portentous psychodrama of transference and resistance.

When he turns to recount the institutionalization of psycho-analysis, in Europe and the United States, the same dynamic of a resistance in others reinforcing the authoritarianism of the theorist recurs. Psychoanalysis must make headway against the opposition of entire medical establishments, in Germany and in France, and if it has succeeded in penetrating the United States it is only in a 'watered-down' form. But at this hinge in his story, Freud is quite dramatically alone: 'For more than ten years after my separation from Breuer I had no followers. I was completely isolated. In Vienna I was shunned; abroad no notice was taken of me. My *Interpretation of Dreams*, published in 1900, was scarcely reviewed in the technical journals'(87). But then has begun the second phase of his life, the antistrophe of discipleship, in which 'my pupils and collaborators have been growing more and more in importance'(101). This might instantly seem like a generous acknowledgment by the supreme theorist of the help he has been receiving from others, but the thought is as yet incomplete; at the moment of writing Freud believed that he was dying, so that the growth in importance of his collaborators exactly matches the decline in his own powers. The acknowledgment

serves to reassure him that 'today, when a grave illness warns me of
the approaching end, I can think with a quiet mind of the cessation
of my own labours'(101). He is secure in the belief that his authority
will outlive him.

Freud is the autobiographer as patriarch. Like Descartes, he is in
the end indebted to no one as the creator of his psychoanalytical
method. At the same time, one might think that he reveals in the
Autobiographical Study an actual *fear* of intellectual indebtedness. He
tells us that he has no gift for what he calls 'philosophy proper', that
he is 'constitutionally' unsuited for it. What 'philosophy proper'
might be, he does not say, but one can only conclude he means that
he has no gift for abstract thought, which would be a remarkable
assertion coming from the master metapsychologist. Among the
philosophers 'proper', Freud goes to the odd lengths of naming two
who have had no influence on him, Schopenhauer and Nietzsche.
Both he allows as having preceded him in achieving insights into the
unconscious mind, but his theory was already in place before, 'very
late in my life', he read Schopenhauer, while the works of Nietzsche
he had positively censored: 'Nietzsche, another philosopher whose
guesses and intuitions often agree in the most astonishing way with
the laborious findings of psychoanalysis, was for a long time avoided
by me on that very account; I was less concerned with the question
of priority than with keeping my mind unembarrassed'(110). The
key word there is surely *laborious*; to Nietzsche's 'guesses and
intuitions' Freud opposes his own hard work, his theory having
resulted not from abstract guesswork but from his clinical encounters.
He is protesting his empiricism, and covering himself finally against
being taken as merely a speculative or abstract thinker by pointing to
the source of his ideas in the concrete experience of the consulting-
room.

I take Freud's desire in the *Autobiographical Study* to emerge from his
story as a physician and not as a philosopher to mark the closing
gesture typical of autobiography, by which the writer affirms his
solidarity with his kind. The story of his singularization can not be
allowed to leave him isolated, as if there were no way back from the
textual fastness into which he has withdrawn. The tension in
autobiography derives from the conflict in it between the will to
apartness and the will to association; and if the evidence of the will to
apartness pervades all autobiographical narrative, then the evidence
of the will to association lies in the existence of autobiography itself,

as the most sociable of literary acts. The manner of performance of that act may vary greatly, over time and from one cultural setting to another, but by forcing numerous canonical examples of auto- biography into the unnatural cohabitation of a study such as this, the theorist can hope to show that this 'disreputable' genre is not without its common principles and practices. And I do not apologize for choosing only canonical examples of literary autobiography for analysis in the pages that follow, rather than looking outside the canon as the fashion currently is, to writers previously unconsidered. There are excellent reasons why certain works become canonical, having to do with their quality and not with the coercive impulses of the canon-makers. The particular autobiographies studied here are works without exception that it is a pleasure to read, quite apart from their uncommon richness as theoretical examples.

CHAPTER I

Augustine

THE PROCESS OF CONVERSION

A human life can be brought to display a meaning only on condition of being turned into a story; once subject to the public order of narrative, it acquires both the gravity of a settled and venerable literary form, and the orientation of hindsight which alone raises the past from an aimless sum of reminiscence into a personal history. If we crave significance for ourselves as historical beings, we can have it only by an intelligent and sequential ordering of what we retain or can recover of our past – in which the autobiographer is a model for us all. A life storied is a life made meaningful, and any life, however vapid, is at least storiable. I begin therefore from the assumption that whoever narrates his or her life is willing its transformation from a lived farrago into a thought whole.

This making meaningful may be called a 'conversion' of merely brute experience, which will be moralized by the attentions of the autobiographer and made exemplary, an improving tale for imitation by others. True narrative autobiography begins indeed with the *Confessions* of Augustine, an unprecedented work of introspection written at the end of the fourth century. Simply as narrative, the *Confessions* tell the story of Augustine's conversion to Christianity, and my argument in this chapter is that, by the extraordinary coherence of its structure, his may serve as the paradigm of all autobiographical stories. The *Confessions* record a conversion and in so doing they also effect one: the profound ideological shift within the author which gives to his narrative its finality exemplifies the shift inherent in narrative as such, as a temporal process inescapably transforming of all that it touches.

The story of Augustine's conversion did not follow closely on the event. It is told not as an urgent, apostolic story, but as a deeply deliberate, philosophical one. Augustine was baptized as a Christian in Milan in 387; his *Confessions* were not published in North Africa until ten or more years later, when he had already been elected bishop of Hippo. It is as if he had put off writing them, in keeping with the strategy of deferment which is so conspicuous in the story itself. It is so in the matter of his baptism, for example: this conclusive event very nearly happened earlier, according to the *Confessions*, at a time in Augustine's boyhood when he was seriously ill and his mother feared for his life. His mother, Monica, was a Christian and wanted her son baptized for the sake of his salvation. But the boy Augustine recovered and his baptism never took place: 'So my washing in the waters of baptism was postponed, in the surmise that, if I continued to live, I should defile myself again with sin and, after baptism, the guilt of pollution would be greater and more dangerous'(1.xi).[1]

This deferment testifies to the prudence and the realism of Augustine's mother, forceful Christian though she was, but who fears that her son is too sensual by his nature to endure without lapsing the self-denial that would be required of him were he to be baptized so young. It is also the necessary precondition of the *Confessions* themselves, which would not have come to be written had he been baptized then, rather than in his maturity and after an exemplary inner struggle. Later in his story, a second opportunity for baptism comes and goes (v.ix), echoing the first, when Augustine falls sick once more in Rome. By now he has grown too 'vicious' to ask to be baptized. He is one of the chorus of mockers, 'a fool who laughed at the cure which you [God] prescribed'. He has laughed, indeed, at the baptism, already narrated in Book Four of the *Confessions*, of his dearest childhood friend, who was baptized when unconscious of a fever, but has surprised Augustine by refusing to make fun of the event once he had recovered consciousness – an episode premonitory of the passivity of Augustine's own progress towards baptism, as a narrative telos known up until the moment of its realization only to God.

His narrative thus incorporates two episodes which threaten to bring about its abrupt foreclosure, but Augustine, unlike some autobiographers, is too serious a determinist to pursue any counter-

---

[1] The translation of the *Confessions* I shall quote from is that made by R. S. Pine-Coffin for the Penguin Classics (Harmondsworth, 1961). The Roman numerals in brackets after each quotation refer first to the Book of the *Confessions* from which it comes, and then to the chapter within that Book.

factual speculations into alternative, unrealized futures for himself. That it was wise for him to have deferred his baptism as he did is borne out by what he has to tell us in the earlier books of the *Confessions* about that very 'pollution' which Monica was afraid of. Much of the story's psychological drama, and its appeal for a modern, secular reader, derives from Augustine's struggle subsequently to overcome his strong sensuality and follow a life of Christian austerity. Read thus, the *Confessions* become, as the British classicist E. R. Dodds rather frostily has it, 'the intimate record of a neurotic conflict'[2] and the deferment of Augustine's baptism foreshadows the much-quoted deferment of his acceptance of the pangs of sensual renunciation, with his 'Give me chastity and continence, but not yet'(VIII.vii). Whether or not this pattern of deferment be characteristic of neurosis, it has in the *Confessions* a profound intellectual basis, as I shall hope to show, fundamental to Augustine's theology, to his philosophy of language, and to his role as the narrator of his own life.

As the account of his 'turn' to Christianity, the *Confessions* have for many centuries remained an edifying document for those who share or who aspire to his Catholic faith, tracing as they do in some particularity and with a precious degree of inwardness the spiritual and intellectual process by which he became a Christian believer. They are a document of self, but traditionally employed for the reassurance or edification of a collectivity, and a collectivity moreover which has as its highest moral imperative the belittling of self. The *Confessions* raise in the peculiar context of Christian ethical teaching the question attaching to all autobiography, of to what extent it is possible to be an autobiographer and yet remain innocent of a culpable self-regard. Autobiographers may claim to be free from vanity, though most must recognize that they are engaged on a voluntary undertaking and that they have chosen to make a public display of themselves. In the case of Augustine, his more resourceful Christian readers can pit the usefulness of the *Confessions*, both as a statement of doctrine and as the record of an imitable, soterial experience, against whatever it might seem to contain of unChristian self-advertisement. Its most eminent translator into English, the Tractarian Bishop Pusey, absolves Augustine from possible charges of

---

[2] E. R. Dodds, 'Augustine's *Confessions*: A study in spiritual maladjustment', *Hibbert Journal*, April 1928, p. 460.

self-display by arguing that he only wrote about himself to the extent that he had to, in order to convey to us the teachings which it was God's will he should convey: 'Such, not an autobiography, is the object of the Confessions; a praise and confession of God's unmerited goodness, but of himself only so much, as might illustrate out of what depth God's mercy had raised him.'[3] That severe interpretation of the *Confessions* seeks to deprive Augustine of his story altogether, as if he had contributed it once and for all to the good of the Christian community; just as, many centuries later, St Teresa of Avila was to write her *Life* only because her confessor had ordered her to, and John Henry Newman to defend himself in his *Apologia* on behalf of the Catholic priesthood of which he was a member.

But the student of autobiography has other, more formal and less topical perspectives on the *Confessions* than these. From the Christian schema of the work I require for now only the notion of conversion. In what does a religious conversion consist? Summarily, in the words of A. D. Nock, in 'the reorientation of the soul of an individual, his deliberate turning from indifference or from an earlier form of piety to another'.[4] This reorientation may or may not be a process drawn out in time. The archetypal conversion of our own religious tradition is that of St Paul, which is narrated in the book of Acts as an instantaneous 'reorientation' of the soul effected from outside, a perfect and sudden enantiodromia. Augustine's conversion is an inner process extended over a number of years of his life and taking up the first eight, narrative books of the *Confessions*. It has its recognizable stages, and meets more than adequately Nock's requirement that a conversion be 'deliberate'.

Whatever the tempo of its achievement, a conversion is literally a turning-point in the story of an individual life. But it does not in narrative terms demand a *break* between the life led by the convert before conversion, and the life he or she has led since. On the contrary, a conversion institutes a potentially dramatic new relationship between past and present, as Saul the persecutor of Christians turns into Paul the Christian evangelist, his reformation made the more compelling by the sinful past which he carries publicly with him (and the near identity of his new name with the old). So it is with Augustine, whose years of devotion to Mani-

---

[3] E. B. Pusey, 'Preface', *The Confessions of St Augustine* (London, 1949), p. xviii.
[4] A. D. Nock, *Conversion: The Old and the New in Religion from Alexander the Great to Augustine of Hippo* (Oxford, 1952), p. 7.

chaeanism and of sensual 'pollution' are emphatically not to be forgotten in the light of his conversion but given a new, perhaps paradoxical value as its necessary if superseded prelude.

From which it is clear that 'conversion' is an essentially narrative process, the record of an individual's turning away from one form of belief and turning towards another which is in piquant contrast with it. Conversion – the distinction is Nock's – is to be distinguished from some casually conformist 'adhesion' to a new system of belief; it transforms not just some of the convert's values but most or all of them. One might say that any well-formed narrative effects a 'conversion', because as it unfolds it transforms an original state of affairs into a different one and as its readers we are in the superior position of being able to relate and compare those states of affairs one to the other, the beginning of the story with its end. This happens, as we shall repeatedly see, in autobiography, whose narrative aims at tracing the process of singularization characteristic of its subject: an original state of anonymity is converted into one, first of social and then of literary distinction.

But the autobiographer does more, he 'converts' his past by making from it a story. What, though, can that past be like in its unconverted state? It does not of course exist, for us, outside of the autobiographical text; it is a hypothesis – or better, a hypotext – which we bring with us as readers of autobiography. It is the pre-textual, wordless reality from which an autobiography has arisen, a potential nebula of thoughts and sensations which both underlies and brings pathos to the stable order of the narrative that we are given to read. When we read autobiography we bring to it our own knowledge of 'life in general', or more poignantly, of our own disoriented lives in particular, as the dark background against which we can better appreciate the narrative's heartening logic.

THE ENTRY INTO LANGUAGE

The only medium in which such acts of 'conversion' are feasible is that of language. All that we can share of the past, even with ourselves, is what we are capable of saying or writing about it, under whatever systematic compulsion we can find for effecting its recovery, be it that of writing a book or of enrolling in a psychoanalysis. The autobiographical 'conversion' of a life can but be a textualization of that pretextual 'life', as well as the conversion of a unique lived experience into the symbolic, shared order of a language. For the sharing of our lived experience verbally with others entails loss as well as gain, when the autobiographer must shape his past to the constraints of language equally with shaping his language to the constraints of his past. The great majority of autobiographers have not paused to see this condition as in any way inhibiting or throwing into question the literary activity in which they are engaged; they have written autobiography as if the nature of the medium in which they did so was without real effect on the activity of writing. There is a convenient blindness in them, or else a Rousseauesque will to transparency, whereby such is the bond of sympathy they hope to establish with their readers that neither party to the autobiographical contract will stop to examine this first of its clauses: that auto-biography is not life itself but a certain artful representation of life.

Augustine was aware as few later autobiographers have been of the exclusively verbal nature of the task he was engaged on. The nature and function of language is a theme central to his concerns in the *Confessions*. As a young man he had been trained for the profession of rhetor, or teacher of language and philosophy, and by the time he wrote the *Confessions* he was a Christian bishop, charged with promulgating from his *cathedra* the Word of God. His conversion has carried him from a secular to a sacerdotal practice of language, a fundamental change of register to which I shall have cause to come back. More than that, however, the unregenerate Augustine holds an explicit theory of language, of how it is first acquired by the human infant and of how it conveys meaning. On this theory rests what I have called his 'strategy of deferment'; it demands analysis.

Augustine is rare indeed among autobiographers for introducing himself into the text while still in the speechless state of infancy. Modern autobiographers habitually equate the birth of their self-consciousness with their 'earliest' memory, an originary trace characterized by its isolation, its triviality and its uncertain date: it is the very sign of contingency and as such an ironic prelude to the rational narrative which is to follow. Augustine is more scrupulous; he first represents himself to us as an infant not because he believes he has actual memories of that preverbal state but because he has since observed it in other infants; he is writing as a philosopher and not as an autobiographer, the first person singular of his text standing here, like that of the Cartesian cogito, for all first persons.

As Augustine imagines the process, the entry into language of the infant begins with the significant responses of the baby at the breast, smiling or crying according to whether or not it is satisfied, and continues in frustration once the will exists for the expression of infantile desires: 'Little by little I began to realise where I was and to want to make my wishes known to others, who might satisfy them. But this I could not do, because my wishes were inside me, while other people were outside, and they had no faculty which could penetrate my mind. So I would toss my arms and legs about and make noises, hoping that such few signs as I could make would show my meaning, though they were quite unlike what they were meant to mime'(i.vi).The human voice here is one more part of the body, able to be 'tossed about' as if it were a limb; its radical differentiation from other bodily functions is yet to come, though come it does as the *Confessions* proceed, until it is at last established as the organ of transcendence itself.

The passage from the preverbal to the verbal state is pictured by Augustine as being inspired by the will to expression of what we must assume to be wordless 'wishes', and this will demands for its satisfaction that the few 'signs' which the infant is capable of using should resemble 'what they were meant to mime'. That is, the theory of language here adumbrated is Cratylist, or founded on the belief – it could as well be the desire – that the signifiers of our language should bear a relation of resemblance to their signifieds. The notion that baby-talk is onomatopoeic in this sense, that its sounds somehow 'resemble' infantile drives, dies hard; it still finds supporters today. But the Augustinian infant is frustrated by his failures in signing, when his signs are found to be unintelligible; and frustrated by another kind of failure also, when the wishes he has managed to express are adjudged 'hurtful' and are therefore not acted upon by those around him. He is embarked on the ordeal of socialization through the acquiring of a common language, a knowledge of which both releases us from the (presumed) frustrations of signlessness and brings us up against the opposition to our own will of the will of others. Augustine's *Confessions* dramatize explicitly a conflict of wills, between his will and that of the God who has other plans for him, and this conflict is foreshadowed in the genetic moment of his insertion into his native tongue. This ambiguous moment of socialization, crucial to any narrative preoccupied, as the autobiographical narrative is, with the formation of an image of selfhood, is one to which I shall come back at the far end of this book, since it recurs in a more explicit form in the writings of my last subject, the twentieth-century French autobiographer Michel Leiris.

Augustine's theory of how a natural language is acquired is familiar to the philosophically minded for having been quoted and analysed by Wittgenstein in his epochal *Philosophical Investigations*. It is a theory of learning-by-ostension:

I noticed that people would name some object and then turn towards whatever it was that they had named. I watched them and understood that the sound they made when they wanted to indicate that particular thing was the name which they gave to it, and their actions clearly showed what they meant, for there is a kind of universal language, consisting of expressions of the face and eyes, gestures and tone of voice, which can show whether a person means to ask for something and get it, or refuse it and have nothing to do with it. So, by hearing words arranged in various phrases and constantly repeated, I gradually pieced together what they stood for, and when my tongue had mastered the pronunciation, I began to express my wishes by means of them. (I.viii)

More than simply the acquisition of a language is being accounted for here; Augustine is also advancing a theory of meaning. According to Wittgenstein, he gives us a 'picture' of language in which 'Every word has a meaning. This meaning is correlated with the word. It is the object for which the word stands'.[5] As a theory of either language-acquisition or of meaning it is very obviously inadmissible, inasmuch as if some elements of a language might be thus learnt ostensively by no means all of them could be, since a great many words of a language do not refer to objects potentially or actually available to us in our immediate environment. Augustine's is an empiricist theory, of a child originally wholly without language being gradually equipped with it on the model of the conditioned reflex, the corollary of which is a 'picture' of language as a nomenclature, or collection of terms for things in the world, as if it were formed exclusively of concrete nouns. No such theory can begin to account for the richness and novelty of actual language-use, even in small children.

As the *Confessions* proceed, a different theory of how words 'mean' comes unobtrusively to replace this earlier one; but the earlier theory is important because it serves to polarize Augustine's thought

[5] Ludwig Wittgenstein, *Philosophical Investigations* (Oxford, 1968), p. 2e.

concerning the nature of language, on which so much in his
metaphysical scheme hinges. The ostensive theory is appropriate to
the first, unredeemed state of his intellectual and theological
evolution. It is a materialist theory of meaning, continuous with the
frustrating, preverbal state of signing in that the proper use of words
has to be learnt from observing what we might now call the 'body-
language' of those around, a language assumed by Augustine to be
universal as an expression of human intentions and hence requiring
no interpretation on the part of the child learning his native language.
These significant gestures or bodily movements alone certify the
meanings of terms. Were those around the infant for some reason
incapacitated from performing them, he could learn no words at all,
since his teachers would then be reduced to explaining one term of
the language by other terms, and the child would have no point of
entry into that language. The Augustinian theory is atomistic,
relying on a one-to-one model of words and things, so that the
paradigm case of linguistic 'meaning' is of one object in the external
world being correlated with one term of the language. Meaning is
understood as a function of individual words and to be learnt from
observing their successful application to the world around us.

This first 'picture' of language is not, however, one which
Augustine intends should last him. It is there to be transcended. In
the same account of the acquisition process from which I have, after
Wittgenstein, quoted, he describes the child as having 'gradually
pieced together' what words stood for by hearing them 'arranged in
various phrases and constantly repeated'. Here there are the
foundations of an adequate theory of meaning, as a function not of
single signs but of whole utterances formed in accordance with the
rules of syntax of the language in question. The point is not dwelt on
in the first book of the *Confessions*; it is, however, this second,
sentential theory of meaning to which Augustine will implicitly shift
in the course of the work.

We are now back with the 'strategy of deferment', in its
philosophical and no longer simply narrative guise. Once linguistic
meaning is seen as a function of whole sentences and not of individual
words, its achievement is deferred : not until the sentence is complete
can we necessarily be sure of what it means. Meaning does not inhere
in this or that element of the sentence, but in the sentence as a whole,
as a well-formed string of words. We have shifted from an atomistic
to a structural conception of meaning ; we can not now confuse what

a sentence means with the naming of some object in the world. (Or alternatively, we can see that the naming of some object in the world is itself sentential, that the pointing finger, accompanied by the word 'chair', is equivalent to the sentence of English, 'That object there is called in English a chair.') If now we are asked what a sentence means, it will be no good pointing or performing the bodily indications which Augustine describes; the only satisfactory answer to such a question is in the form of another sentence of the same, or perhaps a second natural language into which the first can be translated. Meaning has become an abstraction.

LETTER AND SPIRIT

This abstraction may be taken as the model of transcendence which Augustine requires, if he is to 'turn' from a pagan or Manichaean philosophy of God and nature to a Christian one. On the theological level, he must turn from a conception of God as a Supreme Being of human form distinctive only for his dimensions, and of individual human beings as constituents of this larger Being. The Christian Augustine, recalling the benighted twenty-year-old pagan Augustine, who believed that God too must be subject to Aristotle's Ten Categories of substance, reflects: 'But what value did I gain from my reading as long as I thought that you, Lord God who are the Truth, were a bright, unbounded body and I a small piece broken from it? What utter distortion of the truth!'(IV.xvi). There is in such a corporeal theology no room for the supervenience of spirit. The spirit it is, however, which will in due course bestow on the substantial scheme its true meaning. Augustine's Christian God is a creator no longer coterminous with his creation. He stands outside of it or transcends it in just the same way as the meaning of a sentence transcends its material components. The Creator is more than the All since it is by his original, verbal act of creation that the All has come to exist.

The theological model on which Augustine now depends is the orthodox one of matter as opposed to spirit, or substance as opposed to meaning, the substance being what is known to our senses, the meaning what is understood by our intellect. The model may readily be traced to the reading of the Neoplatonist philosophers which Augustine had done in the years leading up to his conversion – or better, as a product of his first, preparatory 'conversion', from heedless self-indulgence to the study of philosophy, effected for him by his reading of Cicero's *Hortensius*. The linguistic aspect is what concerns us here, however. This theological or philosophical model is equally familiar as a 'picture' of language, to preserve Wittgenstein's term, in the opposition we frequently recognize when it comes to determining the meaning of a particular sentence or longer text between the 'letter' and the 'spirit', or between its 'literal' and its 'figurative' meaning. This is an opposition open to all manner of question and argument; but it has existed for at least two thousand years and remains fully operative, and it applies very fittingly to the 'conversion' theory of autobiographical narrative which I am proposing. Once life has been turned into literature, its 'literal' meaning or 'letter' has been transcended, because autobiography is specifically concerned with rendering a life 'figurative'. With a diary, or journal, written intermittently and published without any attempt at its later integration into a narrative, we could argue that a past life is represented in a 'literal' form, or in a form as close to literalism as any writer can come. Not so with autobiography proper, where the piecemeal logging of the past has been transcended in a reflective and consciously literary process of integration, so that we now have the 'figure' or else the 'spirit' of a life, embodied in a narrative oriented from the outset towards its eventual 'meaning'.

This is the specifically autobiographical version of the profound 'turn' so variously incorporated in the text of the *Confessions*. Augustine's own initiation into the vital polarity of 'letter' and 'spirit' is begun when he calls, as an enquiring young proto-Christian in Milan, on that city's celebrated Bishop Ambrose. When Ambrose is not beset by visitors, he fills his time by reading, but silently, to himself. Ancient historians have used this passage in the *Confessions* as evidence whereby to date the radical change from reading out loud to reading inwardly, the assumption being that Augustine records this characteristic in Ambrose because it surprised him.[6] But if he was surprised, he does not say so; rather, silent reading is a practice which has important metaphysical implications for him: 'When he read, his eyes scanned the page and his heart explored the meaning, but his voice was silent and his tongue was still. All could approach him

---

[6] The idea that Ambrose was a pioneer of silent reading seems no longer to be popular among historians of antiquity, who now largely accept that the practice is much older and traceable certainly as far back as the time of Alexander the Great – see the correspondence columns of the *Times Literary Supplement* between January and March 1991.

freely and it was not usual for visitors to be announced, so that often, when we came to see him, we found him reading like this in silence, for he never read aloud'(VI.iii).This is no mere transition from one manner of reading to another. What Ambrose has done is to transfer reading from the corporeal to the spiritual sphere, from the visible world to the invisible. The eye is still required, if the text is to be read, but the voice and tongue that would have once been needed as intermediaries in the determination of its meaning have been replaced by the 'heart'. It is the text which now 'speaks' and not the reader, and the 'heart', as the organ to which the text is addressed, has to be opposed to the eye, whose function is purely sensual and instrumental. The 'heart', that most familiar and robust of bodily metaphors, is for Augustine the intimate receptacle of the truly intelligible, and one is not surprised when, a short time later in the *Confessions*, he tells us that 'I was pleased to hear that in his sermons to the people Ambrose often repeated the text, *The letter killeth, but the Spirit giveth life* … '(VI.iv).

With this opposition of Spirit to Letter there enters into the Augustinian model of textual or sentential meaning scope for uncertainty. The 'letter' of a text, its 'literal' meaning, is the meaning on which we can all of us agree, simply by the knowledge we have of the normal use of the terms of which the text is composed. With the 'spirit' of the text it is different, since not all readers will be likely to find the same figurative meaning in what they read. Spiritual meanings are interpretative, and there is a need for Authority to determine which of them should prevail. The authority of Ambrose has taught Augustine that passages of the Bible which, taken literally, might attract the derision of the mockers, could be interpreted spiritually and have their dignity restored (v.xiv). And this same lesson is invoked almost at the outset of the *Confessions*, in respect of the act of confession itself, when Augustine discriminates between his divine and his all too human audience: 'But, dust and ashes though I am, let me appeal to your pity, since it is to you in your mercy that I speak, not to a man, who would simply laugh at me.' (I.vi). Men are literalists and will laugh at him; God, on the contrary, already knows in his prescience that the text which Augustine is addressing to him is the finished, figurative account of his progress to baptism.

It is a short step only from this opposition between the literal and the figurative to another, of equal significance in the *Confessions*: the opposition between grammar and rhetoric, or the rules of language and the use we make of language. By his own account, Augustine early went wrong when learning Latin in succumbing to the deceitful pleasures of literature. Learning the elementary rules of reading and writing – grammar – had been 'an irksome imposition' and he failed then to understand their practical value. Rather, he responded to such emotive fables as that of the passion of Dido for Aeneas in the *Aeneid*. What as an autobiographer he now deplores is the power of such figments to bring us to experience vicariously the emotions of characters who are not, unlike ourselves, real. (The same anxiety was later to seize Rousseau too, as he tells us in his *Confessions*.) Augustine recognizes that the emotions we feel as spectators in the theatre, or as readers of fiction, may be stronger than those aroused in us by similar events in real life; recognizes, more subtly, that what characterizes such vicarious emotion is that it is invariably pleasurable, that we find enjoyment for example in the spectacle of a fictive sorrow.

That recognition might seem self-defeating for the author of so patently rhetorical a work as the *Confessions*, whose story will be ineffective if it fails to move those who read it. Like all autobiography, the *Confessions* are a demand for attention, written with feeling and in the desire to prompt feeling in whoever reads them. This feeling can but be vicarious, but in autobiography it is no longer misspent on the figments of an author's imagining because the story which is being told is true and whatever it causes us to feel seals the uniquely intimate bargain struck between the writers and readers of autobiography. By first cautioning us against the facile emotiveness of fiction, Augustine is legitimizing the emotiveness of fact, in the interests of the literary genre in which he himself has invested.

Grammar creates meaning, and by recourse to rhetoric we may then exploit what grammar creates. But where in all this is meaning to be *located*? In accordance with Augustine's mature, 'transcendent' theory of language, the meaning of a sentence or whole text exists 'beyond' or 'outside' the material words of which that sentence or text is formed. The words are transcended, they are not discarded; they are 'taken up' as the Hegelians might put it, or 'converted' as I would rather have it here. The medium of language remains absolutely necessary to the communication of meaning, just as Bishop Ambrose, even when 'wordlessly' reading, is only able to accede to the abstract realm of intelligibility through the physical medium of eyesight; but the meanings so mediated are for Augustine something other by their nature than the means of their materialization. The means remain in the world of sense, whereas their end transcends sense and belongs to an immaterial sphere beyond.

Words and meanings are related further as parts to a whole, the whole being the deferred factor of semantic integration, the eventual meaning of the sentence, without whose retrospective power of 'conversion' the parts or individual words making up the sentence would remain a broken collection of sounds – in hard fact they would not even be describable as parts, since even to label them as such is to imply their imminent integration into a whole. By this essentially Platonist theory, meanings, understood as transcendent entities of some unspecified form, take clear precedence over the medium in which they are realized or as Platonists might say 'expressed'; such 'meanings' can not themselves be verbal and can but pre-exist their realization in particular forms of words (as the term *realization* of course presupposes).

IN THE FULLNESS OF TIME

Meanings for Augustine are thus timeless, or absolved from temporality: realized inescapably in time yet conceivable outside of it. The passage from an immanent 'picture' of language to a transcendent one involves an escape from the temporal. In their material aspect words are only capable of being spoken or written successively, in time. Indeed, Augustine is as insistent as the founding father of modern structural linguistics, Ferdinand de Saussure, that the first characteristic of natural language is its extension in time, since no two units of either spoken or written language can be uttered or inscribed simultaneously, and when he turns, in the later, philosophical books of the *Confessions*, to speculate as to the nature of memory and of time, it is the strict linearity of language as temporal extension which Augustine draws on in order to illustrate certain characteristics or philosophical difficulties in connection with both memory and time.

Augustine is perplexed, for example, by the measurement of time, or the ability which we have to compare one period of time with another and to decide whether it is longer or shorter or of the same duration. He approaches the question by envisaging time as being filled with the sound of the human voice or else by the imaginary sound of a human voice – as if the subject were St Ambrose, reading silently but still enunciating the words inwardly – so that we even measure a period of silence by the number of consecutive sounds it might potentially contain. And when he passes on to the tripartite division of time, into a past, present and future, Augustine proceeds similarly, having first established his point of vantage necessarily in the present, as being the only one of these three temporal divisions which is empirically 'real', and having redescribed past, present and future as the mental faculties we all of us have of expectation, 'attention' and memory, 'attention' being our capacity of attending to what is passing through our consciousness here and now.

This unceasing temporal process is in effect a further 'conversion', of the future into the past, and Augustine illustrates it with an apposite verbal, or textual example:

Suppose that I am going to recite a psalm that I know. Before I begin, my faculty of expectation is engaged by the whole of it. But once I have begun, as much of the psalm as I have removed from the province of expectation and relegated to the past now engages my memory and the scope of the action which I am performing is divided between the two faculties of memory and expectation, the one looking back to the part which I have already recited, the other looking forward to the part which I have still to recite. But my faculty of attention is present all the while, and through it passes what was the future in the process of becoming the past. As the process continues, the province of memory is extended in proportion as that of expectation is reduced, until the whole of my expectation is absorbed. This happens when I have finished my recitation and it has all passed into the province of memory. (XI.xxviii)

In this particular entity, a psalm, we have what in his wonderfully acute and enlightening essay on the *Confessions*, the American critic Kenneth Burke calls a 'title-word', containing within itself, and asking to be unfolded in time, the summation of a text.[7] The seminal 'title-word' thus represents a point of intersection between the temporal and what lies outside of time, between the words as sequentially uttered and their transcendent meaning, between time and eternity. The 'title-word' *psalm* is a whole of which each successive syllable of the text as it is uttered is a part, and one might note that the title-word is not usually held to be a part of the text, in so far as when we recite or sing a psalm the word (for) psalm itself will not be uttered. And the transcendent title-word Autobiography

---

[7] Kenneth Burke, 'Verbal Action in St Augustine's *Confessions*', in *The Rhetoric of Religion: Studies in Logology* (Berkeley and Los Angeles, 1970). My debt to this brilliantly original essay is pervasive, and I can not itemize it here.

functions in the same way, relative to the written text over which it presides. In the terms put into currency by Jacques Derrida, it is 'parergonal', a 'framing' device, neither quite 'in' the text nor quite 'outside' it – but raising, very uncomfortably, the question of just what surreptitious spatial metaphors such as 'in' and 'outside' imply in this context.

The psalm in Augustine's illustration stands for a whole which is not only complete but *harmonious*; not for nothing has he chosen for his example a biblical text more accustomed to being chanted than merely said and one moreover to which he has much recourse in the *Confessions*, which contain more than three hundred quotations from this one book of the Bible. For harmoniousness too is a quality attributable to the separate parts of a piece of music by virtue of their successive integration into a whole. In the singing of a psalm the harmoniousness of the whole begins to sound in the very first note and syllable, as 'expectation', and if we extend, as Augustine does, this aesthetic pattern from the literary domain to the cosmic, the same may be claimed of human history, whose separate moments, for all their apparent discordancy, sound for the Christian believer with the promise of an eventual harmoniousness. The faithful must trust that everything which, in the momentary perspective of the unbeliever, seems wrong or disharmonious, will come to be understood as a necessary part of the Great Whole. This is the most ample and imposing 'deferment' of all, since for the harmoniousness of Creation finally to be recognized we must wait for the End of Time. And intermediate between the harmonious recital of a psalm, or transcendence on the small scale, and the harmonious making explicit of God's purpose in human history, or transcendence on the very largest scale, there comes the harmonious narration of a single human life, such as that of Augustine, recounted from the start in the foreknowledge of its sublime culmination.

The assimilation of the aesthetic to the historical is made by Augustine himself, in the conclusion to the paragraph from which I have already quoted: 'What is true of the whole Psalm is also true of all its parts and of each syllable. It is true of any longer action in which I may be engaged and of which the recitation of the psalm may only be a small part. It is true of a man's whole life, of which all his actions are parts. It is true of the whole history of mankind, of which each man's life is a part'(xi.xxviii). Yet in finding this continuity between aesthetic and historical structures of transcendence, Augustine is getting on to what is for him perilous ground. He may have chosen a psalm for his example of a significant verbal sequence, but he could have made his point equally well by using a secular text, such as an extract from the *Aeneid*, by whose fictitious delights he was seduced in his boyhood. The ground is perilous because a chief element of the 'turn' which Augustine is at once recording and enacting in the writing of his *Confessions* is also one from an aesthetic to a religious view of the function of language. The aesthetic view of language is one which he wants us to believe he has now surpassed and to recognize as unregenerate, but this is not so simple given that religion can hardly be practised and certainly not preached without the use of language and, as a consequence, without making certain concessions to aestheticism.

THE REALM OF PLAY

Augustine has almost nothing good to say in the *Confessions* about his education; it gave him what he now knows to have been a false understanding of the function of language. As an instrument language is necessary and neutral: the value which we place on it however is determined by the company we keep. As a clever boy in the provinces, with ambitious parents, Augustine was taught to value the mastery of language for the social and financial rewards it would bring. He was trained as a rhetor and for the professional rhetor language was an end in itself, since he was teaching only its mastery, unconcerned by the reputability of the uses to which it would be put. This is the 'aesthetic' view of language, best exemplified perhaps in the forensic reliance on eloquence as a means of persuasion during the hearing of cases in a court of law. The rhetor is a linguistic mercenary, concerned always with style, never with substance. As a schoolboy Augustine had been taught to admire the writings of authors such as the licentious Roman playwright Terence, whose 'lewdness' was of no account, compared with the exemplary qualities of his Latin. For the rhetor and his kind the transgressions which mattered were those against the rules of polished, successful speaking, not those against the moral laws prescribed by the Christian God.

This opposition between an ethical and a ludic philosophy of language and of life is the central issue of the most celebrated episode from his early life which Augustine recounts in the *Confessions*: of the theft of some pears from an orchard. Seeing what a very small crime this was one is surprised at first by the cardinal importance which he gives to it. Why does he make so much of this larceny and so relatively little of those he remembers having perpetrated on the food-stores of his own home? Its very pettiness as a malefaction betrays the stealing of the pears as an event holding a greater importance for the autobiographer than for the boy. It was not a conventional theft or a rational one, made for gain, or out of an uncontrollable desire to possess the objects stolen. The pears, we are told, were of poor quality, and once stolen they were not even eaten but fed to the pigs. This culpable act appears to have had no end outside itself, to have been what we could now call an *acte gratuit*. Whether or not it was a historical act, that is, a theft which actually took place, we can not know and need not decide. It is important within the scheme of the *Confessions* for stigmatizing a playful or purposeless act as if it were a seriously criminal one. (Nietzsche contemptuously calls it a 'prank', in criticizing Augustine for his Christian servility.[8]) Had he stolen the pears for some ulterior purpose, Augustine would have thought less ill of himself. But he associates crime or sin with play. In the brief description which he gives of his sinfulness as a boy, it is notable how intimately the twin worlds, of the sinful and the ludic, are entwined: 'Many and many a time I lied to my tutor, my masters, and my parents, and deceived them because I wanted to play games or watch some futile show or was impatient to imitate what I saw on the stage. I even stole from my parents' larder and from their table, either from greed or to get something to give to other boys in exchange for their favourite toys, which they were willing to barter with me. And in the games I played with them, I often cheated in order to come off the better, simply because a vain desire to win had got the better of me'(I.xix).

The realm of play is tainted for Augustine, along with the institutions – literature and the theatre – which pander to the ludic impulse. But he acknowledges the compulsion to play, the pull which games and public spectacles exert. Play is tempting. His theft of the pears, indeed, represents his own private Fall into temptation, it is a lapse singularized by its clear biblical echoes. The young Augustine

---

[8] Cited by Pierre Courcelle in his indispensable *Les 'Confessions' de Saint Augustin dans la tradition littéraire: Antécédents et postérité* (Paris, 1963), p. 533. Cf. the urbane remark of Oliver Wendell Holmes concerning the same episode: 'Rum thing to see a man making a mountain out of robbing a peartree in his teens', cited in Peter Brown's *Augustine of Hippo: A Biography* (London, 1969), p. 172.

has laid his hands on forbidden fruit, and is now using this reckless moment to symbolize his 'turn' from a superficial, aesthetic appreciation of life to a serious, ethical one. But when he stole the pears he was not acting alone; a characteristic of the world of play is that it is highly sociable. As a thief he had accomplices and in now reflecting on the reasons why he ever allowed himself to do such a thing he concludes that it was the result of his association with others, that he would never have done it on his own. He wanted to merge unremarked into the gang of malefactors: 'For the sake of a laugh, a little sport, I was glad to do harm and anxious to damage another; and that without thought of profit for myself or retaliation for injuries received! And all because we are ashamed to hold back when others say "Come on! Let's do it!"' (II.ix) In Christian terms, Augustine is weak, a sinner, for not having stood up against the lax morality of the group; he has lapsed into anonymity. But his weakness then is his opportunity now, as an autobiographer, able to single himself out from the nameless group of his associates and to appropriate their collaborative endeavour as a cardinal moment in his private story.

It is a teaching of Augustine's *Confessions*, as also of those of Rousseau, that in association there lies danger for the individual soul. When Augustine's protégé (and eventually fellow-convert) Alypius precedes him to Rome, he succumbs for all his good intentions to the attractions of the circus, from which 'futile pastime' Augustine believed he had cured him while they were both still in Carthage. Alypius is persuaded by his Roman friends to go with them to the arena, where he shuts his eyes to the spectacle until the roars of the bloodthirsty crowd prove too much for him, and he begins to look as well as to hear. But the eye for Augustine is the organ through which the 'heart' or soul is attained, and once he has become a true spectator Alypius can not help himself: 'He fell, and fell more pitifully than the man whose fall had drawn that roar of excitement from the crowd'(VI.viii). For Alypius the circus crowd plays the part of Augustine's young accomplices in the orchard; its contagion has brought about his Fall. Its presence is morally corrosive, temporarily extinguishing the singularity of the candidate for salvation.

This threat of a regressive anonymity explains why, throughout the *Confessions*, Augustine has harsh things to say about laughter, almost invariably presented by him in its most antagonistic form, of derision. As a young law student in Carthage he has 'kept company' with a boisterous set known as the 'wreckers', who terrorized other,

more timid students with their mockery.[9] He has found pleasure in
derision, and felt shame when he hung back rather than losing
himself in the crowd of those bent on displaying it. As earlier in the
orchard, he was unprepared to stand alone and to be looked down
upon by his fellows for not following them.

Nor is derision as yet to be distinguished morally from its opposite,
admiration or praise. For Augustine the convert the seeking of the
second is every bit as sinful as the practice of the first. It was not
always so, however. As a clever student and then as a teacher, he had
learnt to expect praise from others for his rhetorical skills and to
instruct others in the rhetorical means of bestowing it. But the love of
praise is a serious temptation which as a Christian he must overcome.
He must turn away from admiration, court even its contrary, derision
(as by thus confessing himself before men). The passage from an
unregenerate to a regenerate state is marked out by his invocation of
two successive role models, both of them well known rhetors, like
himself at the time of his conversion. The first is Hierius, to whom
Augustine had dedicated the aesthetic treatise (it is lost) which he
wrote in his mid-twenties, before he left North Africa for Italy. He is
excessively vague as to how many volumes this work ran to, but
remembers very well to whom it was dedicated: ' ... to Hierius, the
great public speaker at Rome. I had never even seen him, but I
admired his brilliant reputation for learning and had been greatly
struck by what I had heard of his speeches. Even more than this I was
impressed by the admiration which other people had for him. They
overwhelmed him with praise, because it seemed extraordinary that
a man born in Syria and originally trained to speak in Greek had
later become so remarkable a speaker in Latin, and had also such a
wealth of knowledge of the subjects studied by philosophers'(IV.xiv).
The idolized provincial Hierius is everything that the young
Augustine himself has first aspired to be and then become, a worldly
success in the most sophisticated Italian society. The convert must
break publicly with all that, but still has need of an exemplum, to
show him the way. After Hierius, Augustine invokes the story of a
second celebrated rhetorician, Victorinus, a professor in Rome and
for many years an eloquent advocate of the prevailing paganism.
Late in life, Victorinus has been converted to Christianity and has

---

[9] The Latin term which Augustine uses for these hooligans is *evertores*, which might be literally
translated as 'turners-inside-out'. It thus connects with the various other 'turning' words in
the *Confessions*, including that of conversion itself.

professed it publicly. He has chosen to do so even though he was given the chance to make his profession privately, as a prominent pagan 'who seemed likely to find the ceremony embarrassing': 'But Victorinus preferred to declare his salvation in full sight of the assembled faithful. For there was no salvation in the rhetoric which he taught, and yet he had professed it in public. If he was not afraid of uttering his own words before a crowd of madmen, why should he be frightened to name your Word before your meek flock?'(VIII.ii).

A LANGUAGE BEYOND LANGUAGES

In this conversion of Victorinus, so firmly prefiguring Augustine's own, we pass from a plural to a singular 'picture' of language, from the secular profession of words by the rhetor to the Christian profession of the Word. In the notion of the Word, language acquires a unity and wholeness it was far from having while it was still subject to division and dissipation in time. The story of Victorinus is told to Augustine by the Christian Simplicianus, the form of whose name serves to underline the lesson of singleness – deriving from the Latin *simplus* – that he is used in the *Confessions* to convey. After hearing of Victorinus' conversion Augustine has the will to 'imitate' him, as he earlier had the will to imitate Hierius; but as yet he is unable to do so, because his will is not single but double, the divisions within himself are still unresolved: 'So these two wills within me, one old, one new, one the servant of the flesh, the other of the spirit, were in conflict and between them they tore my soul apart'(VIII.v). Only once the lower, fleshly will has been 'converted' by its assumption into the higher, spiritual will can Augustine be recognized as the servant of the Word.

The Word stands in a vertical relation of transcendence to the empirical spoken or written language-chain. It is the supreme example of a sentential 'meaning'. It both is and is not linguistic, being located for Augustine at the mystical point where the verbal and the trans-verbal meet. This is the mystical scene of God's intervention in the world, from outside of time and space. Indeed, the physical creation, of everything which materially exists, was necessarily a verbal act, that being the one conceivable form of such externality, a pure intellectual contingency. The material world can only have been created by an immaterial agency, if it is not to be thought of, impossibly so far as Augustine is concerned, as having created itself. 'In the Beginning was the Word ... ' The doctrine is well known to us from the opening verses of St John's gospel, and Augustine himself cites those verses in the book of the *Confessions* where he both acknowledges his philosophical debts to the Neo-platonist thinkers he has read and distinguishes their pagan version of the doctrine from the Christian one, involving as this last does the element of Incarnation, or the embodying of God's Word in Jesus. Augustine identifies Jesus with the Word, as the mediator between the empirical and the immaterial worlds, Jesus having adopted the natural language of men and even the devices of rhetoric in a uniquely supernatural purpose.

As author of the *Confessions*, Augustine has himself to perform a comparable role of mediation, having to rely on the material resources of human language to point beyond language, to an immaterial realm of meaningful silence. In the eleventh book, where he is concerned with the question of how the Creation came about, he concludes that the Voice of God alone can have made what was not God, that is, matter. And it is in the act of Creation that the two orders meet, of the verbal and the transcendent:

But how did you speak? Did you speak as you did when your voice was heard in the clouds saying: *This is my beloved Son?* At that time your voice sounded and then ceased. It was speech with a beginning and an end. Each syllable could be heard and then died away, the second following after the first and the third after the second, and so on in sequence until the last syllable followed all the rest and then gave place to silence. From this it is abundantly clear that your speech was expressed through the motion of some created thing, because it was motion subject to the laws of time, although it served your eternal will. These words, which you had caused to sound in time, were reported to the bodily ear of the hearer to the mind, which has intelligence and inward hearing responsive to your eternal Word. The mind compared these words, which it heard sounding in time, with your Word, which is silent and eternal, and said, 'God's eternal Word is far, far different from these words which sound in time. They are far beneath me; in fact, they are not at all, because they die away and are lost. But the Word of my God is above me and endures for ever'. (XI.vi)

Augustine here locates the 'mind' intermediately, somewhere 'above' the transient language of signs and 'below' the signless 'language' of God. The verticality of this metaphorical scheme is a reminder that for Augustine, as his biographer Peter Brown observes, the many and incommensurate natural languages of mankind are the 'outcome of the Fall': 'For the Fall had been, among many other things, a fall from direct knowledge into indirect knowledge through

signs. The "inner fountain" of awareness had dried up: Adam and
Eve found that they could only communicate with one another by the
clumsy artifice of language and gestures'.[10] The eternal Word of God
is the 'language' beyond languages; because it never sounds in time
it is exempt from the process of change and the relativism of history.
It is also, one might note, beyond need of interpretation.

Augustine's dilemma in writing the *Confessions* is to use a merely
natural language for the end of indicating to us the supernatural
realm of the Word. How is he to introduce this vertical dimension to
the story, when the very language in which it must be told is
inadequate to its full telling? The two great climaxes of the *Confessions*,
the first narrative, the second psychological, both turn on the
dramatic opposition between a 'fallen' language of signs and the
signless language of God. The narrative climax is the celebrated
moment in the story when Augustine, on the very brink of his
commitment to Christianity, hears the voice of a child from a house
nearby crying out the words *tolle lege, tolle lege*, or 'take it and read,
take it and read'. This apparently pure contingency he interprets as
(i.e. converts into) a divine command. He goes to his Bible and reads
at random a verse from Paul's Epistle to the Romans: 'Not in
revelling and drunkenness, not in lust and wantonness, not in
quarrels and rivalries. Rather, arm yourselves with the Lord Jesus
Christ; spend no more thought on nature and nature's appetites.'
This heavenly admonition is enough to put an end, finally, to his
doubts in respect of his readiness for baptism as a Christian. That
deferred act is now assured.

Augustine tells the episode with a far keener regard for the trivial
circumstances of the occasion than one finds elsewhere in the
Confessions: for example, 'So I hurried back to the place where
Alypius was sitting, for when I stood up to move away I had put
down the book containing Paul's Epistles.' This is a conspicuous
effort at what we, as twentieth-century readers, know as realism. The
evoking of mundane details serves to anchor the episode in time and
place and to heighten its drama, as a moment when the divine order
of things supervenes on the human order, portrayed at its most
ordinary. It is as if Augustine were here testing our credence, by
giving us every chance to interpret this event in our own, profane
way, as an insignificant accident with none of the huge implications

---

[10] Brown, *Augustine of Hippo*, p. 261.

he is claiming for it and for himself, as the sinner chosen to receive this remarkable 'sign' from God. He is making special demands on that 'charity' which he asks for from his readers: 'For although I cannot prove to them that my confessions are true, at least I shall be believed by those whose ears are opened to me by charity'(x.iii).

But it would be naive to suppose that this famous episode of the *Confessions* is, as told, the plain truth of the matter, a simple recollection; that would be straining our charity too far. Read the exhaustive pages of commentary devoted to it by the French Augustinian scholar Pierre Courcelle, and one finds that the episode is made up of a number of formal elements already traditional in literature by the time when the *Confessions* were written.[11] To take just one of these: children at play were commonly then employed by writers as the source of such divine admonitions as that received by Augustine. He is careful in his case to tell us that the words spoken by the child did not seem to come from any known game played by children (though they are certainly formulaic, as Courcelle shows); but might this not be in order to mark this particular child off from the norm for purposes of realism, as well as to exclude any taint of the ludic at this profoundly serious juncture of the narrative? It appears that scholars have long been divided, over whether the child and its exclamation are memory on Augustine's part or invention. This uncertainty reflects very well the uncertainty which attends on all autobiography when we read it, suspended as it is between recording the particularities of a life and observing literary conventions, which work constantly to approximate that life to fiction. But in the case of Augustine and his conversion, it reflects equally well his own need for duplicity at this moment of the story, since he must present the origin of the words which he hears as *both* human and divine. The child must seem to be undecidably both a real child and an angelic messenger. At what is literally the 'turning-point' of the *Confessions* the two orders of language have to be conflated, and the process of conversion from one to the other suspended at its moment of highest drama.

The exhortation which Augustine receives from his Bible is to continence, and one might be tempted to see this, uninterestingly, as addressing, if not removing, the most stubborn of the obstacles to his conversion, which is the strong sensuality he has been unable to master. But in the perspective of the *Confessions* the notion or ideal of

[11] Courcelle, *Les 'Confessions' de Saint Augustin dans la tradition littéraire*, pp. 127–97.

continence can be interpreted more widely and suggestively than this, as being linked textually with other, less obviously moral notions of containment and of content. Immediately before he hears the voice of the child crying '*Tolle, lege*', Augustine has had a vision of 'the chaste beauty of Continence in all her serene, unsullied joy, as she modestly beckoned to me to cross over and to hesitate no more.' A modern reader is likely to dismiss this resort to prosopopoeia as trite and unnecessary, although revealing as to the extent to which the regenerate autobiographer is prepared to employ the devices of the rhetoric he has supposedly abjured. But that would be unjust to the serene figure of Continence, the effect of whose urgings and encouragement is to turn Augustine in on himself, to bring about the great inward 'turn' from the world outside to the God within of which the *Confessions* is both a reenactment and the evidence.

Continence has been Augustine's muse, in having inspired his autobiography; she has earned her figurative role in the text. The next section of the *Confessions*, following that of her appearance to him, opens: 'I probed the hidden depths of my soul and wrung its pitiful secrets from it, and when I mustered them all before the eyes of my heart, a great storm broke within me, bringing with it a great deluge of tears' (VIII.xii). Here, in germ, is the process of self-communion which will be realized *in extenso* in the *Confessions* themselves; this highly emotional moment of the story ranks as a *mise en abyme* of the work as a whole. Augustine is launched on the path of confession, his attention having been turned by the vision of Continence to the *contents* of his own life, or of what for Augustine, as for any autobiographer, is coterminous with his life, the contents of his memory. That curiosity in respect of the outside world which he looks on as sinful, identifying it with the 'lustfulness' of the senses, can now be turned inwards and intellectualized, the 'eyes of my heart' giving him access not to the perishable attractions of a material reality but to the imperishable truths of God.

How then to discover the 'content' of a life? It can only be managed by a process of exegesis. Augustine is called upon as an autobiographer to 'read' the contents of his memory and to 'convert' them. As an autobiographer he stands in the same relation to his own past as he stands as a bishop in relation to the scriptures: he must save it from the derisory condition of literalism and interpret it figuratively for the benefit of his congregation of readers. The vision of Continence has not so much curbed his lusts as 'turned' them; she has given him the clue as to how properly to conduct his textual integration as an individual. His resource is memory, that mysterious faculty which autobiographers mostly take for granted, as if it were a transparent, unequivocal medium by means of which their present self can be reunited with a formless yet readily textualizable past. Augustine, ever the philosopher, chooses rather to question this faculty, to try to determine its nature. Because only what is present can be said to be real, what we know as the 'past' has no other existence but what we are capable of re-presenting of it here and now: 'When we describe the past correctly, it is not past facts which are drawn out of our memories but only words based on our memory-pictures of those facts, because when they happened they left an impression on our minds, by means of our sense-perception. My own childhood, which no longer exists, is in past time, which also no longer exists. But then I remember those days and describe them, it is in the present that I picture them to myself, because their picture is still present in my memory'(xi.xviii). The writing of a life is thus a re-presentation of what no longer exists, but because that re-presentation is itself necessarily extended in time, as a succession of signs, it too has a past, present and future, it cannot be grasped instantaneously. But its readers may feel when their reading is complete that this 'horizontal' narration of a life has left them with a 'vertical' and unitary image of the narrator, as someone standing outside that life and so not to be altogether identified with it. This is the hypothetical, transcendent 'subject' of any life-story or work of autobiography. The contents of a life, in short, are not the whole story, since we can not grasp the notion of content without also having a notion of a container. And as readers of autobiography we are no different in this respect from authors of autobiography, who must see themselves as something more than merely the sum of their recoverable memories. In reflecting on the workings of memory, Augustine concludes that: ' ... the mind is too narrow to contain itself entirely'(x.viii). The relation of rememberer to memory may thus be assimilated to that of Creator to Creation, the rememberer standing outside his memory and willing it into existence as language.

The second climax of the *Confessions*, to go with the episode of the *tolle, lege*, occurs during the conversation recorded as having taken place between Augustine and his mother, shortly before Monica's death in Ostia, on her way home to North Africa. That death marks the end of the narrative element in the *Confessions*, and as such might be said to stand in the stead of Augustine's actual baptism as a Christian, which is never referred to. In this ninth book Augustine is regenerate. He has turned at last from being 'a vendor of words'; he has turned as well from practising the spoken to practising the written word, having begun, as he tells God, 'to serve you with my pen'; he has turned from seeking for his salvation in the sense-world around him to seeking it in himself: 'For those who try to find joy in things outside themselves easily vanish away into emptiness.' And in his last, spiritually exalted conversation with his mother, the two of them aspire higher and higher in their subject-matter, envisaging what the immaterial world might be like, and the eternity of God. The climax of their conversation comes with a moment of wordless trans-cendence: 'And while we spoke of the eternal Wisdom, longing for it and straining for it with all the strength of our hearts, for one fleeting instant we reached out and touched it. Then, with a sigh, leaving *our spiritual harvest* bound to it, we returned to the sound of our own speech, in which each word has a beginning and an ending – far, far different from your Word, our Lord, who abides in himself for ever, yet never grows old and gives new life to all things'(IX.x).

This is the climax of the conversation but not its finale, since the two of them go on to reflect on the posthumous state of joy of those who have died in the faith, in which the only language to be heard is the silent language of God himself, a state, suggests Kenneth Burke, which is 'the analogue of the infant's speechlessness, when such speechlessness is paradoxically conceived by an adult in terms of language' – he is referring back to the theory of language acquisition advanced by Augustine earlier in the *Confessions*.[12]

The instant of contact which Augustine claims that both he and his mother have had with the godlike language beyond language, or the pure language of Truth and Wisdom, serves as the justification for his narration of his life, which might without this divine sanction seem no more than a rhetorical exercise to be classed with those other exercises that he now sees to have been a perversion, a turning of language to false and transient ends rather than the true, eternal one. By the particular exercise of language which has led to the existence of the *Confessions*, Augustine has realized in time his own discovery of what exists beyond time. The record of his discovery is formally addressed to God; the *Confessions* are written in the vocative case.

---

[12] Burke, *Rhetoric of Religion*, p. 133.

Which being so, the question arises of why Augustine should tell God a story which God already knows? There is a simple answer to this: Augustine addresses God in the knowledge that he will be overheard by men, that his narrative of his life, together with his theological and philosophical reflections, will be of value to others, will stir their devotion and direct it.

But there is another answer to the question also: he addresses God because he wishes to demonstrate the extreme of truthfulness of which human language is capable, and that can only be done through the constant invocation of an interlocutor necessarily absent from the text, God's language being silent. Augustine himself stands in for God in the narrative part of the *Confessions*; he recounts his story from God's perspective. For there is more in the telling of his life than there had been in the mere living of it, more in the spirit of it than in the letter; while he had merely been living it he had not understood the direction in which it was going, nor the way in which God had secretly ordered it. As an autobiographer, he is in the peculiarly godlike position of knowing the future, and knowing it for certain, because the future has now happened. While he was still a pagan, Augustine had been much taken up with the powers of prediction claimed by astrologers and the like, and whether or not they were real. In a passage in Book Four, he tells how he was warned – in vain – against believing in such 'trickery' by a doctor, 'a man of deep understanding':

I asked him why it was then that the future was often correctly foretold by means of astrology. He gave me the only possible answer, that it was all due to the power of chance, a force that must always be reckoned with in the natural order. He said that people sometimes opened a book of poetry at random, and although the poet had been thinking, as he wrote, of some quite different matter, it often happened that the reader placed his finger on a verse which had a remarkable bearing on his problem. It was not surprising then, that the mind of man, quite unconsciously, through some instinct not within its own control, should hit upon some thing that answered to the circumstances and the facts of a particular question. If so, it would be due to chance not to skill. (iv.iii)

At first sight, the doctor's rational explanation of the apparent successes achieved by bibliomancy seems to undermine the later episode in the *Confessions* of the *tolle, lege*, when Augustine himself (following, as he declares, the example of St Antony) opens his Bible at random and interprets what he reads as having a quite momentous

'bearing on his problem'. Is this then a reversion to the gullibility of
the pagans? Far from it; taken together, the two episodes mark the
distance Augustine has travelled in understanding. The 'unconscious' element in his life has been the agency of God, who has
directed him into the path of baptism without his knowing it at the
time. In Book Seven Augustine recounts how he came to be convinced
for himself that the divination practised by astrologers was false, and
that its successes were the product of chance. But this is the
philosophical argument against divination, not the Christian one.
The Christian argument substitutes the notion of Providence for that
of chance, and the notion of divine direction for that of the blind
'instinct' which is outside the mind's control.

The verbal account of his life which Augustine gives in his
Confessions is thus double: it is realized in time and in natural
language for the benefit of his fellow sinners; and it aspires
simultaneously to God, as an index to that transcendental 'language'
which he and Monica have glimpsed during their moment of
mystical exaltation in Ostia: 'And so my confession is made both
silently in your sight, my God, and aloud as well, because even
though my tongue utters no sound, my heart cries to you. For
whatever good I may speak to men you have heard it before in my
heart, and whatever good you hear in my heart, you have first spoken
to me yourself'(x.ii). The autobiographical theme of 'conversion' is
here prodigiously enriched. For not only does the process of
'conversion' symbolize the turning of a life that would otherwise
remain as a chaos of inconsequential accidents into a figurative and
redeeming 'story', it also symbolizes the workings of the creative will
of God himself, whose own autobiography can but be the totality of
human history.

CHAPTER 2

A case to answer: Abelard, Dante, Petrarch

Rousseau begins the fourth of his *Promenades d'un rêveur solitaire* by saying that he has just been reading a work by the Roman author he most admired, the moralist Plutarch: the work in question was a treatise entitled *De Capienda ex Inimicis Utilitate* or (in its 1535 English translation), 'Howe one may take profit of his enemyes.' This is a topic on which by this late period of his life Rousseau was sadly expert; he believed that he had enemies everywhere, and most of all among his former friends, and his autobiographical writings are his response to the untruths he supposes them to have been spreading about him. This was to go against the advice of Plutarch, that we should not rise *to* calumny as Rousseau so unstoically did, but rise *above* it, by keeping silent and striving all the harder to live our lives in such a way as to be beyond reproach.

Autobiography is self-evidently not the way of the quietist, but an expedient by which the writer can reply to the injuries that have been done to him. It is a kind of writing by which to win redress, a forensic genre, the first true example of which, according to the foremost historian of autobiography, Georg Misch, was the *Antidosis* or 'Challenge' of the Athenian logographer and rhetorician, Isocrates, in the fourth century BC. The declared purpose of the *Antidosis* was 'to reveal to those who had mistaken ideas about me, and to posterity, my character, my life, and the sort of education to which I was devoted'.[1] The autobiographer can stand up in court and vindicate himself against whoever may have harmed or defamed him in the course of his life, as well as against the impersonal hindrances that might have kept someone less pertinacious than himself from achieving prominence. He is a narrator who has won through and has correspondingly much to gain from showing how hardly his

---

[1] See Georg Misch, *History of Autobiography in Antiquity* (Cambridge, Mass., 1950), Volume 1, pp. 154–60.

reputation has been gained, in the spite both of a grudging fortune and of human contrariety. The autobiographer's story should ideally be of the *vita travagliata* or 'life of travail' invoked by Benvenuto Cellini at the start of his highly adversarial *Life*.[2]

There is no knowing whether such a *vita travagliata* be God's truth or autobiographer's fable, the legitimate crowing of a high achiever or a belated reparation for slights and frustrations vindicable in no other way. The autobiographer's proclaimed resilience in the face of enmity or misfortune, or surpassing of his professional rivals may have had to wait until now, and the act of writing, to be fully realized: for where better than in a backward-looking story of this kind to indulge a restorative *esprit d'escalier*? Either way, it is the autobiographer's literary celebration of his achievement which gives to his vindication of himself the permanence and dignity of print. The resort to arms may serve a Renaissance bravo such as Cellini well enough in settling hasty quarrels in the streets of Florence, but the resort to letters will serve him better, by duplicating his self-affirming exploits in the new, equally admirable and infinitely more enduring form of art.

The more potentially deterrent the recorded circumstances of his life have been, the greater the autobiographer's merit in being finally in a position to write of them. Only now can the injuries inflicted on him be definitively bandaged, by being laid under a narrative contribution and fitted gainfully into the economy of his life as a whole. In writing, the autobiographer is free to conspire against the circumstances which he believes have conspired against him: the 'plot' of his autobiography is also a counterplot. At its extreme – and the extreme case is that of Rousseau – this redressive posture may verge on the paranoid, with the writer driven to take up his pen in order to defend himself against fantasmal intrigues. At a less intense pitch, it sounds only the soothing note of retaliation. But a touch of paranoia is inspirational in urging the autobiographer to make public the truth about himself, so as to obliterate the false views of him put about by the envious and spiteful. Autobiography as truth-telling has both a moral and an aesthetic claim to make: by its veracity it displaces the false reports previously attaching to its author, and in its fixity as literature it rises above the mutability of daily life.

[2] The words come from the sonnet by Cellini which stands at the head of his *Life*.

Abelard

Nowhere is the potential vindictiveness of autobiography displayed more candidly than in the brief account of his troubled life left behind him by Abelard, the twelfth-century scholastic philosopher, better known to us as a writer from the letters which he exchanged with his former lover, Heloïse. Abelard's *Historia Calamitatum* or *Story of my Misfortunes* may have been eclipsed by that poignant correspondence but it is the more expressive document of the two.[3] The *Historia* too is epistolary, having the form of a letter addressed to an unnamed friend who is in need of consolation and whom Abelard affects to console by the time-honoured method of assuring him that his troubles are as nothing compared with those which he himself has endured: a recognition at the outset that this autobiographer means to stand supreme, having out-suffered other sufferers at the hands of a contrary fate – we learn nothing in the *Historia* of the troubles of the unfortunate friend-cum-rival who has, he claims, inspired him to write it and the assumption among scholars has frequently been that there was no such person, but that Abelard invented him as an excuse first for writing and then for circulating this notably uncharitable account of his life's dealings.

The *Historia* is an 'open' letter, addressed nominally to a single recipient but open to be read by many and written in a polemical intention. The format is one suitable to a practised dialectician such as Abelard. For a modern reader the epistolary falls as a mode of address midway between the spoken and the written, ideally marrying the greater emotiveness of the first to the greater formality of the second. In the hybrid prose of a literary letter we may suppose that we hear the writer's distinctive 'voice', speaking in contradiction of his bodily absence. In the first of her letters to Abelard, the bereft Heloïse herself writes, 'While I am denied your presence, give me at least through your words [...] some sweet semblance of yourself.',[4] thereby employing a topos familiar to her and to her correspondent from their extensive knowledge of the literature of antiquity, which according to Abelard was a strong bond between them. 'Some sweet semblance' of himself is what any autobiographer may hope to

---

[3] The edition I shall quote from here is: Peter Abelard, *The Story of My Misfortunes*, translated by Henry Adams Bellows (Glencoe, Ill., 1958).

[4] *The Letters of Abelard and Heloïse*, translated by Betty Radice (Harmondsworth, 1974), p. 116. Heloïse has already in this letter quoted a classical literary source, Seneca, to this effect, that a letter makes the writer 'present' to the recipient.

deliver, a semblance 'sweet' because designed to earn him the affection of those who receive it.

A theorem of autobiography which I hope to prove in the course of this book is that it is a kind of writing conscious of itself as an invitation to intimacy but of having to achieve that intimacy by an indirect means. Because he writes, and does not speak his life, the autobiographer need never be anything except calm and composed, and may air the most emotional matters confident in having them under control. In the *Historia*, Abelard argues for the advantages of writing over speaking as an instrument of rational persuasion. In the preamble, he reminds his correspondent that he has already attempted to console him in conversation but that, the record of his own misfortunes offering a better means to that end 'than words', he has now determined to write him this letter. For Abelard, seemingly, conversation is 'words' but narrative is not, its status as story being sufficiently imposing to suppress awareness of the medium in which stories are told.

He has grasped the advantage to be had from physical separation even in the conduct of his love affair with Heloïse: ' ... I believed that I could win the maiden's consent all the more easily by reason of her knowledge of letters and her zeal therefor; so, even if we were parted, we might yet be together in thought with the aid of written messages. Perchance, too, we might be able to write more boldly than we could speak, and thus at all times could we live in joyous intimacy.' (16) Absence is thus an inspiration, provided it can be bridged by an exchange of messages, the couple's love letters serving as both product and proof of their shared 'knowledge of letters'. Abelard's insight, moreover, into the increase in boldness that may come with writing, applies not simply to lovers, able in their letters to one another to indulge a fulsomeness they either could not or would not allow themselves in conversation, but to autobiographers, who in writing can rise to a boldness and egotism that would be deemed intolerable in the more tactful and inhibited setting of daily life.

Such boldness is the characteristic mark of the *Historia Calamitatum*. This brief text gives an extraordinary summary of nearly forty years of its author's unmerited persecution, starting when Abelard is adolescent and a student in Paris, and ending when he is in his mid-fifties and the beleaguered abbot of a rebellious monastery in Brittany. If he has not merited persecution, however, he has certainly invited it: his enemies are ones that he has made, by his audacity or independence of mind, as philosopher, theologian and lover. Abelard begins his story, true to autobiographical type, by marking himself firmly off from his siblings – he has a sense of lineage and a wish to show to what extent he has both shared in and departed from its traditions. His father he presents as a man divided between arms and letters, by profession a soldier yet sufficiently in love with learning to have his sons 'taught in letters even earlier than in the management of arms'. Abelard's brothers have followed their father and become fighting men; he, the firstborn, has chosen differently and more pacifically: ' … I was so enthralled by my passion for learning that, gladly leaving to my brothers the pomp of glory in arms, the right of heritage and all the honours that should have been mine as the eldest born, I fled utterly from the court of Mars that I might win learning in the bosom of Minerva. And since I found the armory of logical reasoning more to my liking than the other forms of philosophy, I exchanged all other weapons, and to the prizes of victory in war I preferred the battles of minds in disputation'(1–2).

With this brief volley of military metaphors, Abelard closes the gap he has just opened up between his own course of life and that of his soldier brothers, and one soon learns from the *Historia* that as a theologian and philosopher he has been every bit as militant, and certainly more famous than his brothers, of whom we hear no more. He has surpassed them; no other member of his family is named thereafter in the text. Naming is reserved for his enemies, whose nomination is necessary if they are to be recognized as worthy adversaries of himself. There is William of Champeaux, Abelard's teacher in philosophy, his relations with whom are first cordial and then unhappy, once the precocious student has begun to take his master on in argument and to be 'adjudged victor'; or Anselm of Laon, a renowned theologian whom Abelard seeks out but about whom in the *Historia* he is memorably rude: 'If anyone came to him impelled by doubt on any subject, he went away more doubtful still … He had a miraculous flow of words, but they were contemptible in meaning and quite void of reason'(10). (cf. Augustine on one of his principal adversaries, Faustus the Manichee, noted, he says, for 'his charming manner of speech' and complete vacuity of argument: *Confessions* v.iii). Other of Abelard's adversaries follow in order: Alberic of Rheims, Lotulphe the Lombard, Fulbert the uncle of Heloïse, who eventually plans his castration in outrage at the seduction of his niece, and the great Bernard of Clairvaux.

The story of Abelard's 'misfortunes' is in fact the story of his fame, or of the imposition on his society of his own name. He is in no doubt that his gifts are singular: challenged as a student to expound the most obscure passage in the prophet Ezekiel, even though he has hitherto studied only the 'sciences', he is perfectly ready to do so, and responds scornfully to the suggestion that scriptural exegesis requires time and experience with the boast 'that it was my wont to win success, not by routine, but by ability'. Ability is of course a gift, not something instilled in us by the care of others and Abelard here is introducing a prime topos of autobiography, of the natural endowment that requires no contribution from outside – the paradigm case of which is Descartes, so set on embodying a cognitive aseity. By his victories in philosophical argument Abelard has first distinguished and then isolated himself, victory bringing with it as its tribute the enmity of those he has defeated. His life has been punctuated by the need for withdrawal in the face of persecution, and for seclusion. When William of Champeaux in Paris spreads slanders against him, he retires with his following of students to the 'castle' of Melun, just like a prudent strategist on the battlefield; when things get too hot for him in Laon, thanks to the spiteful reaction of Anselm, Abelard returns to Paris.

But slander and sequestration alike serve to increase his fame; and once again absence turns out to have an advantage over presence. For just as the bodily absence of the loved one may prompt in the suitor a greater courage and address in language, so the enforced absence of the celebrated teacher serves only to increase his charisma. When, as a result of some unspecified illness, the youthful Abelard is forced to return to his native province in the west of France, he declares himself to have been 'sought out all the more eagerly by those whose hearts were troubled by the lore of dialectics'; when, later on, as a teaching brother in the monastery of St Denis, he is obliged by the hostility of the abbot and other members of the community to remove himself to a 'hut', such is the crowd of students who come to him 'that the neighbourhood could not afford shelter for them, nor the earth sufficient sustenance'. If we take these moments of triumphal banishment as premonitory of the solitude of the autobiographer, then we may conclude that the latter's temporary withdrawal from human company in order to write is likewise to be compensated for by the promise of an increase of fame. 'Behold now, the whole world runs after him, and our persecution of him has

done naught save to increase his glory': these are the words which
Abelard puts into the mouths of his enemies, contriving, as any
autobiographer must, to incorporate even the unhappiest contingencies of his life into the telos of his narrative.

The two calamities he has experienced which justify the title he
gave to his work are his castration at the hands of Heloïse's uncle and
the condemnation and formal burning of his treatise on the Trinity at
the Council of Soissons. These are episodes unlike any others in the
Historia for having by his own account brought shame on him. His
relations with Heloïse have been conditioned throughout by his
concern for his reputation. If he marries her, having made her
pregnant, he will be disgraced, and the arguments against their
marrying are rehearsed at unexpected length in the *Historia*, not by
Abelard himself but as if addressed to him by Heloïse. This is highly
suspect. Is he, as an autobiographer, unprepared to admit that
concern at the loss of his own reputation weighed more strongly with
him than guilt at having dishonoured his mistress? His textual
attribution of the reasons for his not marrying to the wronged girl
smack of deviousness: in making her appear so saintly in her concern
for his career and good name, he is exculpating himself from any
charge of selfishness. The reputation which he is protecting is his own
reputation *now*, thirty years after the event. The marriage in the end
takes place, but is conducted in secret, so that Abelard's good name
may be preserved. The feared 'disgrace' comes instead with his
castration. But rather than disgrace, it is ridicule which Abelard very
reasonably fears will now follow him, as a man known to have been
violently emasculated; he looks for seclusion in the cloister. In this
extreme of persecution he can see no honour, only mockery. He has
been assailed in his vanity, as he is a second time when his book is
unjustly condemned to the flames and he is criminalized.

But for an autobiographer there can be no disgrace in having been
disgraced, since to admit to it is a creditable act. Abelard's *Historia* is
an extravagantly vain account of his life, ending not in the calm of
reconciliation with his fate but in crazed accusations against the
monks of the Breton community of which he is abbot, that in their
vicious resentment of his austerity they have tried to murder him by
lacing the communion wine with poison. Abelard's final acquiescence
in the will of God, who has purified his soul by subjecting him to so
great a persecution, rings hollow, except for its suggestion that the

exceptional degree of punishment he has had to endure has been earned by the singular nature of his abilities.

Dante

Where the *Historia* of Abelard is robustly literal, the *Vita nuova* of Dante approaches the condition of allegory, its lived substratum evoked so delicately as almost to deny the 'story' which it contains anchorage in a determinate time or place. Dante's physical setting is thinly furnished – a bed, a frescoed wall, some 'panels' on which he draws figures of angels, are all that the autobiographer requires by way of specific indications of materiality. When dates, ages or the time of day are given, it is patently in obedience to a numerological scheme and not to the accidents of the author's personal history; and the cast of human beings among whom the autobiographer has moved is undifferentiated, faceless. Not once does Dante name the city of Florence, in which the etiolated events of his narrative have taken place, and a reader unattuned to the refinements of allegory might conclude that there never were any such events, that this brief essay in autobiography is purely fabulous. But whatever the veracity of the *Vita nuova*, it is I believe sufficiently realistic in accounting for its own existence to justify the claim that Dante, like Abelard, uses autobiography in a forensic cause, to defend himself against charges to which he was certainly open and which may in truth have been laid.

Read as narrative, the *Vita nuova* tells the story of his passion for Beatrice, from the moment he first set eyes on her when they were both of them children up to, and a little beyond her early death. This is the passion which has dominated the writer's early life and one might suppose that the 'New Life' was that which had begun with his auspicious first glimpse of the nine-year-old girl. Dante's opening words seem to bear this out: 'In my Book of Memory, in the early part where there is little to be read, there comes a chapter with the rubric: *Incipit vita nova*. It is my intention to copy into this little book the words I find written under that heading – if not all of them, at least the essence of their meaning'(3).[5] *Incipit vita nova*, 'A new life begins': Dante's title, it turns out, is not newly coined but copied, from a previous inscription of the story of which he is now about to

[5] The English version I have used is Mark Musa: *Dante's Vita Nuova: A Translation and an Essay*, (Bloomington and London, 1973).

give us the 'essence', though with the important difference that where the original title was in Latin, the new one is in the vernacular. As a 'rubric' in the Book of Memory, the Latin words may be taken to have referred straightforwardly to the new life that had begun for him at his first sight of Beatrice. But the Book of Memory has now undergone a revision, the autobiographer is an older and a wiser man, and he has entered on a second new life founded on a true understanding of the first.

One finds soon enough that the *Vita nuova* contains two stories, and both stories of a 'conversion'. The account of Dante's youthful dependency as the lover of Beatrice is overlaid from the start by that of his eventual recovery from this irrational and unseemly state. As a lover the autobiographer cuts a pitiable figure, forever drooping disconsolately when he fancies his amorous cause to be lost and without control over his own fluctuating moods. But as an auto-biographer he is in an altogether different state, having come to that autarky which all autobiographers are able to enjoy by virtue of their calling. The youthful surrender to a sensual passion can now be recouped by being set within a spiritualized context. To literature goes the task of turning past folly into present, and exemplary Reason.

The relation of Love to Reason in the *Vita nuova* is reflected in the text by the combination there of poetry and prose. Within his prose narrative, Dante has incorporated thirty-one poems, love sonnets for the greater part but also four longer ballads or *canzoni*, which serve as lyrical intermediaries between the writer's present state of self-possession and his earlier volatility as a lover. Each poem is immediately followed by a brief 'division', in which the poet summarizes its themes in a postface modelled on the explanatory procedures of the scholastic philosophers. So if the sonnets and *canzoni* represent a first stage in the autobiographer's mastery of the sentiments which had once ignominiously mastered him, his glosses on them represent a second stage, in which he summarizes in a plain, elementary form the 'essence' of what is in the poem – just as he is giving in the *Vita nuova* as a whole the 'essence' of what had previously been obscurely written in the Book of Memory.

These prose glosses are a part of Dante's strong desire to be *understood* and are one index to his sense of the discrepancy on which this, like any work of autobiography, is founded, between his experiences as they have appeared from within, to himself, and as they have appeared from without, to others. The *Vita nuova* makes the case for behaviour that had been sufficiently extravagant to be deemed out of place, even laughable. For as long as she was alive, no one had known for certain that Beatrice was the object of Dante's adoration, neither Beatrice herself nor any of those around her. He had not been able to suppress all sign of the agitation the sight and thought of her caused in him, but he had managed to disguise its source by pretending to be in love with other women, who have been made to act as a 'screen' or shield for his true passion. But his decoy tactics have been more effective than he wanted, because Beatrice has concluded from the rumours spread about him in her circle that he is a 'vicious' young man and has snubbed him, so precipitating a crisis of melancholy and self-pity.

This, potentially, is the stuff of comedy, a subject more for Boccaccio than for Dante. The lover's decorous deception has occasioned a breach, and his cult of Beatrice has been brought coarsely down to earth, among the gossiping and inquisitive burghers of his native city. As the soulfully pining Lover, he has been a conspicuous figure, and if his friends have worried at the changes in his appearance, 'others, full of malicious curiosity, were doing their best to discover things about me, which, above all, I wished to keep secret from everyone. I was aware of the maliciousness of their questioning and, guided by Love who commanded me according to the counsel of reason, I would answer that it was Love who had conquered me'(7–8). Here already, Dante has hit upon a sounder way to conceal the true object of his passion; instead of human 'screens' or stand-ins he will resort to prosopopoeia, that rhetorical trope – *the* autobiographical trope, according to Paul de Man – of which he turns abruptly aside to offer a defence in Book xxv of the *Vita nuova*. By its means, the historical Beatrice can begin her ascent on to the allegorical plane as the embodiment of Love, there to be joined before long by her devotee.

The jarring didacticism of Book xxv is the strongest indication of all in the *Vita nuova* that Dante is engaged on a task of reasoning and self-justification. The rhetorician has turned aside from his story in order to justify his use of rhetoric: 'At this point it may be that someone worthy of having every doubt cleared up could be puzzled at my speaking of Love as if it were a thing in itself, as if it were not only an intellectual substance, but also a bodily substance'(54). Dante has given Love a body, and caused it to speak, even though this is 'patently false', love being something which occurs *in* substances – it is an 'accident', in the scholastic jargon – not a thing in itself. To personify it as he has done is to employ poetic licence; the Latin poets of antiquity were granted such licence and so now, argues Dante, should poets like himself writing in the vernacular, not least because love is the one proper subject for vernacular poetry.

This is so because 'The first poet to begin writing in the vernacular was moved to do so by a desire to make his words understandable to ladies who found Latin verses difficult to comprehend.' That the *Vita nuova* should itself be in the vernacular, and so much concerned with making Dante's words and past actions understandable, suggests that it too is addressed to women, to those *Donne ch'avete inteletto d'amore*, or 'Ladies who have intelligence of love' whom one of the most exquisite of the *canzoni* begins by apostrophizing. This poem stands at the turning-point of Dante's story, and he describes its occasion with a circumstantiality not to be found anywhere else in the *Vita nuova*. He has been persuaded one day to join a group of ladies 'who knew my heart very well' and who are 'enjoying one another's company'. The atmosphere is animated and candid, and Dante is asked by one of those present to explain his contradictory sentiments as a lover who both longs for and dreads an appearance by the object of his affections: 'Why do you love this lady of yours, if you are unable to endure the sight of her? Tell us, for surely the goal of such a love must be strange indeed'(31). Dante's embarrassed answer is that his 'goal' has changed its nature: 'Ladies, the goal of my love once consisted in receiving the greeting of this lady to whom you are, perhaps, referring, and in this greeting rested the bliss which was the goal of all my desires. But since it pleased her to deny it to me, my lord, Love, through his grace, has placed all my bliss in something which can not fail me.' This unfailing resource, he explains, is poetry, his bliss now resting 'In those words that praise my lady'. To this Dante's acute questioner replies: 'If you are telling us the truth, then those words you addressed to her describing your condition must have been written with some other intention', and the poet departs, 'shamed by her words' and determined that in future his theme as a poet will be 'praise of this most gracious one'.

This episode has brought about the second of the two 'conversions' Dante has undergone and has inaugurated the second of his two new lives. Previously, the topic of his narrative and of the poetry set into it has been his unhappy condition as Beatrice's lover; but from this point on he will leave off treating Love in these low material terms and make of it his ideal, never again writing to Beatrice directly but taking her as the absent object of his 'praise', as more the excuse than the occasion of his art. Like Abelard, Dante has found fresh inspiration in the physical absence of the beloved.

This 'conversion' in both his life and his art has been effected by shame, or by his public exposure to the group of clever and satirical women among whom he found himself, as someone whose poetic intentions had not always been as highminded as he asserts them now to be. The second story told in the *Vita nuova* is that of the genesis of his new, definitive artistic credo, and Dante must tell it in order to show that he is capable of doing so, that his life may not have made sense in the days of his amorous passion but that it does so now. He ends his defence of personification in Book xxv by saying that were a poet unable to strip his poem of its 'images and rhetorical colouring [...] in order to reveal its true meaning', 'this would be a veritable cause for shame' (56). If Dante has been shamed once, into adopting his new idealism, he will not be so again, for in the prose of the *Vita nuova* he has revealed the true meaning of his love for Beatrice, as a sensual and egotistical experience now transcended. Dante has employed autobiography for the edifying purpose of tracing his own liberation from life into art.

Petrarch

Abelard, Dante and Petrarch form a set of three autobiographical writers driven variously by a perceived adversity and ridicule to make explanation of themselves. Like the others, Petrarch too has courted publicity as a lover, having taken for his supreme poetical theme his love for Laura, the young girl whom he had first caught sight of in Avignon in 1327, when he was twenty-three years old. This 'insensate passion' as he calls it comes under long scrutiny in his autobiographical *Secretum*, a work written some fifteen years after that determining encounter.[6] In it Petrarch, like Dante, is looking in retrospect to set himself morally and emotionally outside a passion whose effects in his life have been ambiguous; but he does so not in the univocal form of a narrative but in that of a dialogue – a set of three dialogues, to be exact – in which among other questions the

---

[6] The edition I shall quote from is *Petrarch's Secret, or The Soul's Conflict with Passion: Three Dialogues between Himself and St Augustine*, translated by William H. Draper (London, 1911).

effects for good or ill of his devotion to Laura can be debated between himself and his spiritual alter ego, St Augustine, whose role in the *Secretum* is to condemn the author's ineradicable worldliness and spiritual inertia. Petrarch is looking to undergo a 'conversion' of the Augustinian kind but is without the will-power to bring it about.

In defence of his 'insensate passion', he argues that its moral influence on him was such as to have quite changed his life: 'To her I owe whatever I am, and I should never have attained such little renown and glory as I have unless she by the power of this love had quickened into life the feeble germ of virtue that Nature had sown in my heart. It was she who turned my youthful soul away from all that was base, who drew me as it were by a grappling chain, and forced me to look upwards'(121). The language here is exactly that of a 'conversion' as if copied from Augustine's *Confessions* – the book to which Petrarch was so attached that he carried it with him on his celebrated ascent of Mont Ventoux, loyally opening it at random, with a fine bibliomantic flourish, on the summit.

But this praise of Laura as a force for moral good is only one side of the argument. Under pressure from Augustine – and in the presence of a silent third party to their discussion, the rhetorical personification of Truth – Petrarch is led into an admission that to the first meeting with Laura there has also to be dated the beginning of his 'confusion', or that state of moral and psychological inhibited-ness which it is the purpose of the *Secretum* to elucidate. He is writing because he feels he has gone astray, his life is not as it should be, and it is the fateful encounter with Laura that he now blames as a literal aberration: 'I first saw her and I turned away from my right course at one and the same time'(129). This, however, is the opposite of the impression that he has given in his other writings, in which Laura has been idealized as the object of a devotion from which he has never lapsed. Petrarch has become the captive of his own rhetoric and suffers a barbed reminder from his interlocutor that his true situation in life is the shameful or ridiculous one of the *senex amans*:

Blush, therefore, to pass for an aged lover; blush to be so long the public's jest; and if true glory has no charm for you and ridicule no terror, at least let change of heart come to the rescue and save you from disgrace. For, if I see things at all truly, a man should guard his reputation, if only to spare his own friends the necessity of telling lies. All the world owes this to itself, but especially such a man as yourself, who have so great a public to justify, and one which is always talking of you. (160)

The concern for his own place in the world which Petrarch declares himself anxious but unable to give up is thus concentrated in the figure of Laura, whose given name is very nearly homonymous with that of the bay or laurel, the ancient symbol of the glory with which the competitive artist aspires to be crowned. To disavow Laura would be for Petrarch to disavow the past as a whole and in particular the works of literature by which he has made his name.

This he is not strong-willed enough to do, and the *Secretum* itself exemplifies his readiness, his need for compromise. This is no narrative such as that of his interlocutor Augustine, culminating in a brave statement of his renunciation of worldly goods and pleasures, and the dedication of himself to spiritual ones. It is inconclusive, the dialogue form enabling Petrarch to exhibit his moral weakness in a state of suspense, without resolving it. But then he is attempting to cure himself of the temporal vanity that attends on authorship by writing yet another book, a work which will extend his fame, not disown it. Petrarch knows that he is trapped within a contradiction: he describes the *Secretum* as a work different in kind and not to be classed with his other books, because in it 'My thoughts aim higher.' Rather than give it to the world, he will keep it by him, and reread it when he wants: 'So, little Book, I bid you flee the haunts of men and be content to stay with me, true to the title I have given you of "My Secret"'(5). Yet the very existence and refined formulation of the work betray its author's concern that whatever fresh understanding of his own nature he has come to it should be known also to others. Unlike Augustine, Petrarch is addressing his secular confession not to God but to men, to that public 'which is always talking' of him.

There is misanthropy in the *Secretum*, a nostalgia on the part of Petrarch for the days when he was living in isolation in the countryside, and a bile directed at the life of the city, Avignon being anathematized as 'the most melancholy and disorderly of towns, the narrow and obscure sink of the earth, where all the filth of the world is collected'(97). This autobiographer runs true to type in being so proudly thankful he is not one of the crowd, the 'detestable herd' it has been his wish to escape from ever since the moment of his 'conversion' by Laura. But in the eyes of Augustine the poet's will to seclusion is impure, because its true purpose has been to earn from him the admiration of the very crowd he claims to despise: 'I have observed that no man more than you abhors the manners and behaviour of the common herd. Now see what perversity is this! You let yourself be charmed with the applause of those whose conduct you abominate...'(167–8). But this is Petrarch calling Petrarch to account, and doing so secure in the knowledge that as an auto-biographical subject he will remain in the state of moral suspension he so deplores, having chosen in his vanity to exhibit his weaknesses rather than contend with them in private.

CHAPTER 3

Fame and fortune: Cellini, Cardano

The first question posed by Petrarch in his *Secretum* is whether men are themselves to blame if they are unhappy. It is unhappiness which has driven him to write these dialogues, but his experience of life has been, he believes, of a kind to entitle him to feel miserable. He lays a stock complaint against the mutability of Fortune, 'This stepdame who in a single day with her ruthless hand laid low all my hopes, all my resources, my family and home'(96) – the allusion being to his exile from his native city of Florence – and grumbles in passing about the cruelty with which human hopes are mocked by an adverse fate. But Augustine does not agree that Petrarch has the right to complain; he dismisses the argument from experience as a hackneyed and ignorant one, arguing for his own part that we will our own unhappiness, misfortune being no more than an opportunity which we seize upon in order to feel unhappy, never a sufficient cause of unhappiness. This innovative reply shifts the ground of the discussion from the rhetorical to the psychological plane, and confronts Petrarch with the possibility that he might be other in future from what he has been in the past, were he to abjure the passivity which has led him to blame Fortune for a state of mind it is within his power to change. But he lacks the will to do so. He is caught within a contradiction: the will that is too weak to allow him to respond cheerfully to the bludgeonings of fate is apparently strong enough to sustain him in his melancholia. He is willing his own will-lessness.

Petrarch's contention that his unfavourable experience has entitled him to feel unhappy is a first step along the way to autobiography. He has something to complain about and, by raising the question at the start of his own stealthy collusion with the ruthless Stepdame Fortune, he has found a fresh, ingenious and idiosyncratic form in which to make his complaint. The *Secretum* is a work of literary art whose fixity as an aesthetic object stands in dramatic and reassuring contrast to the instability of life. The autobiographer can indeed make that instability into a powerful narrative resource, by representing the vicissitudes of his life as the peripeteia of an individual drama – and even the most apparently uneventful of existences may be narrated so as to profit from its small reverses of fortune.

Autobiography is written in times of respite from an immediate experience of the world, the autobiographer having found a provisional asylum from the gross intrusions on his consciousness of both history and humankind. A Petrarch can not look back on a life of uninterrupted calm, nor realistically ahead to one in whatever time is left to him, but he has contrived an interval of calm in which to reconsider the values by which he lives. The *Secretum* ends with the autobiographer longing to find permanent shelter from 'the winds of adversity', but having already acknowledged that his craving for 'glory' is too strong, and that the world will therefore always be too much with him. He will remain exposed to the adverse winds which have not blown him unequivocally ill, since it is the ambivalence of his reaction to them which has set him to writing the *Secretum*. A capricious Fortune has been his inspiration as an autobiographer, as it was to be the inspiration of Cellini and Cardano, the two subjects of this chapter.

Cellini

Sixteenth-century Italy is a setting for autobiography which threatens by the splendour of its intellectual and artistic heritage, and by the anarchy of its mores, to reduce the autobiographer who writes within it to nothing more than the impersonal representative of his age. Stendhal, in full reaction against the costiveness of bourgeois Grenoble, thought that renaissance Italy was the place and time into which a venturesome young egotist like himself ought to have been born and that the finest guide to its commendably reckless Zeitgeist was the – newly published – *Life* of Benvenuto Cellini. What he might have allowed is that Cellini the autobiographer is not so much the product of his milieu as its creator, since the *Life* is the one source-book for understanding the spirit of the Italian Renaissance that most of those who read it will have come across.

We should break out from this circular, documentary reading of the *Life* and accord it greater respect as an autobiographical text. Graphic as it is, and passionate, it has been taken also as artless, the work of a man so spontaneous in all his doings as to be capable only of action, never of reflection, or of producing more than a behaviourist's narrative of his past life. But again, the evidence for Cellini's spontaneity of nature comes from Cellini himself; for him it is a quality intrinsic to all of human behaviour, both his own and other people's, a quality which assimilates them to animals – men, popes included, are frequently likened to beasts in the *Life* – and embodies the fickleness of our reception by the world which it is a main part of Cellini's purpose to dramatize.

One person alone stands out against this endemic spontaneity: the Artist. Cellini the man may boast of his headstrong ways, but Cellini the artist is in a different case; he plans, he deliberates and he works. Art and life do not with Cellini fit smoothly together: they are opposed. There is a theory of art to be found in the *Life*, and of the role of the Artist, as someone able by the exercise of his skill to avenge enduringly the hostility and the hardships he has experienced. We do not have to read very far in the story before coming upon an episode in which a sudden, harsh change of fortune proves richly inspirational to an artist. It concerns, not Benvenuto himself but his father. Giovanni Cellini had been an 'engineer', with a great 'skill in making instruments for lowering bridges and for working mills, and other machines of that sort'. But he has not stuck to engineering, he has gone astray professionally and given too much of his time to playing the flute, at which he is also very adept. The father's music-making is resented by his patrons, the Medicis no less, who remove him from his official post:

My father took this very ill, and it seemed to him that they had done him a great despite. Yet he immediately resumed his art, and fashioned a mirror, about a cubit in diameter, out of bone and ivory, with figures and foliage of great finish and grand design. The mirror was in the form of a wheel. In the middle was the looking-glass; around it were seven circular pieces, on which were the seven Virtues, carved and joined of ivory and black bone. The whole mirror, together with the virtues, was placed in equilibrium, so that when the wheel turned, all the Virtues moved, and they had weights at their feet which kept them upright. Possessing some acquaintance with the Latin tongue, he put a legend in Latin round his looking-glass, to this effect – 'Whithersoever the wheel of fortune turns, Virtue stands upon her feet'. (7)[1]

This episode has occurred before Cellini himself was born; it is a family story, of the domestic kind which Augustine also scrupulously

---

[1] The edition I have used is *The Life of Benvenuto Cellini Written by Himself*, translated by John Addington Symonds (London, 1949).

identifies as being told first to him before being now retailed by him.
The sequence of events is of a misfortune to the father – a serious loss
of patronage and of his primary employment – leading directly to the
making of a work of art. It is a story which suits Cellini's
autobiographical purpose extremely well, to the point – how can I
not say? – of mirroring it. His own career as an artist, as sculptor,
goldsmith and medallist, goes counter to his father's intentions for
him; these had been to make of Benvenuto a professional musician,
and on the selfsame instrument, the flute, which had been his own
great distraction, and on this notable occasion his downfall. The
reflexive artefact which the father is led instantly to create, in
response to what he perceives as the injustice done to him by his
powerful patrons, turns art into a medium of revenge, but a medium
elevated by its rarity to a high place. The artist's is a *lasting* revenge.
'If God but grant me to execute my work, I hope by its means to
annihilate all my scoundrelly enemies', as Cellini tells himself later,
just after he has forborn from murdering one of his most persistent
artistic rivals and gone back home to continue work on his heroic
statue of Perseus (351).

More subtly, he embodies this same symbolism, whereby art is
granted the last word over the bitterness of life, in the inscription
which he tells us that he designed for the funereal monument to his
brother, a soldier killed in a scuffle in the streets of Rome. The
brother's real name is Giovanfrancesco, but Cellini has had inscribed
on the stone the name by which he was popularly known, Cecchino
del Piffero, or Cecchino 'the fifer's son'. This name, which is followed
by an ornate epitaph in Latin, he has had incised 'in fine antique
characters, all of which were broken save the first and last', the first
so that it might 'symbolise the great gift God had given him, namely
of a human soul inflamed with divinity, the which hath never broken,
while the second represented the glorious renown of his brave
actions' (97). As thus curiously incised, the brother's nickname
pictures in a summary fashion the narrative which Cellini gives us of
his own life, with the two constants, the given of a soul, and the
achievement of a 'glorious renown', separated by the manifold
adversities of a gruelling lifetime.

This epitaph is remarkable too for Cellini's insistence on having on
it his brother's nickname, not his 'real' name; the Tuscan appellation
of 'Frank, the fifer's son' clashes with the pompous Latin wording of
the epitaph itself. But Cellini has a point to make here, and not for the

first time in the *Life*: that vernacular-speaking Florentines of the
sixteenth century like the Cellinis are true descendants and in
everything the equals of their grand Roman forbears. The mixture of
languages on the monument is an index of this flattering con-
sanguinity, just as the Latin tag inscribed by his father around his
looking-glass has been earlier in the *Life*. Cellini in fact starts his
personal story by constructing a supportive lineage for both himself
and his native city. Florence, he claims, was originally built 'in
imitation of the fair city of Rome' and received its name of Fiorenze
from Julius Caesar, partly because it was a place of flowers (*fiori*) but
also because it was the headquarters of one of Caesar's favourite
'captains', Fiorino of Cellino. Whence the Cellinis, conditioned ever
since by the name they bear to be 'men of valour', though the
gentler, horticultural strain in the name Fiorino is perhaps a hint that
the at least partial 'turn' from arms to art made by Benvenuto
himself was also inscribed in his ancestry. And then Fiorino is also to
be treasured as an autobiographer's role model for having risen to
captaincy out of nothing: Caesar loved him, we are told, 'for having
drawn him from a very humble place, and for the reason that so
excellent a man was a creature of his own'(2). Benvenuto Cellini of
course will do better than that; he is proud of 'having been born
humble', but unlike Fiorino he will rise, as we shall now learn,
entirely by his own efforts and emphatically not as another man's
'creature'.

This early invocation of a Roman model against whom to measure
himself promises that the pervasive theme of rivalry in the *Life* will
have a historical dimension. Cellini competes as an artist not only
with his contemporaries, but with the ancients also, either directly,
by producing work held by connoisseurs to be finer than that which
had been done in antiquity, or indirectly, by copying classical models
so adeptly as to put his contemporary rivals in the shade. He may be
praised by the Pope for the excellence of his workmanship ('The
ancients never had such medals made for them as these'), or, more
deviously, he may so oppress by his originality a rival such as the
Bolognese painter Primaticcio, that the latter must set off for Rome
to make casts of the most admired classical statues there and so prove
the superiority of the ancients in design over the moderns – that is,
over Cellini.

But for all his malevolent intentions Primaticcio can not match
Cellini's own skill as a copyist. When Cellini makes two vases out of

silver for a patron, the latter, a celebrated physician, tells the Duke of
Ferrara, who has admired them, that they are antique vases given to
him with the utmost reluctance by a patient as payment for his cure.
Cellini learns this story second-hand, when he is himself subsequently
visiting Ferrara and is shown earthenware copies of his own 'antique'
silver vases:

Thereupon I laughed, and as I said nothing, Messer Alberto Bendedio, who
was a haughty man, flew into a rage and said:'You are laughing at them,
are you? And I tell you that during the last thousand years there has not
been born a man capable of so much as copying them'. I then, not caring to
deprive them of so eminent a reputation, kept silence and admired them
with mute stupefaction. It was said to me in Rome by many great lords,
some of whom were my friends, that the work of which I have been speaking
was in their opinion of marvellous excellence and genuine antiquity;
whereupon, emboldened by their praises, I revealed that I had made them.
(47)

Nothing could better serve Cellini's self-promotional purposes than
this neat sequence of events, in which a false but highly flattering
origin is first attributed to his handiwork, by a patron who, in
spreading his falsehood, is simultaneously boasting of the very high
value set by society on his own services; after which the artist himself
is permitted a double triumph in two different settings and before two
different audiences, the first enjoyed mutely before a haughty
underling, unworthy of being disillusioned, the second in the ancient
city of Rome and before 'great lords', whose 'praises', it seems, are
the necessary spur to the final revelation of the artist's gratifying
secret. The episode dramatizes very tellingly Cellini's shrewd
management of his artistic reputation, as if the public acknowledgment of his talent were also controlled by him; it also shows how, in
the *Life*, technicalities of art are integrated with the risks and
excitements of a social strategy founded on fearless arrivisme.

The professed object of Cellini's *Life* is one common to many
autobiographies: it is to set an acclaimed public achievement into its
hitherto unknown private context. He is a successful artist bent, as he
repeatedly says, on writing primarily about his art; he will use
autobiography to tell numerous, cumulative stories of how various of
his works, both large and small, came to be first commissioned, then
designed by him, then made and finally admired once they passed
out of his workshop and into the world. These are stories which we
can still attach to such surviving art objects as Cellini's famous statue

of Perseus, exhibited to this day in the Loggia dei Lanzi in Florence
for which he created it and whose difficult casting is described at
length in the *Life*. But to distribute the contents of the *Life*
geographically in this way would be perverse, when the effect of the
book is the very opposite, being to reassemble the artist's scattered
oeuvre in its place of origin. It is a work of re-collection in which the
writer asserts his claim symbolically to repossess all that he has given
up or sold over many years to others.

Here the circumstances in which the *Life* was written come into
play. It was begun when Cellini, as he himself tells us at the start, was
fifty-eight years old and back once again in Florence. The nomadism
of his life as an artist had delivered him finally to the city he was born
in. But this was the year also, according to his biographer Eugène
Plon, when Cellini got himself tonsured, as a first step towards
entering the priesthood – a plan which he abandoned two years later,
in order to have children.[2] Plon's assumption is that he had thoughts
of the priesthood because by this time his circumstances were not
good; he was at odds with his great patron in Florence, the Grand
Duke Cosimo, and short of money. His life was precarious and he felt
ill-served. There is a passage indeed in one of Cellini's other writings,
the *Treatise on Goldsmithing*, where he links the wish to write his life-
story directly to the unfavourable turn his life had taken:

So in my despair I felt sure my bad luck was due to the influence of those
heavenly powers who have dominance over us here below; and in this state
set to work to write my whole life, my origin, and all the deeds I had done
in the world, and I also described the many years in which I had served the
illustrious Duke Cosimo. But on thinking the matter over I was minded how
great princes often take it ill if their subjects complain and tell the truth
about them. So with much heart-burning and not without tears I tore up
what I had written about the part of my life spent in Duke Cosimo's service
and threw it into the fire, vowing that I would never write about it again.[3]

Tact having this time got the better of him, Cellini says that he
turned to writing the present *Treatise* instead. But the *Life*, when it
eventually came, came from an old man with real cause for complaint
against a patron who seems to have been extremely bad at paying his
bills. Cellini lets Duke Cosimo off lightly enough in the *Life*, but then

---

[2] Eugène Plon, *Benvenuto Cellini, Orfèvre, Médailleur, Sculpteur* (Paris, 1883), p. 97.
[3] *The Treatises of Benvenuto Cellini on Goldsmithing and Sculpture*, translated by C. R. Ashbee,
no date or place of publication, p. 55.

he continued to need his favour all through the years when that was being written. At the same time, we may see the *Life* as the protracted statement of a grievance.

I say when the *Life* was being 'written', but that is too hasty a description. For the most part it was not written by Cellini himself but dictated by him. No doubt autobiographies of a kind are being 'written' today by means of dictation, but these will be dictated into a recording machine, at the normal tempo of speech and without those pauses which dictation entails when the dictator must wait for the dictatee to finish before resuming. Cellini's autobiography was dictated to an amanuensis and taken down in longhand, at the tempo of writing. One can only speculate as to the braking and centrifugal effects which this vicarious method of 'composition' might have. The *Life* is 'oral', yet originally spoken with a deliberation approximating it to a written form. Cellini gives his reason for deciding to dictate his story rather than write it himself in a prefatory note to the main text. He had begun to write it down but then desisted, 'reckoning that I was wasting too much time and it seeming to me an excessive vanity (*una smisurata vanità*)'; instead, he has employed a young boy to do the writing for him: ' ... I set him to write, and as I worked I dictated my life to him; and because I derived pleasure from this I laboured much more assiduously and created more works ... '[4]

By his 'excessive vanity' Cellini might mean that writing his story himself was a futile employment of his time (or of the right hand he might be putting to so much better artistic use), or, more interestingly, that he found such a protracted absorption with his own past life presumptuous, an offence against every social code. He would then be raising an interesting distinction for autobiography, since once he had changed to dictating the story of his life to someone else Cellini presumably overcame this inhibiting sense of being engaged on an endeavour too vainglorious to be acceptable, even if the *Life* is a work unequalled among autobiographies in its show of vaingloriousness. The advantages remarked by Abelard in writing over speaking face to face with an interlocutor are countered here by a man who is apparently set more productively at ease by having someone to listen to him. Cellini's amanuensis was not an interlocutor but a deferential hireling, who was being paid to listen to him; but this clerk is also the autobiographer's first audience, a stand-in for

---

[4] Symonds omits this prefatory note for some reason; it is translated here by me, from *Vita de Benvenuto Cellini*, per cura di Orazio Bacci (Firenze, 1901), p. 2.

posterity. Should we then take written autobiography – and auto-biography is a written form by definition – as a literary act more naturally understood as a *vocal* one? If, in company, we take our selves and our past lives for our exclusive topic of conversation, we know we shall not be tolerated for very long, whatever momentary successes we may win by our skill in narration. But the auto-biographer proper offends against no such dinner-table protocol; on the contrary, the less he dwells on himself the less we think of him as an autobiographer. By choosing to speak his *Life* out loud, Cellini is choosing to excel his rival autobiographers in the insolence of this peculiar literary office.

But there is also the practical benefit of his method to be mindful of. The hand which would otherwise have been occupied for very many hours in the writing down of his life-story may be redeployed, once the amanuensis is in place, in doing what it is known for. By preferring to dictate his *Life* Cellini is not simply setting his creative hand free, he is enabling himself to work all the more productively. He finds pleasure in recounting his life, with the result that his sessions of narration contribute to the quality of his art; the activity of autobiography has its part to play in the living of his life, an aspect of the genre too often overlooked (with Michel Leiris we shall have particular cause to return to it). Writing autobiographically may bring comfort to an author psychologically, especially if the writing is in a confessional mode, or professionally, if autobiography be seen as the logical consecration of some public achievement; Cellini is unique in that the writing of his autobiography appears to have inspired him daily in his commitment to the art his career in which was his purported subject-matter.

We should not take Cellini too simply at his word, however, when he tells us that he is straying from the subject of his art and calls his tongue to order. There is more than enough in the *Life* by way of warfare, both personal and collective, of travelling, falling sick, suffering in prison, and the like, to make it seem a cheerfully digressive text, the most purely sequential of autobiographies for being ordered entirely by the chronology of events, whether these be true or imaginary.[5] In fact, it is ordered more by Cellini's pervasive

---

[5] The question of Cellini's veracity has been much debated. His biographer, Eugène Plon, defends him, by citing documentary evidence in support of the autobiographer's own account; Symonds also, in the introduction to his translation, defends Cellini, arguing that even such fantastic claims as that of having at one point in his life acquired a halo, have a

conception of the Artist, as a hero whose mighty talent is to be exhibited not only in the narrow practice of a particular art, but everywhere, in whatever he does or is called upon to do. Take the account which he gives of a typical affray, a quarrel between himself and a soldier visiting Florence, 'a light-brained young swaggering fellow' who has passed some sarcastic remarks about Florentines. A set-to in the street is followed by a challenge to a formal duel, even if this particular quarrel is settled bloodlessly. The episode may well appear to 'diverge' from Cellini's avowed main business as an autobiographer, but the divergence does not make it incongruous. The insulting remarks passed by the soldier have been overheard by Cellini when he is consorting with his own professional kind, with 'painters, sculptors, goldsmiths'; he alone responds to them, thus singling himself out among the artists as a man who will take action in defence of his city's honour. When the challenge is brought to him he accepts it 'very gladly, saying that I expected to complete this job far quicker than those of the other art I practised'. So swordmanship too is an art, at least when practised by himself, and he is able to revert perfectly smoothly immediately this episode is closed to recalling how 'The spirit of honourable rivalry impelled me to attempt some other masterpiece, which should equal, or even surpass, the productions of that able craftsman, Lucagnolo, whom I have mentioned. Still I did not on this account neglect my own fine art of jewellery; and so both the one and the other wrought me much profit and more credit, and in both of them I continued to produce things of marked originality'(42).

Such are what Cellini at one moment refers to as the 'ornaments' of his life-story, thus encouraging us to assimilate the *Life* as a verbal artefact to all those other artefacts which we are to imagine him working on simultaneously in his workshop as he romances, works in which the artist's exuberance in the ornamentation of the piece ends by disguising its function. Purged of its 'digressions', the *Life* would be an austere affair, just as, stripped of the fantastic superstructure which made of it first a royal and then a museum piece, Cellini's celebrated salt-cellar would have been merely one more functional and hence perishable vessel for serving salt.

natural explanation. I see little point in trying in this way to tether Cellini to the ground, when the degree of exaggeration or falsehood in what he writes can never finally be measured, any more than it can with autobiographers far less obviously inventive. Let us say that Cellini has told the *tall* story of his life.

Art survives, and gloriously; it is what rises above the terrible uncertainty of life. And sculpture and goldsmithery, because of the materials they use, are especially durable – this was an argument much used, it seems, in contemporary squabbles in Italy between painters and sculptors as to which was the preeminent art. Art is the product, as I have said, of work and of deliberation, not of the fabulous spontaneity everywhere else characteristic of human activity in Cellini's *Life*. Fortune's wheel may turn but the Artist counters its capricious movements by actually representing it, in a spectacularly stable form. And as the *Life* continues, so Cellini works to create the representation of himself, a various figure, yet concentrated at the last in the monumental consistency of the Artist.

Cardano

Cellini's is the militant response to adversity, of a man pitting his artistic triumphs against his human misfortunes the more graphically to prove his virtue.[6] Sickness, imprisonment, the extreme malevolence of the envious, all are enthusiastically turned to the autobiographer's advantage. In a rare moment of pessimism in his dungeon, Cellini's – typically elaborate – attempt at suicide is supernaturally foiled (224), when he is hurled violently across the room by what he concludes must have been his guardian angel. But this perfunctory call on his tutelary spirit hardly takes away from his sovereign wilfulness as subject and narrator of his arduous life. For Cellini divine protection itself remains a contingency, a momentary intervention in his affairs, rather than a benevolent canopy beneath which he can go about his risky business confident of a safe outcome.

His guardian angel acts in the same abrupt, boisterous manner as Cellini himself, so proving that autobiographers receive divine help in a form consonant with their own nature, their authority extending equally to the supernatural plane. And as with Cellini so with Girolamo Cardano, his Italian contemporary in both life and autobiography. Cardano too has survived into old age through very taxing times, but with none of the panache or heroics of Cellini; and his guardian angel has played a quite different role, as a pervasive rather than an exceptional force in his affairs. In the writing of his *De*

---

[6] 'Virtue' is intended here as the translation of the Italian term *virtù*, to convey excellence both in the appreciation of art and in the living of life.

Vita Propia Liber, or *Book of My Life*,[7] Cardano has come to see that this supernatural agency has regularly 'apprised him of perils impending', and has preserved him by fostering within him that acute apprehensiveness towards both the present and the future which has been the hallmark of Cardano's career. Where Cellini faces adversity down, Cardano tends to out-maneouvre it, and in his autobiography he emerges delightfully as the freakish and neurotic anti-hero, or even, looking far ahead, as the ancestor of that late twentieth-century form of anti-autobiography, in which the writer undermines the genre from within by revealing himself as unfitted for the role of protagonist.

Cardano did not set out to be an anti-autobiographer; on the contrary, he seems to have wanted to write an orthodox life-story. He begins one chapter of the *Book of My Life* by declaring: 'An account of this nature is by its own character a most difficult thing to write, and so much the more for me as I reflect that those who have been wont to read the autobiographical books of writers are not used to seeing such a straightforward narrative set down as I purpose to publish'(49). The heading of this chapter is 'Customs, Vices, and Errors', which already indicates that 'straightforward narrative' is perhaps not the right description to give to the contents of *The Book of My Life*. The element of straightforward narrative in it is in fact scant. Chapter Four is entitled 'A Brief Narrative of My Life from the Beginning to the Present Day – That is, the End of October, 1575', and the text is a hurried catalogue, only a few pages long, of Cardano's many sufferings as a child, and then of his enmities, his professional successes and frustrations, his deprivations and his travails as a physician and teacher. So much, in *The Book of My Life*, for chronology; the principle of order in this life-story, if any, must be looked for elsewhere.

Cardano shares with Cellini the Renaissance wish to associate himself with the first Italians; only where Cellini looks to find an ancestry for himself among Roman fighting men, Cardano is more sophisticated and invokes Roman models not for the living of his life but for the writing of it. He finds an exemplar for his present autobiographical role in Marcus Aurelius, author of the *Meditations*

---

[7] Jerome Cardan, *The Book of My Life*, translated by Jean Stoner (London and Toronto, 1931). This is the only English version of Cardano to be found; it is high time a new translation was made and a scholarly edition published of this remarkable and endearing work.

– and, in his magisterial stoicism, an absurdly unsuitable model for the agitated Cardano – and in the physician Galen. More to the point, he compares his method of composition with that followed by the Roman historian, Suetonius, in whom we have the ancient rival, serving the same function as the artists of antiquity with whom Cellini likes to compare himself. Cardano first criticizes Suetonius, starting his 'Brief Narrative' chapter with the words: 'If Suetonius by any chance could have noticed the method of this chapter, he might have added something to the advantage of his readers'(9). Cardano has improved on Suetonius by introducing chronology into the account of his life, for Suetonius was a biographer of Roman emperors who instead of narrating their lives chronologically grouped his data concerning them in moral categories so as to illustrate the relative weight of their vices and their virtues. But having briefly surpassed his Roman model, Cardano reverts throughout to a broadly Suetonian method, grouping together the events of his life and his habits and characteristics by kinds, and not by reference to the calendar.

This striking, a-chronological method reflects the procedures of the two arts, or sciences, of which Cardano was a known master and anxious therefore, as an autobiographer, to demonstrate his mastery: the arts of medicine and of mathematics. He was celebrated throughout Europe for his skill in both. So far as medicine goes, he records in the *Book of My Life* a number of his diagnostic and curative triumphs – Chapter Forty for example is headed 'Successes in my practice'; and his three failures in fifty-one years of practising are listed separately, among his 'Dishonours'. But more than that, he describes himself throughout the book with conspicuous detachment, as if he were a physician called to attend on his own person – he sets the tone by providing something very seldom to be met with in autobiography, which is a careful (and unflattering) description of his own body, whose flaws and peculiarities are continuous with the flaws and peculiarities of his psychology. The medical note is struck at the outset, where his inauspicious birth is narrated in the form of a case-history, as though he had been midwife to it as well as neonate: his mother had reportedly been given 'various abortive medicines', but the foetus has survived, only to endure when the time comes a difficult birth: 'So I was born, or rather taken by violent means from my mother; I was almost dead. My hair was black and curly. I was revived in a bath of warm wine which might have been fatal to any other child. My mother had been in labour for three entire days, and yet I survived'(4–5). This is the stubborn coming into existence of a physician born to calamity yet able to answer it back by the exactness of his observations and his powers of diagnosis.

It is Cardano's second art, however, of mathematics, of which the formal influence is more subtle and more telling in the *Book of My Life*. In mathematics he was a pioneer, to be credited with discoveries that are now a part of the history of the subject – his *Ars Magna* of 1545 is, according to Oystein Ore, 'as fundamental in mathematics' as Copernicus' contemporary *De Revolutionibus Orbium Coelestium* was in astronomy.[8] Everywhere in his autobiography there is evidence of Cardano's passion for numbers, including in the chapter of 'Brief Narrative', which is notable for its exactitude over dates, precise often down to the day of the month on which something happened. He is fond also of computation, as when he tells us that his visit to Scotland in 1552 on a medical mission took him from home for 311 days, or that his imprisonment in Rome in 1570 lasted 77 days, followed by a further 86 days as a prisoner in his own home, making a total of 162 days (*sic*: his 77 days should in fact have been 76, an error corrected in the overall total). He draws no explicit conclusions from sums such as these, nor does he declare the numbers to be significant. Why then trouble to calculate and to publish them? Because, seemingly, they are the product of *chance*: Cardano's excursion to Scotland might have lasted more than 311 days, or it might have been completed in fewer; the actual number of days that it took is a contingency. But it might also be interpreted as the product, in the mathematical sense of that word, of an incalculable number of individual factors multiplied together. Cardano's state of health, the weather, the ease or otherwise of the roads he travelled, the delays he met with, and so on: such are the broad factors, themselves infinitely subdivisible into smaller factors, which have determined the seemingly insignificant total of 311 days. This chance number contains multitudes.

Behind the publication of it by Cardano there stands a theory of high and consoling importance to him, whereby trivial circumstances must combine in determining the meaningful course of a human life. As his twentieth-century readers, we may applaud his belief that, as we might say, 'nothing is too trivial to record', for it means that he

---

[8] Oystein Ore, *Cardano: The Gambling Scholar* (Princeton, 1953), p. 48.

tells us things about himself we do not expect to learn from a man writing in the sixteenth century (unless piecemeal from his great French contemporary, Montaigne, in his *Essays*). Cardano gives us particulars about his physique, his every least ailment or disability, the way he walks, his diet, the places he has lived in, his feuds with others, his clothes, his dreams, his quirks of temperament, whatever fresh theme comes to his mind in writing.

The Book of My Life is without obvious order, as the chapters accumulate randomly and with them a mass of information, some of it contradictory, concerning the past, present and self-perceptions of its author. But if the whole is disorderly, the parts are not, inasmuch as the contents of each chapter belong clearly together, under such enticing rubrics as 'Those things in which I take pleasure', or 'The disasters of my sons'. To call this peculiar method of composition 'disorderly' is unfair: *The Book of My Life* jolts us only because it has no story-line. It shows that there are more ways than one of arranging a life in order to make of it a public attraction.

Cardano's theory of composition involves treating the raw material of autobiography mathematically. From time to time he pauses in the restless accumulation of small bits of evidence about himself, to state his justification for proceeding in this way. Why all these apparently insignificant facts, catalogued chapter by chapter, by kinds?

It is ever legitimate to draw inferences from even the most insignificant events, when they are uncommonly persistent, since, as I have elsewhere declared, even as a net consists of meshes, all things in the life of man consist in trifles repeated and massed together now in one figure now in another like cloud formations. Not only through the very smallest circumstances are our affairs increased, but these small circumstances ought gradually to be analyzed into their infinitely minute components. And that man alone will be a figure in the arts, in display of judgment, or in civil life, and will rise to the top, who understands the significance of all these influences, and knows how to heed them in his business. Wherefore in any events whatsoever things of apparently no significance ought to be duly observed. (195)

The theory has overtones of the astrology in which Cardano believed and which he also practised.[9] The artist is the man who has learnt to interpret the configurations into which the trifling circumstances of his daily life have chanced to form and who can apply his learning prudentially, for self-preservation. Cardano is the artist as semio-

---

[9] I was sorry but not surprised to learn in conversation with my friend Professor John North, that Cardano's horoscopes are notoriously flawed by his carelessness in casting them.

tician, able to discern signs where lesser men can see only events.
Two aspects of his theory are of particular moment to the theorist of
autobiography. First, the notion of persistence, or repetition, to the
value of which Cardano's practice of grouping his facts a-chrono-
logically bears ample witness. One of the most persuasive theses
advanced by psychoanalysis is that our affective lives are dominated
by patterns of behaviour which repeat, of relationships formed,
dissolved and reformed as variations on a constant motif. In grasping
as he does that self-understanding is hugely advanced by concentrating on those experiences or emotions which persistently recur,
Cardano is opening the way to a modern, post-Freudian form of
autobiography, where chronological narrative is called in question,
as offering a suspiciously comfortable *screen*, behind which the
narrator can find shelter from the pains of unwelcome self-discovery
by failing to give the will to repetition its due. In *The Book of My Life*
Cardano follows an associative path, which enables, indeed en-
courages him to reveal trifling aspects of his behaviour that a go-
ahead story-teller such as Cellini could never have time for.
Cardano's autobiographical method expands his potential subject-
matter quite remarkably, in the direction of the shameful, the strange
or even the pathological: what a shock and a pleasure it is, for
example, to find him recording his need at times to inflict bodily pain
on himself, as a cure for his 'mental anguish'.

The second aspect of Cardano's theory which is important is the
implications that it has for narrative. *The Book of My Life* as a whole
is not a narrative, but it incorporates episodes of narrative, according
to the writer's needs. Cardano recognizes the pleasures of narrative,
even if he practises it only randomly. In a chapter called simply
'Happiness', he gives a delightfully miscellaneous catalogue of the
things that are capable of making him happy; they range from 'rest,
serenity, modesty' to 'keeping abreast of events' to 'continence, little
birds, puppies ... '. But there is one other pleasure or 'good thing'
which he is able to enjoy even as he writes: 'the satisfaction of
recalling an orderly disposition of the past'(123). *Recalling* an 'orderly
disposition of the past', note, not creating one, orderliness being a
particularly reassuring property of life itself. Cardano has indeed
begun this chapter by declaring: 'In the first place I think I may lay
a clear claim to happiness in that all events of my life have come and
passed in an orderly fashion, as if by rule[...] Had this not been the
case and had the numerous commencements of the succession of

events begun a little too late, or a little too soon, or had the conclusion been delayed, my whole career would have been subverted'(119). As a philosophy of life this is pure superstition, but as a philosophy of autobiographical narrative it represents the ideal, of a structure no one piece of which can be removed or displaced without prejudicing the whole. The absence of a master-narrative in *The Book of My Life* is justified obliquely by Cardano's assumption that the narrative orderliness of his life has required no contribution from himself and that he may borrow from it as he likes without calling its existence into question.

Talk of 'happiness' may seem out of place for someone like Cardano, who has had a far from happy life, beset as he has been by sexual impotence in youth, by poverty later, by constant illness, by spite and enmity, by imprisonment, and even by the execution of his eldest son for the murder of his wife. But the 'orderliness' which makes him happy has nothing to do with whether the events ordered have been favourable or unfavourable for him; it is an end in itself, the end of a mathematician. In orderliness Cardano finds an ultimate consolation, as autobiographers always will.

When he turns to narrative it is to dramatize the point that major consequences in life may follow from minor antecedents. Near the end of the book he recalls an episode which might well strike us as the most unimportant event to have been recorded anywhere in the sixteenth century. About to set off on a lecture trip, he loses the brass tip from a garter and has to go back into his house to find another. In looking for one, he comes upon 'the stacks of all the books I had written',[10] which he had meant to take with him and would, but for this unplanned return indoors, have left behind. Then, during his absence from home, Cardano learns that the chest previously containing the books has been burgled and everything in it taken. The conclusion he draws from this sequence of events may seem overdone, even hysterical; but let us just say here that it is theoretical: 'If it had not been for my garter I should not have been able to give my lectures, I should have lost my post and gone begging, so many memoirs would have perished, and I should have died ere long of grief'(259).

Such are life's small chances and such Cardano's means of

---

[10] Chapter 45 of *The Book of My Life* is entitled 'Books Written by Me; when, why and what became of them'. It lists more than 230 items, as various and unpredictable in their subject-matter as one would expect.

exploiting them. *The Book of My Life* turns finally, as does Cellini's *Life*, on the opposition between art and adversity, although Cardano being Cardano he is more inclined to strike a bargain between the two than is Cellini. '*Chance* has no place in art', he declares roundly, and 'is not to be counted on' in medicine, but within a very few lines, he has started to water down this claim, allowing that the doctor's art may be 'subjected to various vicissitudes'. The claim that the medical art has no room for chance could never be rationally upheld; what matters is that Cardano should insist on making it. He does so in order to set himself up against the vicissitudes of fortune, as a supreme medical practitioner able by his experience and skill in his art to rise superior to them.

But where Cellini was able to send art-objects out from his workshop into time and space, to bespeak his lasting achievement, what can Cardano do, to ensure the perpetuation of his name, which he tells us was his very earliest ambition (the first thing he wrote was a treatise on how this could best be done)? However successful he might be in treating the sick, that is a merely practical, ephemeral achievement; he has not contributed to the stock of medical knowledge which will be passed down to future generations. With mathematics it is different; to this pure and universal art he has contributed something of lasting value, since mathematical discoveries can never be supplanted, they are valid once and for all. Cardano's position in the history of mathematics is owed to his work on what we now know as the theory of probability, and nothing could better express his search for some vital equilibrium between the contingencies of life and his own power of responding to them. In his earlier days he had been an addicted gambler, the pitiable victim of Chance; then, aged forty-two (exactitude again), he had turned away from 'pleasure', recognizing that he had only gambled because he required solace in his miseries and lacked 'self-respect'. As the theorist of probability he has established an honourable position for himself vis-à-vis the Chance of which he had previously been the slave; he can not, even now, affect the operations of Chance, but he can hope for fame as the man who first accurately calculated them. In Cardano's mastery of numbers there lies a restorative assertion of self premonitory of that of the autobiographer, who in the Symbolic Order of words can at last turn the hazards of an indifferent Fortune to his own undying advantage.

CHAPTER 4

By force of nature: Herbert of Cherbury, Teresa of Avila, Descartes

Among the 'Five Unique Characteristics' which Cardano claims for himself in *The Book of My Life* is what he calls 'an intuitive flash of direct knowledge'. This is not something he has been born with but it is a gift none the less; it has 'originated about the year 1529', and continued to serve him up until the time of writing, forty-six years later. Indeed, in his old age Cardano has found it to be infallible, and to be invaluable 'as an aid to the composition of books'. Like the other four 'unique characteristics' with which it forms an auto-biographical class, this intuitive power has been visited on Cardano, he has not inherited or had to work for it; and its gratuitousness is matched by its labour-saving effects. For it enables him to know without having to learn, to enjoy knowledge without the ordinary expense of its acquisition. Cardano is a widely knowledgeable man, telling us elsewhere in the book that he is competent in ten out of the thirty-six 'important branches of learning'. And yet he also writes of himself 'as a man even somewhat lacking, in comparison to other men, in natural endowment and education'(163). The story of his formal education is thus one of having triumphantly overcome a double disadvantage – he has neither been born clever, nor efficiently taught. A spectacular example of 'direct knowledge' is his mastery of Latin, a language which he had not been taught but has acquired overnight in his twentieth year, after a single reading of Apuleius.[1] Nor is this the only language he has mastered by such intuitive

---

[1] The work by Apuleius that Cardano refers to is surely *The Golden Ass*, which is among other things a story of initiation into a mystical cult. The theme of initiation suits Cardano's purposes extremely well here, and the introductory chapter of Apuleius' story contains, remarkably, the announcement by its supposedly Greek narrator that 'Then, coming to Rome, by painful labour with no teacher to show me the way I tackled and mastered the native tongue of Roman scholarship.' Given which, it would be nice to think that Cardano chose Apuleius among all the possible Latin authors from whom he might thus miraculously, by no labour at all, have learnt the language as a sly, scholarly joke.

means; Greek, French and Spanish also he knows without having been taught them.

Cardano accords this privileged characteristic of direct, effortless cognition a central place in his make-up: 'This faculty seems, as it were, the most elemental quality of my nature, for it exhibits at one and the same time the essence of all the qualities which compose my nature ... '(165). It is an auspicious quality for an autobiographer to find in himself, economizing as it does on the need for protracted self-examination: his intuitive faculty is an essence, but more than that it is an essence the possession of which enables him to identify whatever other essential qualities he may contain; it is the ideal autobiographical tool. But let us stick to its educational advantages. How seriously should we take Cardano's casual claim that he acquired a reading knowledge of Latin in a single night? Perfectly seriously: it is an autobiographical claim all the more meaningful for appearing incredible. It will find an echo, in due course, in the seemingly rational account given by a twentieth-century autobiographer, Jean-Paul Sartre, of how he first learnt to read. Cardano is anxious to be beholden to no one but himself in accounting for the extent of his knowledge – that is, if we discount 'supernatural' agencies. The single page he devotes to listing his 'teachers' is nugatory. He seems never to have been to school, yet one year after entering the University of Padua, at nineteen, he was debating in public with one of the professors of Medicine. He has learnt all that he knows without the aid of teachers, and in this, I suggest in this chapter, he is an archetypal autobiographer.

First it was Augustine, disowning in the *Confessions* his official education, or else 'turning' it retrospectively, away from the profane ends inculcated and esteemed by the educators themselves and towards his own sacred ends. Then there was Abelard, the precocious dialectician, contending at an early age with his renowned teachers and overcoming them in argument – Cardano is more modest than this, he does not boast of having defeated his professor in their disputation. Cellini again, in his first apprenticeship as a goldsmith in Florence, wastes no time in displaying his superiority; he has 'a liking for the art' and a 'natural bias' towards it, so that 'in a few months I caught up the good, nay the best young craftsmen in our business'(10) – a 'liking' and a 'natural bias' may sound ordinary or casual enough as explanations of his quickness in learning, but we may take them as having real importance for Cellini, since they are qualities freely accorded to him by the power he refers to as the 'God of Nature'. They are a part of that transcendental endowment which enables him to excel his rivals in art without having to pass through any gradual process of initiation.

Lord Herbert of Cherbury

But for a demonstration of Nature's superiority over formal education as an aid to material and intellectual advancement, a more considered source than Cellini is the autobiography of the seventeenth-century English soldier, diplomatist, historian, poet and philosopher, Lord Herbert of Cherbury, whose *Life* was written in the 1640s but only published more than a century later, in 1764. Herbert had a sickly childhood and was not even taught his alphabet until he was seven years old. True to autobiographical type, he then makes up for lost time; within two years he not only knows Latin but is able to write in that language 'an oration of a sheet of paper and fifty or three score verses in the space of one day!' The set theme of this juvenile triumph is the tag *Audaces fortuna juvat,* or 'Fortune favours the bold', words which might stand as a device over Herbert's adventurous story, as he tells it in the *Life*: this first, precocious exercise in composition is auspicious of the one he is now embarked on.[2] Herbert is aged twelve by his own account when he is sent to Oxford as an undergraduate (in fact he was fourteen), and eighteen, and two years married, by the time he leaves the university. He gives few details of his studies there or of any profit he might have derived from them. But having reached the age of twenty-one, he is more forthcoming: 'During this time of living in the University or at home, I did without any Master or teacher Attain the Knowledge of the French Italian and Spanish Languages by the help of some books in Latin or English translated into those idioms and the Dictionaries of those several languages. I attained also to sing my part at first sight in Music, and to play on the Lute with very little or almost no teaching'(17).[3]

[2] Comparably precocious with Herbert is another autobiographer almost contemporary with him, the French soldier, poet and Protestant apologist, Agrippa d'Aubigné, who in his *Vie à ses enfants,* or 'Life Written for his Children', remembers that 'At seven and a half with some help from his lessons, he translated Plato's Crito, on his father's promise that he would have it printed with his childish effigy at the front of the book.' See Agrippa d'Aubigné, *Oeuvres* (Paris, 1969), p. 17.

[3] The edition cited is *The Life of Lord Herbert of Cherbury,* edited by J. M. Shuttleworth (London, 1976).

At this point in the *Life* there ensues a lengthy interruption to Herbert's narrative, which is itself only a few pages old; having reached the age of manhood, he digresses in order to pass on his many precepts concerning the proper education of a Gentleman, both intellectual and moral. First in order of the fields of knowledge whose study he recommends is Medicine, an art or practice in which Herbert claims for himself some expertise. It takes this unexpected precedence among the elements of a good education because of the possible need to diagnose and treat hereditary ailments in infants. Herbert's own sickliness in his first seven years, when it seemed possible that he was suffering from a congenital epilepsy, has conditioned the sequence in which he passes on his educational rules. Medicine also enables him to establish a close rapport with the natural as opposed to the artificial world: having touched on some of the contemporary remedies effective as he holds in the treatment of nurslings, he spares his readers from the full catalogue of his knowledge: 'I could say much more upon this Point, as having delighted ever in the Knowledge of herbs Plants and Gums and in few words the History of Nature'(18). A little later he goes into greater detail concerning his knowledge of pharmacology for, like Cardano, Herbert has had his successes in the treatment of patients given up for lost by other practitioners. His understanding of the ways of Nature is an important part of his intellectual repertoire, even if, unlike Cardano this time, he does not lay claim to any miraculous assistance in its acquisition – Herbert at least admits to having had need of translations and a dictionary in learning other languages.

The curious priority given in Herbert's *Life* to a practical knowledge of inherited ailments in infants brings to the fore another of the thematic oppositions which may be exploited in autobiography: between the innate and the acquired. However set he may be on retracing for us the process of his unaided singularization from among his contemporaries, the autobiographer can still make allowances for the contribution to his success of Nature, or alternatively of what we would now call his genetic inheritance, those parental or ancestral qualities which he declares to have been passed down to him and which are, among autobiographers if not among the population at large, generally taken to have been beneficial. An autobiography is a record of the writer's acquisition of knowledge, wisdom, position – of fame – over part or all of a lifetime, but that glorious record is hardly diminished by the acknowledgment that its subject began with certain assets, granted to him by his birth – or by some supernatural surrogate, in such cases as Cardano – rather than gained by his own admirable efforts. Autobiography plays down the merely given, but need not eliminate it.

Teresa of Avila

Given the choice between acquiring knowledge from other human beings, through education, or from an impersonal source such as Nature or else Life, the autobiographer looks preferably to the second alternative. Experience, not formal schooling, has made him what he is. Or made her what she is: for here I pass to a woman writer for a further, revealing variation on the autobiographical model which is the subject of this chapter, to the *Life* of Saint Teresa of Avila, written in Spain early in the 1560s, circulated privately in her lifetime and first published six years after her death, in 1588. Teresa's *Life* is not all, or even mainly narrative, since a significant part of it is given over to defining, for practical purposes, the kinds and methods of Christian prayer. Rather than addressing herself textually to God, as Augustine does in the *Confessions*, Teresa is handing on to others the procedures by which they, following her, may address God for themselves. The *Life* in fact has a rather different addressee or set of addressees: it was written for her confessors, at their ordering. She is a woman, a member of a religious order, writing her life because she has been ordered to do so by ecclesiastical authority.

The *Life*, however, is not the submissive work that the authoritarian circumstances of its commissioning imply that it should have been. Rather, it hinges on a distinction made a number of times by Teresa herself between two kinds of authority, one formal and founded on hierarchy, the other informal and founded on experience alone. This distinction is also one between the authority vested in men in sixteenth-century Spain, and the very different authority laid claim to by a woman. It arises once Teresa finds that she has come to the end of the confessional part of her commission, and must now turn to the didactic part. The confessors for whom she is writing have the power to publish what she will give them or not, according to how they decide; but she entreats them to publish at least the confession of her great sins, as she believes them to have been, because then the world, which she knows thinks well of her, will be undeceived. This is a simple reversal of that desire I have already alluded to, whereby the autobiographer writes in order to gainsay the prejudicial untruths supposedly current about him with the much more flattering truth. Teresa writes as a paragon of humility, in the conviction of her own sinfulness, though she is alert to the possibility that any such concern for her worldly reputation may be the devil's doing.

When she turns, self-consciously, from the way of confession to that of instruction, she pauses to draw attention to her lack of credentials for fulfilling so presumptuous a role. She asks that whatever she writes from this point on be published anonymously:

> If the rest is shown to anyone I do not wish him to be told whose experience it describes, or who wrote it. That is why I mention neither myself nor anyone else by name and I have done my best to write in such a way as not to be recognized. I beg your Reverence, for the love of God, to preserve my secrecy. Persons as learned and serious as my confessors have enough authority to confirm any good thing that the Lord may grant me the grace to say, in which case it will be His, not mine. For I am not learned nor have I led a good life, and I have neither a scholar or anyone else to guide me. (74)[4]

Here the autobiographical trap has been sprung: Teresa is attempting concealment in the very act of exhibiting herself. Her *Life* effects a conscious transition, from a youth which she presents as having been governed by a worldly concern for her 'honour', to a maturity in which, as a member of an enclosed religious order, she claims to 'care very little what people say or know about me'. The ethic of 'honour', so stringent in Spanish culture of the sixteenth and seventeenth centuries, might seem designed to suppress any urge to autobiography, enjoining as it does an absolute keeping-up of appearances and hence a complete secrecy about the ignoble doings and desires whose publication would bring social disgrace. Teresa takes herself to task for having observed this ethic and in the narrative of her life shows herself growing out of it, as she abolishes the distance between outward appearance and inner truth, by imposing her own revelation of her private self on the world. The ethic by which she replaces that of 'honour' is the ethic of transparency, feasible before God in the form of a confession whatever dangers there may be in observing it in public.

Teresa follows Augustine in presenting her education as a perversion, or as a deferment of God's gracious intentions for her

---

[4] The edition cited is *The Life of Saint Teresa of Avila by Herself*, translated by J. M. Cohen (Harmondsworth, 1957).

which will be righted later by a *con*version. She too has been
distracted by literature. In her home there were two kinds of books,
the 'holy books' which her unfailingly upright father liked to read,
and some of which, she specifies, were in Spanish, 'so that his children
might read them too'; but also 'books of chivalry', in which her
sickly mother found amusement and to which Teresa too became
addicted. This was a secret indulgence, needing to be hidden from
her father, who would not have condoned it, and it leads directly, in
her account of these years of childhood, to what she calls 'an excessive
care for my appearance'(26). From the deceiving of her father, that
model of male authority, she has learnt the dangerously enjoyable
possibility of separating what she knows herself to be from what she
seems to others to be, and where better to learn the ways of duplicity
than from romances of chivalry, whose ability to conflate the real
delusively with the apparent was sufficient to turn the mind of Don
Quijote?

   This is all we are given in the *Life* concerning Teresa's secular
'education'; she has read the wrong books and, again like Augustine,
associated with the wrong people, the company of the corrupt having
corrupted her. Later, however, she comes to read one of the right
books, Augustine's *Confessions*, to which she responds emotionally,
feeling that the voice which Augustine hears in the garden at the crux
of his story was addressed to her also. She has not asked for a copy of
the *Confessions* nor ever set eyes on one before being given a copy,
'seemingly by the ordainment of the Lord'. She is back among her
father's 'holy books', from which she had once defaulted. That the
Confessions should come to her like this, literally as a given, rather
than her being led to them by her own inclinations, is all of a piece
with her presentation of herself as a woman without learning.
Learning is for men, for those in authority, for the confessors whom
she is addressing and who are expert, like her own father, in 'holy
books'. Teresa concedes to these men of the book the power to
'direct' the lives of the 'spiritual', while suggesting that they are not
always or even very often spiritual themselves. In the *Life* learning, or
the intellect, is categorically opposed to the spirit, as a dry, masculine
curb on a passionate, feminine spirituality. As an autobiographer,
Teresa acknowledges that curb even as she destroys its authority over
her, by recounting the singular relationship she has entered into with
a greater authority, that of God.

   If men stand together in the *Life* as a class, having inherited a patriarchal role and a corpus of vicarious wisdom to go with it, Teresa stands out against them, as an individual possessing nothing but her own inalienable experience, which she prizes as 'my only means of knowledge'. This it is which qualifies her to write her *Life*, thereby invading the authoritarian preserve of the book. But there is a conflict for her between the discursive nature of writing and the transcendental nature of the experience she is mainly concerned to make public. The truly singular experience which she has had and of which she must now write is of an immediate communion with God, in prayer and in rare moments of 'rapture', which are distinguishable from communion by their being felt as 'irresistible' and as so excessive a mark of God's favour as to have made Teresa anxious at the time to suppress all outward sign of them, for fear of being talked about. That fear comes from her mistrust of 'the world', a milieu characterized for her by the endemic contradiction which rules there between the outward signs people give of their feelings and the far less honourable inner truth. The 'world' is duplicitous, and even the nuns who have observed Teresa's physical convulsions when she was experiencing her 'raptures' may misinterpret them, and not recognize the sublimity of their source. As signifiers, these involuntary movements are utterances drawn from the language of God, which is unlike natural languages for being unequivocal; for God being and appearance are one.

Unfortunately however, the *Life* itself can contain no such unequivocal signs, no involuntary body-language; natural language will have to serve. Extreme spiritual experiences such as those which Teresa has had are not to be plausibly described, and certainly not to be described in such a form as to deny to their readers the possibility of reinterpreting them. To anyone who is merely *told* of them, her 'raptures' will remain enigmatic, an invitation to part company with the writer and give to her experience a meaning different from that which she claims for it. But here, crucially, the *Life* reenacts in full the mundane experience of its author when she came to describe to her spiritual advisers the rareness of her experience in prayer. They have not taken her simply at her word, doubting whether in her ignorance as a woman she can be a proper recipient for the extraordinary 'favours' she claims to have received. Religious authority exists in order to foreclose on matters of interpretation, and Teresa's confessors are wise to the duplicitous possibility that what appears to her to have come from God may equally well have come from the Devil:

equivocation of this same cosmic order is a constant theme of the *Life*, as a concession made by the autobiographer to the ways of the 'world' she is differentiating herself from.

In speaking face to face with her confessors she has failed in persuasion. But now that she is embarked on the writing of her *Life*, so that the unique experiences she records there may turn others to praise of the God who has saved so great a sinner as herself, she has the power to do better. Her pen may succeed where her tongue has been frustrated. Recounting her dealings with a particular 'pious gentleman' to whom she had earlier gone for spiritual guidance, Teresa distinguishes her verbal power then from what it is now: 'The trouble was that I simply could not describe the nature of my prayer. For not until recently has God granted me the grace of understanding it and describing it'(166).

Once again it is God and not men or books who has raised her to this new level of understanding, and given her the power of persuasion over others. Like Cardano, Teresa has been brought to the mastery of a new language by supernatural means. In it she can write her *Life*, uninhibited now by any sense that as an uneducated woman she has no business doing so. The autograph Spanish text is by all accounts crude, ill-spelt, ill-punctuated, and syntactically uncertain; characteristics which editors frequently and translators invariably succeed in removing. This is a *Life* processed by history, and partially disguised in its incorporation by that bookish community against whose cosmetic protocols Teresa herself was in reaction. Time (and translation) has served to formalize her writing, if by a process continuous with that whereby the immediacy of her experience first became mediated in language.

The *Life* has to do with prayer and prayer, for Teresa, is first a state of mind and then a state of language congenerous with it. The experience of writing can repeat the experience of praying: 'But if the spirit is lacking, there is no more agreement between the words than in so much gibberish, as one might say, even though one may have spent many years in prayer. Therefore it seems to me a very great advantage to be in the state of prayer when I am writing. Then I realize that it is not I that speak, nor is it I that am putting the words together with my own understanding. Afterwards I do not know how I have managed to speak at all. This has happened to me many times'(101). The temporal element here is of great importance. The mere length of her experience – her 'many years in prayer' – does not of itself guarantee that she will be able to write a persuasive account of it. For that to happen the 'spirit' must supervene, and in the same time-saving role as it had for Cardano, in his miraculous acquisition of Latin. For all the spiritual momentousness of her theme in the *Life*, Teresa complains of not being able to find the time she would like in which to write it; again, the intermittence of prayer or 'rapture', and the relapse into mundanity which follows it, is repeated in the intermittence of writing, executed in the intervals of her life in a deceitful 'world'. She has had twenty-eight years of experience of prayer which have now to be compacted into a manuscript a reading of which may take only a few hours. Her own 'understanding' is not up to such a feat of compression, she must allow God to direct her, that God of whom her own experience has been that he 'teaches us everything in a moment in the most amazing way'.

In its inspired condensation of Teresa's experience, the *Life* may serve to spare others the protracted fear and uncertainty through which she herself has passed. As an autobiographer she is providing what she very grievously lacked, a reassuring interpretation of experiences which at the time when she had them were beyond her power of understanding. The narrative element of the *Life* is stronger than it may at first seem; the 'events' which Teresa records are more spiritual than public ones and their sequence consequently does not always appear to matter. But it matters to her because she is taken up with the *progress* of her soul; her story has a destination. Hence the value for others of her tracing autobiographically, in exemplary form, the arduous way she has come and the incomprehension she has met with:

If God leads it[the soul], as He led me, along the path of fear and there is no one who understands it, it is a grievous trial. But it will be very glad to read an account of itself and to see that it is travelling on the right road. It will be a great advantage for it to know what it should do in order to make progress in any one of these states. I have suffered greatly and lost much time through not knowing what to do, and so feel great pity for those souls who find themselves alone when they reach this state. Even though I had read many spiritual books in which these matters are discussed, they are not very explicit. If the soul has not a great deal of experience, it will have as much as it can do to understand its state, however much they say. (100)

In thus recording her own soul's progress and mortification, Teresa has finally usurped the role of those (male) authorities who have failed all along to understand her experience and whose 'spiritual books' are of no help either. By writing the improving narrative of her *Life*, she has closed the divide opened in childhood between the romances of chivalry which she had enjoyed in secret and the 'holy books' it was her Christian – and daughterly – duty to read. In coming to authorship in this form she takes on willy-nilly the role of guide which she assigns throughout the *Life* to those set in authority over her by society and by the church. She finds her own authority in the circumventing of that official authority. If there is a moment of the text approximating to an Augustinian conversion or 'turning', it is Teresa's first experience of 'the grace of ecstasy', when she hears the words 'I want you to converse now not with men but with angels.' Unlike Augustine, she does not put these words into a human mouth; they must be presumed to have been spoken unequivocally by God. Their effect is indeed of conversion: 'Since that day I have had the courage to give up everything for God, who in that moment – for I think it was no more than a moment – was pleased to make His servant another person'(173). This temporal 'moment' marks an intersection of human time with divine timelessness, and the realization in Teresa of another essence. Once she has become 'another person' she has the strength suddenly to give up certain reprehensible friendships and henceforth associate only with the community of the prayerful. And thus inspirited by God she also achieves the autonomy towards which she has been progressing: 'So there was no need for my confessor to give me any more commands.'

Throughout the *Life*, Teresa makes all due concession to the temporal certainties and settled dogmas of the church, well knowing how disruptive of the collective orthodoxy her solitary, mystical experiences are. In her show of modesty and anxiety, she colludes in her own *récupération* by the masculine establishment. Her first editor, Fray Luis de León, was a learned man, a university professor, but also a mystical poet imprisoned by the Inquisition for his translation of *The Song of Songs*, and he was thoroughly sympathetic to his authoress' case as to the singularity of what she reported of her relationship with God. In his preface to the 1588 edition of her works, he wrote: 'So, whenever I read them I wonder afresh: and in many parts of them it is not the mind [*ingenio*] of a man that I seem to hear: and I do not doubt that in many places the Holy Spirit was speaking through her and was directing her pen and her hand....' An ungenerous interpretation of this would be that here is a scholar accommodating the intrusive voice of a mere, uninstructed woman only by presenting her as the channel through which the superior voice of a – masculine – God may be heard. But such an interpretation is partisan, and anachronistic; her editor was on Teresa's side, and is better read as sincerely endorsing the uniqueness of her claims.[5]

Descartes

The quintessentially autobiographical themes I have been illustrating, of the superiority of lived experience over formal learning, and of individual autonomy over a blind obedience to authority, are ones which receive their most lucid and arrogant expression in what Descartes has to say about the formation of his mind – Descartes who notoriously favoured having intellectual commerce with women because he believed that their minds had not been closed as men's minds had by an inflexible education. He wrote no proper life of himself, but he did write his *Discourse on Method*, which was published in 1637, when he was forty-one, by way of an introduction to his three short scientific treatises on Dioptrics, Meteors and Geometry. As a declaration of his methodology in science, the *Discourse* serves to unify the three works which follow it, various in subject-matter as these are; in this it plays the autobiographical role I have already invoked in the case of Cellini, of relocating what might otherwise appear diverse productions in a single place of origin. The *Discourse* is the philosophical prototype of such autobiographical writings as Nietzsche's *Ecce Homo*.

Compared with that truculent work, Descartes' is a quite subdued declaration of intellectual independence – and only of intellectual, not of ethical independence: unlike Nietzsche, he aspires not at all to overturn received moral teachings. But such has been the lasting resonance of the philosophical axioms first propounded by Descartes that many readers of the *Discourse* may never have reflected on just how autobiographical a text it is; in an age like our own when philosophy has tried so hard to rebuild itself on foundations as firm and objective as those of the natural sciences whose assurance it so much envies, we are uncomfortable with the idea that even in the seventeenth century a philosopher should want to justify the form his philosophy takes by reference to the circumstances of his own life. But

---

[5] The Penguin translation does not include Luis de León's preface. I have translated it from the Austral edition of the *Vida* (Buenos Aires, 1946), p. 14.

that is what in the *Discourse on Method* Descartes does. It is an irony on the face of it that the philosophical work which marks the institution of the Cogito, or the universalized first person of epistemology, should have so strong a subjective, autobiographical aspect to it. But that is ironical only if one disregards the element of story in the *Discourse*: for as a narrative it traces this very transition, from the personalized I of autobiography to the impersonal I of philosophy. As an autobiographer Descartes achieves self-promotion on the grand scale.

The advent of Cartesianism in European thought is one of the most decisive of those changes of paradigm which have punctuated our modern intellectual history. It represents a definitive turning inwards, from philosophies of naive realism in respect of the external world, to one of reflexivity, according to which certain knowledge can only be of what is within our minds, not of what may or may not exist independently of them. It represents also the exaltation of what Charles Taylor calls 'the disengaged reason', or that inner, immaterial faculty the possession of which guarantees our relative independence of the physical world as well as our capacity to evaluate our own thoughts and feelings.[6] The new dualism, of rational and embodied intelligences set in a mechanical cosmos, has clear implications when it comes to autobiography, in appearing to certify the writer's freedom henceforth to envisage himself confidently and lucidly as an object. In its autobiographical version, dualism takes the form of an actively rational 'I' examining the past actions and emotions of a passive, pre-rational 'me'; that optimistic ideal of our own potential transparency to ourselves had been born which was to endure well into the twentieth century, until, under the impact of Freudianism, such optimism dissolved and we came to recognize that far from being peculiarly clear-sighted in respect of our own behaviour, we might be peculiarly deluded concerning it.

When he turned as a young man to philosophy Descartes was dismayed to encounter the plurality of existing philosophies, which had accumulated over two millennia without ever achieving the certainty which he himself took to be the proper goal of philosophy. Hence the decision to start the search again, from nothing, in order to establish certain unarguable truths and to set philosophy off along

---

[6] See Charles Taylor, *Sources of the Self* (Cambridge, 1989), pp. 143–58. Taylor stresses the Augustinian side of Descartes in his redirection of our attention from the external world to the mind that 'reflects' it; but Taylor's main concern is with the way in which Cartesianism revolutionizes moral philosophy also, by locating the ultimate 'moral sources' within the human mind and no longer seeing them as inherent in the cosmic order without.

a new, definitive track. But what right had he to engage on this overweening, maieutic task? It would not be enough simply to state the principles by which he believed that philosophy should in future be conducted, he needed also to explain why and how he had fixed on them. The *Discourse on Method* would in part be the story by which he could justify the hugely presumptuous step he had taken, as well as a discursive reenactment of the very process of withdrawal from a supposedly direct but in truth delusive engagement with the external world into the autonomous order and security of his own consciousness, there to found, step by logical step, a new philosophy impossible of contradiction. The *Discourse* is a short, at first sight quite modest piece of writing, altogether out of proportion with its author's prodigious will to singularity.

A first sign of Descartes' desire to break with the past is the language in which he chose to publish it. The *Discourse* was first written in the vernacular, in French, and only subsequently translated into the Latin in which, had he been observing the learned conventions of the time, he would have published it in the first place. When, four years after the *Discourse*, he published the *Meditations*, in which he expanded on the philosophical axioms merely adumbrated in the earlier work, he reverted to Latin. In a preface to the *Meditations*, Descartes explains that he had thought it 'inexpedient' to treat of the two major questions – 'that respecting God and that respecting the human mind' – 'at full length in a French discourse that might be read by all and sundry, lest those disqualified through insufficient mental powers should come to believe that they too might travel by this road'.[7] This implies that the *Discourse* was indeed addressed to 'all and sundry', including those who might lack the intelligence to follow more fully developed philosophical arguments. If Descartes' radical ideas in respect of his method are for everyone, as the notably democratic tendency evident in the *Discourse* suggests, then it seems that they are so only in the summary form which they take there. The attraction to him of demonstrating his own rational independence of thought is tempered by the danger of so doing, when that independence may be construed as inimical to the authority of church and state.

Descartes' decision to publish the *Discourse* in French signals his wish to mark himself off from those who had taught him at the Jesuit

---

[7] See his letter to Lazare Meysonnier, of 29 January 1640, in René Descartes, *Oeuvres, Lettres*, edited by A. Bridoux (Paris, 1953), p. 1066.

college of La Flèche, and from a language able to command assent
merely by its exclusivity, as if what were written in Latin were for that
reason alone more likely to be true. Descartes has a wider audience in
mind, and implicit in his appeal to it in the *Discourse* is an appeal
against the authority of Latin. It is a part of his declared purpose in
writing to invite a written response from those who read him, whom
he asks to submit their objections to his arguments, should they have
any, to his publisher, so that he may take them into account, and
answer them. He has confidence 'that those who rely entirely on their
unspoiled natural reason will be better judges of my opinions than
those who give credence only to the writing of the ancients'(163).[8]
This sounds a humble enough way of doing things, as though the
Cartesian philosophy were to be advanced by cooperative means.
But a different interpretation may be put on it, when one reflects that
to elicit objections to his philosophy publicly is also to expose those
objections, so that what he presumes to be their inadequacy will be
apparent to all. He invites objections in order to rebut them, in the
finest dialectical tradition, the better to extend his own intellectual
authority – his letters contain a great many detailed refutals of
arguments advanced against him and, that I have come across, few
if any acknowledgments of error on his part.

It is important for Descartes nevertheless to remind 'all and
sundry' that his intellectual distinction has not been bought at the
cost of his humanity; like autobiographers in general he will both
trace the genesis of his singularity and protest his solidarity with his
kind. The *Discourse* opens with a strikingly egalitarian proposition:
that 'Good sense is of all things in the world the most equitably
distributed.' 'Good sense' he defines as 'the power of judging well
and of distinguishing between the true and the false.' This is not a
power restricted to philosophers, but, on the contrary, one which is
'by nature equal in all men'. Descartes' reason for assuming this
innate equality in the possession of good judgment is the curious one
that all men believe themselves 'amply provided with it' and all men
are unlikely to be wrong. His is a populist assertion justified on
populist grounds. But whatever its persuasiveness as a premiss of his
philosophical method, Descartes requires the notion of an equally
distributed 'good sense' for his purposes as an autobiographer, as the
most promising point of departure for the story of his own

---

[8] The edition cited is *Descartes' Philosophical Writings*, selected and translated by Norman
Kemp-Smith (London, 1952).

singularization. For if we are all of us equally in possession of this fundamental faculty, how does it happen that so few of us distinguish ourselves by its application? We start equal and end unequal. The opportunity is there to tell us by what singular path or process René Descartes has separated himself out from the crowd of those identically endowed. The moral of his story is that we are not born singular but that we can rise to singularity, and do so by being singularly unencumbered by intellectual debts to those who have been our teachers.

No autobiographer, not even Augustine, comes quite up to Descartes in the ruthless disavowal of a formal education which had probably been very efficient. The narrative part of the *Discourse* opens with a scornful repudiation of the curriculum to which he had been exposed:

From my childhood I have been familiar with letters; and as I was given to believe that by their means a clear and assured knowledge can be acquired of all that is useful in life, I was extremely eager for instruction in them. As soon, however, as I had completed the course of study, at the close of which it is customary to be admitted into the order of the learned, I entirely changed my opinion. For I found myself entangled in so many doubts and errors that, as it seemed to me, the endeavour to gain instruction had served only to disclose to me more and more of my ignorance. (118)[9]

The education he is renouncing has failed on grounds of utility, which is a criterion of ultimate importance in the *Discourse*. Descartes we may now look back on as a prime instigator of that philosophy of so-called 'instrumental reason' which came to dominate western thought and science, whereby the human agent can exploit his new-found disengagement from the external world by acting more calculatingly, after due reflection, within it. His new method is utilitarian; where the philosophy he has been taught in the schools is speculative, his own will be practical and, properly extended and applied, might make of us 'the masters and possessors of nature'. The scope of such an ambition, or prospect, casually expressed as it is in the final part of the *Discourse*, may be set against the apparent modesty of the opening, to measure how fast and how far Descartes has there been travelling along his chosen philosophical 'road'.

[9] I have emended Kemp-Smith's translation very slightly here. He translates Descartes' phrase 'en tâchant de m'instruire' as 'the endeavour to instruct myself', which makes him sound already like the agent of his own own education. I think his active role should be played down at this point, and that the force of the French is better preserved by translating these words by 'the endeavour to gain instruction'.

   The notion of utility introduces a familiar opposition into his scheme, between what may be learnt from books and what from life, the same opposition as Saint Teresa makes so much of, though formulated rather differently by Descartes. She has had no formal education, and defers, sincerely or not, to those who have, to the men; he on the contrary has had an elaborate formal education which has served no useful purpose whatsoever. At the earliest possible moment, he will exchange it for an informal education, effected by a dialogue between himself and the life he observes going on around him: '[...]as soon as my age allowed of my passing from under the control of my teachers, I entirely abandoned the study of letters; and resolving to seek no other science than that which can be found in myself and in the great book of the world, I spent the remainder of my youth in travel ... amassing varied experiences ... and at all times making reflections on the things that came my way, and by which I could in any wise profit'(121–2). Here, in embryo, is the picaresque element of the *Discourse*, or that story which Descartes never told of all that had happened to him during his extensive journeyings around Europe, first as a soldier and then as a systematic student of alien customs and practices. But by resorting in this abstract summary of his travels to the established metaphor of 'the book of the world', he concedes the ambiguity of his claim to have thus obtained an unmediated experience of human life, since it was to circumvent the book as the authoritative model of instruction that he undertook to travel in the first place.

   Descartes alternates in his narrative between the will to expose himself to the world and the will to withdraw from it, or between raw experience and rational reflection. And as before with Abelard, the moments of withdrawal act to underwrite his fame, since it is in the course of those that he first discovers and then publicizes his revolutionary Method. The true creative moment of Descartes' story is that of his taking refuge in a *poêle*, or 'stove-heated room', during a wartime winter in Germany when he was twenty-three years old. This is a place at once warm, secure and solitary, in which he can reflect without distraction. It might have been designed for the discovery of a philosophical method by which to establish sure, incontrovertible truths; the quest for epistemological assurance, which Descartes had failed to find during his education, begins in an apt environment. And once he has thus been set free to commune with his thoughts, his account begins by a prolonged excursion into metaphor: 'Among the first [thoughts] that came to me was this, that often there is less perfection in works composed of several parts and the product of several different hands, than in those due to a single master-workman. Thus we see that buildings planned and executed by a single architect are usually much more beautiful and better proportioned than those which others have attempted to improve, adopting walls to serve purposes other than that for which they were originally designed'(124). The architectural analogy is developed at surprising length by Descartes, before modulating into another, in which he compares the laws of a nation which has been civilized only gradually, 'mainly by embarrassments due to the crimes and quarrels which have formed their adoption', with the laws of Sparta, peculiarly beneficial because they were devised 'by a single legislator'. And as with human laws so with divine ones: the 'ordinances' of 'true religion' are 'incomparably better regulated' for having been made 'by God alone'. The autarkic case is emphatically made and divinely sanctioned; the philosopher too will work alone, knowing that only in this way can a perfectly regulated philosophical system be built. Rather than do as his predecessors have done, and try to use some at least of the building materials they found to hand, Descartes means to start afresh, at the level of the foundations.

Sustained metaphors such as these, taken from architecture – elsewhere he favours military ones – , evidence Descartes' debt to his belletristic education, which has taught him the effectiveness of figurative language, and of narrative. In recounting his exposure to 'letters' in the *Discourse*, he concedes that 'fables charm and awaken the mind; that the histories of memorable deeds exalt it'. Histories, however, he goes on to fault, for exaggerating or otherwise altering 'the import of things' in an attempt to ingratiate themselves with their readers, or else for their misleading omission of the merely commonplace. Rather than exalt the mind by the examples they tell of, such stories are more likely to lead it into 'romantic extravagances'. Of fables, which cause us to imagine as 'possible' events which are not so, Descartes has nothing more to say, unless we take that rubric to include the stories of 'the ancient pagan moralists' on whose pretensions to teach us virtue he is severe. It would seem as if neither 'history' nor 'fables' are fit genres for a serious philosopher to practise. And yet when he reflects in the *Discourse* on what he is hoping to achieve by publishing it, Descartes does not fear so to classify his own essay: 'But in putting forward this piece of writing merely as a history, or, if you prefer so to regard it, as a fable, in which, among some examples worthy of imitation, there will also, perhaps, be found others we should be well advised not to follow, I hope that it will be of use to some without being harmful to anyone, and that all will welcome my plain-speaking'(118).

Whether it counts as 'history' or as 'fable', the *Discourse* is offered as an exemplary story, as all autobiographies must be. The autobiographer may not ask or expect his readers to direct their own subsequent lives differently according to what they have learnt from reading him, but he can but be aware that he is giving them the chance to do so. Descartes, who has found no teacher truly worthy of the title in the course of his schooling, will recount his decision to become the mentor of himself, and in so doing act as our mentor. This is a rhetorical endeavour in whose successful prosecution he must act the littérateur, telling a story of himself and resorting if need be to metaphor rather than to plain statement. He is caught in the same bind as Augustine, of aiming at the persuasion of his readers at the same time as dissociating himself from the traditional means of persuasion. But Descartes finds an escape route, as before, in innateness, declaring that 'eloquence', which he prizes, is a 'natural gift', not something learnt at school, and that 'Those in whom the gift of reasoning is strongest and who are careful to render their thoughts clear and intelligible, are always the best able to convert others to what they propose, even if they speak Breton and are ignorant of rhetoric'(120).

The figurative usage to which Descartes returns most conspicuously in the *Discourse* is that of the 'path' or 'road' which we can all of us be said to follow in the conduct of our lives. This was no doubt an etiolated, commonplace figure even at the time, but Descartes uses it in a strong, inward sense that gives it an unwonted vitality. The particular 'path' that we follow in life is what differentiates us from others and thus enables our singularization. Our endowment at birth may be the same, in terms of 'good sense', but we do not all develop similarly or come to hold the same ideas: but 'the diversity of our opinions is not due to some men being endowed with a larger share of reason than others, but solely to this, that we lead our thoughts along different paths...'(116).[10] And this same, opening paragraph

---

[10] I have emended Kemp-Smith's translation a second time here. Descartes has '...mais seulement de ce que nous conduisons nos pensées par diverses voies', which Kemp-Smith translates as '...but solely to this, that our thoughts proceed along different paths'. But on

of the *Discourse* speaks also of the advantages to the mind, if it would progress, of keeping 'to the straight road'. Within only a few more lines, Descartes writes of 'the great good fortune of finding myself, already in early years, travelling by paths that have led to the reflections and maxims from which I have formed a method' and of how 'in this discourse it will be my pleasure to show what the paths are which I have followed, delineating my life as in a picture (*tableau*)'.

These, then, are mental 'paths', though the metaphor itself looks outwards, beyond the privacy of the mind, to what I earlier called the 'picaresque' element in the *Discourse*, or Descartes' reference there to the years he spent travelling and reading from the 'book of life'. The 'path' is an ideal trope by which to mark this inward turn, as Descartes redeploys it autobiographically to describe the rational process by which he has come to think as he now thinks. It is a figure still in the narrative mode, and ideally appropriate to the linear or sequential method which he recommends as his own in philosophy, involving as that does the division of all difficulties into 'as many parts as may be required for its solution', and the arrangement of his thoughts 'in order', starting from 'things the simplest and easiest to know' and ascending to the more complex ones (129). His model of consecutiveness is the geometrical demonstration, which we might reasonably classify as a proto-narrative, in so far as each of its successive moments has to follow from the accumulation of earlier ones. The *Discourse* is intended to give satisfaction to those who read it, by exemplifying in its own orderly progress the method of whose discovery it is the record.

The 'path' which Descartes has followed is his, and his alone; and at least where philosophy is concerned, the proliferation of alternative 'paths' is a scandalous if also inspirational fact, since it is a challenge to him to impose his 'path' on that of others and establish a lastingly valid philosophy. Descartes is prudent, however, in stressing that his singularity extends only to philosophy, and not beyond it, into the conduct of his life.[11] He recommends no break with the past in terms

---

this occasion the idea of agency is strong in the French and should be kept – hence '... *we lead our* thoughts along different paths'.

[11] A striking feature of the first, and best known biography of Descartes, by Baillet, is the frequency with which it assures us that the philosopher was anxious to avoid any appearance of *singularité*, in behaviour or in dress. Descartes is quoted as criticizing his great philosophical contemporary in England, Thomas Hobbes, fearful by nature yet audacious in print, for having a mind which was 'obstinate and dangerous even in its singularity'. Baillet concedes,

of morality; on the contrary, the first of the four moral 'maxims' to which he holds advises obedience to the local laws and customs, and moderation in behaviour, while the third draws a sharp distinction between that which is in our power to control and that which is not: we have control over our thoughts, not over our fortunes. The *Discourse* itself is an exercise in that clarity and distinctness of thought which is for Descartes the touchstone of philosophical truth; but it is thought turned in on the thinker, thus laying down for future autobiographers a model of intimate transparency, as if it were always possible for the reflective mind to be sure of the truth of what it finds within. It is a model which excludes interference from those parts of the self to which we have no unimpeded access, to the subconscious mind for which Cartesianism leaves no room. To a modern autobiographer, writing after Freud and the deep soundings of psychoanalysis, the *Discourse* will seem a disappointing model, because of the confidence which Descartes displays in his own lucidity towards himself.

Assurance, however, is the very state of mind that he has set out to find, by the unique 'path' leading to certain knowledge. But there are risks attached to the singularity which attends on his philosophical success. In the final two parts of the *Discourse* Descartes first summarizes 'the complete chain of truths' which he believes to follow from the 'primary truths' he has been expounding, and then explains why the treatise in which he had earlier been intending to publish them has not appeared: he has withheld it because he has learnt of the verdict of the Inquisition in condemning the physical theory of Galileo. Inoffensive though he believes his own theories to be, either to religion or to the state, he has prudently kept their detailed exposition to himself. (The treatise in question finally appeared in 1671, after his death; and some of his writings were placed on the Index, for their 'novelty'.) Descartes then enters into what is in effect a debate with himself as to the advantages and disadvantages of publishing his physical ideas. Is it his duty to publish them, if they promise to conduce, as he believes they do, especially in the field of medical knowledge, to the general good, at the same time inviting the cooperation of other savants in his researches? Or should he allow

however, that during Descartes' schooldays 'no affectation of singularity was observed in him, unless that which may have come from the emulation with which he prided himself on leaving behind those of his fellows who surpassed the rest'. See A. Baillet, *Vie de Monsieur Descartes* (Paris, 1691), p. 8.

that his 'speculations' are incomplete, and may be wrong, and keep them to himself? His solution is a compromise: to publish three short physical treatises, preceded by the *Discourse on Method*.

The fundamental issue for Descartes is to decide what is of the greater advantage to himself: should there be wide public knowledge of what he has so far achieved or should he protect the fruitful seclusion in which he lives and works? Following nine years of nomadism in Europe, he has chosen to retire to Holland, because life is safe and well-ordered there and the people show no curiosity towards him. If he publishes them, his ideas will prompt controversy, which might, given what has happened to Galileo, prove dangerous to him, and might also involve him in a time-wasting defence of his arguments against those whom he is sure will have misunderstood them. Descartes shows no respect in the *Discourse* for his intellectual opponents; he claims never to have learnt anything from the objections hitherto raised against him, nor to trust even those 'of very good intelligence' to assimilate his philosophy without distorting it. He undercuts his invitation to his fellow-workers to cooperate with him in scientific advancement by declaring that he could only accept the assistance of paid 'artisans' in the carrying out of 'observations'. The hired hand will carry them out exactly as his paymaster orders, and not, we must assume, be led astray scientifically by any desire to make his own name.

To abstain from publication, however, does not mean to abstain from writing: Descartes will continue to write with a view to being read, after his death. He has found the act of writing helpful: 'Do we not always give closer attention to what we believe will be read by others than to what is written only for ourselves? How often what has seemed true to me when first thought of, has seemed false on my attempting to commit it to writing'(171). He gives two reasons in the closing pages of the *Discourse* for having written and published it. The first is that were he to publish nothing, even though he had earlier been known as intending to bring out his physical treatise, his silence might be interpreted to his discredit – implying that he might be adjudged afraid to publish or else unable to, his researches having led nowhere. Fame Descartes opposes to 'repose', or that peace of mind which he requires in order to follow his own philosophical 'path' and which would be disturbed were he to become too great a celebrity and engaged in controversy. But he knows that he has a certain reputation and must take care to manage it. Indeed, his decision to retreat to Holland in order to work at his philosophy had been taken because he was reputed already to have brought it to fruition; the decision was one to match his real achievement to that prematurely and falsely attributed to him, to live up to a name he had done nothing as yet to merit. This is an unusual variation on the specific autobiographical urge, of ensuring that one's reputation represents one truthfully. Similarly, in choosing to publicize his method in the *Discourse*, he has 'thought that I ought to do my best to save myself at least from having an evil reputation'. His second reason for now publishing, perversely, is one he has already given and then seemingly contradicted, being to encourage others to help him by making comparable scientific 'observations' of their own. This is an autobiographical envoi symmetrical with the democratic overture to the *Discourse*; just as there Descartes has presented himself modestly as having been born with no more and no less of 'good sense' than the rest of mankind, so now, finally, he reverts to the theme of equality, even though the whole thrust of the text in between has been away from parity with others and towards an extreme singularity.

CHAPTER 5

The historiography of self: Vico, Hume, Gibbon

Taking a cue from Descartes himself, one might ask whether in the *Discourse* he is writing as the historian of his own intellectual formation, or as a fabulist, as the kind of story-teller for whom what matters is not conformity with fact or even probability but the moral to be drawn? Bluntly put: do we take the story he tells us to be the truth, or one deceptively fashioned so as, in his own words, to 'change or exaggerate the import of things in order to make [it] seem more worthy of perusal'? Descartes has gone egregiously far in proclaiming his own intellectual autonomy, by eliminating the influence of other minds from the development of his own and reducing the properties essential to the successful philosopher to the barest minimum, of the native 'good sense' common to us all. Can this be the credible history of how his thought came to be what it is? By thus clearing away from his path all evidence of an outside contribution to his philosophy, the self-sufficient Descartes has given us not the honest record but what might better be called the *fabula rasa* of his education.

The greatest figure in the philosophical generation following Descartes thought he had been both right and wrong to turn autobiographer in the *Discourse*. Although he left no such account of his own, Leibniz believed that we understand the thought of others more accurately if we know also the thinking which has produced the thought. In a letter of 1714, he wrote that ' ... it is good to study the discoveries of others in a way that discloses to us the source of the inventions and renders them in a sort our own. And I wish that authors would give us the history of their discoveries and the steps by which they have arrived at them.' Descartes' was an autobiographical initiative of the right kind, but, declared Leibniz, the French thinker had exaggerated his own originality: 'Descartes would have had us believe that he had read scarcely anything. That was a bit too much.'[1]

Vico

This letter of Leibniz, and the desideratum he there expresses, creates a historical link between the *Discourse on Method* and the next piece of autobiographical writing which demands admission to the present sequence: the *Life* of the Neapolitan jurist and philosopher, Giambattista Vico. This was an autobiography rare though by no means unique for having been commissioned – perhaps we should allow that St Teresa's *Life* also was commissioned, since it was ordered to be written by her confessors. The originator of the commission to Vico was the Venetian Count Porcia, and its likely inspirer the censor of publications in that city, Father Carlo Lodoli, who merits an appearance in any conscientious study of autobiography for having early in the 1700s so interested himself in it as a literary form as to have coined a Graecism by which to describe it, of 'periautography', or literally, 'around-self-writing'. The 'proposal' of Count Porcia was that a number of illustrious Italian scholars should each write an autobiographical account telling of 'all the episodes of his life which make it remarkable or curious, so far as they can without shame be published to the world and to posterity', but concentrating on what was good or bad in their education and on their experiences in the prosecution of their particular art or science. The *Life* of Vico is the only one of these exemplary narratives to have survived, having been published in 1728 in Venice as a model of its autobiographical kind, in the first issue of a projected quarterly, *Raccolta d'Opusculi Scientifici e Filologici*, or 'Scientific and Philological Miscellany'. The association in this title of the scientific with the philological is particularly apt where Vico is concerned.

As an autobiographer he writes with the example of Descartes explicitly in view. Like Descartes, Vico prefers to use the vernacular, not Latin, and again like Descartes, in so doing signals a certain parting of the ways between himself and the academic establishment. The major part of the *Life* was written within a very few weeks, in 1725, when its author was professor of Latin Eloquence at the

---

[1] Cited in *The Autobiography of Giambattista Vico*, translated by Max Harold Fisch and Thomas Goddard Bergin (Ithaca, 1944), p. 5. All future references to Vico's own text are to this English translation.

University of Naples, a chair he had held since 1699. He was fifty-seven years old and poorly paid, and two years earlier had failed in open competition to obtain a much better paid and more reputable chair of civil law in the same university. His hopes of professional advancement and recognition were certainly at an end. His intellectual hopes, however, were at their highest; for in 1725 Vico also published the first version of his great and eventually celebrated work of metahistory, the *New Science*. The first part of the *Life* was in fact written immediately after he had completed the manuscript draft of the larger book. Before that could be published, however, its sponsor withdrew on the ground that he could no longer afford to support it. Vico was in crisis. He could not publish the *New Science* himself, because he was too poor and it was too long. With remarkable speed, however, he recast his manuscript, removing from it the great quantity of criticism of earlier thinkers which it contained; this reduced its size by some three quarters and he was able to publish the so-called 'positive' version of the *New Science* late in 1725, at his own expense.

These events are briefly recorded at the start of the second part of the *Life*, which Vico extended at the end of that momentous year (then again in 1728 and for a last time in 1731). I cite them in order to demonstrate the closeness in the dates of composition and the coincidence of intellectual preoccupation between the autobiography and the *summa* containing Vico's epochal theory of human history; the two works fit together. The *New Science* too was written not in Latin but in what Vico himself refers to, in the final part of the *Life*, as 'the vulgar tongue', which he had years before studied in the works of its three 'princes', Boccaccio, Dante and Petrarch. He had adjudged them to be inferior to their Latin equivalents, Cicero, Virgil and Horace, but they still proved able to instruct him. When the time came for his own conclusive and defiant reversion to Tuscan he had made, he boasted, 'splendid use' of that tongue in writing the *New Science* (178). This subsequent finding of high advantage in an act whose value to him had not been apparent at the time is entirely characteristic of the scheme of Vico's *Life*, exemplifying as this shorter text does the scheme which he believed to have been inscribed by God in the course of human history. There is a strongly Augustinian side to Vico, both as a philosopher and as an autobiographer.

Unlike Descartes, he writes in the *Life* in the third person: textually, he is not 'I' but 'he' or else 'Vico'. We may take this as a refusal of the extravagant subjectivity of Descartes, whose narrative 'I' is part and parcel of the exaltation of his own philosophical novelty. Vico appears to be making no such mighty claims on his own behalf, and to have chosen a self-denying narrative device appropriate to his professional milieu and to the terms of the commission from Count Porcia. But as students of autobiography we are trapped within the perspective of our own time, with its peculiar readerly expectations, and unable to be sure of the effect which Vico's relative severity as a third-person narrator of his own life might have had on his contemporaries. There is nothing inherently modest in such a procedure – the first great model of third-person autobiography after all is Julius Caesar's *Commentaries* on his own formidable conquests.[2] But the distancing effect which Vico secures by his use of the third or 'non'-person does establish him as, by contrast with the fabulist Descartes, the privileged yet detached *historian* of his own life, confident in the factuality of what he records without need of recourse to the first-person forms of confidentiality.

He wastes very little time in the *Life* before taking his predecessor to task for having misled his readers: 'We shall not here feign what René Descartes craftily feigned as to the method of his studies simply in order to exalt his own philosophy and mathematics and degrade all the other studies included in divine and human erudition. Rather, with the candor proper to a historian, we shall narrate plainly and step by step the entire series of Vico's studies, in order that the proper and natural causes of his particular development as a man of letters may be known'(113). Here Vico anticipates the profound discordance between his own philosophy and that of Descartes, a discordance which he means should be reflected in the form that he gives to his autobiography. Where Descartes has been mathematical, spelling his earlier life out step by step in the timeless form of a geometrical demonstration, Vico will be historical, tracing his own formation also step by step but with a proper allowance made for the operations of time. The charge that in the *Discourse* Descartes has been guilty of 'feigning', or of writing 'fiction', is entirely consonant with what Vico writes concerning mathematics in the *New Science*, where he compares mathematical knowledge unfavourably with the knowledge – *his* sort of knowledge – of human societies, inasmuch as

---

[2] For the best discussion of autobiography written in the third person, see Philippe Lejeune, *Je est un autre* (Paris, 1980) pp. 32–59, or, for an English translation, in *On Autobiography*, translated by Kathleen Leary (Minneapolis, 1989), pp. 31–51.

the first is exclusively of ideal, never of real objects, to come to know which is the harder, more practical task. At the same time, mathematical knowledge is for Vico a model, because it is knowledge of that which is man-made and hence fully knowable; it is this model which he means himself to apply to an infinitely less tractable yet equally man-made object, which is the evolution through time of political, social, legal and religious institutions. If Descartes' mathematics and physics are taken as the model of the 'old' science, Vico's 'new science' will far surpass them in its scope:

For the first indubitable principle [...] is that this world of nations has certainly been made by men, and its guise must therefore be found within the modifications of our own human mind. And history cannot be more certain than when he who creates the things also narrates them. Now, as geometry, when it constructs the world of quantity out of its elements, or contemplates that world, is creating it for itself, just so does our Science [...], but with a reality greater by just so much as the institutions having to do with human affairs are more real than points, lines, surfaces and figures are. (*The New Science*, no. 349)

It is not too much to say that in the *New Science* Vico lays down the principles by whose adoption each 'people' might write its own collective autobiography, or the story of its coming to be what it now is (to echo Nietzsche). For each separate people passes through the same historical process as if it were alone on earth; the process is internal, not brought about by diffusion, or influence from outside. It is as if the inner, mental autonomy which Descartes had falsely claimed for himself in the *Discourse* were being externalized in time and space by Vico and transferred to a whole people, and as if he himself, as the subject of the *Life*, might stand as an example of just such an evolutionary process.

Descartes has erred as an autobiographer in the same way as historians have traditionally erred, by Vico's lights, by interpreting the past in categories belonging to the present, without attempting to comprehend its true otherness. To the Cartesian autobiographer, the early stages of life pose no problem, they may be seamlessly incorporated with the later stages, in a rational whole; whereas to the Vichian autobiographer, childhood is assimilable to the first, primitive state of human societies and its difference should therefore be recognized, as constituting what Richard N. Coe, in his enlightening study of autobiographical 'Childhoods', calls 'an alternative dimension, which cannot be conveyed by the utilitarian logic of the responsible adult'.[3] We have seen how, with Descartes, the autobiographical subject, like any other human subject, is born rational, he does not have to acquire or be taught rationality, which for Vico is the achievement of maturity, whether for whole societies or for individuals, rationality going with their accession to the 'age of men', which in his tripartite division follows the 'age of Gods' and the 'age of heroes'. It is no good hoping to understand these two earlier ages in the secular, democratic categories of the third; instead, the modern, Vichian historian must 'descend from these human and refined natures of ours to those quite wild and savage natures, which we cannot at all imagine and can comprehend only with great effort'(*The New Science*, no. 338). Vico tells us that it cost him 'a good twenty years' to discover this new historical 'method' of as it were backdating his mind, by the application of which he intended to reinterpret and reorder the full temporal course of human history.

Is he, then, the scrupulous Vichian 'historian' of his own life, able to recover for us successively the stages of his intellectual becoming? He is not; he may come closer to this impossible ideal than a gross defaulter such as Descartes does, but he is unable or unwilling to accord to each moment of the process its due importance. One would never guess from reading the *Life* that, for one thing, he had himself for long been a convinced Cartesian in philosophy, to the point where, as his American editors have it, 'the greatest critic of Descartes was himself the greatest Cartesian of Italy'(36). By the time he wrote his autobiography, Vico was no longer a Cartesian, but there is no admission in it that he has passed through a strongly Cartesian phase. The will to dissociate himself from Descartes, and to associate himself instead with Plato, is stronger it seems than the will to historicize his past in strict accordance with his own principles.

In Vico's case the distinction between the fabulous and the historical lapses, because for him fables are unusually precious items of historical evidence, as memorable narratives surviving from those pre-rational stages of human societies whose *mentalité* is so very hard to recover. 'For by virtue of new principles of mythology herein disclosed', he writes in the preamble to the *New Science*, '[...] it is shown that the fables were true and trustworthy histories of the customs of the most ancient peoples of Greece'. Fables, whether representative of the earliest societal age, of the Gods, or of the

<hr />

[3] Coe, *When the Grass was Greener*, p. 2.

subsequent, aristocratic age of Heroes, can be 'read' for the light they shed on the remote thought processes of those ancestral beings who fabricated and bequeathed them.

In the light of which, we should not be shocked to find Vico's own 'historical' *Life* opening on an episode which is itself fabulous. At the age of seven, he tells us in the work's first few lines, 'he fell head first from the top of a ladder to the floor below, and remained a good five hours without motion or consciousness'(111). Now any story written within a Christian community even today which begins with a momentous fall is sure to bring to its reader's mind another, archetypal story likewise beginning with a Fall: the story of the human race as told in the book of Genesis. Is the accident which Vico reports as having happened to himself an authentic memory or is it a somewhat grandiose invention? There is no way of knowing, nor any need to know; its function as the liminal event of his personal narrative does not depend on its authenticity. If the fall actually happened, then it was what we are accustomed to call a *happy* accident, ideally suited to the autobiographical needs of the writer: it is an accident to be classed with other less physically threatening contingencies of his life all of which conduce ultimately to his advantage.

More than this though, Vico's fall should be read as an event at once particular to his own story and representative of human history on the very grandest scale. As a particular happening, it is the proper object of what Vico calls *coscienza* or 'consciousness', whose subject-matter is the sum of all such historical particularities in so far as they can be authenticated – and those reported autobiographically should be more authentic than most. As a symbolic or representative happening, however, the fall belongs to a higher realm, of *scienza*, whose object of study is the universal, causal principles held to regulate the incidence of particular phenomena. The study of the particular goes for Vico under the name of 'philology', that of the universal under the name of philosophy, and only in the *New Science* will these two – in fact complementary yet all too often in past practice opposed modes of understanding – be brought harmoniously together, there to demonstrate the true, universal aetiology common to all particular human societies. Vico's account of his fall could hardly be more auspicious in embodying the cardinal theorem of his mature philosophy.

It asks to be compared functionally with the emblematic 'frontispiece' that he provides for the *New Science*, which contains an elaborate symbolism of that work's main arguments, and which without his commentary we would be quite unable to penetrate. The frontispiece in fact 'speaks' the first of the three kinds of language which the trinitarian Vico stipulates as having followed one another in the course of human history: 'a mute language of signs and physical objects having natural relations to the ideas they wished to express'. This hieroglyphic language it requires himself to interpret for us in the third, democratic kind of language appropriate to the Age of Men, and in a subtle demonstration of that fundamental error which Vico believes to have vitiated previous attempts at comprehending the origins of modern institutions, of supposing our ancestors to have been in all intellectual respects just like ourselves.

The history through which each of earth's many 'peoples' has to pass – Vico's 'ideal eternal history' in its manifold temporal realizations – is likewise inaugurated by a Fall, which is the relapse into 'bestiality', a state lacking both the power of language and even the most rudimentary social institutions, and experienced by the descendants of Ham, Japheth and Shem in their secular wanderings about the earth following the Flood. This history-less interval of time is the hinge, as it were, by which the orthodox Catholic Vico attaches his own 'Gentile' and unorthodox history to the sacred history taught by the church – it is 'Gentile' because he excludes the Hebrew people explicitly from its scope. The Fall into 'bestiality' is the precondition of the subsequent 'making' of the Gentile peoples; without it there could have been no story to tell, no gradual rise through the successive stages of social development along the principles laid down in the *New Science*. The Fall is thus an infinitely productive event, and a seeming adversity which is transformed by its narrative aftermath into an inspiration.

As the inaugural episode of his life-story, Vico's own tumble from the ladder is of course gloriously discounted by his awareness in recalling it that he does so as the creator of the *New Science*. He has reclimbed the ladder from which he originally fell and has richly contradicted by his intellectual achievement the prognosis of the doctor that he would either die from his injuries or 'grow up an idiot'. The *Life* continues: 'However by God's mercy neither part of his [the doctor's] prediction came true, but as a result of this mischance he grew up with a melancholy and irritable temperament such as belongs to men of ingenuity and depth, who, thanks to the one, are quick as lightning in perception, and thanks to the other, take no pleasure in shallow witticisms or falsehoods'(111). Vico's early 'mischance' has done well by him, in determining his temperament in a favourable direction. (He has only a few lines earlier told us of the 'contribution' made to this temperament by his parents, and by the confluence in him of the 'cheerful disposition' of his father and the 'quite melancholy temper' of his mother; his fall has apparently served to suppress the temperamental influence of the father, and bring out that of the mother.) He may not ascribe his quickness and profundity of mind unequivocally to it, yet these intellectual qualities are made by Vico to be inseparable from the temperament accidentally bestowed on him. Falls both great and small, whether into 'bestiality' or into mere convalescence, thus have a lastingly generative effect. Just as centuries of errant bestiality have led to the historical institutionalization of the gentile peoples, so Vico's recovery from his accident provides him with an impetus for learning. He has to stay at home for three whole years, so delaying his formal education and making his precocity the more conspicuous once it begins. Having gone back to school, he soon finds himself far in advance of his coevals and is able to offer us the admirable spectacle of 'a pupil acting as his own teacher'.

As an account of its author's education, the *Life* is not the corrective to the very arrogant story told by Descartes which it ought to have been. Vico is scrupulous in identifying by name certain of his teachers, even if it is from books rather than men that he has mostly learnt; and he pays his dues among the philosophers at least to Plato. But the most propitious, indeed the idyllic period of his intellectual formation has been that which he spent in seclusion in a castle, as tutor to the nephews of the Bishop of Ischia, where 'he made the greatest progress in his studies'. This tutorship lasted for nine years, which, by another happy accident, is the same length of time which Descartes tells us in the *Discourse* he spent travelling and reading in the 'book of life' following the discovery of his Method during his retreat to the *poêle*. Though he is never guilty of the same extremism as Descartes, in denying his intellectual debts to others, Vico too lays large store by his independence of mind, congratulating himself on 'his good fortune in having no teacher whose words he had sworn by' and for having 'followed the main course of his studies untroubled by sectarian prejudice', 'guided by his good genius'(133). He has eventually come to be called by the nickname of 'the autodidact', an honourable title for any autobiographer to claim, as I have here been arguing.

It is a title which, as Vico himself recalls, he shares with the Greek philosopher Epicurus, to whose thought free reference is made in the *Life*, always so that Vico may show to what extent he dissociates himself from it. He approves of neither the physical nor the moral philosophy of Epicurus, but then he is writing as a finally convinced Platonist, unwilling directly to admit the extent to which he had earlier been attracted by Epicureanism, a philosophy much appreciated in the Naples of his youth even though its adherents were at risk from the attentions of the Inquisition. Vico's dissociation of himself from its materialist tenets in the *Life* is not merely prudential, however; to underpin his *New Science* he requires absolutely what he has learnt from Plato, 'a metaphysical principle, which is the eternal idea, drawing out and creating matter from itself'. Under the influence of Plato: '[...] there began to dawn on him, without his being aware of it, the thought of meditating an ideal eternal law that should be observed in a universal city after the idea or design of providence, upon which idea have since been founded all the commonwealths of all times and all nations. This was the ideal republic that Plato should have contemplated as a consequence of his metaphysic; but he was shut off from it by ignorance of the fall of the first man'(121–2). It has been left to Vico to carry to its logical conclusion the metaphysical scheme of social organization which Plato himself was prevented from fully comprehending, presumably because he had no adequate notion of historical development. The difference between Plato and Vico is that the first was a pagan whereas Vico is a Christian. Vico knows of the Fall not only from reading the Bible but in his own bruised bones, having vicariously re-experienced as a child the chastisement of Adam. He knows also that, as the American philosopher Nelson Goodman wittily and, for my purposes, particularly aptly puts it, 'The Garden of Eden was lost [...], not for sex but for science'.[4] With this knowledge there goes, most important of all, the knowledge of Providence, that divine form of supervision so hearteningly transformative of all old, pagan doctrines of chance or fate. It is by the action of a Christian Providence that such 'mischances' as Vico's childhood fall are turned eventually to his profit; his reference to 'God's mercy' in his

---

[4] Nelson Goodman, *Of Mind and Other Matters* (Cambridge and London, 1984), p. 2.

account of that event is to be read literally.

Providence takes two forms for Vico: the first form is that of the interventionist acts of a transcendent God, and is restricted to the Hebrews, the 'chosen people', whom he excludes from consideration; the second form is of an immanent Providence which directs the course and sequence of Gentile history without the human agents of that history knowing that they are acting as its surrogates. It is by means of this second, pervasive but secret form of Providence that Vico is able to reconcile his religious belief with his New Science, which would otherwise appear as stipulating the autonomous evolution of societies by human agency alone. And as with human societies so with an individual life, such as that of the thinker who has elaborated over many years the scheme of the New Science. In Vico's own story the operations of an immanent Providence must be revealed. They are revealed in the passage I have quoted above, in the phrase 'there began to dawn on him without his being aware of it... '. Such a formulation is perfectly indicative of the role of a Vichian Providence, seen as directing the course of a life without the liver's knowledge. There is a patent contradiction in claiming not to be aware of an idea that has begun to dawn on one; but it is the kind of contradiction that as readers of autobiography we are accustomed to, and happy to swallow. We swallow it because it is born of hindsight, and acknowledges that no autobiography can convey past ignorance save through the prism of present knowledge.

As I have suggested in the case of Augustine's *Confessions*, the secret workings of Grace or Providence in bringing a life to its narrative fruition have as much a rhetorical as a theological importance for the writer. Autobiographical retrospection finds its mirror image in divine prospection. In his *Life* Vico traces for us the genesis of his own providentialism, the largest influence on which has been the theology of Augustine. During his formative time of seclusion in the castle, he has read a certain exposition of Augustine and 'found himself in the very middle of Catholic doctrine in the matter of grace', 'in the very middle' meaning equidistant 'from the two extremes of Calvin and Pelagius'. Calvin was extreme for his iron doctrine of predestination, Pelagius, Augustine's contemporary, for his belief that salvation is to be achieved exclusively by our own efforts – he it was who found fault with the *Confessions* for encouraging Augustine's readers in the passive notion that divine grace would favour them. Vico's Augustinian compromise on this matter is another crucial step towards the formulation of his philosophical system: 'This disposition enabled him later to meditate a principle of the natural law of the nations, which should both be apt for the explanation of the origins of Roman law and every other gentile civil law in respect of history, and agree with the sound doctrine of grace in respect of moral philosophy' (119). Once again, this intellectual discovery is as it were stored, against the time when it will find its rightful place in his scheme, the eventual fruitfulness of such a deferment being assured by the clandestine direction of his life by a benign deity. Vico is among those thinkers – like his engaging contemporary in England, Bernard Mandeville, in *The Fable of the Bees* – who believe that Providence, or some profane substitute for it, invariably turns the actions of human beings from the narrow, local ends they are intended to serve to the accomplishment of larger, more commendable ends of its own. As a fable, his *Life* is improving in just the same way as the *Confessions* of Augustine are improving, in teaching the moral that the true singularity of our lives is underwritten by a higher power.

Hume

The judgment of Benedetto Croce on Vico's autobiography was that it represented 'the application of the *New Science* to the life of its author',[5] and as a narrative account of how Vico came by stages into possession of his meta-historical ideas, the *Life* does indeed assimilate the evolution of his own mind to that of mind in general. Which is what we would expect from the autobiography of a historian, for whom it would be perverse to depart from his chosen method of ordering the past when making a historical object of himself. But Vico's metahistorical scheme is unusually well-suited for adoption by an autobiographer: for the distinction on which so much in it turns, between the locally certain and the universally true, may be elided in autobiography, where the writer's life-story as told by himself raises a sum of certain, empirical facts into a general truth. The 'startling conclusion', as Sir Isaiah Berlin calls it, to which Vico had come was that 'The truth is what is made.'[6] And how better to exemplify that

---

[5] Cited in Fisch/Bergin's introduction to the *Autobiography*, p. 7.
[6] See Isaiah Berlin, *Vico and Herder: Two Studies in the Philosophy of History* (London, 1976), p. 100.

pragmatic insight into the historicity of human knowledge than by fabricating the truthful record of one's own ideological progress? As an autobiographer Vico is the direct ancestor of Goethe, who in his *Poetry and Truth* is similarly and explicitly set on raising the mere facts of his life on to the higher, 'poetic' plane of general truth. By writing his life in accordance with his own meta-historical principles, Vico can take on the role of that covert Intelligence – the Cunning of Reason, as the Hegelians were to call it – which realizes its purpose bit by bit in the historical evolution of the species.

Few historians, however, either then or since, have shared Vico's faith that History as a whole should be conceived of in these coherent narrative terms, and I turn now by contrast to two eighteenth-century historians and autobiographers who very certainly did not: to David Hume and Edward Gibbon, who were of like sceptical mind in rejecting all such Vichian notions of historical finalism. But no historian, however much of a naturalist he might be in philosophical terms, can write history without any preconceptions at all about what history consists in, and even the robustly empirical auto-biographies of a Hume or a Gibbon may be read as oblique essays in historical method.

Hume's autobiography is no more than an essay, of a few pages only, and its brevity is explained at the outset as being its author's defence against a charge of vanity, in choosing to write of himself at all. It was written in 1776, four months before he died, and in the foreknowledge of his death. Hume asked that it should appear at the front of the first posthumous edition of his Works – perhaps, though he doesn't say so, in order to forestall, like Alfieri, the appearance there of an ignorant or misleading biographical account by some strange hand. By its placement as the preface to his oeuvre, one might suppose that the function of this miniature autobiography was to unify his diverse publications by reconnecting them briefly to their vital source. But unification was a peculiarly unHumean concept, for he was the philosopher who (in the *Treatise of Human Nature*, Part IV, Section VI) had called lastingly into question the happy, common-sense belief that the human individual is constituted by a 'self', or a principle of identity which is somehow independent of the flux of his or her conscious experience. Hume had looked within his own conscious experience and found no evidence to support this thesis, only the inconceivably rapid succession of perceptions and 'impres-sions' which he did not believe required the support of a metaphysical 'self'. Sardonically, he allows that others may think differently from him on this vital matter, that another man 'may, perhaps, perceive something simple and continued which he calls *himself*; though I am certain there is no such principle in me'.[7] The autobiographer who disbelieves that he has a continuing self might seem to be in an odd position: for does not autobiography require that the person who writes is the metaphysically *same* person as the person he is writing about? Hume appears to be contesting the assumptions of the genre which he was, however briefly and *in articulo mortis*, prepared himself to practise.

But by contesting our assumptions about human identity, he in fact elucidates the nature of autobiography, even if it is only now, in the late twentieth century, that we have begun to grasp in just what ways. In his autobiographical essay Hume is not 'expressing' a continuous self transcendent to the text but modelling for us the impressionistic, intermittent self of his own philosophy. If there is a continuous self 'behind' what he gives us to read, then it is we the readers who imagine it. The autobiographical 'self' is our customary extrapolation from the evidence we are given, and as such a fiction, or so Hume would have it, derived from a negligent elision of what are in hard fact distinct mental impressions.

He can not prevent us from so reading his essay as to extrapolate from it a conventional non-Humean 'self'; but he can and does make it harder for us than do other autobiographers, who do not doubt that they possess and are able to 'express' a continuing self. 'My Own Life' is serial rather than evolutionary in form and ostentatiously objective, as if the writer stood in no especially privileged relation to the experiences he is recalling. It suits Hume's philosophical purpose very well to adopt the 'death-position', as if the imminence of that cessation were an assurance that the writer is no longer swayed by the petty considerations that might make him an unreliable witness in writing of his own life. 'I now reckon upon a speedy dissolution', he writes, and concludes that 'It is difficult to be more detached from life than I am at present', the 'life' from which he is detached being of course his own, that normally emotive subject-matter that he has just treated with a brazen serenity. 'My Own Life' is indeed a *polemical* essay in autobiography: it offers us the exemplary spectacle of a

---

[7]   *The Philosophical Works of David Hume*, Volume 1 (Edinburgh and London, 1826), p. 321.
This volume also contains Hume's autobiographical essay and is the edition I shall quote from.

philosophical mind unmoved by its own looming extinction. In the words of Hume's biographer, E. C. Mossner: 'He was a philosopher and was determined to die philosophically, and to convince the public that he had died in accordance with his principles – without hope and without fear. *My Own Life*, consequently, is, in part, autobiography and, in part, manifesto.'[8]

Thus even in so spare and offhand an autobiographical performance as Hume's there is an argument to be looked for, or an ideological cast to his story. And first, in the difficult matter of causation. Hume refused to see more in causation than the regular or habitual conjunction of one event with another: that the door always opens when I push it is an empirical fact, not a law of nature. But how is an autobiographer to avoid resorting to those catenary pairings of cause with effect without which narrative would surely founder? He can, like Hume, reduce the temporal relations of his story to ones merely of association, whereby one thing follows on another as its customary, not its logical consequence. I have said that *My Own Life* is 'serial' in form, and the 'series' of which it chiefly consists is of the writer's repeated publication of new works and of their repeated failure to find popularity with the reading public. Circumstances have provided Hume with a recurrent motif of disappointment, which as an autobiographer he turns to his narrative advantage. But even a series such as this requires a thread of continuity, and that is provided by the 'passion for literature' which has 'seized' him early on and been the 'ruling passion' of his life. He can thus restrict his autobiography to being 'little more than the History of My Writings', sub-tended by a 'ruling passion' which is the Humean equivalent of a principle of identity.

The sequence of events which he narrates requires only that this passion be tried by the resistance of circumstances. The theme is set proleptically, at the very start of the essay, where, to ward off the charge that by turning autobiographer he is indulging his vanity, Hume promises us that 'The first success of most of my writings was not such as to be an object of vanity.' (A thinker as subtle as Hume will have known well enough that there may be more vanity in broadcasting our failures than our triumphs, since to broadcast failure is to demand recognition from others that the world has done us an injustice in underestimating our true worth.) There follows a

[8] E. C. Mossner, *The Life of David Hume* (Oxford, 1980), p. 591.

regular association of private aspiration with public rebuff, a regularity made possible by the author's possession of an unfailingly 'sanguine' temperament. So if Nature has bestowed on him the passion for writing, it has also bestowed on him the temperament he needed if he was to survive the early frustrations of his writing career – just as it is now sustaining him in these last days of his life, during which he declares that he has 'never suffered a moment's abatement of my spirits'.

In his disbelief in the reality of a continuous, metaphysical self or 'I', Hume stands profoundly opposed to Descartes. There is no mention of Descartes in 'My Own Life', although there could well have been, for Hume there tells us that his 'plan of life' was laid and his first work written during his three-year 'retreat' in France between 1734 and 1737. This creative withdrawal is a very Cartesian strategy, and remarkably, the greater part of it was spent by Hume at La Flèche in Anjou, the very town where Descartes had received his redundant education from the Jesuits. The reception in England of this first work, the *Treatise of Human Nature*, has established the pattern of disappointment: in Hume's own words (and his own italics), 'It fell *dead-born from the press*, without reaching such distinction, as even to excite a murmur among the zealots.' And the same pattern ensues when he later recasts the *Treatise* as the *Enquiry concerning Human Understanding*, or publishes his *Essays*, his *Enquiry concerning the Principles of Morals*, or his *History of England*, none of which is well received. But 'My Own Life' is still a success-story; the autobiographer comes at last to the 'independency' of mind (and of income) which are his birthright. His success he owes to no one but himself, that is, to Nature, whose double endowment of a ruling passion and a sanguine temperament was all that he required.

There is a singular elevation in the position to which Hume the autobiographer finally lays claim. His 'character', as he himself describes it near the end of the essay, has been one of moderation and easy sociability, exempt from the extremisms disruptive of civility. He has risen above faction. When he first planned his *History of England* he thought of starting it at the beginning, that is at the time of the Romans. But the idea of 'continuing a narrative through a period of 1700 years' frightened him, and he had begun instead with the accession of the Stuarts, 'when, I thought, the misrepresentations of faction began chiefly to take place'. This hardly seems like the decision of a historian aiming at impartiality, but the autobiographer would nevertheless have it that 'I thought I was the only historian that had at once neglected present power, interest, and authority, and the cry of popular prejudices.' But in place of the applause he might have expected as a tribute to his evenhandedness, he has met with fury: 'I was assailed by one cry of reproach, disapprobation, and even detestation; English, Scotch, and Irish, Whig and Tory, Churchman and Sectary, Freethinker and Religionist, Patriot and Courtier, united in their rage against the man, who had presumed to shed a generous tear for the fate of Charles I. and the Earl of Strafford'(ix). All these partisan groupings are united against a man for whom a *natural* sympathy outweighs the parochial claims of any cause or affiliation; by posing disingenuously as the man of sensibility Hume is able to show what a singular figure he cuts in an age of gregarious enthusiasts.

The Hume of 'My Own Life' is not so much above faction as scornful of it. When he turns to belabour Whig historians – for promoting what we now refer to as the 'Whig interpretation of history', which sees the Glorious Revolution of 1688 as the narrative telos of seventeenth-century English constitutional history – it is very much as a Tory, happy to have braved their 'senseless clamour'. The end, however, is in serenity. For all the earlier descriptions of the hostility he has aroused, Hume comes at the last to the contradictory conclusion that 'both civil and religious factions [...] seemed to be disarmed in my behalf of their wonted fury'. He knows full well that his religious, philosophical and historical opinions have been profoundly unpopular and subversive, and that this testamentary document itself will not be well received by those looking for some evidence in it of a softening of his scepticism in the face of death. But Hume is finally asking that we should find his own amiability and moderation of temper reflected back at him by the society in which he had lived, which has learnt a greater civility from his example. He lays claim to a rare blamelessness of life inasmuch as his friends have never had cause to 'vindicate any one circumstance of my character and conduct', while such enemies as he has made, the 'zealots', may have invented stories against him but without being able to get others to believe them.[9] In attaching this eirenic envoi to his account of a

---

[9] It is worth remembering in this regard that Hume had earlier suffered from the pathological suspicions of Rousseau, whom he befriended in Paris and whose asylum in England in 1766 he helped to arrange. But like so many of Rousseau's friends, Hume was later accused by the man he had helped of being his enemy and of harbouring malicious intentions against

contentious life, Hume has given full measure to the autobiographer's stock desire to be finally forgiven for having chosen in his vanity to celebrate his independence of others.

Gibbon

Hume has an argument in the *Treatise* designed to appease if not to remove the common fear of death, foreseen as an irrevocable extinction: why, he asks, should we dread our non-existence after death when we are untroubled by our non-existence before birth? Why is the one void so much more fearful than the other? The argument is ineffective since, to use the narrative terms appropriate to my present context, the eternity of non-existence preceding our birth has had a most desirable denouement, to wit the advent of ourselves, whereas that which succeeds our death will have no experienceable denouement at all; it is not the endless state of non-existence in itself which frightens us, but the present prospect of it. Hume, however, is offering us his own ingenious anaesthetic against this prospect: of using a populous – a historian's – past for a distraction from a blank, us-less future.

Unlike lesser mortals, the sceptical autobiographer can face the prospect of his posthumous exclusion from the world supported by the knowledge that what he is now writing will survive him, perhaps by many generations of sympathetic readers. The future void is made habitable in imagination for bearing his imprint. What, however, of the other void, or that stretch of time which has passed before he was born? That may be populated more substantively, by being made to contain the autobiographer's pedigree, or the earnest of his own presence secreted in the annals of his family. The autobiographer is free to select among his forbears those with whom such a voluntary association reflects well on himself, and even to recruit outsiders to his lineage if he wants, like Cellini, to find glorious precedents for his own triumphs. But Cellini is merely tentative in this respect compared

him. The dealings between the two philosophers, culminating in a massive, accusatory letter from Rousseau to Hume, are included in *The Philosophical Works of David Hume*, Volume I, pp. xxxv–cxxi, and make extraordinary reading. Hume was anxious that an account of them be published because he had heard that Rousseau was at work on his 'memoirs' and intended his own version of the story to be the first in circulation. In the event, Rousseau made no mention of this quarrel in the *Confessions*.

with Edward Gibbon, who in the *Memoirs of My Own Life* provides himself with a richly supportive stemma.[10] Gibbon is with Hume in justifying himself by an appeal to Nature: he believes that it is *natural* for a man to want to search out ancestors for himself. The proof of this is his own disinterestedness in the matter, since he can derive from his ancestors 'neither glory nor shame'. The phrase is devious and thoroughly Gibbonian, a first example of many in his autobiography of how he will demonstrate his superiority by use of what Roland Barthes once identified as 'a mechanism of double exclusion', whereby we first posit 'a bi-partite universe' and then present ourselves as achieving 'its divine transcendence'.[11] Gibbon is adept at using Nature for his autobiographical alibi, or as the blameless determinant of his character, his career as a historian and his method in writing of himself.

In fact, Gibbon constructs two lineages for himself in the *Memoirs*, the first in his role as autobiographer, the second as a member of the family Gibbon. He allows, like Hume, that there must always be some vanity in writing about oneself, but at once finds an excuse for doing so in the line of illustrious predecessors who, from Antiquity onwards, have left some written memorial of their lives. These variously autobiographical authors, from Pliny the Younger to his own contemporaries, Colley Cibber and 'the philosophic Hume', constitute his literary family tree so far as the work he is embarked on is concerned, and he is fully prepared to compete with them, ending this supposedly apologetic sweep through literary history with the words: 'That I am the equal or superior of some of these Biographers the efforts of modesty or affectation cannot force me to dissemble.' The implication of which is that truthfulness counts for more than social protocol, that he would be breaking his autobiographical contract with us were he to pretend to hold a poorer opinion of himself than he holds in fact.

The terms of that contract Gibbon has already stipulated, in assimilating the autobiographer to the serious historian: 'Truth, naked unblushing truth, the first virtue of more serious history must

---

[10] The edition of the *Memoirs* I shall refer to is that of Georges A. Bonnard (New York, 1969). Gibbon himself produced no definitive text, but left at his death in 1794 what his executor, Lord Sheffield, described as 'Six different sketches, all in his own handwriting'. These 'sketches' have been assembled in different ways by different editors, in order to form a consecutive narrative; the Bonnard edition may not be definitive but it appears to be the most rational to date.

[11] Roland Barthes, 'La critique ni-ni', in *Mythologies* (Paris, 1957), pp. 162–4.

be the sole recommendation of this personal narrative.' This sturdy promise, coming from the author of the *Decline and Fall of the Roman Empire*, might give one to expect that in the *Memoirs* he means to be as fearlessly prurient in what he tells of his life as he had been in chronicling the centuries of imperial decadence. But on the contrary: as the historian of himself Gibbon is unfailingly prim and flouts no taboos, unless in recording the weakness or plain absence in himself of the filial feelings he might have been expected to show or at least claim to have felt. He touches only lightly on the 'indelicate topic' of 'the pains and pleasures of the body', and favours 'a discreet reserve' on the subject of money, even if he is ready to mourn on his own behalf the large capital loss suffered by his grandfather as a director of the collapsed South Sea Company, and complain of the improvident habits of his father. But even if no reader of the *Memoirs* can have much sense of coming in them upon the 'naked, unblushing truth', there are striking occasions in the text when Gibbon prefaces some autobiographical datum with an assurance that he feels able to publish it without 'a blush', as if in doing so he were braving convention or even inviting ridicule for his conscientiousness in making these discreditable admissions. He enjoys playing the confessional game, while revealing rather little.

One such occasion occurs in the drawing up of his second lineage, of the family Gibbon. 'I do not blush to descend', he writes, from 'a younger branch of the Gibbons of Rolvenden.' Why the defensiveness here, why might a blush have been thought in order in signalling this particular association? Because these Gibbons had migrated from the country to the city early in the seventeenth century, they had abandoned their place as landed gentry and gone instead into trade: the 'naked, unblushing truth' is that the historian's line has not been exclusively genteel as he might have wanted, but mercantile also. Only one branch of the Gibbons has been in trade, however, the rest have been gentlemen for many generations past, and Edward Gibbon follows them piously back as far as the fourteenth century, itemizing their most prominent members. Yet the distinguished ancestry which he finds to celebrate in the *Memoirs* was not, as it happens, his own, but that claimed for himself by one John Gibbon, a seventeenth-century member of the College of Heralds, whom Edward Gibbon took to be his great-great-uncle. He found eventually that John Gibbon was nothing of the kind, but he never rewrote these unhistorical pages of his memoirs, which are the more revealing for being inauthentic, as an index to the historian's willingness uncritically to appropriate for himself a flattering and ancient lineage.

An autobiographer may within obvious limits recruit the forbears that he believes he deserves, as having a character and achievements prophetic of his own. Gibbon's is an extreme case of this practice, and it is a nice touch that he should have adopted a herald for his prime historical informant: not only does this mark his respect for the profession of genealogy but, taking the word 'herald' in its other common sense, it identifies this particular historiographical ancestor as looking promisingly forward to himself. Gibbon likes families to go back a long way, and he likes them to have acquired merit in the same fashion as he has acquired it, in practising the arts of peace, not of conflict. His exotic ideal is the family of Confucius, 'in my opinion the most illustrious in the World', which 'has maintained above two thousand two hundred years its peaceful honours and perpetual succession'. This eirenic theme he at once expands on genealogically by moving closer to home, first according the poet Edmund Spenser pre-eminence among the family of Spencer (with which he was not connected), above even the famous Duke of Marlborough, and then allotting the novelist Henry Fielding to a branch of the Habsburg family no less. This second imaginary linkage he uses to justify the conclusion that 'the Romance of Tom Jones [...] will outlive the palace of the Escurial and the Imperial Eagle of the house of Austria'(5). There is no suggestion of irony in Gibbon's promotion of these genealogical fancies, which illustrate the value-system of the 'philosopher', whereby literary is to be ranked above martial fame, and his own great work of literature recognized as earning him the pre-eminent place among the Gibbons.

It is as the author of the *Decline and Fall* that Gibbon has become the author of the *Memoirs*: against the millennial collapse of an empire he will now set the rise to fame of its historian. The autobiography will account for the history, by concentrating on the growth of the historian's mind and tastes: 'the review of my moral and literary character is the most interesting to myself and to the public; and I may expatiate without reproach on my private studies since they have produced the public writings which can alone entitle me to the esteem and friendship of my readers'(89). So far as his 'literary character' is concerned, Gibbon records in some detail the reading that has gone towards his intellectual formation; he is closer to Vico than to Descartes in allowing the early influence of other minds on his own, whatever the distance by which he may subsequently have surpassed them. He has had an education, of sorts. He allows, if only 'by Analogy', that the rudiments of knowledge must have been inculcated in him by others. But curiously and, for his autobiographical purposes, auspiciously, his first tutor, to whom he went at the age of seven, turns out to have been the author of a 'Philosophical fiction' entitled *The Life of Automathes*, which was published one year after Gibbon became his pupil. This is the story of a boy, 'the son of a shipwrecked exile', left alone on a desert island, who grows up into 'a self taught though speechless philosopher'. The eighteenth century had a liking for such fables, in which the author speculated as to the possibility of a child receiving a 'natural' education and as to what its moral outcome might be. If *Automathes* is sympathetic to Gibbon, this is not only because it was the work of his former tutor and thus connected with himself, but also because its theme suits him well as an autobiographer, concerned to demonstrate the 'natural' growth of his inner Genius.

Gibbon is with Hume in refusing to see the course of a human life as providentially ordered; 'Our lives are in the power of chance' is his complacent philosophy, the more easily adhered to for his own favourable treatment by chance, he having been born into an 'honourable and wealthy family' in a 'free and enlightened country'. He has 'drawn a high prize in the lottery of life'(186). Chance presides therefore at our birth, though we can take credit for what we accomplish thereafter. Gibbon, like Cardano, has in his time been a gambler, if without the mathematical knowledge that might have enabled him to transform his moral frailty into a scientific project. The determined gambler, however, may stand in the same relation to chance as the historian does to historical facts. In his first published piece of writing, the *Essai sur l'étude de la littérature*, Gibbon compares the conception which a 'philosophical mind' takes of history to that which the Marquis de Dangeau had of play, 'who discerned a system, connections, a sequence, where others saw only the whims of fortune'(*Essai*, xlviii-xlix). The pattern so discerned is one of cause and effect, which it takes a superior mind to discover amidst the apparent chaos of historical events, or what Gibbon describes in the *Memoirs* as 'the loose and scattered atoms of historical information'. The historian's role is synthetic, but what he synthesizes is not the past *an Sich*, but the past as already ordered by his historical predecessors. Gibbon is aware of, and undeterred by, the pure *textuality* of history; indeed, it is the textuality of the past that opens the way for his own gigantic effort of synthesis, which will relegate the work of earlier historians to the status merely of the atomized sources of his own work.

As he tells it in the *Memoirs*, Gibbon's life has been directed, not from without but from within, by a natural propensity for the study and writing of history. He contests the opinion of Sir Joshua Reynolds (accused in this merely of following 'his oracle Dr Johnson' – an oracle between whom and Gibbon there was strong mutual dislike) that there is no such property as 'original Genius', or an innate leaning in people to 'one art or science rather than another'. Gibbon knows better: 'Without engaging in a metaphysical or rather verbal dispute, I *know* by experience that from my early youth, I aspired to the character of an historian'(119). It is no doubt proper that a Genius for historiography should emerge thus retrospectively, in the historian's own narrative, as a natural if indeterminate power which has conditioned his life without his knowing it at the time. In this respect, there is little to choose between Gibbon's (or Hume's) naturalism and Vico's providentialism as determining influences on their narrative.

Genius is for Gibbon the strongest imaginable principle of individuation. 'A composition of Genius must be the offspring of one mind': so he reflects when writing of the time he had spent as an undergraduate in Oxford. The thought is inspired by the presence on the shelves of the college library of vast collective volumes produced within monastic communities. It contains a twofold antithesis, first between works of literature or history achieved by collaboration and those written by a single author; and second, a more local opposition, between the industry represented by these earlier tomes and the spectacular indolence of the quasi-monastic community in which Gibbon then found himself, at what is now Magdalen College. Both contrasts redound to his own advantage, as the immensely industrious and solitary historian whose Genius is already at work secretly within him. This Genius is the free, informal element in Gibbon, unconstrained by any obligation to others or by their authority over him. His education has been got randomly and unofficially from books, not from those employed to teach him. He has been cared for and encouraged, though never directly taught, by the one relation for whom he shows sympathy in the *Memoirs*, his aunt Catherine, 'the true mother of my mind as well as of my health'. As a sickly child, burdened with a 'crazy frame', he has flourished intellectually during the enforced interruptions to his formal schooling, when he 'was allowed without control or advice to gratify the wanderings of an unripe taste' and when his 'indiscriminate appetite subsided by degrees in the Historic line'(41).[12]

The historian has thus been formed in absentia as it were, and the distinctive expansion of his intellect and learning has depended on the autonomy allowed to him by his physical failings. Gibbon's first formative withdrawal has been not into a Cartesian *poêle* but into the seclusion and independence of his bedroom. These small but productive absences from ordinary society evolve later into a larger, conclusive absence, when as an adolescent he is dismissed by his father into exile in Switzerland, where he was to spend 'four years, ten months, and fifteen days' – his positively Cardano-like exactness in measurement underlines the importance Gibbon wants to attach to that period in the *Memoirs*. He had been banished to Lausanne following his reckless conversion to Roman Catholicism and to the acceptance of such dogma as that of transsubstantiation, which he now professes himself unable to believe that he ever believed. This was a moment of immature folly or of an absurd 'Enthusiasm', whose incomprehensibility to the mature autobiographer is testimony to the urbane rationality that is now his hallmark. The young Gibbon had been converted to Popery not by meeting other people but by reading books, and in Lausanne, where he was the lodger and pupil of a Calvinist pastor, he has converted himself back again, by taking thought: the whole inner process has been of his own ordering.

The Swiss years it is which have made Gibbon: 'Such as I am in Genius or learning or in manners, I owe my creation to Lausanne: it was in that school, that the statue was discovered in the block of marble; and my own religious folly, my father's blind resolution produced the effects of the most deliberate wisdom'(86). Here autobiographical hindsight is exerted sardonically, to show that hindsight is simply that, not the elucidation of a foresight somehow inherent in events themselves but the free imposition of a later date which can take pleasure in the incongruity of cause with effect.

---

[12] Gibbon's 'crazy frame' was also a very unprepossessing one, and the phrase might be read as a rueful euphemism. The frequently reproduced silhouette of him, assuming it was not made in a spirit of caricature, suggests that he was both very short and very fat. One nickname found for him in France was that of 'Monsieur pomme de terre', while Samuel Johnson, himself no beauty, is recorded by Boswell as having expressed 'disgust at his ugliness'.

Instead of a clairvoyant Providence having determined the prosperity of his life, Gibbon would rather see it as hinging perversely on his own folly and his father's blindness. In doing so, he is exploiting a historian's concern with causality for ironic effect, not implying that such a concern is mistaken; once again, there is no contradiction between his metahistorical schema and the Vichian one, since Vico too might endorse the beneficial perversion of merely human intentions whereby folly turns out to be indistinguishable in its effects from wisdom.

Gibbon describes his exile in Lausanne as a 'fortunate shipwreck', a phrase that can but cast the mind back to the fable of *Automathes* and the self-teaching castaway. Rewording it to suit myself, I shall describe Gibbon's Lausanne years as those of his successful alienation, or decisive singularization of himself from his native setting. In Switzerland he has entered on that steady transcendence of doxa and of faction any genuine subscription to which would rob him of his full identity. Having recanted his Roman Catholicism, he takes communion again as a Protestant, but in a spirit of empty conformism; he has in fact outgrown all sectarianism or care for doctrine: 'It was here that I suspended my Religious enquiries, acquiescing with implicit belief in the tenets and mysteries which are adopted by the general consent of Catholics and Protestants'(74). 'Implicit belief' is a delightfully characteristic notion; Gibbon is now *above* religion, forever exempt from any lapse into Enthusiasm, just as later on in the *Memoirs* he affects to have been above party in the course of his membership of the House of Commons, where he has sat unspeaking but with profit, the future author having there found himself sitting in 'a school of civil prudence, the first and most essential virtue of an historian'.

In Lausanne – the town where he later returned to live and to write, his inheritance from his father once secured – Gibbon has alienated himself also from his native language. He has learnt to think and to write in French, the language of a people whom he believes to be marked by a 'national urbanity'. He is proud to have written his first literary work, the *Essai sur l'étude de la littérature* in French, and when he later contemplated and began his history of medieval Switzerland, he again wrote in French (cf. his letter to Hume of 25 October 1767: 'The five years [...] which I passed in Switzerland formed my style as well as my ideas; I write in French, because I think in French; and strange as it may seem, I can say with some shame, but with no affectation, that it would be a matter of difficulty to me, to compose in my native language [...] when I have finished the work [...] I will endeavour to put it into an English dress; at the risque perhaps of appearing a foreigner to my own countrymen, and of betraying myself to foreigners for an English-man.')

But the French language has also carried dangers for Gibbon: in now condemning the one completed book of his abandoned Swiss history, he says that 'I was conscious myself, that my style, above prose and below poetry, degenerated into a verbose and turgid declamation'(142). In style, as in everything else, he must avoid extremes and, having first posited what these extremes are, embody their transcendence. Thus, when he comes to write the *Decline and Fall* he is able, after many experiments, to 'hit the middle tone between a dull Chronicle and a Rhetorical declamation'. This, we can assume, is the ultimate synthesis of inborn English virtues with the acquired virtues of the French, of staunch empiricism with a sociable urbanity. The historian Gibbon is neither English nor French but both, or neither, and his *Memoirs* form the narrative of how he made his escape from these limiting categories.

Gibbon narrates his life as an ascesis of indifference: not for nothing does he write of his experience in Lausanne as having revealed the 'statue' in 'the block of marble'. As an autobiographer he has aimed at and achieved a certain stoniness, a certain *desirable* stoniness as my final subject in this book, Michel Leiris, would argue. He has liberated himself from the encumbrances and attachments, whether to persons or to parties, which would have encroached on his autonomy or disturbed his calm. He has recognized, and defeated, the two great threats to his serenity: the need for money and for sexual satisfaction. So far as money is concerned, Gibbon has finally realized his inheritance and, typically, found it ideally adjusted to his needs, a middling fortune which had it been larger or smaller might have led him into indolence or depression, and prevented him in either case from becoming a historian. As for his sexuality, he has been at risk from that only once, again in Lausanne, where he fell briefly in love with Susanne Curchod (later to become the wife of the great Swiss banker and Louis XVI's finance minister, Jacques Necker, and the mother of Madame de Staël). 'I need not blush at recollecting the object of my choice, and though my love was disappointed of success, I am rather proud, that I was once capable of feeling such a pure and exalted sentiment'(84). In the end this tepid passion has been sacrificed to good sense, or else self-interest: Gibbon's father 'would not hear of this strange alliance' and since he was still dependent on his father for money, Susanne was let go – in the celebrated formula, 'I sighed as a lover: I obeyed as a son.' Nowhere else in the *Memoirs* does Gibbon suggest that sexual desire ever imperilled his self-command, and in his marmoreal account of the episode of Susanne he disqualifies it as a topic suitable for an autobiographer, since 'it less properly belongs to the memoirs of an individual, than to the natural history of the species'(84). With biology there appears the threat of a regression into anonymity, which would undo the autobiographer's gratifying advance into conspicuous selfhood.

CHAPTER 6

Rousseau

TO MOVE THE HEART

Autobiography of Gibbon's gentrified kind pays its dues to sociability, not simply in the execution of the autobiographical act itself,
but in the reasonable bounds which the writer sets on his will to
singularity, confined by Gibbon to the achievement of financial
autonomy, to an avoidance of close human attachments or partisan
'enthusiasm', and to the progressive manifestation of his literary
Genius. He is too consciously the 'philosopher' ever to admit to
harbouring the abrasive, unsociable passion of a Rousseau, who as an
autobiographer brings a new, near pathological urgency to the desire
to establish before posterity the true measure of his uniqueness.
Where Gibbon has teased us, with hints of being about to publish the
'naked, unblushing truth' about himself, only to reveal in the end his
incapacity for anything so vulgar, Rousseau will abandon all such
nice adjustments between living and writing: with him man and
autobiographer must seem to be one. And as both he means to be
unique: Rousseau the man is by his nature like no other who has ever
lived, Rousseau the autobiographer will, in the completeness and
candour of what he discovers, distinguish himself unashamedly from
all the autobiographical writers there have been in the past. And as
if that were not enough, the life which is narrated in his *Confessions*
turns out to have been uniquely difficult, fate too having been
coopted by the autobiographer to assist in his singularization.

As I suggested at the start of this book, Rousseau demands more
openly and aggressively than any other autobiographer that we
should not read what he has written about himself as if it were
literature. When we meet with the abundance of his autobiographical
prose – in the *Confessions*, the three dialogues of *Rousseau juge de Jean
Jacques*, the *Rêveries d'un promeneur solitaire*, along with a number of

remarkable fragments – we must bear in mind the grievance which he felt against both the *abbé* de Condillac, who was the chosen depository of his dialogues, and the fashionable guests at his public readings from the *Confessions*, who were not as moved by what they heard as he required them to be. (That the readings apparently lasted for up to seventeen hours at a stretch may help to explain the woodenness of the reaction to them.) Rousseau directs his auto-biographical writings at those who are sufficiently like-minded with himself, the unbudgeable friend of justice and of truth, to be prepared to grant him their time and their concern, so enabling him to avoid what, in the preamble to the dialogues, he calls 'the ultimate indignity, that the depiction of my life's miseries should be an object of entertainment for anyone'. But if his own contemporaries let him down in this regard, who are we, two centuries later, to do any better?

Rousseau is unusual, probably alone among the great auto-biographers, in having read publicly from his autobiography, as if he were anxious to sample the response of posterity from among the living. He did so in order to try and *enforce* that sympathy and attention which he craved from his audience by his own physical presence, in accordance with the belief that he held in the emotive power both of discourse and of the human voice. There is a first paradox here, that the man for whom, as we shall see, immediacy was all, should have believed so strongly in the power of a mediate discourse to *move* its hearers. That belief he states in the opening chapter of his *Essai sur l'Origine des Langues*, where he argues that the body-language of gesture or 'movement', which is addressed to the eye, is at all times superior to the vocal language of sounds, which is directed to the ear, except when the speaker's need is 'to move the heart and to fire the passions'. In illustration, Rousseau offers the example of a person grief-stricken, the mere or immediate sight of whom will not affect us so very deeply, but who, once allowed to spell out his or her feelings, will cause us 'to dissolve into tears'. In such a case discursive language is being true to its origins, as Rousseau sees those, it having come into existence not for the statement of human needs but for the expression of human feeling. And as an auto-biographer that is the purpose to which he too would like to put it.

Autobiography, however, is a written form of address and so has lost the moving immediacy we might be prepared to grant to the grief-stricken person speaking his or her woes in front of us. Nor can that loss of immediacy be reversed by the autobiographer appearing in person before an audience, to recite his woes from a prepared script. He is no longer grief-stricken; from a sufferer he has turned into a performer, a histrion, successful or not according to the virtuosity of his performance rather than by the perceived force of his sincerity. By performing his autobiography as he did, Rousseau was underlying the inescapable theatricality of such writing, in the practice of which we make a spectacle of ourselves. Like Augustine, he recognized – see the *Lettre à M. d'Alembert sur les spectacles* – that simulated emotion on the stage is better able to move us than the real emotion of real people in real life; his dilemma as an autobiographer is how to stage in words the moving spectacle of his own *real* emotions, whose history, rather than that of the facts of his life, it is the declared aim of the *Confessions* to narrate. The way of escape from that dilemma can only be into solipsism, with the frustrated auto-biographer warming as he writes to the ineffable delight of recollection, and reliving discursively states of emotion that may be indicated to others but never fully shared with them. Thus, when he experiences an immediate pleasure in the fixing of his mind and his text on the idyllic days of his life with Mme de Warens, Rousseau seems very happily resigned to keeping it for himself: 'Indeed if it all consisted of facts, deeds, and words, I could describe it and in a sense convey its meaning. But how can I tell what was neither said, nor done, nor even thought, but only relished and felt, when I cannot adduce any other cause for my happiness but just this feeling?'(215).[1]

In his *Essai sur l'Origine des Langues*, Rousseau remarks the ambiguity of conventional language, or what – ironically enough, from any Rousseauesque perspective – we would now call natural language. Animals do not have it, and can make no progress; men do have it and therefore do make progress, 'whether for good or ill'. And if that ambiguity applies to natural language as a whole, it applies more pertinently still to the written form of it. Writing, for Rousseau the writer, is both a very good and a very bad thing. It is a very good thing inasmuch as in writing he can make up for his deficiencies in talking before strangers. By his own admission, Rousseau was in company neither a fluent nor a persuasive talker, but shamefully

---

[1] The English translation of the *Confessions* I shall quote from is the generally excellent one made by J. M. Cohen for the Penguin Classics (Harmondsworth, 1953). Where Cohen seems to me to have missed a nuance of the original important to my argument, I have given the French word or words he has translated in square brackets.

tongue-tied and potentially ridiculous. He may have been able to *recite* from the *Confessions* before other people but he could never have improvised before them, the written text alone affording him the necessary self-possession. The text is thus interposed, as a mediate presence between himself and others which will save him from the silence or incoherence of high embarrassment. It acts as a 'supplement', that ambiguous annex so important to Rousseau's conceptual system which is both surplus and substitute, at once an enrichment and a *pis-aller*.[2] When, in Book Ten of the *Confessions*, Rousseau finds himself obliged to call on Madame de Luxembourg, wife of the Maréchal on whose estate and largesse he is currently living, he is conscious as usual of his own awkwardness in society and particularly so on this occasion because this 'great lady' is known to be 'exacting in conversation'. The inhibited man must look to the prolific writer for a way out: 'An expedient occurred to me for saving myself the embarrassment of talking to her; and that was to read aloud'(484). Rousseau reads to her from the novel he has recently finished, *Julie, ou La Nouvelle Héloïse*, and the reading is splendidly successful, its author becoming an instant favourite with his listener. The effect is of a seduction by the nervous author of his imposing female reader, brought about by his own presence and by the persuasiveness of his voice, the same seductive effect which Rousseau hoped to achieve later in his life, as the reader out loud of his *Confessions*. The sad lesson of the two performances taken together is indeed that the feigned emotion of characters in a novel proves more immediate – or more *touching*, which is the ultimate condition of immediacy for Rousseau, gestural language itself having derived he thought from a 'language' of actual touch between persons – than the real emotion recollected in autobiography.

The substitution of a written text for his own spontaneous presence is, then, an unhappy shift forced on Rousseau by the confusion which takes hold of him socially and which acts as a disguise, so that the strangers whom he happens to be with misjudge him on the strength of his faltering tongue to be a simpleton. To this extent he is an autobiographer *malgré lui*, a man who, differently constituted, might have succeeded in appearing before others exactly as he believes

---

[2] The notion of the 'supplement' as a crucial element in Rousseau's ideology is a main theme of Jacques Derrida's fascinating and hugely illuminating essay on Rousseau in *De la grammatologie* (Paris, 1967), to which anyone who now writes about Rousseau should be largely indebted.

himself to be, so that there would be no discrepancy to trouble him between his two self-images, that 'true' one which he alone possesses and the 'false' one which he 'shares' by projecting it into the keeping of others. In the *Confessions* Rousseau makes much of a typical slight *balourdise* or piece of clumsiness, when he has spoken for the sake of speaking and said something witlessly impolite. It has been met with silence, and silence he will invariably interpret as hostile, such is the prodigious reach of his self-concern. His gaffe has been doubly contradictory, first of his physical appearance, 'my face and my eyes', which he believes to promise better than he delivers, and then of his real intelligence and his real wish to be sociable, rather than the farouche person he appears to be because of his timidity. He is literally, in his own judgment, not *himself* when he is with others, so that the solitude into which he has withdrawn, both as a man and as an autobiographical writer, is the precondition of his textual reappearance as, at long last, his true self. The mediacy of writing is thus both sacrifice and salvation: 'I should enjoy society as much as anyone, if I were not certain to display myself not only at a disadvantage, but in a character entirely foreign to me. The role I have chosen of writing and remaining in the background [*de me cacher*] is precisely the one that suits me. If I had been present, people would not have known my value; they would not even have suspected it'(116). Nowhere else within autobiographical writing is the cycle out of which that writing emerges, of presence to the world, followed by absence from the world, followed by a symbolic re-presentation to the world, more pointedly traced out.

Autobiographers may write without having first suffered as Rousseau did from the paranoid conviction that the images of them held by other people must at all costs be repossessed and revised in their own favour, but they must still write in the desire to impose a settled image of themselves of which they approve, and as the subject of their own text secure their absolution from those heteronomous impressions which they have left behind with others in their less deliberate moments of socializing.

FROM FEELING TO THOUGHT

If autobiography entails stepping provisionally aside from the world, the better to measure oneself against it, then Rousseau was an autobiographer *avant la lettre*, well practised in the voluntary seclusion of himself. There is I think only one event in the *Confessions* which he dates to the exact day when it took place: on 9 April, 1756, he abandoned Paris to go and live at the Ermitage, the pastoral refuge fitted out for him by his admiring patroness, Mme d'Epinay. On that momentous day, 'I left Paris never to live in a town again.' Towns from now on are the damnable locus of corruption and artifice, and no fit setting for a man who might have taken for himself the title of 'Citizen of Geneva' but whose ideals of citizenship were too exalted for him to endure for long the reality of urban life. (Rousseau went back to live in Paris none the less, and spent the last eight years of his life there.) As refuges go, the Ermitage was not so very remote: a bare twenty kilometres out of Paris to the north. Rousseau's high-minded removal of himself from society was thus an equivocal gesture. At the Ermitage, and after he had had to move from it, to nearby Montmorency, he was sufficiently far from the Town to have made his point, and sufficiently close for the point to be taken by those for whose benefit he had made it. His calculated apartness could be read as the austere reproach of the virtuous man against the degraded life led by those he had left behind. There was provocation in Rousseau's notorious *retraite*, and he was inviting by it the ridicule of those inveterate socializers from whom he had parted, ridicule being a form of attention which he valued and could use as evidence that he, the exile, was in the right, and they, the incurably gregarious ones, were in the wrong. He is with Augustine in seeing derision as a tribute paid by the collectivity to the morally superior individual.

But Rousseau did not become a writer only once he went into voluntary exile; he was already a member of the literary community of Paris. They it was indeed he was breaking with, the sardonic, superficial 'côterie Holbachique' or 'd'Holbach set', who predicted that he would not be able to tolerate the perpetual quarantine he had arranged for himself in the countryside. He had published things before 1756, most notably his two *Discourses*, on 'Progress in the Arts and Sciences' and on 'Inequality'; but it was in his new Crusoe-like state of enislement that he became truly productive. In the next six years he published the works that he is mainly known by: the *Social Contract*, the *Nouvelle Héloïse*, *Emile*. At the end of this time, his voluntary exile turned however into an enforced exile, because of what he had used these years to write and to publish. *Emile*, the didactic novel which contained Rousseau's radical programme for the 'natural', hands-off education of the young (shades of Gibbon's

Automathes), and the statement of his equally 'natural' religious creed, was condemned by the Sorbonne and a warrant went out for his detention; he sought safety first in Switzerland and then in England.

That an easy, notorious and productive isolation should have thus led to an unhappy exclusion from France was a reversal of fortune which, as an autobiographer, Rousseau is quick to endow with its own punitive logic; the ideas whose publication in *Emile* had set authority against him were the ideological expression of his own bucolic self-sufficiency, so that their condemnation by the Parlement in Paris extends inevitably to a condemnation of his chosen way of life. It is a sentence passed on the man just as much as on the writer, so reflecting at a high, institutional level the hostility against him which Rousseau had earlier attracted by his decision to live apart, in a simple, 'natural' domesticity. The inclination of the autobiographer – of any autobiographer – being to personalize whatever he records as having befallen him, Rousseau can flatter himself that he has become the cynosure of a malevolence no longer local but national. Later, as the diffuse antagonism by which he imagined himself to be beset cohered in his mind into a universal 'plot', he was able to claim that one of the ringleaders, along with his former friends, Grimm and Diderot, was the duc de Choiseul, the chief minister of King Louis XV.

Rousseau presents his decision to 'conceal' himself by writing as a rational one, founded as it was on his humiliating incapacity to display more directly his true moral and intellectual worth. But it can not have been a decision consciously taken at a given moment of his life in Paris. In the text of the *Confessions* it takes the form of a reflection based on long observation of his own nature, not that of a datable memory; the episode which has given rise to it, of his conversational gaffe when talking with 'two great Ladies', occurs anachronistically, having taken place many years after the period of his life he is here ostensibly narrating, when the future career that was thought best to 'suit' him had been not literature but the Catholic priesthood. Rousseau calls up this episode proleptically by way of illustrating the fundamental disunity of his being, in which warm and impetuous feelings have cohabited destructively with a slow and uncertain brain: 'It is as though my heart and my mind did not belong to the same individual.' Heart and mind are not merely unalike – *presque inalliables* in Rousseau's description, or 'almost unalloyable' in a literal English translation – they are in opposition, for the immediacy of his feelings actually clouds the deliberations of his brain. If he is to think to some rational end and to his own satisfaction, he needs the sang-froid which comes from privacy, and he needs time. Emotion is thus opposed to order, including, as he will subsequently demonstrate to us, the distinctive order of narrative. On at least two occasions, in the later stages of the *Confessions*, Rousseau assures us that such is the strength of his emotion as he recalls the painful experiences he has had after his flight from France in 1762, that his narrative can but suffer: 'The further I go in my story, the less order and sequence I can put into it. The disturbances of my later life have not left events time to fall into shape [*s'arranger*] in my head. They have been too numerous, too confused, too unpleasant to be capable of straightforward narration'(574). Thus whatever confusion we may meet with in the chronology of this final Book should be put down to its author's loss of sang-froid. For he has in fact had just as much *time*, which was his second requirement if he was to achieve mastery over his feelings, for the composition of these pages as he had for the earlier ones.

But to assert that one is in a state of high agitation is not to be altogether *in* such a state; whoever so asserts is sufficiently self-collected, as we say, to make the assertion. In the double game which he has chosen to play at moments such as these, Rousseau brings out the full ambiguity which writing has for him, as the orderly medium which both connects him with his past and makes him conscious of his distance from it. It is not the medium ideally suited to recounting the story that he wants to tell, of his feelings. In such assertions as the one I have just quoted, to the effect that his emotional state at the moment of writing must interfere with his observance of narrative conventions, he is approximating writing to speech, and in particular speech as he himself has experienced it, he as we know having been rendered inarticulate by the quickness and force of his feelings. There are times, however, when it seems that that is just the state into which he would like now to relapse, as evidence that, writer though he be, he remains the same potentially embarrassed person. The disorderliness with which the narrative of his troubles is threatened is wilful, it is not a fatality; it is a darker version of the repetitiveness with which Rousseau flirts at the start of Book Six of the *Confessions*, where the opening theme is his perfect happiness in the company of Mme de Warens at Les Charmettes. So moving is the memory of those days to him as he writes that he would wish to perpetuate it: 'What shall I do to prolong this touching and simple tale, as I should like to; endlessly to repeat the same words, and no more to weary my readers by their repetition than I wearied myself by beginning them forever afresh?'(215). By this empty threat of flouting the proprieties of writing, and immobilizing his narrative so as to perpetuate the enjoyment he himself is taking in it, Rousseau shows how facile it is to say, as we often hear it said, that an autobiographer 'relives' his past in the writing of it. The autobiographer alas knows differently; to narrate one's past is to be driven through it without stopping, when the deeper pleasure would come from being free to arrest its progress.

The 'conversion' of a life into a story means passing from the ardent immediacy of experience to the cool mediacy of language, or from feeling to thought. This transition may well be seen as imitating that which we all of us make as individuals as we mature, in a personal recapitulation à la Vico of the history of our species. For Rousseau in particular it recapitulates the evolution of language, or that institution which distinguishes man from beast and has, for good or ill, made progress inevitable. In the *Essai sur l'Origine des Langues* (Chapter Five: 'Of Writing'), he sees language as having evolved through time away from its primary use for the expression of emotion and towards a secondary use, for the formulation of ideas – a development which has taken place *pari passu* with the supplementation of speech by alphabetic writing, envisaged by Rousseau as a graphic representation of the sounds of language. 'As needs increase and things become more complex and enlightenment spreads, language changes in character; it becomes more precise and less passionate; it substitutes ideas for feelings, it speaks no longer to the heart but to the reason.' Rousseau is not so foolish or so contradictory as to regret this evolution, of which he is himself making the fullest use in the *Essai* from which these ideas are quoted. He knows that he is also a thinker, a party to the age of Enlightenment though profoundly anxious to mark off for himself a distinctive ideological space within it.

The pragmatic decision to substitute writing for speaking can not in itself account for the kind of writer that Rousseau has become, in his didactic role as philosopher. For that there has to have been another origin, and given that by the time he came to write the *Confessions* his philosophical publications had brought him both glory and persecution – had worked for both good and ill – that origin too must be suitably ambiguous. Rousseau has in fact undergone an experience of conversion, an Augustinian 'turn'. His own preferred term for it was of a momentary 'illumination', a description recalling the 'great light' witnessed by the unregenerate Saul on the Damascus road, but promissory also of the new career of didacticism to which Rousseau was about to turn, as an agent furthering the spread of enlightenment. The scene is well known. Rousseau like Saul is on the road, on the way from Paris to Vincennes, to encourage his friend Diderot, who has been incarcerated there by order of the king for the 'intemperateness' of his materialist ideas. The themes of exile and of punishment are well found for Rousseau, as yet projected on to his fellow writer, but eventually to be incorporated in himself. Too poor to pay for a carriage, Rousseau is on foot, a form of mobility peculiarly inspirational in setting him thinking. It is exceptionally hot, he is tired and in a very emotional state – a state far more forcefully described in the second of his four 'Letters to M. de Malesherbes' than it is in the *Confessions* themselves. Reading as he walks, he comes upon the notice advertising a prize offered by the Academy of Dijon for an essay on the question 'Whether the progress of the sciences and arts has served to corrupt or to purify morals.' The effects of this announcement on him are extraordinary: 'The moment I read this I beheld another universe and became another man.' Having reached Vincennes, he asks Diderot if he should enter for the prize and is encouraged to do so. 'I did so and from that moment I was lost. All the rest of my life and of my misfortunes followed inevitably as a result of that moment's madness' (328).

Purely as a crisis or turning-point, this episode of 'conversion' is not unique in the *Confessions*, because Rousseau likes to punctuate his narrative with doleful markers, to the effect that 'this was when my troubles really began'. The series of these fateful moments is inaugurated when he is still a boy of fifteen in Geneva and fails to get back from an excursion with friends one evening before the drawbridge into the town is raised. The autobiographer uses this memory to demonstrate his freedom to range forwards in time: 'I trembled as I watched its dreadful horns rising in the air, a sinister and fatal augury of the inevitable fate which from that moment awaited me' (49). That augury is once again, as with the announcement that he has read in the paper on the way to Vincennes, equivocal. The adolescent Rousseau decides after a night spent outside the walls not to return inside his native city, there to complete his servile apprenticeship as an engraver. His companions choose incarceration, he chooses an errant and improvident freedom, so dissociating himself from the servility and fellowship of work. In the reconstruction of this crisis, as in that of Vincennes, accident plays its part, opening the way to that counterfactual speculation dear to both writers and readers of autobiography: Supposing the drawbridge had still been down? What if Rousseau had failed to see the Dijon Academy's announcement? In Rousseau's scheme, contingencies such as these must be accorded a determinant role in his story so that he may look back on himself as having been as much a passive as an active protagonist.

These are crises in his story precious to Rousseau for enabling him to crystallize in their telling his self-pitying version of hindsight, whereby a stark juxtaposition of past and present will expose the fatuity of optimism in a malignant world, and a punitive future be hurried into view to block out the innocent promise of the present. At liberty suddenly from the tyrannical master to whom he has been articled in Geneva, the boy sets off into the countryside intoxicated by the prospect of his independence and of what he will accomplish in life: 'Now that I was free and my own master, I supposed that I could do anything, achieve anything.' But the road up is the road down, as Hegel very nearly said and as Rousseau in effect does say, by prefacing the hopes he attributes to his fifteen year-old self by the black forebodings which he should have had about the future course of his life. And it is the same with his account of the 'illumination' of Vincennes, more than twenty years later. First we are given the bad, post-dated news, that the decision to compete for the Academy prize was the 'moment's madness' that has ruined the rest of his life; and only then the good news, that once it had been taken he entered on a remarkable period of prolonged mental excitement, in which 'My feelings rose with the most inconceivable rapidity to the level [*ton*] of my ideas'(328). But this apparently benign intellectual ferment must then, by the perverted logic of Rousseau's account, be reinscribed as the sufficient cause of that career in literature which was to end his privacy and bring persecution on him.

Rousseau is the arch catastrophist among autobiographers, the cheerless denouement of whose story requires preparation by a series of premonitory inflections. The episode at Vincennes is the more stagey – operatic might be the word – for giving off a distant but perceptible sound of music. It involves a dramatic change of tempo: along the road to Vincennes Rousseau has taken out his newspaper in order to slow himself down, as if the mediacy of print were essential for such a small act of will on his part; then, on the far side of the climactic decision, we get the 'inconceivable rapidity' with which his feelings rise into unison with his thoughts. In both the short rallentando along the road and the sustained accelerando that ensues, body and mind are synchronized, or else harmonized, given that in the second instance his feelings and his ideas have risen explicitly to the same '*ton*', which can best be translated as 'pitch'. As a theorist and composer of music, Rousseau was the advocate of melody as against mere harmony, because melody, and especially song, by its directedness animates and spiritualizes what would otherwise remain a lower pleasure, satisfying the senses alone. Melody moves us, according to Rousseau, by mimesis of our emotions, which it articulates, so transforming the sounds of music into affective signs. In moments such as the crisis at Vincennes, the text of the *Confessions* becomes particularly melodious, as Rousseau plays on our emotions in order to harmonize them with his own. But his whole auto-biographical venture, like that of Augustine earlier, can be read as a musical composition: in Rousseau's case as an articulation of its subject's feelings intended as mimetic of his emotionally tumultuous life. In his exalted state after Vincennes, he has found a rare harmony: the two 'almost unalloyable' elements of his nature, his ardent heart and his reluctant brain, have come into unison and have remained so for several years. But for Rousseau the confirmed melodist harmony is not gain but loss, since it is a state recalcitrant to narrative; he will invoke but not develop it; the aria must resume.

The two related episodes on which I have been dwelling have one other far from casual element in common: they both display Rousseau as a pedestrian. In the first instance during his adolescence, he is caught outside the town because he has been off wandering, on a *promenade* with friends; then, the decision once made not to go back, he sets off wandering again, into the nearby countryside, the temporary freedom of an afternoon off exchanged now for what in his imagination is a permanent freedom. Again, outside Vincennes, the walking is an integral part of the causal chain, as I have suggested, since if he had not been walking he would not have read the notice in the newspaper, and if he had not read the notice ... For Rousseau there is a vital association between the movement of his body and the activity of his mind, the first, he tells us, having been peculiarly conducive to the second. It is as if he had wanted to recapitulate in his own behaviour his theory of the evolution of natural language; for if this has originated, as he argues that it did, in the immediate, tactile contact between two human bodies, and has then evolved into a visual medium, of bodily gestures and movements made between individuals now further removed from one another physically, then someone like Rousseau who perambulates as he thinks to himself is regressing along the evolutionary chain, back to the stage where the movements of the mind could still be deduced from those of the body. Thought as a mental function is mimetic of the corporeal function of the limbs, and if physical movement induces it, then by a Rousseau-esque logic, thought in its turn can *move* us, as its addressees – to complete the virtuous circle we should perhaps read the *Confessions* only when ourselves out exercising.

Elsewhere in the *Confessions* Rousseau reveals his habit of composing his books in his head, when out walking alone or else lying sleepless in bed. These are his times of release into independence and into an audacity of thought impossible for him otherwise. Out walking or travelling on his own, he no longer suffers the world, he takes a symbolic possession of it: 'I dispose of all Nature as its master'(158). And the unimpeded command of language of which he is capable in writing is restorative of the phantasmal mastery he has exercised over Nature. Time too he can now call to order, because the writer, like the traveller, can spin things out or speed things up, indulging, if he is Rousseau, in the doubtful pleasures of procrastination: 'In telling the story of my travels, as in travelling itself, I never know how to stop'(167). In his last literary avatar, as the author of the *Rêveries du promeneur solitaire*, he carries the notion of pedestrian self-sufficiency to the limit, since by now he is not only first rehearsing and then writing down his audacious thoughts in solitude but also acting as their delighted and sympathetic reader, the most compliant audience he can imagine for them being himself. He has come as close as he can to autism, to that 'hearing-oneself-speak' which Derrida takes to be the false paradigm of all such linguistic immediacy.

THE NATURAL ORDER

In Rousseau's vagabondage there is autarky, and in autarky a verbal inspiration, the contagion of independence spreading from body to mind to language. In the exchange of an ordered society for the random companionship of the road, Rousseau becomes both freedman and writer. It is by the tongue, or by its inescapable surrogate, the pen, that he will come in the end to fame and to disaster, so that the truly momentous initiation of his life is that into language. But our first coming to language lies beyond the reach of memory; it is not to be recovered and told honestly as an event in time. Augustine incorporates it into his story only by behaving as a philosopher and proceeding by analogy: it can only have been for me as it was for all infants. Rousseau is too possessive of his own gifts to relapse into the anonymity entailed by Augustine's scrupulousness. He bides his time and makes of the freeing of his tongue a memorable event of his adolescence.

This liberating episode occurs during the months that he has spent in Turin after his baptism there as a Catholic.[3] The penniless, sixteen-year-old boy has found work as a footman in an aristocratic household, where his real talents are unknown, except to himself. His servile status and his timidity are both against him, especially once he has come to feel desire for the young grand-daughter of the house. There is only one way open to him to attract this patrician girl's attention, which is by saying something to impress her. He does so twice over, first by countering some disobliging remark made against him by her brother with 'so neat and smart an answer that she noticed it and threw me a glance', and then, more theatrically, by revealing himself as more knowledgeable than all those present – bar the head of the family – by correctly interpreting the family motto, which happens to be in French. On this formative occasion his mute acquiescence in the given state of things has been overcome; by speaking he has established himself at his true worth in front of others and has given the lie to the state of servility in which he is provisionally trapped. It is a moment of high importance to him:

They all looked at me and exchanged glances in silence. Never in my life had I seen such astonishment. But what flattered me more was to see a look of

---

[3] This episode of the *Confessions* is the subject of a wonderfully full and persuasive commentary by the greatest of living scholars of Rousseau, Jean Starobinski. See *La Relation critique* (Paris, 1970), pp. 98–153. This is the most remarkable *explication de texte* known to me, and my debt to it here is large.

pleasure on Mlle de Breil's face. That haughty young lady condescended to throw me a second glance, every bit as precious as the first. Then, turning towards her grandfather, she seemed to wait almost impatiently for him to give me the praise which was my due. Indeed he did compliment me so generously and whole-heartedly, and with such an air of pleasure, that the whole table hastened to join in the chorus. That moment was short, but it was in every respect delightful. It was one of those rare moments that put things back in their proper perspective [*dans leur ordre naturel*], repair the slights on true merit and avenge the outrages of fortune. (96–7)

This same delectable restoration of the 'natural order' is Rousseau's deepest desire as an autobiographer, the only difference being that publication of the *Confessions* will effect the permanent restoration of that order, whereas his triumph in Turin was a mere vicissitude. His correct reading of the motto turns on a question of etymology, or on establishing the history of a particular word, which is to elucidate the truth by narrative means; the episode of the motto may stand as a *mise en abyme* of the *Confessions* as a whole.

The 'natural order' is that which has been determined by, and is thus altogether gratifying to, Rousseau himself, and the sanction of Nature is called for if he is to convince us of that order's unassailable primacy over the false order imposed on his life by the slanders and machinations of others. At Turin he avenges the humiliations he has had to endure in silence by speaking audaciously out; in the *Confessions* he will do the same, and on a grand scale. That autobiography serves to settle scores we already knew, from reading Abelard, or Cardano, or Vico; with Rousseau the urge for an autobiographical vindication is absolute.

But if the desirable Mlle de Breil has been brought for once to attend to and admire the young lackey, the boy's etymological coup is instantaneous. After it, his timidity at once returns and, made the more nervous by having entered on this new relationship, he spills water over the girl and by his clumsiness regresses beyond the point from which he had begun.[4] As throughout the *Confessions*, every up must be followed by a rapid down. Rousseau's formulation of this particular regression is striking: 'Here the romance[*roman*] ended.' He then goes on to generalize from his failure with Mlle de Breil to reflect on a subsequent lifetime of such failures, in bringing his

---

[4] This spillage might be read as a symbolic act of masturbation, or a discharge denoting frustration, masturbation having a large part to play in Rousseau's erotic economy, in the typical role of 'supplement' to the 'natural' act of sexual intercourse with a woman.

amours to a successful conclusion. But his momentary escape from the false condition in which he has been living has been ruefully equated with a fiction. It is at once true and yet too good to be true. For the brief interlude during which Rousseau has held the stage, real life has proved as gratifying to him as anything that he might imagine; his initiation into the mastery of language is a literally fabulous event in which reality coincides with fiction and the 'natural order' thus briefly restored is seen to derive not from the world as we experience it but from the world as we find it represented in books.

Rousseau is true to autobiographical type in having been brought up on stories. But where other autobiographers – the severely episcopal Augustine, or the severely practical Teresa – have put fiction behind them, he has been unable to do so. He has in his time written against fiction, condemning it for a lax and evasive pastime unworthy of a serious mind, but he has himself been seduced by it, has even written fiction, though acknowledging as he did so – according to the *Confessions* – that the gratifying scenes he was making up were a facile counterweight to the tribulations of his real life.

Effeminate genre that Rousseau declares it to be, fiction has come down to him from his mother. She has died giving birth to him, but she has left behind some novels, and reading these in early childhood has had a decisive influence on him. We might see these books as taking the place that his mother should have taken; reflecting by the unreality of their contents the child's primal loss. As intermediaries, or as a love offering from the absent mother, they open the way to Rousseau's own work of fiction, *Julie ou la Nouvelle Héloïse*, which he has written, he would have us believe, with a great reluctance, but because he is too weak to deny himself the voluptuous company of its two female characters – and too weak, once the novel is written, not to read it aloud to real women so as to play vicariously on their feelings.

But his first exposure to fiction has not been woman's work alone; he has read the books left behind by his mother in the company of his father:

I felt before I thought: which is the common lot of man, though more pronounced in my case than another's. I know nothing of myself till I was five or six. I do not know how I learnt to read. I only remember my first books and their effect on me; it is from my earliest reading that I date the unbroken consciousness of my own existence. My mother had possessed [*laissé*, i.e., left] some novels, and my father and I began to read them after our supper. At first it was only to give me practice in reading. But soon my interest in this entertaining literature became so strong that we read by turns continuously, and spent whole nights so engaged. For we could never leave off till the end of the book. Sometimes my father would say with shame as we heard the morning larks: 'Come, let us go to bed. I am more of a child than you are' (19–20).

Heart before head: this enduring priority of his life and thought alike has been fixed for Rousseau in the curriculum of his first reading, fiction having been allotted the role of teaching him to feel, not to think. And that his 'unbroken consciousness' of himself should date from the time of this first exposure to stories implies a further mimesis, whereby now, as an autobiographical subject, he will imitate by his continuous presence before us, his readers, the fictive heroes who first seduced him. But the pleasures which come from fiction must for Rousseau be guilty ones; they are not manly pleasures, and the father who should have represented for him the Reality Principle has led him astray by fostering in him the will to escapism.

But there has been another, stricter side to his literary education. By the age of seven, the novels have all been read, and it is time to turn to the 'good' books in the house. These are men's books, passed down from his maternal grandfather, and their role is corrective, they will be morally and intellectually bracing after the effeminate pap. The boy now reads Bossuet, Ovid, Fontenelle, La Bruyère, Molière, and reads them not with his father but *to* him, as the father works; this is no longer a covert, escapist night-reading, but reading in the light of day, curricular, a precocious advertisement of the future 'Citizen of Geneva'. The author whom Rousseau has then favoured above all others is that autobiographical favourite, Plutarch, whose moralizing 'Lives' he has read and reread, and which 'did something to cure me of my passion for novels'. He was ideally susceptible to these virile fables, and imbibed and expounded in conversation with his father the austere republican virtues, so developing in himself 'that proud and intractable spirit, that impatience with the yoke of servitude, which has afflicted me throughout my life, in those situations least fitted to afford it scope'(20). The encounter with Plutarch has exalted him, like the moment of 'illumination' at Vincennes: heart and head have entered into unison and the young Rousseau forgets his timidity in a typical act of *folie*. Unlike the knowing young Sartre when his time comes, he has identified with the virtuous and predestined subjects he reads about, to the extent of laying his hand down on a hot stove in painful imitation of Mucius Scaevola, who did the same, according to Plutarch, after having infiltrated the Etruscan camp in order to kill their king and succeeded in killing only the king's lieutenant. We may be impressed, or we may be suspicious, that this particular child should have taken for his role model a man celebrated for having gone to an extreme of self-punishment.

This collaborative course of serious reading may have made Rousseau contemptuous of womanish fictions but it has confirmed his trust in the effectiveness of stories. He can from now on observe the distinction between useful and non-useful stories, or the kind of stories told by Plutarch, which have a clear moral purpose, and the kind of stories told by the novelists, who aim to amuse, not to improve. In the fourth *promenade* of the *Rêveries*, where he traces a rational borderline between truth and falsehood, Rousseau exonerates fables from the charge of mendacity on the ground that they are confessedly fabulous and so take no one in, falsehood being defined by an intention to deceive and to profit by deception. But the fabulous achieves its useful effects by the same dangerous means as the idlest of fictions, by drawing its readers or hearers out from the actual and into an imaginary world, a world fit for Plutarchan heroes. The 'proud, intractable character' which has formed in Rousseau in obedience to his fabulous regime of reading is itself a figment, an imaginary or contrived self too pure and uncompromising ever to be accommodated in the fallen world of which the autobiographer is about to give us an account. It is a narrative convenience, the writer's insurance that as the bearer of a character so adamantine he will always be separate from the flux of his experience.

What is untrue, but of no advantage to whoever proffers it, whether in the ordinary exchanges of social life or in the practice of literature, is for Rousseau excusable. He can excuse himself for writing fiction because his intention in doing so is not to deceive. But more than that, fiction can serve a moral end as a kind of writing peculiarly well adapted to teaching virtue to a vicious society, one of whose notorious vices is the taste for fiction, whether printed or spoken, in the form of rumour and calumny. But even so, when in the *Confessions* he becomes the author of *Julie*, Rousseau appears as the novelist *malgré lui*, taking up the very literary genre he is known for having previously condemned as 'breathing love and indolence' and, on notably Augustinian grounds, as arousing in its readers strong but sterile emotions which the dramas of real life fail to awaken in them. Writing fiction is in part a shameful pleasure for Rousseau, just as reading it had once been for his father. It is a distraction inspired by his timidity, an unnatural introversion of mental and erotic energy very like masturbation, that other 'supplementary' pleasure which Rousseau both valued and condemned for the phantasmal mastery which it offered him over desirable and compliant women. But against the satisfactions which he gets from keeping company day after day with his female characters as he writes, there can be set the lessons of virtue which *Julie* will teach when published. His self-indulgence as a writer finds its justification in the service he gives as a moralist, as it will do later and more strongly still with the *Confessions*. And when his readers are moved to tears by his deceitful mobilization of their feelings, this will be a legitimate means of enforcing the comparison he would make between the desirable but untrue society represented in the novel and the undesirable but real society to which those readers will soon be returned.

In the *Confessions* the utilitarian ambitions of the novelist are carried further, the excessive indulgence of self which autobiography invites calling no doubt for a more extreme remedy. The ideal 'society' which is held up now for the reader to admire is the moral being of the autobiographer, the man who is not as other men are but the voice of Nature. As the hero of his own fabulous narrative, Rousseau represents himself from within as he truly, transparently is, in contra-distinction from a society false through and through for being opaque and deceptive. The autobiographer himself is the personification of truth, alone able to tell us what the true intentions were 'behind' the actions he is known to have taken. Up until now he has been the prey of fictions, of lying fictions invented by others for their advantage and his disadvantage. It is known that all five of the children he has fathered have been abandoned, put into homes for foundlings; the story is put about that he is a monster for having done such a thing. But that is a false story, the work of spiteful enemies such as Voltaire. The true story – and what a lame one it turns out to be – must be told by the autobiographer, who alone knows what his intentions were; in the event, to save these children from an even worse future, of being raised by their mother's degraded family. The autobiographer has the supreme advantage over the novelist in being thus able to introduce the real world into his story so as to correct it explicitly there and then, rather than doing so only by the indirections of fiction.

In the end, it is we who are asked to decide by Rousseau whether he is right and the world wrong, or whether it is the other way round. The decision is all or nothing. Autobiography here turns openly forensic: he will give us all the evidence about himself, we must then judge him. Truth and rhetoric he has kept separate: 'My role is to tell the truth, but not to get it believed.' But pledges of truthfulness as insistent as those made by Rousseau say differently; that he cares more for credibility than for veracity. The truth-teller must still compel attention, by artifice if need be, his only defence against which is to admit it, as Rousseau does, confessing that even in his autobiographical writings he has 'disfigured' the truth here and there by a shameful 'ornamentation'. Such extremes of honesty in an autobiographer are aggressive, they make it particularly hard for us to judge him in any way other than that which he is imposing on us. We can but declare him if not innocent then forgiven, his transparency being beyond compare. It is no surprise that when, after the *Confessions*, Rousseau went back to autobiography, by writing the dialogues of *Rousseau juge de Jean Jacques* he should have chosen there to play all the judicial roles himself, of prosecutor, counsel and presiding judge. As readers of the *Confessions* we are asked to sit in judgment not simply on the autobiographer in his heroic transparency, but also on ourselves, Rousseau having set us an example of candour and completeness of self-knowledge which we can all profit from in the examination of our own lives. This is the high utilitarian value of autobiography as he so enthusiastically practises it.

THE FALL INTO REFLECTION

There exist two preambles to the *Confessions*. From one I have already quoted in the Introduction to this book; it forms the opening paragraphs of the work as published. But Rousseau also wrote an earlier, longer and less hectoring version, now preserved with the alternative Neuchâtel manuscript of the *Confessions*. In this he lays less store by the uniqueness both of himself as a man and of the autobiographical form he has chosen, and more by its moral ends.[5]

---

[5] This preface can be found on pp. 1148–64 of the Pléiade edition containing the *Confessions*: see Jean-Jacques Rousseau, *Oeuvres complètes*, Tome 1, *Les Confessions, Autres textes autobiographiques*, edited by Bernard Gagnebin, Marcel Raymond and Robert Osmont (Paris, 1959).

He starts as any *moraliste* might, by observing that whatever knowledge we claim to have of why other people behave as they do is for the most part a projected self-knowledge, and that self-knowledge itself may be supposititious (for anyone but himself). Self-knowledge is uncertain because it is purely internal, we have nothing to compare it with; we may be mistaken as to our own nature and motives, which makes self-knowledge a fallible guide in determining the motives of other people, when we imagine them acting from the same motives as would impel us in their situation. Rousseau here redraws solipsism as a vicious circle: in order to have true knowledge of others we first need true knowledge of ourselves and in order to have that we first need true knowledge of others. How are we to break out from this epistemological trap?

The answer is, through the rare service offered to us by the autobiographer. What we need is an example of someone who has come to genuine self-knowledge and is ready to publish it: Jean-Jacques Rousseau, 'a sort of being apart'. This being apart writes out of a long and hurtful experience of being misjudged by others, who have attributed to him motives he has not in fact had but which are, of course, the motives they themselves would have had for acting similarly. It seems that Rousseau's self-knowledge has been certified by his exposure to these false interpretations of his behaviour, which are also his proof that other people do not inhabit the same moral universe as himself, that their motives are not his. This is a lesson he will now pass on, by playing the part of specimen Other to a whole benighted society. We can know our own 'hearts' by 'reading' in that of someone else and learn that not all hearts are alike, that we should not judge those of others by our own: 'I want to attempt so that if we are to learn to appraise ourselves, we have at least one piece of comparative evidence; so that everyone can know both himself and one other, and that other will be me'(1149).

The Neuchâtel preface to the *Confessions* reads more reasonably than the published one, yet it is equally as presumptuous in setting the autobiographer up as a moral exemplar, or even as a saviour, for were the transparency he promises us in the representation of himself to become the norm, societies would be purged of the accretion of falsehood and artifice that literally de-natures them. Such an autobiography as Rousseau's is the healing instrument that we all of us require, a fable to be read by generation after generation as their ideal 'piece of comparative evidence'. Its acknowledged artifice is redeemed by its dedication to the cause of Nature. But the role of saviour also involves sacrifice, for in the course of his exemplary fable the autobiographer will reveal shameful things about himself such as no one before has revealed. The autobiographer's great candour is the more estimable for what it has cost him. The pleasure of writing the *Confessions* must be paid for by the punishment – inflicted, Scaevola-like, by himself – of letting other people know things that are to his discredit.

With Rousseau the 'inward turn' of autobiography is made under an imaginary duress. He must spread the truth about himself so as to bely the slanders spread against him by others. The plot that has been mounted to misrepresent him is in his eyes a tribute levied on the resentful many by his singularity, the plotters having been brought together by the recognition that his *bizarreries*, as he himself gladly names them, are witness to his greater moral refinement. Their desire is to recapture him for the pragmatic, cynical morality of the group. But by writing the *Confessions* he will foil them, on both counts: he will now substitute his incontrovertible truth for their falsehoods and he will go so incomparably far in the revelation of his previously hidden self as to reconfirm his entitlement to his apartness. This auto-biographer has come to write in the gratifying knowledge that he is a being of a different, because finer moral constitution from others, and that the autobiography which he writes will be unlike any so far written. In the Neuchâtel preface, Rousseau is scornful of the literary tradition against which the *Confessions* must be judged if their originality is to appear: 'Histories, lives, portraits, characters! What do they amount to? Ingenious fictions built on a few external actions, on a few spoken words relating to them, on subtle conjectures in which the Author is seeking much more to shine than to discover the truth'(1149). These trite, inanimate forms are no adequate container for a life as novel in thought, word and deed as that of Rousseau; they convey not what is unique about their subjects but what is classifiable about them, they sacrifice the original to the familiar. To be reduced to a *caractère* is to become one more entry in a roster of well-known social types and a living proof of the invariability of human behaviour.

If there is literature to be made out of a life, then let it be made by the person uniquely placed to transgress the bounds of such bookish convention: the subject himself. Rousseau is a writer, and the writer who allows himself to be written about by another writer suffers not only misrepresentation but also a partial eclipse, his biographer being also his rival in literature and certain therefore to usurp some part of his subject's light so as to 'shine' the more brightly himself. Authorial vanity is of greater account than biographical truth; self will occlude self. But only for as long as subject and biographer are two people; combine them in an act of autobiography and authorial vanity will pass from being the screen which obscures the subject to being our guarantee that the subject is now appearing in all his truth. As the author of the *Confessions* Rousseau may take to himself the glory of being shiningly truthful.

The enemy of enemies for him there is Grimm, once his intimate in literary Paris but now the vile orchestrator of the 'league' against him. Grimm is charged above all by Rousseau with a systematic failure in reciprocity: Rousseau has been generous, supportive, confiding towards him, but Grimm has been the opposite of all these things towards Rousseau, mean, defamatory, secretive. When Grimm becomes the lover of Mme d'Epinay, Rousseau's patroness at the Hermitage, the liaison is an open one, to everyone except Rousseau. Mme d'Epinay has revealed it to her husband even, but will not talk about it with himself, and Rousseau knows why: 'I understood that this reserve was due to Grimm, to whom I had entrusted all my secrets but who did not want me to be privy to any of his'(432). Within the scheme of the *Confessions* this 'reserve' is immoral, it condemns Grimm, even though the 'secret' which is being withheld on his instructions is public knowledge. Rousseau alone is, or may be supposed to be, in the dark, and Rousseau has been one of Grimm's closest friends. The failure in reciprocity is a failure in transparency: Grimm is opaque, his morality is that which Rousseau finds peculiarly abhorrent, an 'inner doctrine' according to which we should do exactly what we feel like doing and whose implications for society are so outrageous that it has to be kept concealed. It is Rousseau's most bitter complaint against the *philosophes*, that the philosophy they profess in their writings is not that which they live by privately.

But if Grimm is so secretive and duplicitous, how can Rousseau know the truth about him? In his own case inner and outer doctrines are one, so he can not look inside himself for evidence of a similar division by which to explain the hypocrisy of Grimm. Such a truth can emerge only through *confession* and Grimm has indeed confided it, to his mistress, Mme d'Epinay, and she in turn has confided in Rousseau. The act of confession is infectious. Rousseau's reaction to what he has learnt about Grimm has two stages: first he assumes that the revelation of Grimm's secret 'doctrine' has been a mere *jeu d'esprit*, but he comes soon to see that the doctrine does indeed regulate Grimm's behaviour, as he now knows to his cost, he having been a principal victim. Rousseau's first – immediate – reaction has been friendly, it reflects his own uncorrupted good nature: Grimm is a man given to wit but not to wickedness; but Rousseau's further reaction is sombre, it is the fruit of experience and of reflection, and it corrects the optimism of his first reaction. The morally downward movement from one interpretation of Grimm to the other is that from immediacy to reflection; it is the movement which humanity itself has made, in its Fall from a benignly natural into an antagonistic social state: 'With reflection the man of nature ends and "the man of man" begins', in the words of Jean Starobinski.[6]

The 'man of man' is infected with the disease endemic to any society, with *amour-propre*, which is for Rousseau the most corrosive of emotions, and a corruption of the entirely beneficent feeling which has preceded it in his evolutionary story of the human heart: *amour de soi*. This is the unreflective, loving passion which drives us to seek our own happiness; it is natural and it is good – identifiable perhaps with the 'primary narcissism' postulated by Freud. Trouble only starts when 'obstacles' arise to prevent our happiness and we turn our attention to the removal of those rather than to the achievement of happiness itself. The obstacular is the intermediate. These obstacles tend of course to be other people, or rival happiness-seekers, with whom we engage in close and unfriendly competition. For as long as we are impelled purely by *amour de soi*, we are exempt from such internecine warfare, but once lapse into *amour-propre* and we are condemned to negativity. *Amour-propre* in Rousseau's reading of it is secured by the belittlement of those around us and by the looking for enjoyment not from doing good to ourselves but from doing harm to others. This opposition, of a good *amour de soi* to a bad *amour-propre*, is very obviously the opposition of the autobiographer to his enemies. He is all the one, they are all the other. He is the overflowing source of a natural benevolence and the seeker after happiness, they are a

---

[6] Jean Starobinski, *Jean-Jacques Rousseau: La transparence et l'obstacle* (Paris, 1971), p. 42.

spiteful set representative of society in general in their preference for harming him rather than seeking their own happiness. He in short is the supreme obstacle by whom they have been distracted.

Judged according to Rousseau's own morality, the *Confessions* are a sadly fallen work. For how can autobiography express a simple *amour de soi*, that blissfully self-absorbed pursuit of happiness which knows no distraction? Autobiography is called into existence by the very obstacles which impede such a pursuit and pervert *amour de soi* into *amour-propre*. The *Confessions* themselves are a monument to *amour-propre*, a model of autobiographical vindictiveness in which the writer is constantly dramatizing his moral superiority over those whom he has conscripted to serve as his enemies. Autobiography may be composed *in absentia*, but its practitioners know the joys of what Kenneth Burke calls 'symbolic action', or that release of tension by dramatic means which according to Burke is the main purpose of all literary work. Rousseau makes much autobiographically of his aptitude for 'retirement', because the closer he can come to self-sufficiency in living the more he is absolved from acting directly in the world. His actions have been misunderstood; he will cease from action, and claim thereafter that by doing nothing he has at least rendered himself harmless.

But the strategy of withdrawal is an invitation also to *reflect* on what has happened to him: in his fastness the 'man of nature' is free to indulge himself as 'the man of man'; withdrawal is an invitation to live out in his own person that turning of his gaze on himself which Rousseau elsewhere sees as having first made man aware of his superiority over the other animals and proud in that awareness. The birth of the faculty of reflection announces the growing distance between natural man and social man or, as I would transpose those terms here, autobiographical man and social man, autobiographical man being that hyper-reflective being who is empowered to recount the full story of his own progress from an idyllic oneness with nature to an unjust isolation within a world of artifice unaccommodating of him. Reflection may not have been a blessing to early man but it is a blessing now to Rousseau, for by its help, and by the mental work which it has brought with it, he will contribute to the enlightenment of his kind.

By confessing himself in his full transparency he will triumph lastingly over those who have set obstacles in his way. Autobiography may be a form of writing directed to the satisfaction of the writer's *amour-propre*, but he will use it, uniquely, for the expression of his *amour de soi*, or true self-love. *Amour de soi* can itself serve as the agency of his revenge over those who have no sense of it: in the Seventh Promenade of the *Rêveries* Rousseau meditates on the *fantaisie* which has seized him in his old age, for collecting and identifying wild flowers and plants, and declares that this solitary, disinterested, innocuous habit is a way of ensuring that no 'leaven of vengeance or of hatred' can 'germinate' in his heart. Except that he instantly adds that the very pleasure which he takes in botanizing *is* his revenge over the plotters who have driven him out from the society of men, since 'there is no more cruel way of punishing them than by being happy in spite of them'. *Amour de soi* can have no value in itself, for it belongs within no system of values; it acquires value only once it has been drawn into that corrupt system of comparisons and relations born of *amour-propre*.

CONFESSION AS PERFORMANCE

Rousseau is embarked in the *Confessions* on the self-defeating task of restoring 'the natural order' by an artificial means, as he had restored it briefly at Turin by making so bold as to speak. There would be no need for such a restoration had he not suffered in his *amour-propre*. An injustice has been done him which only he can right. A working model of such a rectification is offered to us in the first book of the *Confessions*, where Rousseau recounts the traumatic episode of the broken comb. This has occurred when he was a young boy and a pupil boarding with a Protestant pastor, Lambercier, in a village near Geneva. This in the *Confessions* is a time of deep, edenic contentment for Rousseau, which ends catastrophically, when he is punished for a fault he has not committed. A comb belonging to the pastor's sister, Mlle Lambercier, has been broken, and he is accused of breaking it. A confession is demanded, but refused; the youthful devotee of Plutarch stands firm, he will not save himself by a falsehood, even though it be to his physical advantage. He is beaten and his moral universe is overturned, with this first invasion of his mind by the idea of injustice.

On this occasion Rousseau might have confessed but chose in his virtue not to; as a consequence he has received the punishment which should by rights have been visited on someone else. His shattering experience of injustice thus involves him suffering by proxy, a role in which he has specialized. Even before the affair of the broken comb he has interposed between his enraged father and his brother, to take on his own body the blows meant for his sibling, just as later on he endures the bruising assaults of local schoolboys whose real target is the cousin who was then Rousseau's constant companion. These are moments of commendable self-sacrifice recorded in the *Confessions*. To them must be added two other such moments which were not recorded there, but which Rousseau subsequently revived in the *Rêveries du promeneur solitaire* (in the Fourth Promenade). Both involved childhood friends as well as painful injury to himself. On one occasion his fingers had been trapped in some machinery, on another he had been knocked insensible by a blow from a club during a game. Rousseau was both times in pain but both times kept quiet as to how his injuries had been caused, to save the friends who had caused them from punishment; and he even makes the extraordinary claim that 'a hundred other' similar accidents had happened to him of which he had not written in the *Confessions*.

His reason for keeping silent about them had been so as not to show himself there in too meritorious a light. But he has now finally revealed two at least of these apparently habitual accidents, so that we may think triply well of him: first for his generosity at the time; then for having in his modesty left them out of the *Confessions*; and lastly for having now revealed them, his truthfulness being of such an order as to oblige him to *confess* such experiences, meritorious though they be. Rousseau's desire is to compel our admiration at each moment in this cumulative sequence. He is exploiting to the full the gap between the two narrative 'orders' that Paul de Man distinguishes as the 'cognitive' and the 'performative', or that gap constitutive of autobiography in general, between the historical 'facts' which the writer recounts, and the autobiographical act of recounting them.[7] Confession in our Christian culture is a very strongly performative act, a solemn performance rooted in church ritual and made dramatic by the avowal within it of shameful actions, thoughts and feelings which the person confessing would in all other circumstances have kept to himself. Rousseau may have taken over Augustine's hallowed title for his autobiography, but his own *Confessions* are secular; they lack the element of praise of God which is so prominent in Augustine. His performance is a recog-

---

[7] See Paul de Man, *Allegories of Reading: Figural Language in Rousseau, Nietzsche, Rilke, and Proust* (New Haven and London, 1979), especially the final chapter, 'Excuses (*Confessions*)', pp. 278–301.

nizably modern one, each disclosure of which might in principle be headed by the words 'I confess that ... '. We read autobiography intelligently when we keep in mind that our one access to the 'cognitive' order of the writer's life is by way of the performative, that whatever 'facts' the text contains are there by authorial fiat.

I go back to the broken comb. In this episode of the *Confessions* Rousseau is confessing to not having confessed, despite an invitation to do so by those who believed him guilty. His refusal to confess is very staunch, very creditable. But what of his confession now, fifty years later, that he would not confess then? This is not so creditable, if it shows him in so meritorious a light; perhaps he should have refused once again to confess, once again setting principle before pleasure. But in any case the shame attaches not to the 'fact' or event itself, but to its narration. There is a second, similar event in the early part of the *Confessions*, recorded as having been more traumatic still for the adolescent Rousseau: the episode of the stolen ribbon. This time, instead of refusing to confess to a crime of which he is innocent, the young Rousseau refuses to confess to one of which he is guilty. And far from saving, as has been his virtuous wont, a guilty party from a merited punishment by the sacrifice of his own person, he has allowed a guiltless party to suffer for his fault. Rousseau has himself stolen the ribbon in order to give it flirtatiously as a present to a pretty fellow servant, Marion; it is found on him and in self-defence he charges *her* with having given it to *him*. Both young people are dismissed from the household, but Rousseau has been troubled ever since by thoughts of what dire things may have befallen Marion in later life. He has been ready to admit to others that he had once committed 'a terrible deed', but only now is he admitting to the ignoble form which it took: 'The burden, therefore, has rested till this day on my conscience without any relief; and I can affirm that the desire to some extent to rid myself of it has greatly contributed to my resolution of writing these confessions'(88).

Rousseau has acted badly not because he is wicked but because he is weak; confronted publicly with the innocent girl he has borne false witness against her, because to have confessed the truth would have been too shameful. This is the *mauvaise honte*, or 'wrongful shame', which has mediated so harmfully in the course of his life between the inner and outer man, and has caused him to behave in blameworthy ways preserving of his *amour-propre*. But for the presence of such an 'obstacle' there would have been nothing for him to confess, because his real innocence of nature would have been reflected in his innocence of behaviour. The purpose of the *Confessions* must therefore be to evacuate the shame which he has felt at these culpable moments and which the autobiographical act will revive, since Rousseau assures us that his emotions fluctuate as he writes in consonance with the emotions he is recalling. His desire in writing is to purge himself by this tardy but sincere abasement.

By suffering now in the act of writing, the autobiographer is offering a symbolic reparation for having failed to suffer when he should have done. With the ribbon, it was the intimidating proximity of other people which overcame him and made him act dishonourably; in the absence of other people he will now make textual amends. But those amends are *only* textual, they may restore the transparency of the man who is making them, they do nothing for the long vanished victim of his small crime. Confession, as de Man reminds us, exculpates, it is made in the interest of whoever practises it; and we can never be sure that what is being confessed to is true: '[...] how then are we to know that we are indeed dealing with a *true* confession, since the recognition of guilt implies its exoneration in the name of the same transcendental principle of truth that allowed for the certitude of guilt in the first place?'[8] De Man's scepticism, in his dauntingly subtle analysis of the Marion episode, runs to the extreme of taking the theft of the ribbon to be no more than an excuse for Rousseau to fulfil his real desire in writing, which is to expose himself symbolically, to 'parade his disgrace'. In such a reading, the wretched Marion herself becomes the indifferent plaything of an autobiographer happily caught up in the dialectic between repression and revelation, as he now reveals not simply the truth that he was blocked from revealing then, but also his previous inability to reveal it. This is to sacrifice the 'cognitive' altogether to the 'performative' order of the confessional text, and few of us would want to move so far in that direction as de Man. It is for cognitive satisfactions that we first go as readers to autobiography, and only in the second or reflective instance that we construe the idiosyncrasies of the performance.

Rousseau himself was extraordinarily wise to the advantages for an autobiographer of harmonizing the one order with the other. Writing a life is not an instantaneous act, it is a performance which takes time

---

[8] De Man, *Allegories of Reading*, p. 280.

and is itself narratable, either as an element in the autobiographical text or as a separate codicil to it. Autobiographers do not stop living in order to write and their perspective on their own past must change all the time. But they may choose to work with or against this process, recognizing that their feelings and thoughts are changing from day to day, or trying to suppress that knowledge, in the interests of presenting themselves textually as gratifyingly coherent wholes. Rousseau for his part recognized that the autobiographical performance belonged also to the 'cognitive' order; that the way or 'style' in which he chose to write his life was itself further factual evidence about him. But a recognizable 'style', in the usual sense of the word, was the very thing he needed to avoid, since 'style' is to be identified by its uniformity, it is an imposition. Rousseau declared himself to have been not one person in the course of his life but many, and above all contradictory persons, a unique plurality admirable for fitting within no known categories of human being. A performative 'style' which was homogeneous would do away with the hectic variety of the life it was imposed on. His intention, rather, was that the unevenness and emotional dramas of his past should be immediately reflected in the unevenness and emotionality of his narration. The gap between past and present was to be closed: 'By giving myself up both to the memory of the impression received and to my present feeling I shall portray the state of my soul twice over, to wit at the moment when the event occurred and the moment when I described it; my uneven, natural style, here quick and there diffuse, here reasonable and there wild, here serious and there cheerful, will itself form part of my story'(Neuchâtel preface, 1154).

Rousseau's trust in the mimetic capacity of his style might seem like an extreme expression of that nostalgia supposedly inherent in all autobiography, for the writer to be reunited performatively with his past. But there is another, more interesting aspect to it. On his first removal to the Ermitage, Rousseau had numbered among the literary projects to be worked on in his retirement there a treatise on what he called *la morale sensitive* or 'le matérialisme du Sage' – 'the Wise Man's materialism'. This was not in the end written but its argument is outlined in the *Confessions*. The starting-point was to have been the inconsistency of behaviour which he had observed in himself, whereby he appeared to change his nature from one day to the next. One day he could resist temptation, the day after not. This was a painful admission of weakness for an *honnête homme* like himself;

what could be the reason for this moral disunity? Rousseau blames it largely on the sense impressions we receive from our environment, which constantly 'modify' our moral behaviour without our being aware of it. To be more consistently virtuous therefore, we need to change not ourselves but our surroundings, to make them more favourable to our moral aspirations. This programme of reform is highly Rousseauesque in its shifting of moral responsibility from the agent to his setting, since in an ideally organized environment we could not but be virtuous. Such were Rousseau's dreams of a passive goodness. But in autobiography, unlike in life, the writer's environment may be arranged to suit his desires and its secret modifications of his behaviour made fully explicit. The relationship between past 'impression' and present 'feeling' of which Rousseau writes in the Neuchâtel preamble, is also that between the autobiographer's 'external objects' and the 'state of soul' they condition in him. In autobiography, one might argue that Rousseau's utopian programme is realized.

The pleasure to be got from writing the *Confessions* is also surely an erotic one. Among the temperamental contradictions from which Rousseau has suffered most in his life is that between sensuality and shyness. He has desired women ardently but has not been man enough to possess them. He has found solace in the 'dangerous supplement' of masturbation – 'that bizarre taste' as Rousseau, rather bizarrely (or possessively), calls it. He does not use autobiography as others have no doubt used it, to enjoy in imagination the sexual conquests debarred to him in fact, but for the more pathetic purpose altogether of confessing his inadequacy. The first, foundational erotic 'impression' which he receives in the *Confessions* is that of sexual arousal brought on by corporal punishment, and a punishment made more than ordinarily shameful for being administered by a woman. To this event he attributes the 'bizarrerie' of his subsequent erotic life, and its culpable introversion. His environment has conditioned him falsely. Or at least, it has done so up until now, for in the confession of this childhood punishment he will presumably re-experience the shame and the sensual excitement which he experienced at the time. The difference is that now, as an autobiographer exposing his shameful secrets to public view, it is by his own hand that he is being punished, he having finally discovered the literary means to play all the parts in his life's drama himself.

CHAPTER 7

Subject to revision: Alfieri, Goethe, Stendhal

The intensity of Rousseau's desire to establish the incontrovertible truth about himself is such as to censor the interval of time between the experiences of which he is writing and the present moment of their recovery. To draw attention to this temporal gap might cast doubt on his credibility as a witness, might, worse still, invite others than himself to fill it, with alien explanations of his actions. Rousseau is adamant that he is re-experiencing his past, not indifferently recording it and he assures us more than once in the *Confessions* that his memory is weak, that he has never been able to memorize things – when he had tried to learn his lines for a part in a play, he found himself having to be prompted throughout. But as an autobiographer, delivering his own and not another author's lines, he can remember copiously, prompted only by the few personal documents from which he quotes. He can not help remembering indeed; autobiography is his *passion*, in the full sense of that word, as the past comes crowding back without him having to go in search of it. The faculty he can rely on is the affective memory, which he regards as infallible and as abolishing by its immediacy the space that would otherwise open between past and present, in which the reflective consciousness might begin to play, sounding the fatal note of discontinuity and hence of doubt.

Because he is reviving feelings, not remembering facts, Rousseau need not question the authenticity of his recollections, nor consider the extent to which what he is now writing is the imposition of his mature judgment on experiences that were barely or not at all comprehensible at the time when he had them. Rousseau suits himself – and impresses us as his late twentieth-century readers – by assuming that the design of an adult life is inked indelibly in during childhood and adolescence; but he is deceptive in eliding that fledgling past with his grown-up present, as if man and child were coeval. He refuses to exercise the autobiographer's privilege of applying the rationality and insight of age to the confusions of youth, and when he tells us in the course of the *Confessions* that it is we, as his readers, who must sit in judgment on him, since he, the writer, can do no more than set down what he has felt and done, this is not simply a self-deluding invitation to us to judge him morally, it is an invitation also to perform in his stead the specific autobiographical task of imposing on his past life the grand design he himself claims to be too near-sighted to be able to perceive.

Autobiographers ask for our attention, and for our trust, they do not usually ask for our help in understanding them. If they express ignorance as to their own nature or, like Rousseau, an inability to do more in writing than mimic the volatility which has marked both his inner and his outer life, that is a feint, a surrender of authorial initiative which may momentarily restore the autobiographer to the community of expectant outsiders like ourselves but which we can hardly believe in when to do so would kill our curiosity as readers. Autobiographers may start out by wondering, explicitly, about what their lives have been, or who, really, they themselves are – as Stendhal so delightfully does. They may be sincere in doing so, or merely arch. In either case, we expect from them an answer, to have an idea by the time we have finished reading them of what they at least *think* their lives to have been, and their nature. Nowhere in the large and serious corpus of Rousseau's autobiographical prose does there sound the grace-note of irony, or that wry distancing which in autobiography is the writer's admission that his present self is sufficiently removed in time and sentiment from his past selves to savour their strangeness. Rousseau the intense visionary of the past must now give way to three strikingly rational writers who belong together in this chapter for having practised the potentially pathetic genre of autobiography in a strongly *re*-visionary way.

Alfieri

'As to the style of these *Memoirs*, dictated by the heart and not the head, I shall let my pen run on and write as spontaneously and naturally as possible. This will best suit my modest theme'(3).[1] These are the closing words of the brief Author's Preface to the *Memoirs* of

---

[1] The (abridged) edition I have cited is Vittorio Alfieri, *Memoirs*, The anonymous translation of 1810, revised by E. R. Vincent (London, 1961).

Vittorio Alfieri, the eighteenth-century Italian poet and tragedian. In their promise of spontaneity they might seem to belong to the new autobiographical age of effusiveness, or the Rousseauesque compulsion to *épanchement*. But Alfieri did not like the way in which Rousseau wrote. He admired the man for 'his upright and independent character', but what little he had read of Rousseau's work he found tedious, 'owing to the labour and affectation of sentiment evident throughout all the productions of this author'(124). Alfieri had once turned down an opportunity in Paris of being introduced to this 'odd and difficult man', fearing that in his pride he would only repay Rousseau in kind and with interest for the discourtesies the other would be likely to show him. Alfieri has had a better idea: 'Instead therefore of cultivating an intimacy with Rousseau I formed what was much more interesting to me, an acquaintance with the works of the most celebrated characters in Italy, or perhaps in the world. I purchased during my stay in Paris a collection of the works of our principal writers both in Prose and Verse [...].' This is a turning-point in Alfieri's story: rather than add to his human acquaintance, he turns to books, and to Italian books, thereby resuming the language and the culture into which he had been born but had later come to feel ashamed of. The rejection of Rousseau is an important moment in his maturation.

That Alfieri should distinguish so sharply between Rousseau as moral being and as writer lets us know that here is an autobiographer who will not connive at any sentimental conflation of man and text, of the kind to which Rousseau aspires in the *Confessions*. Alfieri's own rhetorical strategy will not be Rousseau's, he will not demean himself by any 'labouring or affectation of sentiment'. In one respect at least, he is an anti-Rousseau. Where Rousseau was sustained by the desire to contradict the false and hostile stories he believed to have been put about concerning him, Alfieri is inspired, so he says, by the wish to pre-empt a biography. He presumes that a new edition of his works will be brought out soon after his death, and knows that the custom then is for the publisher to commission a flattering life of the author, to puff whom is to puff the oeuvre and so increase the edition's sales. So just as when reading Rousseau's *Confessions*, it does to keep in mind the ominous projections of scurrility to which they are a response, we do well in reading Alfieri's *Memoirs* to imagine the version of his life that he is *not* writing. In this autobiography too there is a more or less concealed dialectic, between what the writer wishes to impose on us as the truth about himself and what other, less scrupulous and less well-placed writers might be imposing by way of falsehoods about him. Only where Rousseau sets the record straight by making himself out to be a far finer person than we could otherwise have known, Alfieri is gaining his advantage by doing just the opposite: by demonstrating that he is a man undeserving of a panegyric. As an autobiographer he means to be neither hard nor soft on himself, but to commend himself to us at the outset for his impartiality.

The greater part of the *Memoirs* was written by Alfieri in Paris in 1790, when he was forty-one years old. This may seem rather early in a lifetime to be turning to autobiography. But Alfieri had good reason; this was both a gratifying and a discouraging moment for him. It was gratifying because there was then being printed in France a collected edition of all that he had so far written, his poetry, his prose writings and his tragedies. He had been remarkably fertile in publications since turning to literature barely a dozen years before, so that a collected edition would add his name to the pantheon of Italian writers and add volumes of his own making to the thirty-six he had bought almost twenty years before, when he had forgone the meeting with Rousseau and bought a set of his native classics instead. But it was also a discouraging time because of what was happening socially and politically in France, where the one-year-old Revolution had begun to dismay Alfieri. He, the apostle of liberty and would-be toppler of tyrants, now saw all manner of insolence and intolerance on show in revolutionary Paris, and feared, very reasonably, for the future. France was on the way to betraying 'the holy and sublime cause of liberty'.

In both literary and ideological terms, the moment was one for Alfieri of a wholesale revision. Where his writings were concerned, this was called for by the fact of their reprinting in a new, collected edition. They could on no account be reprinted as they stood; Alfieri was seemingly quite unable ever to reread his own work without seeing the need to alter it, alteration meaning improvement. If he had not made changes to the existing texts before they went to the printer, then he did so when he got the proofs. Small wonder that it took him in all some three years to see his collected works through the press. The tragedies began to be set in 1787, by a printer in Paris. But this printer insisted on the author paying for all proof changes so Alfieri switched to another, more accommodating printer. It may be that he was no more than averagely pernickety among authors in behaving as he did – he falls some way short of Marcel Proust, for one, that relentless scourge of the typesetters. But in Alfieri's case the urge to alter what he had written is not simply an authorial tic but a recurring autobiographical theme. It is one manifestation of his obsession with freedom; Alfieri will not be bound even by the words he has himself written, at least for as long as he remains free to improve on them. When, the edition of his collected writings still not complete, he believes himself to be dying from a severe attack of dysentery, he is distressed first at the idea of leaving his 'beloved mistress',[2] and then of 'relinquishing that fame for which for ten years I had toiled in a kind of frenzy and the foundations of which I had scarcely laid'. The fine frenzy of creation may be the condition of authorship but its unexamined product is not what a proud tragedian like Alfieri means to be judged on. He must not die before he has given his works a last revision: 'I was fully conscious that none of my works were so perfect as I could have rendered them had more time been allowed me'(256). This was to keep possession of his writings to the end, and to preserve them from corruption by ignorant or careless printers.

The same goes for the *Memoirs* themselves. Having first written these at an age when he might well have thirty or more years of life left to him, Alfieri can look forward to their revision in the fullness of time. He promises us that he will put this 'trifling production' aside until he is sixty or so, when 'I must certainly have terminated my literary career': 'Then I shall revise it with all the cold objectivity of old age'(263). The process of revision is thus one of increasing impartiality, as the strong and prejudicial emotions of youth recede. When eventually, in 1803, only a few months before he died, Alfieri wrote a short continuation to the *Memoirs*, the same theme instantly returns: 'Having reread, in Florence, the biographical sketch I had written in Paris thirteen years before at the age of forty-one, I now endeavoured to improve the style and clarify the text'(265). Later, he says that should he be prevented from giving his memoirs a last polish he will burn them – though how he was to know which polishing would be the last, he does not say. This passion for revision

---

[2] This was the Countess of Albany, as yet still the wife, though on the point of becoming the widow, of Charles Edward Stuart, the Young Pretender. Alfieri lived with her for the last twenty-five years of his life and celebrates their companionship very touchingly in the *Memoirs*, as a relation freely entered into and involving no oppression of either party by the other.

might seem hardly to fit with the spontaneity and naturalness in writing which he declares will be his method in his original preface. Yet it is surely the corollary of that initial, unreflective fluency; as an autobiographer Alfieri wishes not simply to have second thoughts, but to be seen to have them, to revise what he writes for publication so that it represents him as he is *now* and not as he may once have been.

Any such autobiographical strategy as this is inherently deceptive, inasmuch as the transition in the writer from an unreflective to a reflective posture is itself the product of reflection. The spontaneous, natural man we meet with only in the guise of an attitude transcended. But Alfieri's whole narrative is determined by this transition: his life as he tells it has been one in which a first period of heedless pleasure-seeking gives way to a second period, of hard and mindful intellectual effort. The *Memoirs* are in the finest auto-biographical tradition in revealing its subject as having turned from one manner of life to another which is in dramatic contrast with it. Alfieri presents himself as a *convert* to literature, which was not a career he had been born to. His wealthy Piedmontese family has had no aesthetic interests and his schooling has been – predictably, I think I am entitled to say by this stage – a nonsense: the second section of the *Memoirs* carries the subtitle 'Comprising eight years of unproductive education' and is contemptuous of teachers, institutions and curricula alike. More deterrent still has been his lack of a language in which to feel at home. He has been brought up to speak French and to feel embarrassed by his poor command of Tuscan, or Italian, that 'divine language which I mangled in the most barbarous manner every time I was obliged to use it'(64). The turn to literature is also a passionate turn to Tuscan, and a furious, vindictive rounding on everything French, whose culture Alfieri repeatedly scorns in the *Memoirs*.[3]

The turning-point of Alfieri's life has come in his mid-twenties. Up until then he had written nothing, beyond some humorous pieces – in French – for an informal society of Piedmontese friends. He has

[3] By the time he came to write their continuation, his vindictiveness had grown, the French armies having by now invaded northern Italy, an event which Alfieri commemorated by writing a bitter little book called *Misogallo*, in which he poured out his contempt for these uncouth 'founders of republics'. He had ten copies of this work transcribed and hidden 'in different places' during the French occupation, 'to ensure that, if I could not live free and respected, I should at least die revenged'(289) – the motive of a true autobiographer.

been a traveller, a soldier, and a lover of horses and of women; in sum and in his own description, an 'idler'. But to be idle is not to be free, and independence is as much the declared goal of this auto-biographer's life as it was that of Hume's, or of Gibbon's. Alfieri has been subordinate as a soldier, and enslaved as a lover; but if he has freed himself from the military by resigning his commission, he remains trapped, like Augustine, by his sensuality. A crisis is at hand. It breaks when his mistress of the hour, whom he no longer cares for, falls ill and he attends at her bedside, silent and bored. At which moment of wordless suspense there occurs the Augustinian contingency which is to reorient and redeem his life: 'a few sheets of paper fell accidentally into my hands and on which I began to scribble without any determinate plan' (142). The scene is one of extraordinary passivity: Alfieri has neither looked for paper nor looked to start writing. This is clearly a portentous interlude in the life of a hitherto directionless man who is henceforth to be imbued 'with that true, strong, almost excessive love for learning and decisive action' (138).

The eclipse of life by art, or of his ailing mistress by his scribblings, echoes Alfieri's earlier choice of books over the person of Rousseau. His first, bedside composition is a dramatic dialogue involving Cleopatra. But this rough draft spends the next twelve months under the cushion of a chair, because he is not yet free of his erotic attachment and has to conceal what he has written. Only on the point of final liberation from his attachment, does he recover and reread his inspired and premonitory draft, and notices for the first time the similarity between the state of his own feelings towards his mistress and those of Mark Antony towards Cleopatra. That is, with the passage of time, reason can be called in to explain the product of a blind spontaneity or literary automatism, and reveal to him that the relation between brute experience and its projection in art is one open to a potentially interminable deliberation.

Reason and art go together for Alfieri because both set him free. Previously he had found himself so addicted to his tiresome mistress, that he had had to order his manservant to tie him down, to prevent him visiting her. But then he has hit upon a second, better expedient: he has dressed up as Apollo and sung bad lyrics of his own composition in public, with a view to making his attachment seem ridiculous and thus easier to shed. This derisive public image of himself is the preparation for a more glorious one, once he has become a true writer

– it is an image open to revision. And now it is that Alfieri sets out freely and objectively to revise the manuscript which he has, in an unusually literal sense of the phrase, been sitting on all this while: 'No sooner had this idea passed through my mind than, forgetting my mistress, I began to scribble, patch, change, cut, add, continue, start again, go nearly mad over this ill-starred *Cleopatra*'(148). He has begun in literature as he means to go on, by reworking first thoughts which he finds unworthy of him and whose import he has not fully grasped at the time when he had them.

Hence the regularity with which in his autobiography he marks the distance between past and present by the explicit rationalization of some long past action or emotion. When, for example, he recalls having grieved at his early separation from the sister of whom he was very fond, it is not so as to revive the tears and unhappiness of early childhood à la Rousseau, but rather to fix the place of this particular moment within his sentimental economy: 'Upon reviewing the sensations which I then experienced I find they are similar to those I afterwards felt when, in the heyday of youth, I was compelled to separate from my beloved or from sincere friends to whom I was ardently attached'(8). Not always is the element of taxonomy in autobiography, whereby the writer ranges over the whole of his past in order to classify emotions, events and people's characters by their similarity, made so obvious as it is by Alfieri. He believes that a thorough knowledge of self is to be obtained not by holding to philosophical theories but by paying due attention to the small circumstances of one's own life and finding in them a telltale consistency. The *Memoirs* are offered as a proud lesson in how to rise by the reflexivity of art above captivation by the moment.

At forty-one Alfieri foresees making a last revision of his life-story in the 'cold objectivity of old age'; but at fifty-four, when he wrote the coda to his *Memoirs*, his mood was neither cold nor objective, but heatedly gallophobic. He had reason to be so: a French mob had threatened him before he managed to escape from the country in 1792, and a French army had subsequently marched unwanted into Italy, finally occupying Florence and causing him to abandon his home there. But Alfieri's fury against the French is also a fury against his own younger, Frenchified self, who had spoken French, and had even tried writing in French, before he became so ardently Italian. 'Cold objectivity' is in any case not an end-state of mind to be looked for from the intemperate hedonist that Alfieri had for so long been.

He is in fact suspiciously hard on himself when describing the unregenerate time of his 'idleness', so desirous is he, as a by now experienced playwright, to bring out the contrast between himself then and himself now.

The most theatrical episode of the *Memoirs* is that of an amorous escapade in London, which has the rakish Alfieri dashing from the opera-house to fight a duel in Green Park with the husband of his mistress, receiving a flesh wound in the arm and then hurrying bloodstained back to his box in the theatre. The story of this daring amour is told with free reference to the extravagance of its hero's emotions at the time, when he was 'rendered so desperate that I acted like a man who had nothing further to lose' or else 'agitated by all the demons of hell' – the duel and the imbroglio that has occasioned it serving as an apt substitute for the action on the stage of the opera-house from which Alfieri is temporarily absent. But the story ends in disillusionment, when Alfieri discovers belatedly that the woman towards whom he has acted with such insouciant gallantry has also been the lover of her husband's groom. Yet again, he has cause to revise his interpretation of what has happened in the light of his further knowledge, so that the episode exemplifies the pattern of the *Memoirs* as a whole. His absence from the opera-house and risking of his life has been a naive mistake, the stage having more lasting and trustworthy satisfactions to offer him than the duelling-ground.

Alfieri's revenge for the betrayals of real life is to accentuate the emotional divide between his present and his past: if the young Alfieri has been famously hot-blooded, then the older Alfieri will be studiedly cool. Nothing could be further from the desire of Rousseau, to feel again in writing the strong emotions that have distinguished his life. If emotion returns for Alfieri, it does so in a denatured form: 'My feelings were so indescribably vehement that even now, as I write in frigid middle age, I shudder at the recollection'(107). In that 'shudder' he passes judgment on his youthful vehemence, giving us to assume that he is the happier for not re-experiencing it. But if with time and the desire for self-mastery he has outgrown his callow subjection to such affairs of the heart, he can not as an autobiographer neglect their attraction for his readers. The episode of the duel is the most exotic and most circumstantially narrated of any in the *Memoirs*, and it is told with an openness which stands in bold contrast to the uxorious discretion with which Alfieri writes of his long attachment to the Countess of Albany. But then that attachment continues, it is not, unlike the attachments of his volatile youth, ready yet to be expelled and placed in the showcase of his memoirs.

The dramatic crux of the affair in London is the moment of anagnorisis, when the caste-conscious Alfieri learns from his mistress that she has previously been the lover of a groom. The hold she has had over him and which she continues to have, is now all the more humiliating. Her scandalous revelation effects an ironic revision of everything that has gone before, when Alfieri had seemed to be acting in all the innocence of patrician venery. But there is a further irony to follow, when he discovers that his mistress has confessed her previous affair to him not out of guilt but only because the London news sheets already have the whole story, including his own part in it, so that its publication is imminent; she is merely forestalling and hence mitigating that eventual disclosure. Alfieri has given this story a central place in his autobiography in part because 'it made a great noise at the time'. It is a story known to some already and a good story, richly serving the autobiographer's purpose of displaying its narrator in a seductive light. But its lesson is as much aesthetic as ethical, being that the passage from innocence to experience represents not only a moral advance but also a fine subject for a revisionist drama, in which we must wait for the last act to learn the full sense of what we have been watching.

Goethe

As agreeable short stories wrapped inside the longer story, an autobiographer's love-affairs may irradiate an otherwise prosaic regime of fact with the allure of fiction, and may serve too as ideal demonstrations of the command that he now possesses over his past, as he narrates these potentially febrile episodes with an easy detachment, their impetuosity countermanded by the poise of their narration. Alfieri, the reformed gallant, can look indulgently down as well as back on a youth where he had put the gratification of his body before the improvement of his mind. The *Memoirs* are the story of an escape, from a sensual and social dependence characteristic of that thoughtless class from which the wellborn writer has singled himself out by his writing. Alfieri has no cause to regret the vain dissipations of his youth because without them his autobiography would be, almost literally, only half the book it is, and the energy which he now invests in literature would seem like an impulsion first found by him in manhood, rather than the glorious sublimation of an energy previously misspent in the pursuit of a facile pleasure.

The cardinal discovery to which Alfieri had come was that high literary use might be made of his own most ardent experiences, that a tormented Antony is ideally placed to imagine a tragic Cleopatra. Such a discovery is ironic, in the Goethean sense of that slippery term: it bespeaks elevation, since the writer who is capable of formulating it has risen sufficiently clear from entrapment by his feelings to grasp their possibilities as aesthetic subject-matter. Young love for Goethe, as for Alfieri, is something for the autobiographer to be observed fighting free of; it is an important moment of the initiation into his literary profession. In his *Poetry and Truth*[4] Goethe recounts several youthful flirtations, any one of which might have grown into a permanent attachment but all of which come to nothing, leaving him free finally to enter on to his manhood experienced but unimpeded.

Goethe's early liaisons have been decorous, they are a bourgeois world away from the rash entanglements of an Alfieri. They serve none the less as very effective intervals of narrative concentration in a text where the element of story is never strong and often wilfully occluded, for reasons that I shall come to. Their attraction as love-interest was well recognized by Goethe's reverent interlocutor, Eckermann, who in his *Conversations with Goethe* (see the entry for 10 August 1824) says that he has been looking at a draft of the later books of the autobiography, in which Goethe writes of the last, most serious and hence most independence-threatening of his three attachments, that to Lili. Eckermann is keen that Goethe should now work up this draft and has decided that 'The whole has much of the character of a novel. A graceful, tender, passionate love-affair, cheerful in its origin, idyllic in its progress, tragic at the end through a tacit but mutual renunciation, runs through four books, and combines them in an organized whole.' His advice was to make the most of Goethe's relationship with Lili, on the mimetic grounds that

---

[4] I shall use this literal English translation of Goethe's German title, *Dichtung und Warheit*, even though the one commonly available translation of the work, that made by John Oxenford back in the 1840s, will be found listed as *The Autobiography of Goethe*. Oxenford's subtitle however is 'Truth and poetry: from my own life'. It is remarkable that no good modern translation has yet replaced his – a sign perhaps that Goethe's is not seen as one of the more inviting of the classical autobiographies. The edition I shall quote from is that first published in two volumes by Henry Bohn, (London, 1848). Oxenford's translation is also available in a two-volume edition published by the University of Chicago Press in 1974.

his 'captivation' long ago by her could now be replayed so as to captivate his readers. The advice was not taken; the love-interest of Goethe's autobiography remains subordinate.

It does so because it is representative there only of the subjective pole of a work schematically arranged so as to plot the auto-biographer's emergence from the exclusive self-concern of youth into that active engagement with the outside world which for Goethe was the proper business of the grown man. *Poetry and Truth* is thus one more work of autobiography in the course of which the writer may be seen to have 'turned' from one philosophy of life to another, even if it contains nothing so dramatic or disruptive as a 'conversion'. For Goethe an individual must be shown as developing evenly and continuously, in a process of vital exchange between himself and his environment, like one of the botanical growths of which he was so close a student. In his autobiography he uses his particular story to illustrate general laws of human development, thereby raising it from a merely empirical into a 'poetical' process. The story ends with his departure from his native Frankfurt for Weimar at the age of twenty-six, which was certainly the turning-point of his life viewed historically, or from outside, since it was as counsellor for half a century to the ducal regime there that Goethe became a truly celebrated German citizen. But his leaving Frankfurt was a turning-point of a more intimate kind also, since it marks for Goethe the conclusion of his inner development and the start of what he called his 'conflict with the world'. All that we have for the many years of his activity after 1775 are his 'Annals', a rather sparse, intermittent set of diary entries which comment on the 'results' of his conflict with the world. *Poetry and Truth* is the writer's farewell to the romantic but unsociable age of introversion.

Writing in old age of himself when young, Goethe occupies an 'ironic' vantage-point from which he can oversee both past and present, both self and setting, without appearing to favour the claims of either. In *Poetry and Truth* young Goethe impinges on the world and the world impinges on young Goethe, all in the lofty mind's eye of the sage of Weimar. Goethean irony is the manifestation of that 'elevation of mind' which he had once found to admire in Goldsmith's novel, *The Vicar of Wakefield*.[5] This was a book he first

---

[5] Stendhal too knew this novel, though he, unlike Goethe seemingly, saw through its sentimentality. One of his joke proposals for the title-page of his autobiography would have described the *Vie de Henry Brulard* as a 'Roman imité du *Vicaire du Wakefield*', this wildly

met with when it was read out loud to him by Herder, the philosopher, on an occasion recorded in some detail by the autobiographer. Herder's method of reading, according to Goethe, was strikingly flat and undramatic, and thus out of tune with the sentimentalism of the text. But Goethe had responded feelingly to Goldsmith's story all the same; 'I felt like a man, like a young man; everything was living, true, and present before me'(I. 370). This naive response is not at all to the serious Herder's taste; he has no time for those who respond to artifice as though to a phenomenon of Nature, and as a corrective draws his hearers' attention to the way in which the fiction is constructed. Herder's is the role – my own role here, needless to say – of the arid theorist: 'It will be seen from this that he regarded the work merely as a production of art, and required the same of us, who were yet wandering in that state where it is very allowable to let works of art affect us like productions of nature.' That is a state which Goethe has long ago transcended, but not in order to ally himself with Herder, who has shown himself in this small episode too much the philosopher and too little the man of feeling. Goethe himself will be the combination of the two, able to appreciate what Nature, or reality, supplies to Art – its subject-matter – and what Art supplies in return, which is form. Even at the time of the reading from Goldsmith, he has had an inkling of this transcendent role, since he has refused to be 'perplexed by Herder's invectives' and has continued to admire Goldsmith's novel without knowing why. Now he does know why: it had left him with the impression of being 'in harmony with that ironical tone of mind which elevates itself above every object, above fortune and misfortune, good and evil, death and life, and thus attains to the possession of a truly poetical world'(I. 371). This 'truly poetical' world is that which transcends the frequently opposed worlds of Nature and of Art, and the world to which *Poetry and Truth* is meant for our own introduction, for in this ironic narrative of his early life Goethe will pay his dues to both Nature and Art by enacting the metamorphosis of the one into the other.

Irony transforms and in doing so moderates the emotions on which it alights; the old, autobiographical Goethe will not be moved by the strong feelings, whether pleasurable or painful, of the young Goethe,

unsuitable English model having been chosen as a decoy for 'MM. de la Police', whom Stendhal imagined might not take kindly to his cynically free-thinking and anti-monarchist account of his life.

that figure whom he occasionally refers to in a patronizing departure from the first person as 'the Boy' or 'the Youth'. As a work of literary art, *Poetry and Truth* finds its own reflection in the works of literary art that Goethe has written in these early years: most conspicuously, in *The Sorrows of Young Werther*. This he had written at a time of acute unhappiness. For several years past, he had been toying with what he calls the 'whim' of suicide, and had gone so far as to experiment by sticking the point of 'a handsome, well-polished dagger' into the skin over his heart when lying in bed. But 'handsome, well-polished' daggers are clearly collectors' pieces, rather than the tool of the impulsive suicide; the sorrowing young Goethe had 'laughed myself out of the notion'. But suicide was now a theme suitable for elevation into 'poetry', and all that was lacking for its poeticization was 'an event, a fable' that might cause his still disturbed thoughts on the subject to cohere; that is, the outside world must connive at his project. The precipitating event occurred: the suicide of Karl Wilhelm Jerusalem, a young littérateur whom Goethe knew and who had killed himself out of a hopeless love for a married woman. The love he felt for a girl engaged to be married to someone else had been the reason for Goethe's own suicidal feelings; Jerusalem was an ideal surrogate, having gone through with the intention Goethe himself had ended by mocking. He could now write *Werther* with 'all that warmth which leaves no distinction between the poetical and the actual'(I. 511). The book was finished in four weeks, and Goethe gave it to his friends to read: 'upon whom it produced an effect so much the greater, as, contrary to my usual custom, I had told no one of it, nor discovered my design beforehand'. These friends have reacted to it in just the same artless, unHerderian way as he had reacted to *The Vicar of Wakefield*:

Yet here again it was the subject-matter which really produced the effect, and in this respect they were in a frame of mind precisely the reverse of my own; for by this composition, more than by any other, I had freed myself from that stormy element, upon which, through my own fault and that of others, through a mode of life both accidental and chosen, through design and thoughtless precipitation, through obstinacy and pliability, I had been driven about in the most violent manner. I felt, as if after a general confession, once more happy and free, and justified in beginning a new life. (I. 511)

Here is irony indeed: Goethe has turned reality into Poetry and his readers have turned Poetry back into reality; he has purged himself of violent emotions by instilling them vicariously in others, which is to give back transformed to the outside world what the outside world has given to him, in a perfectly Goethean act of exchange.

Wertherian suicide represents for the regenerate Goethe a disastrous concentration of the self within the self, and as such it makes a strong theme for 'poetry', since the writing and publication of a work of art reverses that concentration and restores the communion of the self with others. The commerce between reality and Poetry is thus one version of that regular process of contraction and dilation, or of systole and diastole, of which Goethe finds evidence everywhere in nature and which he takes to be characteristic of the cosmos and of whatever supernatural Power has fixed its laws. This double movement may be successive but it is also contradictory. As a dualism of attraction and repulsion Goethe observes it in human beings, in Herder for one, who can be both charming and cantankerous, drawing others to him at one moment and pushing them roughly away at another, in order to withdraw into himself. But whatever the threatening influences may be which impel us to contract in this way, a contraction of the self demands or entails an eventual expansion, or re-opening to the world.

Werther is that: the writing of it is for Goethe an expulsion or, as one might in these post-Freudian times want to say, a therapeutic excretion of emotional matter the retention of which would perpetuate a state of social maladjustment. The troublesome matter of depression and suicide is evacuated into *Werther* just as he says in the *Annals* that he later evacuated the matter of the French Revolution, associated in his mind with 'the most horrible apparitions', by transforming 'the whole event' into an opera (*The Grand Kophta*, see the *Annals* entry for 1789). Artistic tellings or transformations of his psychic storms are the sedative of which the emotionally volatile young Goethe is much in need. But they are more than merely sedative, they are also cognitive, because by externalizing in the form of literature what has been most affecting him he increases his understanding of the world around him. This is the 'tendency' that has marked his life:

[...] namely the tendency to turn into an image, a poem, everything that delighted or troubled me, or otherwise occupied me, and to come to some certain understanding with myself upon it, that I might both rectify my conceptions of external things, and set my mind at rest about them. The faculty of doing this was necessary to no one more than to me, for my natural disposition whirled me constantly from one extreme to the other. All, therefore, that has been confessed by me, consists of fragments of a great confession, and this little book is an attempt which I have ventured on to render it complete (1. 240).

Goethe's final remark here concerning the function of *Poetry and Truth* (which is not everyone's idea of a *little* book) carries us back to the preface, in which he explains that he has undertaken it in answer to a request from a friend, who had thought that the various contents of the newly published collected edition of his poetry were 'without connexion' among themselves and hardly seemed 'to emanate from one and the same writer'. Their author's commentary was needed to explain how the different poems had come to be written and how they fitted together. Here we meet again with the Nietzschean, or Cellinian, mode of autobiography, as a literary act inspired by the desire phantasmally to reassemble the scattered products of a lifetime (Goethe, interestingly, was the first German translator of Cellini's *Life*). In Goethe's own case, it would be more appropriate to say that autobiography's function is to concentrate by narrative means a notably expansive oeuvre: to be the prose systole of his poetic diastole.

In the event, *Poetry and Truth* performs this function only for the first few years of Goethe's writing life. It does so by re-establishing the chronology of his early writings, of which there had been no indication in the collected edition, as well as the personal and historical circumstances of which these poetical works had been the topical transformation. Goethe is giving us the inside story, but doing so in accordance with his own contextual principles, whereby what is happening inside him at any point reflects what is or has been happening around him, while his lengthy digressions into external events reflect his growing capacity to assimilate them for his private literary purposes. Read as a Bildungsroman, *Poetry and Truth* narrates the moral education of a youth for whom the absorptive and the reactive roles are to be brought systematically into balance. Goethe the autobiographer will occupy the equivalent of that favourite space of the boy Goethe in Frankfurt, the 'birdcage' or 'frame' on the ground floor of the family home, which communicated directly with the street and acted as a sort of turnstile between the domestic and public spheres.

Public events may quite take over Goethe's narrative, as in the many pages which he gives to a description of the festivities in

Frankfurt at the time of the election and coronation there of the German emperor, Joseph II, as the 'King of Rome'. This oppressively full reportage seems to exemplify the maxim which he says he adopted when writing of his travels: 'to *deny* myself as much as possible, leaving the object to imprint itself as purely and integrally as could be on my mind'(*Annals*, entry for 1789). At the time of the coronation Goethe was fifteen: do we believe that he was as precociously capable of abandoning himself to these ceremonial events as their description in *Poetry and Truth* suggests that he was? Hardly. But there is more to his exhaustive retailing of them than an exercise in self-denying objectivity. The boy has been commissioned by his father to keep a diary of what he sees, and he does so – the possible implication is that Goethe is now drawing on that ancient document, supposing it has survived. But it is not out of obedience to his father that he attends so dutifully to these historic scenes, but in order to be able to report on them to the girl with whom he is concurrently infatuated. With Gretchen he can adopt the imposing and seductive role of narrator, not only describing the events but also explaining them, by reaching beyond externals to 'the inner course of things'.

This particular episode of *Poetry and Truth* ends badly for Goethe, because it coincides with his own disgrace. He has been associating with a group of young people from the lower orders in the city who are suddenly now exposed as disreputable if not actually criminal. Gretchen is among them, and she, he learns, has looked on him as no more than a child. Goethe in his misery contracts into a 'passionate solitude', a state of being dramatically out of keeping with the carnival togetherness he has been witnessing in the streets. The cure for this unhealthy condition is a narrative one. The boy confesses first his own involvement with this dubious group of friends, he then 'refreshes' himself 'by the relation and repetition of the minutest circumstances of my past happiness', and finally the tutor appointed to look after him, 'like a sensible man, saw it would be better to make me acquainted with the issue of the story, and that too in its details and particulars, so that I might be clear as to the whole, and that with earnestness and zeal, I might be persuaded of the necessity of composing myself, throwing the past behind me, and beginning a new life'(I. 181–2).

Goethe's success as the interpreter of the coronation stands, however. By being able to deduce its implicit rationale, he has shown

himself singularly gifted at penetrating beyond externals to the
'essence' of the event. The event itself is linear, or narrative, being
extended in time and requiring that each stage follow in order from
the previous ones, so fulfilling the form of the ritual. It is peculiarly
suited to Goethe's demonstration, for displaying an Aristotelian
'entelechy', or the progressive disclosure to the world of a hidden
principle of organization. The parallel between the coronation of the
emperor and the sequence of his own early life is obvious: the
adolescent reporter is in training for the role of objective adult
autobiographer. In his success in reaching beyond the merely visible
phenomena of the world to their inner explanandum Goethe provides
himself with an autobiographical foil in the figure of Lavater, the
Swiss pastor and pioneer physiognomist, who makes a number of
appearances in *Poetry and Truth*, but whose pretensions at the
correlation of people's psychic and moral attributes with their facial
appearance Goethe dismisses, Lavater being gifted with intuition
only, not with the overarching 'idea' which could raise his intuitions
into a scientific system. Lavater is a failed version of Goethe himself,
working along the right lines in seeking to establish organic
connections between the moral world and the world of sense, but he
was defeated, says Goethe, because he was 'Utterly unable to take a
comprehensive and methodical view'. He could not represent
outwardly, in the form of an objective theory, the undoubted 'unity
of his inner being' (II. 140).

In Goethe himself inner and outer beings are ideally in tune, and
together make a whole which is in tune with the cosmos. As the
cosmic heart pulses, systole followed by diastole, so too does his. In an
early promise of this harmonious arrangement, he begins *Poetry and
Truth* by telling us how the planets stood at the moment of his birth.
He was born precisely at noon, 'as the clock struck twelve', which is
excellent timing for the coming into existence of so Apollonian a
figure (and the hour too, at which the darkling Werther, with a
suggestive symmetry, shoots himself). Goethe's horoscope was favourable, unlike that of poor Cardano, who almost became a 'monster'
because of the discordant arrangement of the planets at his moment
of birth. According to Karl Weintraub, Goethe had read Cardano's
autobiography more than once and borrowed the astrological motif
from it; but uses it himself symbolically, 'to underline his deep
conviction that an individual fate is jointed into the juncture of a

moving world'.[6] Autobiographers may be suspected of fixing their horoscopes to suit themselves, by disposing the planets post hoc to accord with what they are about to tell us of their life's fortunes and their inner nature. There is a playful anthropomorphism to Goethe's description of the astral scene – e.g., 'Jupiter and Venus looked on him [the sun] with a friendly eye, and Mercury not adversely; while Saturn and Mars kept themselves indifferent' – but we should surely take this astrological exordium to his life-story seriously, as conscripting into his scheme those metaphysical powers which he is about to embody.

For as an autobiographical subject, the young Goethe is remarkable for his passivity. He is 'the planless youth', and as such the immature, congenial but now distant harbinger of the amused autobiographer, who, like Alfieri, has in coming to manhood acquired the power of decision and ceased from being the merely driven youth. Goethe has achieved independence, as autobiographers must, but the urge to independence is inscribed in each one of us by Nature. The life-process of which this 'planless youth' is the representative is one of a natural 'unfolding', in which latent capacities are either brought to fruition or else left to wither, depending on how hospitable or otherwise the world proves to them. The dynamic of the life which is recounted in *Poetry and Truth* asks that the apparently purposive Will of which any human individual is an expression do battle with circumstances which are themselves the expression of Chance, or that contradictory, 'demonic' aspect of life on whose reality Goethe insists. This autobiographer would have us see him in youth as the privileged site of a metaphysical drama, the true author of which is the contented ironist, happily assigning responsibility for the vicissitudes of his story to forces too mighty to be questioned.

Stendhal

Before becoming a man of his time, Goethe has been a boy of his time, and made to take drawing lessons: with typical typicalness he has been introduced by his father to the plastic arts 'according to the

---

[6] Karl J. Weintraub, *The Value of the Individual: Self and Circumstance in Autobiography* (Chicago and London, 1982), p. 352. For Weintraub, as for another of the more penetrating writers on autobiography, Roy Pascal, Goethe is a paragon of the genre, for the balance he strikes between self and non-self in the narration of his early life. Pascal's title, *Design and Truth in Autobiography* (London, 1960), is even more obviously modelled on Goethe's title than is Weintraub's subtitle.

principles of a modern theory of education'. Not until he was forty years old and in Rome, he told Eckermann (entry for 10 April 1829), did he realize that he had no real talent for drawing, on the interesting ground that 'If I drew anything, I had not a sufficient inclination for the corporeal. I felt a certain fear lest objects press too much upon me.' His idea of objects was at risk seemingly from the sight of them, and the hand which should have mediated between conception and perception was not sufficiently skilled for its task. Unlike in writing, in drawing Goethe was not master enough of his means to represent things in a desirable equipoise between the real and the ideal.

But he has grown up in his own words as 'a creature of the eye', fulfilling Roland Barthes' specification of the artistic realist, as someone who is constantly holding up a picture-frame to the world. Goethe has seen virtual works of art all around him and has set about fixing them on paper, by drawing awkwardly from nature. The drawings he has made may not be good as art but they have value of a topical kind: they can bring back to him what had been in his mind when he did them: 'Thus plants and flowers of the commonest kind may form a charming diary for us, because nothing that calls back the remembrance of a happy moment can be insignificant; and even now it would be hard for me to destroy as worthless many things of the kind that have remained to me from different epochs, because they transport me immediately to those times which I remember with melancholy indeed, but not unwillingly'(1. 188). The young Goethe's drawings thus form an objective album, an archive whose particulate images the autobiographer can use to mobilize and punctuate his memory – and in so doing, allow the eye to steer the brain in the impulsion of the writing hand.

Goethe might also have used these images in an exactly contrary way: to arrest the movement of a brain too mercurial to consent easily to any methodical narration of the past. He might have used them, that is, like Stendhal, my third objectivist in this chapter, whose principal volume of autobiography, *The Life of Henry Brulard*, is remarkable – unique, to my knowledge – among autobiographies for containing a great many maps and diagrams drawn by the autobiographer's own hand. There are 175 of these in total, scattered singly or in clumps through the text, showing for the most part rooms and streets in Grenoble or in Paris, the two urban settings with which Stendhal is mainly concerned. They are carelessly drawn but freely and often engagingly captioned, and they date not from the past but the present, having been made by Stendhal as he wrote. The first editors of *Henry Brulard* left some or all of them out, as being either redundant or demeaning (as well as expensive to reproduce). But they were very wrong to do so; these scrawled illustrations have much to say about the rhetorical stance of this, the most delectably offhand of all the great autobiographies.

Just like Goethe, the young Stendhal[7] has been made to take lessons in drawing by his father, as a boy in Grenoble, the bourgeois setting for his childhood his hatred for which lends a bracing malevolence to his autobiography. Drawing had then been 'ridiculously' taught according to Stendhal: all red chalk and parallel hatchings, with no concern for what mattered, line. But his lessons had been a precious escape for the repressed boy; they got him out of the house, where he was otherwise confined and tyrannized over, by a mean, caste-conscious father and a bigotedly respectable aunt. To go alone to visit his drawing teacher is briefly to run free in the streets. It is also to dissociate himself from his philistine father and associate himself with his mother, the beloved figure whose death in childbirth when he was only six years old the autobiographer takes as marking the start of his 'moral life', he having then been criticized by his aunt Séraphie for not showing sufficient grief. (Stendhal's 'moral life', of which *Henry Brulard* is to be the public record, has thus been instituted by an act either of pride or of timidity, since he has hidden the deep grief he in fact felt and passed therefore as unfeeling; the specifically autobiographical task of undoing that original concealment is one that Stendhal enters on with pleasure.) His mother had shown skill at drawing, and there were heads drawn by her to be seen in the house, as a pictorial bequest to the mourning son.

Stendhal had himself shown no skill at drawing but he has in time made a formative artistic discovery: that good drawings must be

---

[7] I shall refer to Stendhal here as Stendhal, rather than as Beyle, his real name, even though we are dealing with an autobiography, where one would expect the real name to be used. That he should have chosen to write the story of his life under a second assumed name, different from that under which he wrote his novels, is very characteristic of Stendhal's levity in respect of the protocols of authorship. The most authoritative French editor of *Henry Brulard* assumes that he took the name Brulard from a distant cousin of his maternal grandfather, in order to associate himself more strongly with this, the admired side of his family – see Stendhal, *Oeuvres Intimes*, Tome 2, edited by V. del Litto (Paris, 1982), p. 1361. Stendhal's own preferred title for the work, of *La Vie de Henry Brulard écrit par lui-même* is clearly modelled on the title given to Cellini's *Life*, the first full edition of which had been only recently published. Stendhal knew the work, admired it and cites it as an example of a memoir long delayed in the publication, as he speculates that his own may be.

good likenesses. This he has found out by comparing a mountain scene drawn by his teacher with the perceived reality; he has been 'illuminated' by the resemblance of one to the other. And here the autobiographer inserts a rudimentary sketch, indicating not only the scene in question but also the point from which it had been drawn. As a draughtsman he thus transcends, Goethe-like, both subject and object, by rising to that imaginary point of vantage from which he can illustrate the line of sight joining the two. The higher the viewpoint the more objective the view. But if Stendhal the auto-biographer climbs high at times above the terrain of his past, it is not in order to gaze complacently down on it in some Goethean spirit of reconciliation but rather to display the pettiness and abjection of contemporary bourgeois existence. He loves high places, both in themselves – his grievance against Paris when he first arrives there, is that there are no mountains to be seen – and as metaphors, as the geological counterpart of that rare elevation of mind and spirit of which he offers himself in *Henry Brulard* as an exemplar.

His sketch-maps are at once mnemonic and labour-saving. They bring objectivity and sequence to the private or 'moral' experiences to whose locations they are an index; and in their particularity they are evocative for a reader as they will have been to the writer, in fixing the precise layout of the Beyle family home or the disposition of familiar buildings and streets. Just as important, they save the writer the trouble of having to reconstruct these domestic or other settings in words. Stendhal assures us more than once in *Henry Brulard* of the 'abhorrence' he feels for physical description in prose; he was not among those early nineteenth-century French writers who admired the elaborate topographies of Sir Walter Scott. Physical description wastes time and words which can better be spent on the rapid but exact notation of his thoughts and feelings. The casual diagrams which replace it are the visual evidence of his wish not to bore us, and to spare us the extended, immobile prose periods into which less considerate writers are led – they are the equivalent in his autobiography of those strings of *etc*s to be found in his novels, where he resorts insolently to aposiopesis at the end of a sentence as if we knew without his having to demonstrate it how he meant to go on. Stendhal is an autobiographer ostentatiously concerned with socia-bility; he will not compound the unavoidable egotism of writing so much in the first person by being long-winded, and in *Henry Brulard* he gives us a convivial display of *esprit*, or that esteemed quickness of mind which had come upon him suddenly, so he says, in the winter of 1826 when he was in Paris. His 'wit' has been his ticket to social acceptance and once endowed with it he has been able to improvise conversationally and to shine in the salons.

Stendhal, then, is no Rousseau: he has not failed in company and taken to writing instead, to show himself there at his true, unrecognized worth. But the *homme d'esprit* too may appear socially as something other than he knows himself to be privately, and so it is with Stendhal, who in *Henry Brulard* uses autobiography to counter the wrong impression of him he supposes to be held in the society he has frequented. Unsurprisingly, he writes with the model of Rousseau's *Confessions* in mind, even if for Stendhal the correction of untrue suppositions about himself is a minor, not an obsessional theme. Soon after he set to work on *Henry Brulard*, he wrote to tell his publisher in Paris that he was writing 'a book which may be a great piece of stupidity; it is *My Confessions*, apart from the style, like Jean-Jacques Rousseau, only more outspoken'; and in the course of the book itself he acknowledges the *Confessions* as a 'masterpiece' of autobiographical writing while at the same time distancing himself from their over-emphatic author by his own inability ever to play the 'charlatan' – even if by doing so he might relieve the 'insipidity' of what he was writing! *Henry Brulard* may nevertheless be read in part as a corrective document in the Rousseau tradition. Stendhal's reputation in society, as crystallized by himself, is of a man both cheerful and insensitive, and very successful with women; we shall now learn differently, that he is exceedingly sensitive and, where women are concerned, timid; as a lover he has been mainly a failure but without letting on. In this, he says, he answers to the current characterization of a melancholic.

So does this scrupulous Don Juan cut himself seductively down to size. But if he has known timidity and melancholy as a lover, as a writer Stendhal knows neither; in writing he can be bold, as in the confession of his amorous fiascos. A failure confessed is a failure glorified. But there is nothing at all Rousseauesque about the style in which this autobiographer chooses to tell of himself. Where Rousseau is grave and leisurely, Stendhal will be light, practising an agile colloquialism and brashness of manner intended to lift the curse from all the 'I's and 'me's the autobiographer is forced into using. *Henry Brulard* exhibits the speed of its own composition: it was written over a period of some four months, in the winter of 1835–6 (the close on

40,000 words of the *Souvenirs d'égotisme*, which had preceded it, took Stendhal only fourteen days). Stendhal not only writes quickly but lets us know, as an autobiographical fact of some weight, just how quickly, by counting up the number of pages he has filled in a single session. In spontaneity there is truth: 'In order to try not to tell lies or to hide my faults, I have obliged myself to write these memoirs twenty pages at a sitting, like a letter'(452).[8] To be spontaneous, in writing as in living, is to be for Stendhal morally superior, and raised above the calculating careerists all around him, who gain advantage by precaution, by acting always with a view to some profitable end.

And together with this flaunted speed of writing, there goes his habit of keeping his readers close beside him in the present by recording the date and sometimes the place too where this or that passage has been written. There is no going innocently back into the past in *Henry Brulard*; we keep getting the writer's reminders that what we are reading is today's perspective on the past and as such subject to the caprices of an active mind. The method is established in the work's opening sentence: 'I was standing this morning, October 16th, 1832, by San Pietro in Montorio, on the Janiculum Hill in Rome, in magnificent sunshine. A few small white clouds, borne on a barely perceptible sirocco wind, were floating above Monte Albano' (etc. one is tempted to add, to this perfunctory piece of description).[9] Which seems very compellingly immediate and precise, with the writer having come straight from one pleasant vantage-point to another, at his Roman work-table. Yet this deictic opening is deceptive for being factually false. *Henry Brulard* was begun not in 1832 but three years later, in 1835, so that this setting of the Roman scene belongs if anywhere in the *Souvenirs d'égotisme*, though even if it had appeared there it would still not have been true because on the October day he specifies Stendhal was not in Rome but travelling in the Abruzzi. The exactitude of his incipit is a trick, but it situates the writer winningly where he wishes to be, midway between precision and insouciance.

So if Stendhal's spontaneity is real, the precision he affects is not; it is for show. He does not want to be thought of as concerned with chronology, because the accurately dated narrative is one from which

---

[8] There is no easily procured English translation of the *Souvenirs d'égotisme*; when quoting from them I shall give the page numbers of the French text in the Pléiade edition of the *Oeuvres Intimes*, and make my own translation.

[9] In the case of *Henry Brulard* itself, I shall quote from the English translation made by Jean Stewart and B. C. J. G. Knight, *The Life of Henry Brulard* (London, 1958).

the living and breathing narrator is most effectively expelled, unable to play the determining role which this autobiographer insists on playing. Against the precision with which Stendhal dates the successive moments of the manuscript's composition, we should set a conspicuous imprecision as to exactly when certain events took place: recalling the death of his maternal grandfather – a man he looks back on with rare goodwill – Stendhal is unable to date it securely to within six years, and such uncertainty pervades *Henry Brulard*, as if chronological precision were beneath him or beside the point, exactitude of moral or emotional discrimination being of far greater importance to him than fidelity to the calendar.

Stendhal gives us dates, but without himself certifying them. Why, one asks, does he bother to play the chronological game at all? Because he does not want, or pretends he does not want, to be seen as *vague*. Vagueness is for Stendhal immoral, and he couples it with hypocrisy as one of his 'two pet aversions'. This linkage might seem puzzling, were it not for the context in which it is made: he is writing of his adolescent 'passion' for mathematics, which he had prized as a subject because they left no room for either hypocrisy or vagueness. Mathematics are true and they are exact, as Stendhal the auto-biographer intends to be in the narration of his life. It is in fact by the successful study of mathematics that he has first marked himself off and then made his escape from the stultifying provincialism of Grenoble, and moved in 1799, aged sixteen, to Paris, to take up a place which his mathematical abilities had won for him at the new foundation of the Ecole Polytechnique. Mathematics have been the means to a totally desirable end, and that end once achieved, he has dropped them: he does not go to the school but into the Napoleonic army instead. Mathematics have formed an ascetic prelude to a life of risk and of pleasure.

In *Henry Brulard* he pays continued lip service to mathematical ideals – as in his sketch-maps, with their air of a geometrical demonstration – since his declared purpose in writing autobiographi-cally is to establish the stable coordinates of his character. Yet to do this is to go against the grain of the volatile life he is pleased to have led. Stendhal has lived erratically, in accordance with his reckless motto: 'I take at random whatever fate puts in my way.' But now he is into his fifties and perhaps serious in wanting to know what he might learn about himself from a sustained adventure in retro-spection; once he has turned autobiographer his motto might after all be recast to read 'I take at random whatever memory puts in my way.' He had begun the *Souvenirs d'égotisme* by asking leading questions about himself: 'Have I drawn all possible advantage for my happiness from the positions chance placed me in during the nine years I have just spent in Paris? What sort of man am I?...'; and he puts them again in *Henry Brulard*: 'What have I been? what am I?', and answers 'I should really find it very hard to say'(2). But these are not questions asked on the spur of the autobiographical moment; the writer is in fact *remembering* having asked them, at that fictitious inauguration of his task at the church of San Pietro in Montorio. He has taken them from stock, to act as the conclusive rationale of an inconclusive man.

Stendhal is at one with Alfieri in using the review of his past to graft the explanations of maturity on to the doings or events of youth. Writing of the 1780s and 90s in 1835 has recovered forgotten fragments of his past, which are not continuous but, in his own analogy, like pieces of a damaged fresco, with the bare brickwork showing between the surviving patches of colour. The analogy suggests that his memory works visually, in restoring to him as he writes images themselves inviting of his own commentary – which makes it the more reasonable to see his many diagrams in *Henry Brulard* also as functioning mnemonically. The commentary supplies what Stendhal calls 'the physiognomy and the why of events', though unlike Alfieri this playful autobiographer allows that his tardy explanations may be wrong, that the one sure truth is in the 'very clear' images of the past which he has in his head, not in the gloss he puts on them.

Stendhal follows Rousseau in protesting the ineffability of happiness, or indeed of all strong emotion. What he is able to tell of in his autobiography is the pursuit of happiness, the famous 'chasse au bonheur', not the experience of it. This has been and remains the presiding, distinctive motif of the life which he is narrating. His singularity is in the absolute simplicity of his hedonism; he has sought only pleasure, never gain nor authority. But how is he to objectify this vital pursuit without seeming to mummify it in the description? Stendhal's answer is to mock his own efforts at objectification even as he makes them, thereby investing the experiences in question with their full prestige. He does so in the alfresco recapitulation of his love-affairs. Two months before beginning his autobiography, he had, he says, been sitting above Lake Albano and has there traced a string of initials in the dust, of the first names of twelve women with whom he has had liaisons – this perishable and teasing index he reproduces, inevitably, in the text. But now, in writing and therefore on reflection, he first reduces the twelve names to those of the six women he has loved, and then reduces it again to four, so as to try to decide for which of these six he had felt the 'greatest passion'. This is precision right enough, and in an unpromising area, but Stendhal offers a reason for attempting it: 'I am trying to destroy the spell, the DAZZLING character [*le dazling* in the French] of events, by thus considering them in military fashion. This is the only way I can hope to reach the truth about a subject which I cannot discuss with anyone'(12). Unable to proceed as an autobiographer by a technique of resection, with a friendly interlocutor to put him straight, Stendhal plays the game of objectivity with himself, and with us, knowing that he need never let his narrative harden into complete certainty.

As a seeker after happiness, he distinguishes himself without trouble from the doleful setting into which he had been born and from the joyless generation of his contemporaries. He is in no doubt that his is a superior mind and sensibility unfitted to the times and to the country of which it was his misfortune to be a native. Fifty-two years old he may now be but he has not gone back for a second on the scandalous attitudes that he had first adopted in his childhood. His first – well-found – memory is of biting his grown-up cousin on the cheek when she offered it to him graciously to kiss (cf. Gibbon's first memory, which is of shouting out the name of his father's political opponents in revenge for a whipping he had been given). And if he recalls the guillotining in Grenoble under the Terror of two army officers, it is so that he can restate the '*pleasure*' (he uses the English word) that event had given him at the time, as a precocious republican and anti-clerical only too conscious that where he felt pleasure his reactionary father and aunt felt only horror. But having shocked the local conformists then, Stendhal will shock the wider community now, by defiantly endorsing in middle age the irresponsible gloating of the boy: 'I am *encore* in 1835 the man of 1794.' (This sentence I quote exactly as Stendhal wrote it: I will come back in a moment to these detours into English.)

So when occasion offers he insolently abandons all pretence at wisdom and elides the present with the past, denying that time has changed him for the better (that is, the worse), and demonstrating a real permanency of character. But if Stendhal has remained through all this time the passionate, anarchistic boy he then was, his contemporaries have not. He exploits the temporal freedom allowed him by autobiography to savage effect in rapidly summarizing the lives of many of those whom he has known in his, and their youth, in order to damn them for having capitulated to an ignoble careerism. They have put the pursuit of power and money before the Stendhalian pursuit of happiness, and how he, the impoverished but independent autobiographer, looks down on them for it. One example among many: in Grenoble as a boy his best friend had been Félix Faure, whose first name he sometimes translates ironically into English as 'Happy'. Faure, however, knows nothing any more of happiness. Instead, he has played the bourgeois game: he is now a peer and a judge, passing harsh prison sentences on republican plotters whom Stendhal thinks deserve a pension. In 1835 his judgment on his erstwhile companion is merciless: 'Selfishness and a complete lack of the least trace of generous feeling, combined with a disposition as gloomy as that of an Englishman, and the dread of going mad like his mother and sister, made up the character of this schoolfellow of mine. He is the most contemptible [*le plus plat*] of my friends and the one who has made the largest fortune'(314).

Viewed against success-stories of this degrading sort, Stendhal's own story is that of the contented outsider. Rather than fear madness, Félix Faure should have welcomed it, because madness – *la folie* – is for Stendhal an admirable, Romantic state of mind. But the French are deficient in *folie*, hence his own wish to seem, as unFrench as possible. If he suddenly changes in *Henry Brulard* from writing French to writing English (of a kind), it asserts a wilful foreignness, even if Stendhal found the English, as opposed to their – or at any rate Shakespeare's – splendid language, a sad, and sadly industrious race. His preferred association was with the lazy but also passionate south, with Spain and with Italy. 'Spanishness' is an entirely desirable quality for Stendhal, and he has inherited some of it, from his great-aunt, Elisabeth, 'a tall, lean, dried-up woman, with a handsome Italian face, and a character of extreme nobility, with the over-refinement and conscientious scruples of a Spaniard'(51). She has been the exotic source of his Don Quixotism, or that naive dreaminess which has kept him apart, and scornful of all sordidly pragmatic human activities. As for Italianness, that is everywhere in *Henry Brulard* as it is everywhere in Stendhal's oeuvre. Like a Cellini or a Gibbon, he toys with a 'family romance', imagining that the good or maternal side of his family, the Gagnons, had originated beyond the Alps and been forced to take refuge in Avignon in the seventeeth century, 'having committed some small murder in Italy'. The writing of *Henry Brulard* began and ended in Italy, and the story that it tells ends also in Italy, with the narrator's arrival in Milan with the French army in 1800. This for Stendhal was an epochal moment, for Milan was to be the city where he found the keenest happiness and the most attractive way of life; it was the ideal cure for the penances of Grenoble. So if the autobiography appears to end with a typical casualness, the author having stopped writing on the day that he received his *congé*, allowing him to return to Paris from his consular post in Civitavecchia, it ends on the highest note imaginable.

Nor, in *Henry Brulard*, does Stendhal celebrate his alienation only in space; he celebrates it in time also, by his repeated allusions to a readership far in the future, of whose tastes he can have no idea and who may or may not like or even understand what he has written, after the passage of many years. To the manuscript he attached a delightful series of testamentary notes, saying what he wanted done with it; some of his directions are serious, some are not – in one note he asks that if none of a list of four Parisian booksellers wants to publish it within five years of his death the manuscript should pass to 'the oldest bookseller living in London whose name begins with a C'. To whom then was *Henry Brulard* addressed? To himself in the first place, as all autobiography must be, and then to whatever other choice Stendhalian souls might one day respond to it. As to when that day might come, rather like in his chronological dealings with the past, Stendhal puts up dates at random, 1880, 1900, or 1935; true to his motto, he will let chance decide. In the event, *Henry Brulard* was not published for the first time until 1890, thus neatly bisecting the first two of those arbitrary dates; and the age which then discovered it felt flattered to have been selected in advance by this anachronistic writer as a fit recipient for his anachronistic life-story.

CHAPTER 8

The representative mind: Mill, Newman, Darwin

Stendhal's jubilant restatement past the age of fifty of his boyhood detestation of the class of *bien-pensants* breaks with autobiographical convention. We expect the autobiographer to extend his past life before us cumulatively, stage by stage, as he advances towards the maturity out of which he is writing, not to collapse his present middle age regressively into his adolescence as if the long interval of time between the two had failed to mature him at all. Stendhal, however, acknowledges the extraordinary cycle of historical change that has convulsed Europe since his boyhood, only to stand dismissively aside from it, its splendid promise having evaporated so far as he is concerned in disillusionment. The old clerical and monarchical order, whose violent dissolution he had looked forward to when he was young, and which first the events of the French Revolution and then those of the Napoleonic Empire seemed to have removed, has long since resumed in France, isolating the unrepentant writer as an anachronism amid the dismal ankylosis of the Restoration, in which there can be no place for someone so happily retarded as Stendhal. In *Henry Brulard*, he offers himself to the future as an impenitent throwback to the past, or else as the cynical embodiment of a youthful hope betrayed. But in either guise, he is a historically rooted product of the encounter between a thinking individual and those large and anonymous events valuable to him autobiographically for having determined the evolution of his ideas.

Whether he embraces them or not, the ideological changes that have occurred in the society around him are an invitation to the autobiographer to play the role of representative intelligence or sensibility. The chronological account of how his own ideas have evolved through time may be taken as reflecting the moral and intellectual mobility of the age, and the writer be granted the exemplary status of what *marxisant* literary critics used once to call a 'historically significant individual'. We move here into a particular form of intellectual autobiography, in which by constant cross-reference between his own moral and mental evolution and that of the time, the autobiographer appears to abdicate his singularity in order to serve as a lay-figure evocative of a contemporary group or generation. But as I have suggested in the case of Goethe, the seeming modesty of such an abdication is illusory, since by working to personify a collectivity, the writer is presuming even beyond ordinary autobiographical limits, as someone abnormally open to the intellectual influences of the time and abnormally clairvoyant and capacious in his ability to serve as their final synthesis.

Mill

John Stuart Mill loses no time in his *Autobiography* in exchanging his role of simple individual for that of topical exemplar:

> I do not for a moment imagine that any part of what I have to relate, can be interesting to the public as a narrative, or as being connected with myself. But I have thought that in an age in which education, and its improvement, are the subject of more, if not profounder study than at any former period of English history, it may be useful that there should be some record of an education which was unusual and remarkable, and which, whatever else it may have done, has proved how much more than is commonly supposed may be taught, and well taught, in those early years which, in the common modes of what is called instruction, are little better than wasted. It has also seemed to me that in an age of transition in opinions, there may be somewhat both of interest and of benefit in noting the successive phases of any mind which was always pressing forward, equally ready to learn and to unlearn from its own thoughts or from those of others. (1)[1]

John Stuart Mill the pedagogical guinea-pig, and John Stuart Mill the tirelessly progressive thinker: here are two transcendent roles for the autobiographer to fill, and both of them as the dutiful servant of the community, the notion of public benefaction being necessarily to the fore in the deontology of this arch-Utilitarian. (He has a third motive also in writing, stronger than either of the others, which I shall leave aside for the moment.) To which one might add his exemplary role qua autobiographer, in wanting to subordinate the egotistical gratifications of writing of himself to these high didactic ends. By the time that he wrote the *Autobiography*, Mill's philosophy had expanded

---

[1] The edition of the *Autobiography* from which I have quoted is that published in the World's Classics, edited by Harold Laski (London, 1969).

beyond the parched Benthamite creed it had earlier been, to find room for such non-utilitarian pleasures as the cultivation of literature, and his insistence on justifying the literary enterprise on which he was bound on utilitarian grounds points to a tension in Mill between the writer and the philosopher, or between the self-conscious individual and the outward-looking social mission for which he had been educated.

Mill's education as a boy had indeed been 'unusual and remarkable', so much so that his account of it forms the most idiosyncratic part of his life-story. He was trained for intellectual leadership not by being sent out to school, in the normal way of socialization, but by being taught privately by his philosopher father, and by ruthless and intensive methods aimed at forming his mind in the shortest time possible. The consequence was an astounding precocity, in both the extent of Mill's knowledge and his power of abstract thought.[2] James Mill had taught his son to think, and John Stuart Mill now adjudges that 'in the main his method was right, and it succeeded'. He has learnt to think, and to think for himself, as he is quick to make clear, so that even as a boy he had not invariably agreed with his father's views. The general lesson that we are asked to draw from his peculiar experience is that young minds are capable of absorbing far more than we think – or than was then thought; educational expectations and hence systems of schooling might be transformed were this lesson to be absorbed and more demanded of schoolchildren. Mill attempts to make his own remarkable case the more persuasive as an illustration by claiming that his innate intellectual gifts were 'rather below than above par', so that the credit for his precocious attainments goes all the more decisively to his father, whose methods have been able to make up for what Nature had failed to provide. The notion that a child of below average intelligence might be able to achieve what the boy Mill achieved, to the point of arguing the principles of political economy with his teacher at the age of twelve, is absurd, as Mill well knew. In proposing it, he is inviting contradiction, or an assurance from outside that his education was in fact unique and he himself uniquely apt to be its recipient. But if the singularity of what he has been

---

[2] One writer on Mill, F. A. Hayek, cites a study in which he was reckoned to be the greatest child genius of all time, though, as Hayek notes, the evidence for Mill's precocity comes from Mill and is unusually full and convincing for that reason. See F. A. Hayek, *John Stuart Mill and Harriet Taylor: Their Friendship and Subsequent Marriage* (London, 1951), p. 30.

through as a boy has made of him the intellectual leader he knows himself now to be, it has done so at a price; his education is not a self-contained part of his story, but the ambivalent prelude to all that has been right and wrong in his subsequent life.

The second representative role which Mill aspires to play in the *Autobiography* is that of a mind 'which was always pressing forward, equally ready to learn and to unlearn from its own thoughts or from those of others'. The 'successive phases' through which this ideally critical mind has passed are the index to its receptivity, or in other words its freedom, the mind that is open and discerning in respect of all current thought being alone qualified to serve as object lesson in an age of 'transition in opinions'. Not that all ages are ones of such transition, for in Mill's meta-historical scheme human societies alternate over time between ages of transition and ages of dogmatism, or between 'organic' and 'critical' periods, which in their relative fixity or inconstancy of beliefs together form the repeating pattern of a society's moral and intellectual evolution. This alternation between the 'organic' and the 'critical' – reminiscent of Goethe's 'systole and diastole' – finds a suggestive reflection in Mill's actual practice of writing, all of his books he tells us having been written by a 'system of double redaction', combining 'better than any other mode of composition, the freshness and vigour of the first conception, with the superior precision and completeness resulting from prolonged thought'(188). In writing, the autobiographer can but pass from the 'critical' to the 'organic' position, as his prized openness and mobility of mind becomes in retrospect a fixed principle of his life-story.

Mill's own philosophical evolution he shows to have been a conscious quest for completeness, by which to overcome the partiality of the narrow utilitarianism he had learnt from his father and from Jeremy Bentham, his first exposure to whose ideas he records as 'one of the turning points in my mental history'. Their impact on him was that of a 'religion': he had adopted uncritically the Benthamite principle that the ethical good is what promotes 'the greatest happiness of the greatest number', or the philosophy known as the 'felicific calculus'. All human actions are to be judged not by their private motives but by their public consequences, according to the contribution they make to the common good. The young Mill has become a zealous Utilitarian and would-be reformer of society, convinced that social ills of all kinds must yield to the rational legislation argued for by public-spirited activists such as himself. Over the course of his life, however, his philosophy has modulated into one of Individualism, and the schematic benevolence of his utilitarian years into something close to misanthropy – not that Mill himself comes even close to calling it by such a pejorative name.

He has begun to grow out of his sectarianism, precociously as ever, at the age of eighteen: 'I left off designating myself and others as Utilitarians, and by the pronoun "we" or any other collective designation, I ceased to *afficher* sectarianism. My real inward sectarianism I did not get rid of till later, and much more gradually'(96). The philosophy which Mill now holds, as an autobiographer, is one which insists on a strict separation of the inward from the public aspects of life, and if he is, politically, what he calls a Socialist, he is also a libertarian Individualist, believing that happiness is to be found closer to home, in the cultivation of the self, free from coercion or interference from others. And with that cultivation of the self, there goes in the *Autobiography* a repeated disgust with the 'low moral tone' of English life, which Mill compares unfavourably with the 'free and genial' atmosphere of France. He has ended in elitism and as yet one more autobiographer bent on signalling his spiritual alienation from the society into which he had been born.

But the *Autobiography* is also a strangely meticulous record of the contribution which Mill would have it that other minds have made to the formation of his own. His third, and according to him the most important, motive in writing it has been 'a desire to make acknowledgment of the debts which my intellectual and moral development owes to other persons; some of them of recognized eminence, others less known than they deserve to be, and the one to whom most of all is due, one whom the world had no opportunity of knowing'(1–2). In the event, Mill goes well beyond simple acknowledgment in exalting the remarkable capacities for original thought and sound philosophy first of his father and then of Harriet Taylor, his close friend during the lifetime of her husband and subsequently his own wife, 'the one to whom most of all is due' and whose moral and intellectual sway over himself he celebrates so fulsomely as to make one wonder whether his deeper and unconscious wish is not rather to damn her with excessive praise.[3] If there is an

[3] The editors of the magnificent University of Toronto edition of the *Autobiography* print a table showing the number of pages it devotes to Mill's acknowledgment of his

element of revelation in the *Autobiography*, it is this: John Stuart Mill, the distinguished philosopher of society, is letting us know what we did not know before and could not have known otherwise, that far from being his own his ideas are not to be distinguished from those of Harriet Taylor, who had published nothing under her own name. As in the case of his father, Mill ascribes to her a part so astoundingly large in his own achievement as to seem to be bent on self-abasement rather than the acknowledgment of intellectual debts.

In behaving as he does, Mill might be thought to disprove the thesis I have been advancing that autobiographers write in order to proclaim not their indebtedness to others for their life's achievement but their own ascendancy, or in extreme cases their intellectual autogeny, à la Descartes. How is this to be reconciled with Mill's ostentatious concern to come before us as intellectual debtor? Simply enough, when one reflects that publicly to acknowledge one's debts is also to be free of them; and when an acclaimed thinker and public figure such as Mill acknowledges all that he has got from others with so large a show of scruple he will be seen to be acting graciously, in bestowing his commendations from the stronghold of his own intellectual pre-eminence. Graciously or, in the sceptical perspective of the theorist, questionably, since Mill goes so wantonly far in trying to distribute that pre-eminence among others, rather than keeping it for himself.

The most direct claim to originality which he makes on his own behalf in the *Autobiography* is as an intellectual mediator. He has always had 'a humble opinion' of his powers 'as an original thinker' – 'except in abstract science' he at once goes on, which is no mean qualification, given what he knew himself to have achieved in logic, economics and political science – 'but thought myself much superior to most of my contemporaries in willingness and ability to learn from everybody; as I found hardly any one who made such a point of examining what was said in defence of all opinions, however new or however old, in the conviction that even if they were errors there might be a substratum of truth underneath them, and that in any case the discovery of what it was that made them plausible, would be

'debts'. Eighteen of his moral or intellectual creditors are named, and the space allowed for acknowledgments varies from nineteen and a half pages in the case of his father, to fourteen pages in that of Harriet Taylor, to half a page only for lesser lights – though it has to be said that, especially in the passages concerning his father, Mill's praise is tempered or even contradicted by his qualifications. See John Stuart Mill, *Autobiography and Literary Essays*, edited by John M. Robson and Jack Stillinger (Toronto and London, 1981), p. xvii.

a benefit to truth'(205). At first sight this again seems a modest position to take, of someone able to find compensation for being unoriginal himself in his peculiar ability to grasp the originality in the thought of others and to play a valuable role intellectually in interpreting it lucidly to the community at large. But Mill is in fact setting himself up as more than a self-effacing interpreter of alien ideas: the gift that he has goes beyond the explication of those ideas to their evaluation; he aspires far higher, to be the arbiter of their truth. It is he who will decide what is true and therefore worth preserving from among the intellectual productions of the time, and what is false and should therefore be dismissed. This is the proudly transcendental role I alluded to before, with Mill's as the judicial intelligence in which the thought of the age is first concentrated and then sifted, according to its philosophical credentials.

The claim of unoriginality is made in the context of a characteristic passage concerning the influence which Harriet Taylor has had on the evolution of his ideas. Mill has been fulfilling his lesser role as mediator in examining the ideas of thinkers as different from himself in their metaphysical and theistic presuppositions as Coleridge, Carlyle and the Germans. Their ideas are not merely different from his but opposed to his, they are the philosophical opposition. But Mill believes there may be truth mixed up with so much patent error and that he may be able to extract that truth and make it palatable to the empiricists and rationalists, or to his own 'side in philosophy'. Such is his habitual, diplomatic way: as midwife to the truth he can show that his philosophical adversaries are not altogether worthless. But with the advent of Harriet Taylor this discriminatory role is no longer required of him: '[...] when I came into close intellectual communion with a person of the most eminent faculties, whose genius, as it grew and unfolded itself in thought, continually struck out truths far in advance of me, but in which I could not, as I had done in those others, detect any mixture of error, the greatest part of my mental growth consisted in the assimilation of those truths'(206). Harriet Taylor's liberally provided and unarguable 'truths' must be fitted into the existing scheme of Mill's own thought; her role autobiographically is thus that of *supplement*, providing in both the moral and the intellectual spheres what Mill perceives himself as having hitherto lacked.

The story that is told in the *Autobiography* is one of completion. It begins with the dangerously partial education inflicted on Mill by his father. James Mill had trained his son's mind and neglected his emotions. John Stuart Mill distinguishes himself from among his siblings in being the one child of the family who has felt no love for the father, only loyalty and more often fear, an emotion which Mill does his best to turn now to good account by protesting its usefulness pedagogically, on the grounds that indulgent teachers are less effective than ones who are feared. Notoriously, there is no mention in the *Autobiography* of Mill's mother, beyond the ambiguous remark that James Mill's marriage had been among the 'disadvantages' of his life. Mill's own life as he recounts it has been starved of femininity, of any inclination to tenderness or cultivation of his feelings. The effect of his narrative is to create a vacancy in himself, which must wait for the auspicious addition to his person of Harriet Taylor if it is to be filled.

Before that can happen, however, Mill has a 'crisis' to endure, an ambiguous moment in early manhood during which his programmed intellectual advance is at once arrested and enlarged: the chapter in which it is described is headed 'A crisis in my mental history. One stage onward', to show, in true autobiographical fashion, that the bad moments of a life contribute equally with the good towards its upward movement. At the age of twenty Mill has suffered a severe depression – the first of a series which punctuated his adult life, but asked to do duty for all of them in the *Autobiography*, as introducing the theme of disequilibrium into the story. Mill is in depression, unable to help himself and without anyone he can look to for help outside himself. 'My father, to whom it would have been natural to have recourse in any practical difficulties, was the last person to whom, in such a case as this, I looked for help' (114–15). He was 'the last person' because the breakdown is the unintended consequence of his father's plan of education and his son could see 'no use in giving him the pain of thinking that his plans had failed, when the failure was probably irremediable'. To spare his father pain at a moment when he was suffering acutely himself is self-sacrificial in a very Millian way.

In depression he has endured isolation (not a word is said about his mother, as a possible source of comfort or advice) and an intensified self-consciousness. Mill has attributed the crisis to the hypertrophy within him of his powers of analysis, which had become over-developed from the abstract bias given to his education by his father. He had been brought up with a life's-aim, of being a 'reformer of the world', or of furthering and actually implementing the radical political, social and ethical ideas inherited from his undeservedly obscure and impotent father, but with the fall into depression he was no longer able to feel that such an aim was worth realizing, or that its realization would bring happiness to himself. That is, he has been made aware how very personal an aim it had been, as the potential source of his own happiness rather than benefitting the world as a whole. Such a loss of affect is an ordinary enough symptom of depression, but in Mill's case it has called dangerously into question the philosophy in which he had been raised. His father's doctrine so far as moral education was concerned had been one of associationism, whose object was to associate pleasurable or painful emotions with particular thoughts or actions, according to whether these were perceived as good or bad. But finding himself suddenly in a state of apathy, Mill is able to grasp the artificiality or arbitrariness of the associations he had been taught to accept between the beneficial and the pleasurable, which may be successfully inculcated in the young but can never be shown to be *natural* associations and hence universal or indisputable. They are liable, that is, to dissolution by analysis.

Thus in his moment of mental crisis, one element in Mill's education has served to undermine, or to deconstruct another: the analytical Mill has triumphed over the associationist Mill. The analytical Mill is of course the author of the *Autobiography*, who provides us with a very logical account of his depression and of its aetiology. He is careful, however, to as it were backdate this analysis, by two or three parenthetical insertions in the past tense which imply that the explanation we are reading is one which occurred to him at the time, not one for which he has had to wait for the insights of middle age before writing. And by setting it back in the past, Mill raises doubts as to whether or not he still accepts that his own explanation is the right one. But then a prime effect of his mental crisis has been to set limits on the value of his analytical gifts, which he will never repudiate but which from now on are to be balanced by 'the cultivation of the feelings'. The masculine, analytical element associated with his father is now looking to be supplemented by the feminine or emotional element whose traditional representative, the mother, has been altogether excluded.

Convinced in his self-consciousness that his crisis is a peculiar and therefore intractable one, induced by the 'idiosyncrasies' of his education, Mill has thought of suicide. After some six months of unhappiness, however, 'a small ray of light broke in upon my gloom'. He has been reading – 'accidentally', as he oddly puts it, almost as if this immovable secularist were inviting an angelic, *tolle lege* interpretation of the episode – the 'Memoirs' of the eighteenth-century French writer Marmontel and has been moved to tears by a sentimental passage in that work where the boy Marmontel promises to work to be the protector of his hard-pressed family. The family is hard-pressed because the father has just died, and one does not have to read Mill's *Autobiography* in too zealously oedipal a spirit to think it remarkable that he should find the beginnings of a cure for his stubborn depression in the story of a boy who has been liberated into a life of achievement by the death of his father.[4]

For the repressed young Mill, such reading is extra-curricular, an amusement, not a duty; it is a promising point of entry to the complete, balanced self that he will start to become, by the incorporation of those human qualities whose development had been denied him. This healing departure from routine has in fact been foreshadowed in the account of his education, where Mill writes of the 'voluntary exercise' to which he had been 'much addicted' as a young boy, of 'writing histories', a narrative relaxation practised on extraordinarily serious subjects, such as the History of Roman Government, and encouraged by his father as 'a useful amusement'. But if his father has encouraged this writing he has not asked to see it, with the result that it has represented for the boy an unaccustomed release: 'so that I did not feel in writing it I was accountable to any one, nor had the chilling sensation of being under a critical eye'(12). This childhood escape from supervision into the recreation of story-telling comes to proper fruition only once Mill's crisis is past, and the need is there to expand the sources of his pleasure as well as his notions of utility.

Ironically, if he has enjoyed writing histories as a boy, he has not at all enjoyed writing poetry, which he has done not from choice but out of compulsion, his father having forced him to it, inevitably, as a useful talent, since verse can be more forcible and expressive than prose and since 'people in general attached more value to verse than it deserved'. This is an irony because later on Mill has come to look

---

[4] An earlier reader of Marmontel's *Mémoires*, Stendhal, had derived an exactly opposite lesson from them to Mill, to wit that he would do well, passionate young man that he was, to cultivate some of Marmontel's *lack* of feeling. See his Journal entry for 7 *frimaire an XIII* (28 November 1804).

on poetry as a very necessary part of his own culture, thus going against the scornful condescension displayed towards it by his father and the dismissive attitude of Bentham, quoted by Mill as having declared that 'all poetry is misrepresentation'. He has found on the contrary that he needs poetry; it was the metaphysician Coleridge, in his 'Ode on Dejection', who had for example expressed the most truly the distress he had himself endured in his mental crisis – and in doing so had demonstrated the commonness of that experience, in contradiction of Mill's despairing belief that it was both peculiar to himself and irremediable. Having previously opposed the poetical to the logical, he has reformed and begun on that 'internal culture of the individual' which was in no way a repudiation of the analytical mode of thought in which he was so adept but rather its corrective complement, by whose development he might aspire to transcend the sharp division he had himself instituted, between the logical and the humane, and so represent in fullness, as had Harriet Taylor in her lifetime, the finest possibilities of humankind. As an autobiographical subject, John Stuart Mill offers himself as the ideal representative of a generation, the voice no longer of a prejudiced class or of a partisan philosophy, but of the truth. In the *Autobiography* at least he has lived up to his father's plans for him.

Newman

When he comes in the *Autobiography* to record the writing of his foremost philosophical book, the *System of Logic*, Mill presents it as an oppositional work, directed against the popular but pernicious 'German or a priori view of human knowledge'. He had produced 'what was much wanted, a textbook of the opposite doctrine – that which derives all knowledge from experience, and all moral and intellectual qualities principally from the direction given to the associations'(190). In this staunch empiricism he was defending a genetic or 'narrative' view of human knowledge, since by Mill's lights there can be no knowing without a having got to know, or a communicable story of our cognitive transactions with the world around us. A Millian epistemology has no place for non-narratable processes such as 'intuition', by which we come to knowledge without public accountability, since what we know intuitively we are not prepared to argue over nor further to explain. Kantian, or a priori philosophies were distasteful to Mill for encouraging people to leave unexamined the origins and history of the 'inveterate' beliefs which they hold and of 'every intense feeling' which they feel: they are the support of 'enthusiasm' and prejudice, and the enemy of progressivism. The inveterate and the intense are alike contemptible categories for Mill, as both philosopher and autobiographer, because the beliefs and feelings that might be so described remain unregulated by reason and the task of the Millian autobiographer is to rationalize the past history and present state of his mind without remainder.[5]

Mill's is the history of a mind confident in its own excellence and in its authority to give a lead and to arbitrate in an age of wide ideological change, which for weaker minds must be disorienting. In the *Autobiography* Mill is writing as individual and also as individualist, and by overlaying the singular role of autobiographer with the respectable, corporate role of philosopher, he can avoid the stigma of being thought simply egotistical for having volunteered the story of his life. He is the lay version of my second example in this chapter of an autobiographer writing as the overt representative of a philosophy or creed, John Henry Newman. Newman's *Apologia pro Vita Sua* consists in its narrative part of what he entitles the 'History of my Religious Opinions'. He wrote the *Apologia* as a religious convert, having left the Church of England into which he had been baptized for the Church of Rome nineteen years earlier, so that, like Augustine, the story he tells is of a 'turn', with the form of a foregone conclusion, its known, indeed notorious, end in his conversion being the public state of affairs a private justification of which he feels called on to give. As with the pattern of deferment in the *Confessions* therefore, so in the *Apologia* Newman's formal entry into the Catholic Church is preserved for a denouement, to be led up to with the utmost deliberation, not for the triumphalist or missionary reasons of an Augustine, but for forensic reasons, Newman having been induced

---

[5] In subtle ways, Mill establishes a superiority over Harriet Taylor even in the act of eulogizing her. Having just written that he received far more from her intellectually than he could hope to give, he then comments that, as someone 'who had at first reached her opinions by the moral intuition of a character of strong feeling, there was doubtless help as well as encouragement to be derived from one who had arrived at many of the same results by study and reasoning'(159–60). Mill's role of reasoner, and of a reasoner moreover who has *already* formed many of the same opinions as she holds, gives him a double precedence over Harriet, and if one applies to her the severe things he says subsequently about the pernicious effects in private and public life of the reliance on intuition, his portrayal of her becomes decidedly ambivalent. What I wish to stress here, however, is Mill's role as the genetically minded one of the two, who can only think his way, and never jump to a conclusion.

into autobiography by the publication against him of what he took to be a slander. Like Rousseau, only with genuine cause, he had a true story to publish by which to expunge a false one.

The *Apologia* was written as an episode in a polemical exchange between Newman and Charles Kingsley, author, Anglican clergyman and bitter anti-Catholic. Early in 1864, Kingsley published a book review in which he condemned in passing the historical role of the Pope and of the Catholic Church, finding them to be authoritarian, arbitrary and morally compromised by their this-worldly ambitions. He also invoked the name of that Church's best-known and most influential English adherent, the apostate Newman. Kingsley complained that the Catholic clergy had never regarded Truth as a virtue 'for its own sake' and that 'Father Newman informs us that it need not, and on the whole ought not to be.'[6] That is, Roman Catholics, unlike Kingsley's fellow Anglicans, justified departing from the Truth when it served their sectarian purpose to do so; the Truth was not one, and sacred. Newman read and took objection to this scurrilous misrepresentation of his own views and of the teaching of his Church. He protested to the editor of the journal in which it had appeared, exchanged letters with him and with Kingsley, and then published the offending passages together with the correspondence as a pamphlet. He at once drew from his adversary an answering pamphlet, entitled 'What, then, does Dr Newman mean?', in which Kingsley justified his earlier criticisms, and which was in turn answered very robustly and in extenso by Newman, in a series of seven weekly pamphlets that were later collected, with some alterations, to form his volume of autobiography, which appeared in the following year, under the title of *Apologia pro Vita Sua*.

The narrative substance of the *Apologia* is the four weekly instalments that together make up the 'History of my Religious Opinions', dated successively 'up to 1833', 'from 1833 to 1839', 'from 1839 to 1841', 'from 1841 to 1845', headings which bring out Newman's strong chronological intentions and scruples as an autobiographer. These four historical chapters are followed by

---

[6] The offending passage from Kingsley's review (it was of Froude's *History of England*) is given on pp. 5–6 of the Oxford edition of the *Apologia pro Vita Sua*, edited by Wilfrid Ward (London, 1913). This edition contains both the original, 1864 elements of the *Apologia* and the integrated text of 1865, together with the pamphlets by Newman and Kingsley which preceded it. My page references are to this edition.

another which is conspicuously a-chronological, having the title 'General Answer to Mr. Kingsley', or alternatively, 'Position of my Mind since 1845'. By this formal arrangement Newman sets a limit on the diachronic impulsion of the *Apologia*, whose author's religious opinions have ceased to evolve with his entry into the Catholic Church. This is an autobiography in which the story ends prematurely therefore, before the book is complete, again like Augustine's *Confessions*, Newman having stopped the clock at the culminating moment of his religious development. Since that moment had occurred nineteen years earlier, he is being provocative to his Anglican readers in implying that in this long interval his religious opinions have not needed any further revision, he having finally subscribed to the doctrinal authority of a Church whose authoritarianism was a main source of Protestant complaint against it. Newman's premature abandonment of narrative echoes that of Mill, the long final section of whose *Autobiography* is entitled 'General View of the remainder of my Life', as if this was to be understood en bloc rather than genetically, like the earlier part of his life, a shift of perspective justified by Mill on the grounds that he has 'no further mental changes to tell of, but only as I hope, a continued mental progress' (187) – as if progress were somehow to be had without change.

Newman's need for narrative in the *Apologia* is paramount, because the serious charge levelled at him by Kingsley was that he was already a Catholic in everything but name even when he was still a beneficed clergyman in the Church of England. He had concealed his true religious opinions in order to corrupt his impressionable young followers and persuade them too to become Roman Catholics. The charge is of his duplicity, so that he must defend himself by an assertion of his integrity, or unity, and establish it by narrative means. By writing the true, year-on-year history of his gradual change of mind, he can rebut the slanderous conflation of his successive doctrinal positions by Kingsley, and reveal himself in the role of scrupulous pilgrim making his way out of one ecclesiastical association and into another without ever having once misled those around him as to the state of his beliefs. Newman's story of his 'turn' will be without peripeteia, because he wants to demonstrate the *logic* of his change of mind, this having arisen 'from the working of my own mind, and the accidents around me'. He requires no angelic interventions along the road to Rome. Indeed there is little overt providentialism in the *Apologia*, save in subdued instances as when he remarks that the storm occasioned by the publication of a contentious Tract was providential in saving him 'from an impossible future'. When Vichian opportunities offer, to find, looking back, a super- natural purpose operating without his knowing it in the direction of his life, Newman does not take them. He rejects the double reading of events which providentialism requires, emphasizing, for example, that when he found himself drawing conclusions 'favourable to Rome' from principles he had preached as an Anglican, this was a difficulty for him, but that the principles had been preached 'honestly'; to suggest otherwise would be to allow that the charge of duplicity was reasonable, even if Providence might be blamed rather than Newman himself for having made him into a Catholic before his time.

Newman assimilates the history of his mind to that of institutional Christianity, whose doctrines and practice have evolved over the centuries in answer to changing circumstances. Against that of Kingsley, he has come to a historical conception of religious Truth, as something disclosed not unequivocally once and for all but gradually, in accordance with the principle of the 'Economy', or that prudential 'dispensation of the truth' which can see even the Christian revelation as requiring to be wisely timed. By the principle of the 'Economy' an evolutionary strategy is imposed on the will of God himself, who had waited many centuries before introducing the Gospel to the world 'and thereby gradually prepared men for its profitable reception'. It is this same divinely sanctioned and prudent strategy which determines Newman's own story. This eventuates in the long static section in which he gives the 'position' of his mind since his conversion, but at issue throughout it is the opposition of a static to an evolutionary understanding of Christianity. The divided communions between which Newman is in transit in the narrative part of the *Apologia* embody for him the rival claims of Apostolicity and Catholicity. The Apostolic claim of the Church of England is that it represents primitive Christianity in its uncorrupted form and is therefore doctrinally continuous with the Gospel; the Catholic claim of the Church of Rome is that whatever its doctrinal deviations from antiquity it represents the living community of Christian believers from which the Church of England had long ago seceded. The opposition is of Faith to Church. The young, Anglican Newman is very strongly of the Apostolic party, the objective of the Oxford

Movement, of which he was a prime mover, having been the restoration of the 'ancient religion', which had been secured by the Protestant Reformation but 'had well nigh faded away out of the land, through the political changes of the last 150 years'(145). The Movement stood for Faith and against an Anglican Church which it believed was collapsing into an unChristian liberalism. It was deeply reactionary in denying that Christian teaching might legitimately evolve, in departure from what was seen as its Gospel purity. To such an outlook, the principle of the 'Economy' could but have seemed a heresy.

Newman's eventual adoption of that principle must itself therefore constitute a prudential step in his religious evolution. In the *Apologia* he defends the 'Economy' against the arguments of Kingsley, for whom it comes under the immoral heading of expediency. Newman himself allows that the principle is open to abuse, and that it may 'carry men away into what becomes insincerity and cunning' – the very faults of which Kingsley had sought to convict him. The risk is there because, by analogy with the supreme Economist, God, whoever exercises it does so with a view to a desired end and may seem to be sacrificing moral scruple to temporal ambition. It is a hazardous principle for an autobiographer like Newman to admit to, seeing that the end of the narrative on which he is embarked is known both to him and to his readers, and the successive steps by which he has approached it will very likely appear directed knowingly towards that end, however much he may protest otherwise, that they were in fact taken in ignorance of it.

But the teleological principle of the 'Economy' can be subsumed under another, more general principle, which is that of the evolution of thought itself. In the course of his own developmental story Newman comes to adopt the principle of Doctrinal Development, which, he says, 'had been a favourite subject with me all along'. (At the actual moment of his secession from the Church of England he had been at work on a book on the subject, but had left it unfinished, as if his own conversion might stand for its logical conclusion.) The hope of the Oxford Movement had been to reinstate a 'primitive' form of belief, hallowed by its conformity with Christian origins, and this hope in turn had expressed the principle that, as Newman puts it, 'antiquity was the true exponent of the doctrines of Christianity and the basis of the Church of England'(127). In converting to Rome he does not of course need to abandon this desire for continuity with an original Christianity, only to adopt a different expression of it, by accepting that between those origins and the present time there lay historical changes in doctrine which could not be simply annulled, as in the utopian, a-historical programme of the Oxford Movement. Where that had looked for continuity without history, Roman Catholicism offers continuity with history, acknowledging as it does all the changes in doctrine which have intervened since Christianity began:

> I saw that the principle of development not only accounted for certain facts, but was in itself a remarkable philosophical phenomenon, giving a character to the whole course of Christian thought. It was discernible from the first years of the Catholic teaching up to the present day, and gave to that teaching a unity and individuality. It served as a sort of test, which the Anglican could not exhibit, that modern Rome was in truth ancient Antioch, Alexandria, and Constantinople, just as a mathematical curve has its own law and expression. (290–1)

This triumphant imposition of a diachronic perspective, in the smooth and plotted continuity of a geometric curve, transcends the drawn-out opposition in Newman between Faith and Church. His separation from a doctrinally corrupt Anglican Church has ended in his incorporation into a Roman church now recognized as answering to his earlier requirement of a connection with antiquity. And as with the Church so with himself, as an autobiographer: the narrative part of the *Apologia* applies the 'principle of development' very exactly to his own mental life, asserting its continuity, the legitimacy of the changes through which it has gone, and the supreme value of recording their history, as the one true because realistic way of returning to our origins.

And just as the Principle of Development has bestowed 'unity and individuality' on Catholic teaching, so the narrative act of auto-biography bestows it on the writer. Newman has been accused of duplicity; in telling his story he restores his unity, the charge of duplicity having hinged on a deceitful foreshortening of that story by his accuser, who had refused to recognize the distance separating its end from its beginning, or Newman's Catholicism from his Angli-canism. Newman has acquired the unity of a narrative subject and to that extent he is a whole. But a whole that is extended over many prose pages, as the writer follows through the logic of his mental changes, remains in danger of being received in the etiolated or dispersed form of a referent, and the rhetorical force of the *Apologia* of being weakened by its author's inability to introduce himself within it bodily, in tangible demonstration of his living and breathing oneness. Even as he writes, Newman recognizes the insufficiency of writing to represent substantively the vital process of his change of mind: 'For myself, it was not logic that carried me on; as well might one say that the quicksilver in the barometer changes the weather. It is the concrete being that reasons; pass a number of years and I find my mind in a new place; how? the whole man moves; paper logic is but the record of it'(264).[7]

The unified Newman of his autobiographical text is at best representative of, but not identical with the 'whole man', who is debarred by the nature of textual things from appearing there in person. Nevertheless, Newman exerts every rhetorical means to present himself integrally, starting with the prefatory section of the *Apologia*, entitled 'True Mode of Meeting Mr. Kingsley', where he unifies the separate accusations which have been made against him by interpreting them as 'illustrations of one and the same great imputation': that he is, in a word, a 'liar'. And having thus simplified the charge, he decides it is not to be turned away seriatim, by analysing it into its several components and answering these one by one, but combatted rather by 'a corresponding antagonistic unity'. This 'antagonistic unity' will be himself. By means of a brief exegesis of what Kingsley has written, he greatly enlarges the ground of their disagreement beyond the textual to the integrally human:

Yes, I said to myself, his very question is about my *meaning*; 'What does Dr. Newman mean?' It pointed in the very same direction as that into which my musings had turned me already. He asks what I *mean*; not about my words, not about my arguments, not about my actions, as his ultimate point, but about that living intelligence, by which I write, argue, and act. He asks about my mind and its beliefs and its sentiments; and he shall be answered [...].

My perplexity did not last half an hour. I recognised what I had to do, though I shrank from both the task and the exposure which it would entail.

---

[7] Any Derridean or deconstructionist reading of the *Apologia* starts here, in Newman's anxiety concerning the power of writing, as opposed to speaking, to do what he requires it to do, and make his case for himself unequivocally. An illuminating essay on this aspect of Newman, from which I have profited, is Michael Ryan's 'A grammatology of assent: Cardinal Newman's *Apologia pro vita sua*', in George P. Landow, ed., *Approaches to Victorian Autobiography* (Athens, Ohio, 1979). Ryan brings out well the opposition in Newman between the 'good writing' he desires and the 'bad writing' that is all he can achieve, or between his desire to give us to hear the 'inner voice' of conscience and the need to be satisfied with the 'external voice' of logic or thought.

I must, I said, give the true key to my whole life; I must show what I am that it may be seen what I am not, and that the phantom may be extinguished which gibbers instead of me. I wish to be known as a living man, and not as a scarecrow which is dressed up in my clothes. (99)

This is written like a true autobiographer, with that generic hint of megalomania in the desire to annihilate the influence of a previous misrepresentation by the incontrovertible truth and fullness of one's own textual advent. By offering the 'whole man' as his means by which to erase a partial slander, Newman is over-reacting. But he has prepared the way for the exaggeration of his response by rewriting Kingsley's charges of equivocation as what he calls 'a simple, a broad, an intelligible, to the English public a plausible arraignment'. The highly intellectual and rhetorically adept Newman imposes a forensic simplicity on the proceedings the better to display his intellectual and rhetorical superiority.

The second property accruing to a narrative subject, be this subject a Church or a human being, is 'individuality', which is Newman's view and the view of every autobiographer. It might however seem that Newman would wish to play down his singularity, because he is writing in the *Apologia* not simply as an individual but as a Roman Catholic, or the representative of his new confession. Newman versus Kingsley is Catholic versus Anglican. The charges laid by Kingsley are those traditionally made against Catholics by Anglicans, and Newman answers them on behalf of all Catholics, adverting on a number of occasions to his representative status as apologist, with 'a duty, to myself, to the Catholic cause, to the Catholic priesthood, to give account of myself without any delay'(88). But he does not thereby mitigate his singularity; rather he accentuates it, because read as a narrative the *Apologia* records the lonely passage of an individual from one communion to another, it is the history of a man emerging from the anonymity of one religious group and making his way into the anonymity of another. He is the e-gregious traveller between con-gregations.

The aim of the Oxford Movement had been to formalize a Via Media, or a kind of Christianity intermediate between Anglicanism and Catholicism, a transcendent, neither-nor church as it were. This aim has been 'absolutely pulverized' for Newman by the nearest he comes in the *Apologia* to an Augustinian turning-point, which is one inspired by Augustine himself. He has come across Augustine's formula asserting the authority of the Church in doctrinal matters,

'Securus judicat orbis terrarum' ('the verdict of the world is conclusive'), and this has struck him in his hour of uncertainty with an unprecedented power 'which I had never felt from any words before'(213). Newman takes Augustine's words as being 'a final sentence' against all secessional bodies, including the Church of England, and to be equivalent in their influence over himself to the *tolle lege* once heard by their author in his hour of uncertainty. But if the Via Media no longer exists for him as a legitimate halfway house doctrinally, it may survive metaphorically, as the description of his own autobiographical movement between houses. As a narrative subject, Newman embodies the Via Media even as he travels it, being neither still fully Protestant nor yet fully Papist.

Conversion is a solitary act, an act which singularizes. Newman has been accused by Kingsley of seeking in his duplicity to convert others beside himself, and from within the Church of England, with the aim of some mass defection. But the singularity of his true course between churches now becomes an element in his defence: 'I wished to go to my Lord by myself, and it seemed an absurdity to my reason to be converted in partnership'(310). As an Anglican Newman has found followers, but without ever seeking them; he is able conscientiously to claim that he has travelled alone. Yet singular or not, his personal religious history is the *type* of religious – or indeed political – history in general, in exemplifying that 'continuous picture of authority and private judgment alternately advancing and retreating', or the agonistic pattern which finds its resolution when wilful and passionate human beings are 'brought together into one by the beauty and majesty of a superhuman power'(344). Here the autobiographer's unification of himself by means of narrative comes to seem positively portentous, and Newman's resolution of the ideological conflict within to be the prototype of some ultimate transcendence of human history.

Newman's transcendence accords with precedent elsewhere in this book, in being grounded in mediacy. In his years of religious neither-norness he acts both as an individual and as the personification of the Middle Way, whereby Christian factionalism might be overcome. In this second, representative role he may be likened to his own 'middle race' of 'daemons', or intermediate – and very Goethean – entities, whom he posits as 'the animating principles of certain institutions', and as accounting for the differences in behaviour of 'bodies politic and associations' and of 'the individuals who compose them'(130).

These for Newman seem to be real beings, 'unseen intelligences' midway between the human and the divine, between good and bad, between heaven and hell. They stand in a relation of soul to body in respect of the institutions which they animate, and hence in the relation of transcendent meaning to material text. In the *Apologia* Newman reveals his own 'unseen intelligence', or the rationale of his actions in a particular period and province of his life. It is as his own 'daemon' or 'animating principle' that he achieves integration and transcends the inanimate logic of the words on the page.

The *Apologia* represents an individual who has passed successfully through a process of disassociation followed by reassociation, or through an interval of heroic loneliness. Newman's self-imposed individualism as an autobiographer has been prefigured by the individualism of the contentious Tracts he had once published, when pitting the imperatives of Faith against the monolithic authority of the Church. The historical model which had been offered to him in encouragement in those days was that of Martin Luther, whose bold exertions as an individual had produced vast institutional changes. As an individual Luther may have lost, but his cause had gained: the lesson of his life as suggested to Newman by one of his friends is that 'This is the way of things: we promote truth by a self-sacrifice.' It is the lesson he himself would like to teach by publishing his *Apologia*. The volume's collective cause is that of Catholic Truth, the self that must be sacrificed in its defence is his, its inwardness having now been made over into a public possession. Newman's generic role is that of the autobiographer impelled by his duty to an institution into a self-communion which he experiences as an ordeal, but who is enabled by his membership of that institution to construe his individual mental history as that of a saving aberrancy.

Darwin[8]

Autobiography is a robustly capitalist genre, advertising the accumulation of gainful experience by which the author has been raised into the elite class of those sufficiently approved of among their contemporaries to write their lives. Autobiographers come before us as the successful bankers of their past, and very patently so when the lives that they write are as progressive as those of Mill or of Newman,

[8] This section has benefited from the comments made on a draft of it by Dr Michael Neve.

for whom any losses incurred in the course of time are turned smoothly into gain and work towards the one, profitable end. Mill may have lost the great inspiration of his moral and intellectual life, Harriet Taylor, but so completely has he absorbed what she had to teach him that it is as if she were still there, as a part of himself. And Newman has had to abandon the Church in which he had been raised and into which he had been ordained, as well as the security of his social and academic position, but no pathos attaches to that loss in the *Apologia*, whose author is now the Catholic priest, Father Newman, and debarred from any sentimental identification with his former Anglican self.[9]

To complicate this simple model of an existential calculus, I turn to Charles Darwin, whose brief autobiography, written in old age, might well have carried the title which Newman gave to his novel, 'Loss and Gain'. In life, Darwin was a man careful with money and careful too in recording its comings and goings, his surviving ledgers apparently listing every smallest domestic transaction. In the autobiographical record which he left he is similarly concerned with registering not only what has accrued to him in his lifetime but what he has had to pay out. The outgoings are not of course pure loss; autobiographically there can be no such thing, the autobiographical act transmuting real loss into symbolic gain. The great gain of Darwin's life has been the scientific eminence which is his qualification for writing an autobiography; the great loss has been the dulling or disappearance in him of certain tastes from which he had once had much pleasure. Gain and loss are integrated by the one being shown as the corollary of the other.

---

[9] Soon after his conversion, Newman had published a novel whose subject was also the defection of a young Anglican to the Catholic Church. He called it *Loss and Gain*, the Loss being all that its hero, Charles Reding, has to give up – a close family, friends, a comfortable middle-class career – in order to achieve the Gain of his conversion. For Newman the *Apologia* stands to the fiction as Catholicism stands to an inadequate Anglicanism. The supreme Gain to which his fictional hero comes, in the final pages of the novel, is the 'Great Presence' of Christ in the sacrament at the first Catholic mass he witnesses. This is the fullness of presence that Protestantism can not understand, let alone deliver. Protestantism is all 'outside without inside' as one of the novel's dissatisfied Anglicans puts it. But so, inevitably, is a novel, the story which Newman himself describes in the *Apologia* as 'simply ideal'; *Loss and Gain* is all 'outside without inside' for containing none of the real people whom Newman had known in Oxford; and for not containing the author himself. In fiction there can be only 'scarecrows', without life or reality, whereas in autobiography we can meet with 'the whole man', really present on the human level as Christ is really present on the supernatural level in the Catholic sacrament. The incalculable Gain for Newman in the *Apologia* is to be there in person and to have relegated the notion of Loss to the past and to the insubstantial realm of fiction.

Darwin's autobiography may be read, as it is written, in broad Darwinian terms.[10] It is not, therefore, a wholly cheerful story, for, as conceived by Darwin himself, the slow, blindly experimental diversification of living forms which constitutes Evolution has entailed much suffering, with entire species undergoing extinction as new species replace them, and with survival conditional on success in the grim, Malthusian competition for resources. If the story of Evolution ends well, it does so only on balance, and Darwin (unlike many Darwinians since) refuses to tell it in triumphalist terms, as if the large element of morbidity which it contains were of no lasting account. In the summary of his evolutionary beliefs which he gives in the *Autobiography*, he argues that were there not a preponderance of pleasure over pain in the experience of living, propagation would have died out and the animal creation have lapsed. The mere existence of pain and suffering, however, is famously hard to reconcile with faith in a beneficent God, but it may be reconciled, according to Darwin, 'with the view that all organic beings have been developed through variation and natural selection'(52). This is so because pain and suffering may now be seen as aiding in the perpetuation of the species, being 'well adapted to make a creature guard itself against any great or sudden evil'. Pain and suffering have their positive evolutionary contribution to make, therefore, as states to be avoided. But they can also work against life: should they become chronic, says Darwin, their effect is to produce in the sufferer a potentially fatal inactivity. The vital antithesis which Darwin here institutes, between pain and pleasure, apathy and exertion, isolation and association, is one which finds systematic reflection in the structure of the *Autobiography*.

This is a rather perfunctory work, some 30,000 words in length and written for the most part in two months of 1876, when Darwin was sixty-seven. Like Vico's autobiography, it was written in response to a commission, a German editor having asked Darwin 'for an account of the development of my mind and character with some sketch of my autobiography'(8). The autobiography is thus the product of his international fame. But Darwin turns decisively away from the public sphere at the start, by declaring that he is writing for his own amusement and because it 'might possibly interest my children or

[10] The edition I shall refer to is that published in the Oxford English Memoirs and Travels series: Charles Darwin/Thomas Henry Huxley, *Autobiographies*, edited by Gavin de Beer (London, 1974).

their children'. He himself would have been interested to read 'even so short and dull a sketch of the mind of my grandfather written by himself'. The sheer authorial tactlessness, in promising his readers, be they family or not, something 'short and dull', is very much part of Darwin's autobiographical scheme, modesty having its part to play in the disarming of his adversaries (a matter I shall return to). But by at once invoking both his grandfather and his own children and grandchildren, Darwin imposes an evolutionary perspective, placing himself intermediately, as the living but transient link between the generations of his line. The grandfather in question was Erasmus Darwin, his father's father and a celebrated evolutionist and materialist, who at the end of the previous century had published a prose epic entitled *Zoonomia, or The Laws of Organic Life*. Charles Darwin says that he had admired this work when he first read it, but that when he reread it, years later, he found it very disappointing, 'the proportion of speculation being so large to the facts given'(27). That proportion is one which he reverses in his autobiography, in respect of his own scientific work, by presenting himself not as the supreme theorist of evolution but as the supreme accumulator of scientific facts, with the theory literally as their after-thought – the stance, as we have earlier seen, of Sigmund Freud.

Darwin's stance towards his autobiographical task is more than simply scientific or objective; he ends his opening paragraph with the promise: 'I have attempted to write the following account of myself, as if I were a dead man in another world looking back at my own life. Nor have I found this difficult, for life is nearly over with me.' This donning of a funeral mask in order to write is reminiscent of Hume, with the important difference that where Hume was indeed dying at the time, Darwin was not (he was to live for six more years). The ostensible claim is to dispassionateness, or to the uninvolved posture appropriate to the scientific fact-gatherer, even when – or especially when, given the temptation to fictionalize it – he is recounting his own life. This is the autobiographer in the Alfieri role of forestalling a biographer, whose task he is perfectly well able to perform and to prove his moral worth by doing so without favouring himself. In Darwin's case, however, there is more than objectivity at stake. By writing as one of the living dead he wishes us to suppose that his vitality is exhausted, and that the brevity and dullness of what we are about to read stem from the physical and emotional state to which his life of scientific work has reduced him.

No autobiographer before Darwin, and only Freud perhaps among autobiographers since, has had in the course of his life so deep and seismic an impact on the intellectual outlook of his times. The publication of the *Origin of Species* of 1859 had a dreadfully uncomfortable new story to tell of the animate creation and the wasteful and capricious means by which it had evolved. It was for most, Darwin included, a god-less story, the methods of natural selection seeming not to belong to a well-meaning or even a well-organized deity. Yet as a young man Darwin had himself envisaged going into the church; he was a country vicar *manqué*, who had once taken the Genesis story literally but now finds the Anglican creed 'unintelligible'. The religious position he adopts in the *Autobiography* is agnostic (to use the term perspicuously coined by his friend T .H. Huxley). He declares that he has passed gradually into disbelief without ever feeling any distress at what he was having to give up. But what he had given up easily, others could not; Darwin knew that Darwinism had caused acute religious distress by discrediting orthodox Christian accounts of the creation and of the modus operandi of God, as well as making it very hard to see the human creation as any different in kind from the animal, with the consequent loss of such specific and reassuring human privileges as that of personal immortality. As early as 1844, fifteen years before the *Origin* was published and at a time when he believed that he was dying, Darwin had written to his friend Joseph Hooker, that the theory of the variation of species was beginning to take shape in his mind, and that he was now 'almost convinced (quite contrary to the opinion I started with) that species are not (it is like confessing a murder) immutable'.[11] Who or what had had to be murdered is unclear, but the metaphor is an unwontedly vigorous one, suggestive both of aggression in Darwin and of guilt.

In the *Autobiography* the continuing ideological storm to which the theory of natural selection has opened the way rages off-stage, with the prematurely deceased Darwin as its spectator rather than its prime mover. Autobiographically, he is the man of peace and his shamming dead a strategy learnt from his study of the natural world, where threatened creatures employ instinctive devices of conceal-ment in order to survive the lethal attentions of their enemies. For Darwin an autobiographical text functions as protective colouring.

[11] In a letter to J. D. Hooker of 11 January 1844. See *The Correspondence of Charles Darwin*, Volume 3, 1844–1846 (Cambridge, 1987), p. 2.

He congratulates himself on having personally avoided controversy and goes on eirenically to forgive those with whom he has good cause to quarrel: 'My views have often been grossly misrepresented, bitterly opposed and ridiculed, but this has been generally done as I believe in good faith'(75). So does the grand theorist of the struggle for existence rise above that struggle, by refusing to be drawn into it, but instead, like a true autobiographer, takes on the transcendent role of the man who is above party and who can insulate himself from conflict by generalizing the virtue of good faith to the point where even those who have 'grossly misrepresented, bitterly opposed and ridiculed' his views are deemed to possess it. Darwin may be thought strangely determined here to give no offence.

The *Autobiography* is a hugely benevolent piece of writing, which makes full display of its author's humaneness. This is a quality by which Darwin lays great and explicit store. He doubts whether it is innate, as logically he should, since humaneness is a quality which goes against the Darwinian grain in being opposed to the cruelty endemic in the process of natural selection. But of all the productive pleasures by which 'sentient beings' are guided, the keenest for Darwin is 'the pleasure derived from sociability and from loving our families'(52). Not surprisingly therefore, the locus of humaneness is found to be the family, and the Darwin family in particular, where it has been transmitted by association. His own untamed instincts as a hunter-gatherer had been domesticated in childhood, first by his sisters, who had taught him not to take more than one egg from a nesting bird, and not to impale live worms on his hook when angling. But these small lessons had only moderated his instincts, not removed them. He has grown up to be a sportsman none the less, and a dedicated shooter of birds and other game. He is happy enough in this role until the day when his father says to him – and his words are apparently quoted verbatim by Darwin – 'You care for nothing but shooting, dogs and rat-catching, and you will be a disgrace to yourself and all your family'(12). These are unkind words, spoken by 'the kindest man I ever knew, and whose memory I love with all my heart'. The son concludes that his father 'must have been angry and somewhat unjust when he used such words'. This paternal commination takes effect only later, however, during the voyage of the Beagle, when Darwin finally realizes 'that the pleasure of observing and reasoning was a much higher one than that of skill and sport. The primeval instincts of the barbarian slowly yielded to the acquired tastes of the civilized man'(45). We are invited to read his career in science that is, as the sublimation of the barbaric career he might otherwise have followed with gun and rod, and the conspicuous kindness of his father as a narrative 'event' or turning-point, articulating the 'primeval' and the 'civilized' life.

Darwin's father dominates the early part of the *Autobiography* physically as well as morally. He is not only 'the kindest man I ever knew' but also 'the largest man, whom I ever saw'. He is a man of great bulk and regular 'high spirits', a very positive expression of the life-force. Not so his son, whose own life has been marked by low spirits and chronic ill-health. Compared with his father, as he himself has portrayed him, Darwin must go down as degenerate, as representing a serious decline in the fitness for survival of the family Darwin. Nor does this physical and psychological declension end with himself, because he has passed it on to his children, whose uncertain spirits and health reflect his own.[12] And far from contemplating the next generation of his family in terms of gain, he contemplates it in terms of loss, nominating only one of his children in the pages of the *Autobiography* and she the one who has died, his daughter Annie, who had died in childhood and of whom he had written a memoir at the time. Her loss he records, poignantly, as a 'very severe grief', saying that 'Tears still sometimes come into my eyes, when I think of her sweet ways'(57). When writing of the death of a child, Darwin is no longer able to write as if he were himself dead.

In the *Autobiography* the evils of pain and of death are reduced, if far from justified by their integration into Darwin's evolutionary design, in which the avoidance of them becomes a main strategy in physical survival. Almost forty years earlier, however, at the age of only twenty-nine, Darwin had written an autobiographical fragment of a few pages, in which these twin, dark themes stand strikingly out, without as yet being eligible for theorization within a larger scheme. The fragment opens with an autobiographical topos: 'my earliest recollection'. This turns out to be a memory of physical injury, when Darwin was accidentally cut by his sister. His relation to this primal scene is ambiguous, in so far as it both does and does not seem to belong to him: 'My memory here is an obscure picture, in which

---

[12] To a correspondent in 1872, he wrote that the 'greatest drawback' to his life's happiness was that 'several of my children have inherited from me feeble health'. See *Charles Darwin: His Life told in an Autobiographical Chapter, and in a Selected Series of his Published Letters*, edited by his son, Francis Darwin (London, 1902), p. 280.

from not recollecting any pain I am scarcely conscious of its reference to myself'(3).[13] One might ask, in Wittgensteinian vein,[14] what it is like to 'recollect' a pain as one's own; would it mean feeling it again, in the act of recollection, as a Rousseau might hope to do, and so establish proprietary rights in it? There is no such desire in Darwin. On the contrary, the inability to refer the pain to himself is the incentive he is looking for autobiographically, as the curious rather than the concerned observer of his past life.

But when death is the topic this impassiveness is not so easily sustained. The death that dominates this autobiographical fragment is that of Darwin's mother. He declares that he remembers very little about it, even though he was eight and a half years old at the time and one of his sisters, who was a year younger, remembers it in detail. He expresses no guilt at his own absence of memories of a presumably painful experience, only curiosity at the different ways in which different people remember. His early recollections are characterized by being 'connected most closely with myself' whereas his sister's are connected with others. Thus, at the point where emotion might be in order, Darwin reverts to science and to classification, by identifying the property that distinguishes his memories from those of his sister. The scatter of childhood scenes of which the fragment consists here finds its unifying law.

The fragment contains another evocation of death, one that is the more troubling for having no intimate reference to Darwin himself. It was not the death of anyone he was close to or even of anyone he knew, but death happening to strangers and being made into the subject of a narrative. 'Some very early recollections are connected with fear at Parkfield and with poor Betty Harvey. I remember with horror her story of people being pushed into the canal by the towing rope, by going the wrong side of the horse. I had the greatest horror of this story – keen instinct against death'(4). A death told has

---

[13] This autobiographical fragment is printed in the de Beer edition of the *Autobiography*, though not in the earlier Francis Darwin editions.

[14] Pain being the example which Wittgenstein uses in the *Philosophical Investigations* in his repeated probings into the relation of language to bodily sensation and the question of the privacy of such sensations. Darwin's inability to recollect his own pain places him in the position of Wittgenstein's observer trying to 'imagine someone else's pain' by analogy with his own, that is, a pain he does not feel by analogy with one he does feel – except that at the moment of writing, Darwin is not in pain and so compounds the difficulty by needing to imagine what it is like to feel pain in himself. That he should be struck by his failure to recollect any pain is odd: should we assume that he would have *liked* to do so, so as to revivify the scar left on his body by the injury done to him by his sister?

proved more emotive than a death actually lived through. We come back here to the recognition made by both Augustine and Rousseau, that the staged, or narrated, mimesis of pathetic events has a greater power to move than the direct experience of them – a recognition to make any autobiographer happy. Darwin is with Rousseau this once, in remembering 'with horror' the story of which he as a small boy had 'the greatest horror', horror, unlike physical pain, being open to such intimate recovery. But even in this instance, Darwin can not forbear to add the brief annotation of the working scientist, by ascribing the horror he had felt, and is able still to feel, to a 'keen instinct against death'. With that telegraphic afterthought he turns himself from an individual subject into a specimen, and amortizes the perturbing memory in question by taking his reaction to it to be sound evidence of the universal instinct for survival.

The life which Darwin remembers in this fragment to have begun in pain has also been led in pain; it has been a life regulated by ill-health, at least since he returned from his five-year voyage of researches aboard the Beagle. Even before the Beagle had put to sea, he had been alarmed to get heart pains and palpitations, and had gone all the way north at the last moment to Shrewsbury, to consult his father. And once back in England, he had settled to a life of intellectual labour broken only by the insistent headaches, fevers and fits of vomiting which frequently prevented him from working. Darwin himself construed his unhappy bodily state so as to make it seem to reflect the warring state of creation as a whole. The struggle for existence was inscribed within his divided person: 'The noodle and the stomach are antagonistic powers' was his lapidary diagnosis of the organic war within. Yet the poor health which impeded his work also facilitated it. By Darwin's own admission, it protected him from intrusion and from the demands of sociability – and eventually of fame. Society exhausts him and his unruly 'stomach' can keep him safely at home – as the symptoms he had suffered at Plymouth on board ship had attempted to do. We can say that Darwin has been sickly to his own advantage, so as not to have to do what it would have cost him to do. He has avoided, above all, having to go to the funeral of his father, for whom his love and admiration were so great; this is another death kept autobiographically at a safe distance. (One of Robert Darwin's greatest gifts had been for diagnosing and treating his patients in what we would now call psychosomatic terms; but his son makes no attempt in the *Autobiography* at any psychosomatic diagnosis of his own symptoms, even though the role he shows them as having played in his working life makes such a diagnosis by others inevitable.)[15]

More remarkably still, Darwin gives this ill-health as his reason for not having abandoned science for philanthropy. He recognizes that 'the social instincts' are the highest that a man has, and that 'If he acts for the good of others, he will receive the approbation of his fellow-men and gain the love of those with whom he lives; and this latter gain undoubtedly is the highest pleasure on earth'(55). This altruistic creed is the culmination in the *Autobiography* of the humaneness he had imbibed as a boy. Yet a natural scientist like himself can not claim to have been acting for the good of others, and one remembers at this point that Darwin had originally been meant to follow his father and to practise medicine, the one directly philanthropic science. But his fragile constitution had not allowed him to: two hauntingly 'bad operations' witnessed as a medical student have so disturbed him as to prevent him going on with his studies. The science of the natural world in which he has specialized has been a *pis-aller*, a substitution of one study for another such as to induce guilt. As the theorist of natural selection Darwin has certainly not received 'the approbation of his fellow-men', quite the reverse, he has been reviled by many of them. But he has, he says, been guided by conscience and does not regret giving his life to his science. And yet: '[I] have often and often regretted that I have not done more direct good to my fellow-creatures.' His 'sole and poor excuse' for not having done so is his weak health, and a 'mental constitution' which had made it very difficult for him to divide his time. He could never have been a part-time philanthropist, only a full-time one. And if his conscience is clear at the last, it is thanks to that tissue of infirmities that have together determined his professional life.

The Darwinian contest between head and stomach has ended in victory for the head: progressive thought has subsumed regressive emotion. But the stomach had gone on resisting because it was fighting for its life, as the seat of those warmer feelings and responses which the autobiographical Darwin tells us have atrophied. Over the

---

[15] Much has been written about Darwin's ill-health, of which he himself kept a meticulous record covering some six years, so far unpublished. Scholars divide into those who interpret it physiologically and those who interpret it psychologically. The medical interpretations are reductionist and therefore stultifying, the psychological ones inevitably suggestive. A good, informative account is in Ralph Colp Jr, *To Be an Invalid: The Illness of Charles Darwin* (Chicago, 1972).

course of his life he has lost that 'poetic' faculty which John Stuart Mill realized in his depression that he had been starved of by his education and set out to cultivate. Darwin's first mention of this faculty in his own case occurs in connection with another death: as a small schoolboy he has watched – he does not say why – the burial of a soldier, a scene which 'deeply stirred whatever poetic fancy there was in me'(10). Since this is the same 'fancy' whose loss he mourns later on in the *Autobiography*, one can but remark that its association here with a burial is premonitory. Darwin is writing as a dead man and what has died are those parts of him which would have prevented his sense of having been mechanized, his mind seeming 'to have become a kind of machine for grinding general laws out of large collections of facts'(83). The sacrifice that this gigantic scientific achievement has imposed on him is the loss of 'the higher aesthetic tastes'. The pleasure he had formerly taken in reading poetry has gone, so has his taste for pictures and for music. Liking has even turned to disgust: 'I have tried lately to read Shakespeare and found it so intolerably dull that it nauseated me' – an indication that the troublesome stomach remains active.

This desolate admission finally introduces into the *Autobiography* the very element of pathos which its author's one-sided intellectual development had seemed to preclude. But Darwin has not lost all his higher aesthetic tastes; even into old age novels have given him 'a wonderful relief and pleasure'. 'A surprising number have been read aloud' to him, as stories had no doubt been read to him when a child, and his one, childlike, stipulation if he is to enjoy them is that they should end happily. In stories which come out well there is therapy for him, and in the role of story-teller a kudos of which he himself had become aware as a boy of eight or nine when, as he writes in the autobiographical fragment, he had been 'a very great story-teller – for the pure pleasure of exciting attention and surprise'(5). As the grand theorist of natural selection, Darwin might be thought to have told the supreme scientific story, by transforming an enormous array of patiently collected and seemingly miscellaneous facts into the constituents of a single narrative. The *Autobiography* is the story of that story, and as such it too ends happily, in the assertion of gain over loss and of the sociable instinct of the author over the prudent urge to concealment.

CHAPTER 9

The attraction of style: Stein, Nabokov, Sartre

Darwin ends the brief preamble to his *Autobiography* with what is at once a cautionary clause about the quality of his prose and an advertisement of its sincerity: 'I have taken no pains about my style of writing.' He does not wish his autobiography to be read as if it came from a writer, when to write is to enter literature and thereby sacrifice authenticity to artifice. Darwin is like Rousseau in prizing immediacy above reflection, and takes negligence in respect of style to promise a greater honesty of recollection. This assumption suits him both as the self-effacing gatherer and orderer of natural historical data, and as the homely and beneficent paterfamilias, who is addressing the account of his life to his children and has no need of the trickeries of 'style', which we exploit in order to ingratiate ourselves with strangers. To take no pains about one's style is not, however, to aspire to write entirely without style, in some impersonal language of nature such as scientists may crave (or even believe that they have found); it is to write unreflexively, attending as little as possible to the act of writing, so that what comes to mind comes in its 'pure' state, uncorrupted by the foreknowledge of its publication. A concern with style would for Darwin represent a vicious distraction from his responsibilities as the painstaking chronicler of his past, since the integrity of his memories would be put at risk by cosmetic attempts to enhance their effectiveness.

The conception of style clearly implied in Darwin's brief remark is that which sees it as a surplus-value, a quality expressly added to a piece of writing by the skill of the writer in order to patent it and make it more attractive to whoever reads it. On this view, style is decorative and it is deliberate, and to cultivate it in the writing of autobiography might well seem morally questionable to someone as scrupulous and wary as Darwin. But there is an alternative conception of literary style by the application of which an indifference towards style can be recuperated and shown in fact to *be* a style – in the event, Darwin's style. This is the view which holds style to be, not a detachable nor merely auxiliary quality of writing but 'organic', a truly inherent and distinctive quality, and as such the textual index of a writer's uniqueness. 'Le style est l'homme même', in short. Happily, that most celebrated definition of style as self-expression was coined by one of Darwin's great predecessors in natural history, Buffon; and how faithfully does Darwin live up to it in the *Autobiography*, whose extreme plainness and modesty we readily take to be conveying the essence of Darwin the man.

Darwin thus enters literature even as he protests – by implication – that literature is not where he wants to be, since literature is unthinkable without 'style'. In this he is the unlikely precursor of the third and last of the autobiographers I shall consider in this chapter, Jean-Paul Sartre, who had very different reasons from Darwin for wishing not to be thought of as a literary figure but who could find only a literary means to protest his non-literariness. Sartre too takes 'style' to be the crux: where there is style there is literature, and a Sartrian 'bad faith'; where there is no style, we can be given the simple, effective, revolutionary truth.

But the way to Sartre lies through the autobiographical writings of two other twentieth-century writers, Gertrude Stein and Vladimir Nabokov, for whom style is not some shameful bourgeois net-curtain, to be hung over the autobiographer's window in mitigation of its transparency, but the most prestigious and valuable of a writer's possessions, to suppress which in writing an autobiogaphy would be a kind of mendacity. Stein in the event does partially suppress her style, as a concession to market forces; Nabokov does not, he flaunts it. But both recognize a writer's style to be an autobiographical statement par excellence and accord it priority in writing. They are the heirs of Rousseau in heeding as they do the rhetorical potentialities of style, but where he saw style as a variable quality, determined by the nature of the subject-matter, they see it as a constant and as itself determinant, the attractive signature of an autobiographer's authority over his or her past.

Gertrude Stein[1]

The titles which Gertrude Stein gave to her books were as idiosyncratic as their faux-naïf syntax and their meagre punctuation. Her first volume of autobiography had a title making it seem to be the work of somebody else, her second one is construable only as an oxymoron, its two apposed elements being patently at odds with each other. The misleading title is *The Autobiography of Alice B. Toklas*, a volume which appeared in 1933, with no author's name on the title-page and looking unequivocally like an account of her life written by Alice B. Toklas.[2] It opens as that: it is written in the first person and makes instant reference to Toklas's family origins and early life in the United States. But on only the second page Toklas begins to move aside, when her hitherto nondescript life in California is broken into, first by the San Francisco earthquake and fire and then by the more enduringly seismic impact of her first meeting with the Stein family. Thereafter, Toklas survives textually as a self-effacing narrator charged with giving a reverent account of her imperious companion, Gertrude Stein, with whom she has lived for the past twenty-five years. Only in the book's final lines is its true authorship officially admitted. Toklas is now said to have promised Stein that she would write an autobiography but she has too many other things to do – menial things, as housekeeper, gardener, needlewoman, secretary and vet – to find time for the magisterial role of author, which belongs to Stein herself: 'About six weeks ago Gertrude Stein said, it does not look to me as if you were ever going to write that autobiography. You know what I am going to do. I am going to write it for you. I am going to write it as simply as Defoe did the autobiography of Robinson Crusoe. And she has and this is it'(*AT*,

---

[1] This section has benefitted from the comments of Professor Wendy Steiner.

[2] We do not expect the titles of autobiographies to include the name of the autobiographer and may well feel suspicious towards any which do, as in the case of *Alice B. Toklas*. They fall into a different category from titles such as *The Autobiography of an Artisan*, which indicate the author's social role but not his name and are intended quasi-anonymously, as expressing the writer's solidarity with his class or trade. Stein's title echoes that used in the previous century by William Hale-White, for *The Autobiography of Mark Rutherford*, a splendid book generally classed and therefore read as a novel, even though the story which it tells, of a young nonconformist's loss of religious faith and consequent unhappiness, is one in most known respects applicable to Hale-White himself. Hale-White continued to write – essays and novels – under the name of Mark Rutherford, so that *The Autobiography* may also be read as the story of the making of an (assumed) name; indeed, there is much discreet play with proper names in the book, in which various characters are discovered to be living under names different from those they were born with.

337).[3] Writing was not usually done so quickly for Stein, nor was what she wrote so easy to read: in this respect *The Autobiography of Alice B. Toklas* is already a book apart and she as its subject a person apart, if we are to take her identification of herself with Robinson Crusoe at its full value.

What Stein has written approximates to autobiography in the third person, though it is markedly different in its high presumptuousness from the obvious American precedent for such a format, the earnestly self-doubting *Education of Henry Adams*. But by feigning to transfer authorship to a close and informed observer of her life, Stein has in fact achieved what is more perspicuously described as a first-person biography, and as such a formal innovation unique of its kind. This arch but in her hands robust experiment in self-writing may be explained by the major aesthetic 'turn' which she describes having taken earlier in her life as a writer. The subject-matter of her writing has been changed by a visit to Spain happening some time in the 1910s: 'She says hitherto she had been interested only in the insides of people, their character and what went on inside them, it was during that summer that she first felt a desire to express the rhythm of the visible world'(*AT*, 160). Thereafter she has set herself to find an exact verbal notation for the material world, whether human or inanimate, although as an autobiographer she is faced with the new problem of materializing some part at least of what goes on inside herself.

Psychologically speaking, Stein has become a literary behaviourist, preoccupied as a writer with what *shows* but even more with how it comes to show. In the best autobiographical tradition, she presents this as a sudden, radical 'turn' in her life, brought about by the experience of Spain, but it might also be traced further back, to her time as a student of psychology, when she had conducted, and herself taken part in experiments in 'automatic writing', that once fashionable exercise in 'pure' creativity. The 'automatic' writer writes supposedly without regard for the formal constraints of rhyme or reason, as if she were the involuntary stenographer of the subconscious and whatever she writes the immediate expression of her inmost feelings. But Stein's experiments were a failure, leading her to the conclusion that except under hypnosis there can be no such thing

---

[3] Page references (marked *AT*) are to the first popular edition of *The Autobiography of Alice B. Toklas*, published in John Lane's Week-End Library (London, 1935).

as 'automatic writing' because whoever tries it does so in the knowledge that they are being invigilated, if only by themselves, thereby reinstating the very censorship by the conscious mind that it had been the purpose of the experiment to remove. She herself had been a peculiarly, indeed a uniquely bad subject because she 'never had subconscious reactions', and it is this bluff, Cartesian confidence in the total transparency of her mind which has inspired her as a writer. Contemporary critics of Stein may have concluded that writing as off-puttingly strange and obscure as hers could not be deliberate and must therefore be 'automatic', whereas the opposite was in fact the case: her writing is hyperconscious and aims at an exact representation of the visible, pared of all those subjective associations which blur the hard outlines of objects and people. The motto she has been tempted to take for her letterhead is the most celebrated of Steinian definitions – and never was a definition more definite – 'a rose is a rose is a rose is a rose'. That was the pronouncement of a tough-minded literary hygienist, calling for the suppression of metaphor in our descriptions of the natural world.

Following her stylistic 'conversion' Stein has begun 'to describe the inside as seen from the outside'(*AT*, 210): hence the strategy which she adopts for *The Autobiography of Alice B. Toklas*, where to make the point more graphically that this is to be the *outside* story of her life she gives it to be told by someone else. By her sustained impersonation of Alice Toklas, Stein can sit audaciously to herself as to a portraitist, accepting to be an object among objects – even if she gives no physical description of herself, as the hypochondriacal Cardano once did, in what may strike us as an uncanny, specular moment of diremption. For Stein, the painter is an ideal, because he paints only what he sees, and only in the present tense, because his subject, whether animate or inanimate, has no past nor future but is represented in the instantaneity of an image. The writer, working in the temporal medium of language, has no such good fortune, and can but acknowledge the unwanted successiveness of prose. The verbal portraitist can only envy the portraitist in oils, as when Stein herself sits to her friend and rival Picasso in *The Autobiography*, for a portrait whose making and reception, in her account of them, are intimately related to the making and reception of her own work. She has sat for the painter an extraordinary number of times, between eighty and ninety, as if to impose on him that very temporal dimension which she suffers from as a writer. Picasso indeed has been led to complain that she has changed her appearance in between sittings, that the time element is disrupting his work; but he has in the end abstracted an image from all the faces she has shown him and produced a portrait to be admired by the progressive few and ridiculed by the benighted many (its technique having been greatly influenced by an African mask that he had seen in Spain in the meantime!) And all the time he has been painting her, Stein has sat forming sentences in her head: she has been a creative sitter, silently composing in rivalry with the artist – and anticipating the same ambivalent response towards her experimental methods.

The writing of autobiography may have all manner of therapeutic effects on the writer, privately in the easing of psychic injury or confusion, publicly in the acquisition of a new social and professional standing. As an avant-garde writer Stein's singularity has lain in the uncompromising difficulties of her 'style'; but as an autobiographer she condescends to define her singularity rather than to demonstrate it. *The Autobiography of Alice B. Toklas* was the book by which she became a widely read author. It may be the story of a dauntless aesthetic pioneer, but it is told in an only mutedly pioneering manner, as befits the sociable genre into which she had moved. *The Autobiography* was a popular book for the gossipy account which it gives of Stein's expatriate life in the advanced artistic circles of Paris up to and during the First World War. It mediates geographically between continents and aesthetically between philosophies of art by telling 'how two americans happened to be in the heart of an art movement of which the outside world at that time knew nothing'(*AT*, 35). The 'inside' which is seen from the 'outside' is more the private commerce between members of this movement than the inside of Stein herself, who is present not as psychological subject (or object) but as sympathetic patron, fellow practitioner and now literary portraitist, with a focal role in respect of the group comparable to that of a John Stuart Mill or a Father Newman.

In time, the avant-garde artist or writer can expect to be recuperated into her culture, once her egregious methods have become more or less familiar and intelligible. And autobiography, as I have been arguing all along, is that form of writing by the practice of which the writer hopes to promote his recuperation, by the culture or society from which he has earlier marked himself off. And so with Stein, in her two volumes of autobiography. Her belief is that artistic methods originally perceived as 'ugly', such as those employed by

Picasso or by herself, will eventually come to be perceived as beautiful, and the bold artistic pioneer will be embalmed as a 'classic'. Such canonization is both a threat and a temptation to her, a threat because it implies the mortification of her vital experiments in 'style', a temptation because to be a 'classic' is to enter literary history. Against the high-minded singularity of Art she acknowledges the corrupt but profitable populism of 'Mammon', into whose service she will be drawn by the writing of autobiography.

If Stein began as an autobiographer by imitating the unadorned style of Daniel Defoe, she continued by imitating the style of Gertrude Stein. Her second volume, *Everybody's Autobiography*, appeared in 1938, five years into her celebrity as the author of *The Autobiography* and this time with her name on the title-page. The success of the earlier volume had altered her relationship to her literary vocation, freeing her to exult in her popularity where before she had exulted in her creative solitude. By writing an autobiography she has duplicated herself, as the mediatrix of her own proudly rebarbative oeuvre. Suddenly she has become a literary lion, a position which she unashamedly likes, but she can not go so far as to allow that her facile, sub-Steinian *Autobiography* is the true explanation for her lionization. Much of *Everybody's Autobiography* is taken up with a cloyingly circumstantial account of a campus tour of the United States following the success of *The Autobiography*, but Stein maintains there to a New York publisher that the 'extraordinary welcome' she has been receiving 'does not come from the books of mine that they do understand like the Autobiography but the books of mine that they did not understand'(*EA*, xiii).[4] She can appease her guilt at having sunk into facility by proposing autobiography to herself as the thin end of an aesthetic wedge, by publishing which she can insinuate her difficult writing into the prominence she is certain that it deserves.

Facility explains the perverse title she found for *Everybody's Autobiography*, in the preface to which Stein observes that 'Anyway autobiography is easy like it or not autobiography is easy for any one and so this is to be Everybody's Autobiography'(*EA*, xi) – though Everybody's Autobiography is clearly not going to follow Everybody's rules of punctuation. The title is perverse for being counter-autobiographical. Only a Somebody can write an autobiography, and *Everybody's Autobiography* has the ring of anonymity, seeming to

---

[4] References to *Everybody's Autobiography* (marked *EA*) are to the first edition (London, 1938).

present itself as the life-story of no one in particular, the very crowd from whom an autobiographer will stand out. But this autobiographer is in the mould of Descartes, she is the devious egalitarian who had written in the earlier volume that 'The important thing, she insists, is that you must have deep down as the deepest thing in you a sense of equality'(*AT*, 234), yet who now offers herself as the surrogate of all the world in a mightily capacious, Walt Whitmanesque gesture of incorporation.

Stein is in no doubt of her peculiar fitness to execute this ample autobiographical programme, for she has a theory by which to articulate what she writes with the need for self-expression of an entire generation or cultural moment: her theory of 'composition'. This term she uses in a sense akin to that which it can have in philosophy, where it refers to the extension whereby a statement about an individual member of a class is made to apply to the class as a whole. Composition thus understood is a bridge between the one and the many of which that one is the representative. Each generation or cultural moment, according to Stein, has its distinctive 'composition', made up of everything which *shows*: 'The only thing that is different from one time to another is what is seen and what is seen depends upon how everybody is doing everything.'[5] By this definition, simply to act or move is to 'compose' and the idea that any one individual might be large-minded enough to identify what is distinctive about a particular period's 'composition' seems fanciful.

But Gertrude Stein is not an ordinary individual and her representational powers are boundless. In her vast, unreadable epic entitled *The Making of Americans*, what began as the history of her own American family expanded into one of the whole nation, its overweening author having decided to pursue a scientific programme of induction from the known to the unknown, on the assumption that the laws of psychology were such 'that one could make diagrams and describe every individual man and woman who ever was or is or will be living'(*EA*, 231). Only a 'genius' could aspire so high, which is what Stein by her own account is and why she feels peculiarly empowered to stand in as an autobiographer for the silent majority. Early on in *The Autobiography* we are told straight out that Gertrude Stein is one of the three geniuses – the other two being Picasso and the philosopher Alfred North Whitehead – whom Alice Toklas has

---

[5] Gertrude Stein, 'Composition as explanation', in *What are Masterpieces* (New York, 1970), p. 30.

met with in her lifetime, and that before setting out to write her autobiography Toklas had projected a memoir of 'The wives of geniuses I have sat with', 'wife' to a genius being of course her own role in both the home and the text. As to what genius exactly is, we are told in *Everybody's Autobiography* that it 'is the existing without any internal recognition of time'(*EA*, 210). And since the distinctive 'composition' of the age, which it is a genius's peculiar responsibility to identify, is itself determined by what Stein calls that age's 'time-sense', the logic of her position appears to be that because she lacks any inner 'recognition of time' she is uniquely able to recognize the 'time-sense' of others.

It behoves autobiographers to be essentialist in their beliefs about the self, and Gertrude Stein is certain that she at least possesses an essence, or as she would say, an 'entity', a monadic, immutable kernel of being which is by its nature autistic because it is disconnected from all other selves. This 'entity' is the subject who writes but it can be realized objectively only in the problematical form of a textual 'identity', which is an 'entity' seen from outside and therefore unstable. For the good reason that, in autobiography, she is giving other people to see the varying 'rhythms' of her inner life, Stein can not be sure that this extended organogram can prove her 'identity'. Identity is recognition from outside; as she likes to put it: 'I am I because my little dog knows me'(*EA*, 50). But that her poodle should wag its tail when it sees her hardly proves that She remains identically She from moment to moment as her text grows. Her 'entity' is punctual and recognizes no relation with either the past or the future; it is constitutionally ill-adapted to writing an autobiography (or any other kind of narrative): 'That is really the trouble with an autobiography you do not of course you do not really believe yourself why should you, you know so well so very well that it is not yourself, it could not be yourself because you cannot remember right and if you do remember right it does not sound right and of course it does not sound right because it is not right. You are of course never yourself'(*EA*, 53).

With Gertrude Stein's puzzlement or doubt concerning the claims of memory and of identity, autobiography enters on its Age of Suspicion. Her one certainty is of *now*, of the moment of writing, and the temporal aspect within which she should ideally remain is what she calls the 'prolonged present'. A narration conducted on these terms could but be of the successive movements of the writer's mind as she writes, and the illusion of orthodox narrative, by which past events are told as if they were past and complete in themselves, rather than as a function of the present, would be lost. But in her autobiographical practice, Stein compromises – 'Mammon' *oblige*: she knows the power of stories to attract. There is chronology in *The Autobiography of Alice B. Toklas*, a dating of events and an acknowledgment of the public calendar. Yet there is the evidence also of her desire to go her own narrative way, and to be constantly 'beginning again' as she puts it, rather than beginning only the once far back in the past and moving gradually from there towards the present. She tampers with the chronology, she does not destroy it, by making the events of chapter 3 precede those of chapter 2 in historical time and the events of chapter 4 precede those of chapter 3. Apart from which there are her constant small asides, her 'Well anyway's, which in recalling us to the narrative matter of the book in fact bring out her deliberate failure to sustain it. In *Everybody's Autobiography*, where she is writing of experiences very much closer to her in time, the chronological element is reduced, and Stein moves closer to her ideal, of a narration which is itself the centre of attention rather than subservient to the past. In this sequel, autobiography as narrative has begun to dissolve, and to come closer to the form of a *journal intime*.

The doubtful facility attaching to autobiography shifted Stein's prose style towards the condition of spokenness, which was a serious infringement of her proclaimed protocol of writing. In her life, she was prized in company for her talk and as a raconteur, but as the theorist of literature she refuses any easy continuity between talking and writing: 'I talk a lot I like to talk [...] but and this is very important very important indeed talking has nothing to do with creation.'[6] The argument is that definitively made by Proust in *Contre Sainte-Beuve*, that real literary creation is the product not of the shallow, social self, which we display to others face to face, but of the 'moi profond' or 'deep self', to which the writer has access only in his undistracted solitude. The writer is not to be identified with the man – or woman. But how as readers are we to tell the creative and the merely conversational apart? By the difference in style; Stein intends that her writing should be unmistakeably *writing*, and not a graphic imitation of talk. She admires, she says, those cultures – she cites the

---

[6] Gertrude Stein, 'What are masterpieces and why there are so few of them', in *What are Masterpieces*, p. 84.

ancient Egyptian – which have had two languages, a hieratic language for use on 'exalted' occasions, and another, casual language for everyday. As the making visible of what she, a genius, has inside her, literary creation demands a fittingly exclusive language or style, and by her own bold and timely provision of one, she will fulfil her pioneering role in the expression of the contemporary age: '[...] and it is only comparatively lately that it is true that the written language knows that that is of no interest and cannot be done that is to write as anybody talks because what anybody talks because everybody talks as the newspapers and movies and radios tell them to talk the spoken language is no longer interesting and so gradually the written language says something and says it differently than the spoken language'(*EA*, 4–5).

Given which, it is ironic that some of those who read *The Autobiography of Alice B. Toklas* when it was first published and who knew Toklas, claimed to have been able to 'hear' her voice in the mannered simplicities of its style. But the suggestion that she had carried her feat of ventriloquism to the extreme of alienating herself from her own 'style' would have scandalized Stein, for whom the mimicry of speech in writing meant the mimicry of the banal and the transient and must always remain sub-literary. The apartness which is the price, or privilege, of genius is supported linguistically by her apartness as a faithful anglophone living among the French. French is the language in which she can socialize, English that in which she will write, and as a writer her isolation profits her. Asked in *The Autobiography* (i.e. asking herself) whether she ever reads French:

No, she replied, you see I feel with my eyes and it does not make any difference to me what language I hear, I don't hear a language, I hear tones of voice and rhythms, but with my eyes I see words and sentences and there is for me only one language and that is english. One of the things that I have liked all these years is to be surrounded by people who know no english. It has left me more intensely alone with my eyes and my english. (*AT*, 94)

In *Everybody's Autobiography*, she complains of the French that they write for the ear, not for the eye, and as a result achieve only banality. Living among them has fortified her sense of her own 'entity' as a writer whose sentences are to be *seen*, because the seen endures while the merely audible passes.

Gertrude Stein's theory of writing is too arrogant for her to concede that a form of writing so facile as autobiography might ever count as literature; it is written in the silence and abstraction which are the conditions of creativity but in a style or language hybrid between the hieratic and the oral, because the need to vindicate her uncommon creative achievement has now displaced the former need to exhibit it. Autobiography is vulgar and retarded in its methods, but as a 'composition' of its author's life it has an attraction for others which the far loftier 'compositions' of a whole age or generation may alas not have. And because autobiography is a convivial kind of writing, in stooping to it Stein need not hide her enjoyment of her worldly success. Success has come from writing and she can now perpetuate it in the 'prolonged present' of writing: 'I do always like to be a lion, I like it again and again, and it is a peaceful thing to be one succeeding'(*EA*, 277).

Nabokov

Vladimir Nabokov would have been bitingly contemptuous of the 'facility' with which Gertrude Stein produced the 300 or more pages of *The Autobiography of Alice B. Toklas* in only six weeks – as well as of the plainness of style to which she had descended in order to write them, compared with the riddling complications of her more developed manner. For the choosy Nabokov there could be no appearing in print in mufti; everything published as having come from him must be in his 'style', even the answers ascribed to him in interviews having to be called in and groomed by himself before publication. His defence was that of Rousseau, that in conversation or in company he could not do himself justice verbally and must appear less fluent and less masterful than he would wish;[7] whereas in absentia, as a writer, he could soar stylistically, unhampered by the pressing needs of the conversational moment. But where Rousseau degraded writing to a *pis-aller*, as the standby of a tongue-tied man, Nabokov dedicated himself buoyantly to the written language, knowing it to be an infinitely richer and more distinguished medium than the spoken.

Nabokov always flaunted a cheerful iconoclasm towards his great predecessors in literature, but there was one writer whom he felt

---

[7] These remarks apply to Nabokov as a user of English, which was not his native language and in which facility may therefore have been less of a possibility for him than it would have been in Russian. But he was often witheringly rude about translations of his own work, unless they were done by himself, or by his son under his supervision.

obliged in his own interest to commend: Flaubert, that most celebrated of all martyrs to literary 'style', for whom the creation of a tolerable paragraph might be the work of weeks and of innumerable rewordings. For Flaubert writing had a labour-value, as it did for Nabokov, and the affinity between the two of them, as writers of a superior fastidiousness, is celebrated by Nabokov in his autobiography. The human intermediary between them is Nabokov's father, whom he has admired very greatly as a man but whose occasional writings on legal and political subjects he finds 'rather monotonous' compared with 'his colourful, quaint, often poetical, and sometimes ribald, everyday utterances'(177).[8] The father is in this the opposite of the son, having talked more engagingly than he wrote. He had also been an admirer of Flaubert – as well as of Stendhal, Balzac and Zola, 'three detestable mediocrities', according to Nabokov, presumably because they wrote too much and too quickly. But the manuscripts that Nabokov *père* has left behind are unreasonably clean and as unlike any that the toiling Flaubert could have left as they are unlike his son's, 'penned in a copy-book slanted, beautifully sleek, unbelievably regular hand, almost free of corrections, a purity, a certainty, a mind-and-matter cofunction that I find amusing to compare to my own mousy hand and messy drafts, to the massacrous revisions and rewritings, and new revisions, of the very lines in which I am taking two hours now to describe a two-minute run of his flawless handwriting. His drafts were the fair copies of immediate thought'(178). The father, however, had not been a writer but a public figure, as lawyer, professor and liberal politician; 'immediate thought' was what the world demanded of him. His son by contrast, a resolutely private figure, prizes language in its luxurious, impractical uses, when it is brought to create and display what his Russian contemporaries, the Formalists, referred to as its specific 'literariness'.

Nabokov's ancestor in autobiography must be Alfieri, the arch reviser, who conceived of autobiography itself as an artistic means by which to go back and set right his youthful carelessness in living. But

[8] Page references are to the 1966 New York edition of *Speak, Memory*. The publishing history of the two versions of Nabokov's autobiography is complicated by the fact that the earlier version, published in the United States as *Conclusive Evidence*, appeared in Britain at the same time under the title of *Speak, Memory*, the title under which both the American and the British editions of the final version were published, Nabokov's publishers having turned down his suggested title of *Speak, Mnemosyne*, on the grounds, he says, that 'little old ladies would not want to ask for a book whose title they could not pronounce'!

with Nabokov the act of revision is more complex, for between the autobiographer and his early life there stands his own earlier vision of that life. His autobiography, *Speak, Memory*, was published in its final version in 1966, and bears the subtitle, 'An autobiography revisited', because it is in fact the revision of an earlier volume called *Conclusive Evidence*, which had appeared in 1951. To those with a naively realist, Darwinian view of autobiography, this will seem treacherous: between brute 'life' and finished text, we have here interposed an earlier text, causing reality to recede even further, behind not one curtain of words but two and the words, what is more, of a celebrated literary dandy. This worrying double regress is compounded by the trafficking between languages which has been incurred in the preparation of the definitive version. *Conclusive Evidence* had been written in English but then translated by Nabokov into his native Russian, so that he has had two earlier autobiographical texts from (on) which to work, one in his adopted and one in his mother tongue. In his 1966 Foreword, Nabokov amusedly recapitulates the serial process of translation through which his final text has passed, without the least hint that this unusual compositional history need be thought to impair the transparency of his recollections: 'This re-Englishing of a Russian re-version of what had been an English re-telling of Russian memories in the first place, proved to be a diabolical task, but some consolation was given me by the thought that such multiple metamorphosis, familiar to butterflies, had not been tried by any human before'(13).

We should, I think, take the word 'diabolical' here in a strong sense, of something like mephistophelean, and not in its weak one, as if the task in question had been merely arduous or disagreeable. Nabokov is far from complaining at what had been asked of him but likening his powers of evocation in autobiography to those of a Faustian magus able to summon up unreal sights more pleasing to the mind's eye than any real ones. In the course of *Speak, Memory*, its sly narrator slips in and out of his tempter's costume, reminding us each time he does so that the delightfully 'diabolical' task on which he is bent is that of establishing the priority of art over reality. In Nabokov's case there is a pathos in this, because he is writing as an exile and using autobiography explicitly as an art-form by which to gainsay the state of loss in which he has long been obliged to live. At the age of eighteen he had been driven irrevocably out from both his native land and his native language. He has had to live out of Russia and, eventually, to learn to write in a second language. He has 'lost' the past with a peculiar completeness, because he is unable to return in the body to the edenic topography of his childhood and adolescence.

The impossibility of making a real return is the inspiration for making this unreal one; art must deliver what history refuses, and the interposition between the real landscape of Russia and his present recollections, of his earlier vision of that landscape in *Conclusive Evidence*, makes the subordination of historical datum to artistic design appear the more flagrant and thus the more consoling. Recalling in *Speak, Memory* a return home to St Petersburg from a year spent abroad at the age of six, 'my first *conscious* return'(his italics), Nabokov remarks that it now seems to him, sixty years later, 'a rehearsal – not of the grand homecoming that will never take place, but of its constant dream in my long years of exile'(97). This cruel reversal, by which a real return is transsubstantiated into a preview of very many imaginary ones, is the defiant trick by which this autobiographical Prospero declares his hand, as an artist singularly masterful in the arrangement of his unrealities.

None of this shows in Nabokov's imperious title, whose suggestion is that Memory has been given its orders and must now provide, with the autobiographer as no more than its obedient secretary. But Nabokov is as dead set against automatism in writing as was Gertrude Stein: it is he, not Memory, who will do the speaking, though in a 'style' conspicuously far removed from any which might be thought imitative of speech.[9] In the event, Nabokov's memory does not speak, it *shows*: *Speak, Memory* is the most consistently and triumphantly pictorial of all autobiographies, a book in which Memory seems to be nostalgic for the fullness of perception, and to be striving to 'revisit' a vanished topography substantively, in denial of its own merely vicarious condition. But much of what Nabokov gives us to see from a supposedly distant past is too real to be true, too graphically exact to quite *belong* to the past. Rather than perceptions, these images aspire to resemble the (all too) memorable pictures shown to us in dreams. Nabokov's images, however, are not given but

---

[9] Although *Speak, Memory* is the only autobiography known to me which is addressed to another human being: it is not merely dedicated to Nabokov's wife Vera, but sporadically and discreetly apostrophizes her. In the final chapter, apostrophe turns into full-blooded invocation of the epistolary kind: e.g. 'The years are passing, my dear, and presently nobody will know what you and I know.' The effect is that inevitably of Augustine's *Confessions*, of a story overheard being told to a listener who already knows it.

made, and as such are the conscious constructs of his 'style'. There is no invocation of the subconscious in *Speak, Memory*, a mythopoeic domain of which Nabokov was acidly dismissive and whose fabled dragoman, Sigmund Freud, he liked to refer to as 'the Viennese quack'. Nabokov admits that he has been subject all his life to 'mild hallucinations', but only to mark such passive, febrile visions categorically off from the conscious 'hallucinations' authorized by the artist, 'the bright mental image (as, for instance, the face of a beloved parent long dead) conjured up by a wing-stroke of the will; *that* is one of the bravest movements a human spirit can make'(33). Since his own great visual sensitivity had originally been fostered by his mother, it is her parenthetical influence that we may choose to see as presiding over the pellucid retrospections of *Speak, Memory*.

Nabokov's 'bright mental images' are too compelling in themselves, as forms of words, to be experienced simply as an array of gorgeous pointers to a lost domain beyond. To look beyond them is in fact a discomforting experience because they open only on to that dire vacancy which Nabokov evokes in the very first words of the text proper: 'The cradle rocks above an abyss, and common sense tells us that our existence is a brief crack of light between two eternities of darkness'(19). This might well rank as the most forbidding of all autobiographical incipits. But the verbal semblance of one particular 'brief crack of light' which it introduces has been made by Nabokov not in submission to this cheerless philosophy but in rebellion against it. Unlike the pseudo-democrat Descartes, he cites 'common sense' not in order to endorse its findings but in order to contest them. He dislikes and distrusts 'common sense' for being common; a rare artist such as himself need not feel bound by it. Having shortly reminded us of the threat of oblivion under which we all of us live, Nabokov then comes forward as a rebellious 'chronophobiac', writing in the hope that there may be more dimensions to time than 'common sense' supposes and that by imposing creative patterns of his own upon it, he may even be acting in imitation of some lordly, supernatural counterpart, responsible for ordering our macrocosm along attractively Nabokovian lines.

The proof of artifice is in pattern, or design, and it is design which, in *Speak, Memory*, assimilates the 'style' of the writer to that of Nature. Nabokov's analogy in his Foreword between the changes through which his text has passed and the metamorphoses undergone by a butterfly is more than an advance reminder that he has led a lesser but still notable career as a lepidopterist; it goes deeper, to an analogy between the design with which he has informed his text to that visible in the colouring and configuration of a butterfly – the fragile insect, be it remembered, whose power of metamorphosis has made it into a traditional symbol of immortality and thus the ideal emblem for a work of autobiography. This bringing together of his two careers, as writer and as natural scientist, is a first indication that in *Speak, Memory* Nabokov will envision his memories with the same passionate attention to their specific resemblances and differentiae as when sorting specimens in a laboratory. He groups his memories as it were by taxa, or by themes, going one by one through the tutors whom he had as a boy for example, or correlating across time and space his varied experiences in early life of trains and railway-journeys. This thematic arrangement weakens but does not neutralize the impulsion of his narrative. There is progression in *Speak, Memory*, because the narrator is moving towards two climactic moments of exclusion, first from Russia in 1917–8 and subsequently from Europe, the denouement of his story being his taking ship for the United States in May 1940. The committed aesthete has been formed by the catastrophes of history (and not least by the assassination of his father in Berlin, after the Russian diaspora, by a political fanatic).

The aesthete's response to such vulgar, overmighty events as the Bolshevik Revolution is to admit them to his story only in miniature, as the source of local memories, peculiar to himself. For the instrument through which Nabokov likes to re-view the past is the microscope, at the bottom of whose 'magic shaft' the details of things can be made to appear with a captivating acuity, and the whole of some object be reduced to no more than the hypothetical ground of the visible part. (It is no doubt ironic that the microscope should also have been the optical instrument to whose workings Freud, the 'Viennese quack', likened those of the human consciousness.) Nabokov goes repeatedly in his autobiography to the vocabulary of optics in order to make it seem that what he has lost and means to regain is not time but a place. With him the forgotten or the imperfectly remembered becomes the invisible or indistinct. The 'diabolical' reworking of *Conclusive Evidence* as *Speak, Memory* has thus produced a greater *clarity* in his iconography of pre-revolutionary Russia: 'I revised many passages and tried to do something about the amnesic defects of the original – blank spots, blurry areas, domains of dimness. I discovered that sometimes, by means of intense concentration, the neutral smudge might be forced to come into beautiful focus so that the sudden view could be identified'(12). 'Intense concentration' might be thought a state of mind favourable to an autobiographer, and to be productive of memory images of the utmost veracity; but the blurred scenes so intensely concentrated on by Nabokov acquire in the result an uncanny sharpness of line, testifying not to their reliability but to what he calls 'certain camera-lucida needs of literary composition'.

The camera lucida was a mirroring device used in drawing by which the reflected images of objects were projected on to a sheet of paper; as a representational aid it was the forerunner of the camera.[10] Nabokov invokes it in recalling the drawing lessons he had as a boy, which only came to fruition later, when he was drawing the butterfly genitalia illuminated in his laboratory microscope. We are to conceive of his technique of description in *Speak, Memory* as the equivalent of the passionate precision which was his objective then. Except that now the images he is projecting are of what no longer exists; the writer's camera lucida is a trick. But what it is able to do is to give us to imagine more than we can actually see: like all autobiographers Nabokov is an adept of synecdochism, of that putting of parts for wholes which is both a staple of rhetoric and the essence of sympathetic magic, or the desire to master an intangible reality by manipulation of some tangible emanation from it. It is a form of magic which Nabokov practises openly, never pretending that it is other than magic.

The imagined and the seen complement one another in *Speak, Memory*, in which the twin virtualities of representation, whereby reality is either reduced in scale or enlarged, are mutually supporting. To adopt Nabokov's own metaphorical terms, lantern-slides combine with microscope slides, the one showing less the other more than the so-called naked eye. He has sat through dismal lantern-slide lectures as a boy, and found the slides, as projected on to a screen, both 'tawdry and tumid'; but once held up to the light by hand they were transformed into 'translucent miniatures, pocket wonderlands, neat little worlds of hushed luminous hues'(166). The effect of these clarified scenes, so much smaller than life-size, is to 'fire the fancy', the mind enlarging on what the eye has been shown. But the fired

---

[10] As Roland Barthes recognized in the remarkable book which he wrote on photography and on the effects which photographs had on him personally. See *La Chambre claire* (Paris, 1980) *passim*.

fancy is recalled to order when we turn from the lantern-slide to the microscope, and from reduction to enlargement. Fancy now makes way for fact, as, in the instrument's revealing beam of light, 'an insect's organ was magnified for cool study'. By moving between these two opposed kinds of representation, Nabokov the auto-biographer can play both the novelist and the natural scientist, prompting the 'fancy' by his powers of evocation and then compelling us to attend coolly to the details of what is being set before us. In *Speak, Memory* he occupies that commanding position which he defines as 'a kind of delicate meeting-place between imagination and knowledge, a point, arrived at by diminishing large things and enlarging small ones, that is intrinsically artistic'(167).

Nabokov's autobiography achieves unity not through the continuity of its narrative but by the consistency of its 'style'. This had been true of *Conclusive Evidence* before it became true – perhaps, given the work of revision that he had done, truer still – of *Speak, Memory*. To an editor of the *New Yorker* (who had just turned down a story he had submitted, on grounds easily deducible from what follows), he once wrote, 'Several pieces of "Conclusive Evidence", for instance, which you were kind to admire were merely a series of impressions held together by means of "style". For me "style" *is* matter.'[11] Style thus becomes the artist's paper-thin ark in which to navigate the 'abyss' of time, that disagreeable vacancy which threatens in the blanks between the memories he has been able to recover and assemble. The autobiographer's enemies are ignorance and oblivion, and his work is an exemplary one, of anamnesis. He is inspired by knowing that those inimical tracts of past time which as yet appear tenantless may be colonized by finding memory images with which to plant them, the concentrated effort of recollection having the effect of awakening their 'sleeping beauties' – a trope once used, according to Nabokov, by hopeful cartographers, to populate the emptinesses on their maps.

But it is cruelly clear that time can not be defeated by anamnesis alone, for however many images from the past we are able to gather, to arrange them conventionally in a unilinear sequence is to play by the enemy's rules and connive at our mortality. Nabokov the illusionist plays by other rules, collapsing time now and again on principle from a fatally linear into a more hospitable 'folded'

[11] He was writing to Katherine A. White. See *Vladimir Nabokov: Selected Letters* 1940–77, edited by Dmitri Nabokov and Matthew J. Bruccoli (London, 1990), p. 116.

pattern. The 'compositional viewpoint' here is that of Proust in *A la recherche du temps perdu*. That mighty work too Proust asked should be envisaged as a 'composition', in terms either of an architectural structure or a musical one, whose linearity as a text was contradicted by an internal scheme of repeating motifs (as well as by the circularity of a narrative whose denouement lies in the narrator's turning to write the novel we have been reading). But where Proust is wholly serious in finding an absolution from time in such small sensorial recurrences as the taste of a cake dipped in tea,[12] Nabokov is not, he is playful, not wanting for steepling metaphysical conclusions to be drawn from his reliance on a self-conscious artistic device. Indeed, one might suspect him of parody in such episodes of *Speak, Memory* as that when he twice stumbles over the tea-things on the floor of his tutor's room in Cambridge, on occasions separated in time by some seventeen years – it would have been apt had a trodden *madeleine* then been found among the wreckage.

This repetition is one of the 'folds' in time that the autobiographer has effected, whether or not his cue had been given him by the facts of his life. The 'fold' conjures away by elision the seventeen years which had passed between the first upsetting of the tea-tray and the second, though in Nabokov's case, unlike that of Proust, the repetition is not used to reclaim an entire chain of other, metonymically linked memories. For Nabokov, time is only hidden, it is not abolished, a repetition such as this offering him a way in to what he writes of as his 'stereoscopic dreamland', not to some mystical, time-free realm of being. But as the prize exhibits of the autobiographical quest, his recurrences transcend the primary process of remembering. In another, less farcical but still humorous example, he introduces a Russian general who had once, when Nabokov was a very small boy, been on the point of showing him a trick involving a row of matches, only to be stopped by an aide-de-camp bearing an order for him to 'assume supreme command of the Russian Army in the Far East'. Fifteen years later, after the Bolshevik coup, this same general, now disguised as a peasant, has happened to stop Nabokov's father in the street and asked him for a light. 'What pleases me', writes the

---

[12] The famous *madeleine* is not so banal an object as it may seem. In real life the formative experience of involuntary memory which Proust had found so uncannily restorative of moments in his boyhood had come from tasting something truly banal, a piece of dry toast dipped in tisane. His subsequent elevation of this into a *madeleine* acquired for the experience the religious connotations of the word, which is the French form of Magdalene (and the name of a fashionable church in Paris).

autobiographer in commenting on this extravagant and shapely coincidence, 'is the evolution of the match theme: those magic ones he had shown me had been trifled with and mislaid, and his armies had also vanished, and everything had fallen through [...]. The following of such thematic designs through one's life should be, I think, the true purpose of autobiography'(27). The autobiographer has himself pulled the trick in the performance of which the luckless general had been interrupted.

Once in thrall to the coruscations of Nabokov's 'style' in *Speak, Memory*, one may cease to worry whether these 'designs' are the product of life itself or a 'diabolical' invention. They are another way of converting time into space, by conscripting separate temporal moments into a textual simultaneity, and this for Nabokov is the role which it falls to the poet to perform. Posing briefly as Vivian Bloodmark, 'a philosophical friend of mine', he reflects further on his double autobiographical role as poet and as scientist, giving it as Bloodmark's opinion that 'while the scientist sees everything that happens in one point of space, the poet feels everything that happens in one point of time'(218); the poet is the 'nucleus' of 'trillions' of trifling events happening simultaneously in many different places and associable only in thought, as in the miraculously reflexive 'aleph' in Borges's story of that name. The writer, for Nabokov and Borges alike, is a magician, like the dextrous tutor described in *Speak, Memory* who made coins seem to disappear by holding them between sheets of identically ruled paper. Yet having described in detail how this trick was done, Nabokov goes on to remark that 'Coincidence of pattern is one of the wonders of nature'(157), in an indication that amateur conjurors and the 'contrapuntal genius of human fate' may as fellow-artists share the same saving secret.

Nabokov's cryptic allusion is to the natural phenomena of mimicry in insects and other creatures, which he has observed in butterflies and of which he refuses to take a merely Darwinian view. Mimicry may serve to protect the creatures which practise it by enabling them to remain invisible to their predators, but for Nabokov it goes beyond any such utilitarian or evolutionary function, into the useless virtuosity of art:

'Natural selection', in the Darwinian sense, could not explain the miraculous coincidence of imitative aspect and imitative behaviour, nor could one appeal to the theory of 'the struggle for life' when a protective device was carried to a point of mimetic subtlety, exuberance and luxury far in excess of a predator's power of appreciation. I discovered in nature the nonutilitarian delights that I sought in art. Both were a form of magic, both were a game of intricate enchantment and deception. (125)

In this Romantic analogy is to be found Nabokov's justification for the exotic form which he has given to his autobiography. His exuberant display of 'style' in *Speak, Memory* far exceeds the generic need, of protecting the autobiographer against the encroachments of oblivion. But the poet can claim backing for his superfluities of language from the scientist, for whom the mere urge to survival is too prosaic an explanation of mimetic phenomena. A non-utilitarian Nature is an auspicious model for a poet-autobiographer to imitate, especially when in a clever mimesis there may lie the ultimate luxury of immunity from the oblivion which common-sense declares to be our unhappy fate.

Sartre

If Nabokov was a parsimonious granter of interviews, too protective of his 'style' to be caught in public without it, Jean-Paul Sartre was exceptionally liberal, having given well over a hundred published interviews by the time of his death in 1980. As an impromptu occasion, the interview answered very well to Sartre's wish to be uninhibited, talking with the combative frankness of a man for whom topicality was not to be prejudiced by niceties of 'style'. This was to act in what Sartre himself once taught us to recognize as 'good faith', in circumstances which allowed no room for self-deception. But it is easier to talk in 'good faith' than it is to write in it, when the writer is actor and audience in one, and has ample time to adjust his performance should he disapprove of what he finds himself writing. Sartre wrote a very great deal over his lifetime, with a terrible and compulsive fluency which left him little time for the second thoughts he preferred not to have. But by his own definition, not all of this writing was of the same kind, for at some never quite determinate point after 1945 Sartre had ceased to be a 'literary' figure and become a political one. He had found 'commitment', and writing henceforth must serve a pragmatic end, as a means to change the world by changing the minds of those who read him. 'Literature' was correspondingly now to be a pejorative term, applied to what was written by self-confessed fops such as Nabokov. 'Style' in writing was taboo, it was the stigma of the bourgeois writer, who had condemned himself to the narcissistic pleasures of introversion.

It was in order to recant publicly on his bourgeois 'literary' heritage that Sartre wrote an autobiography, *Words*, which is in the purest autobiographical tradition in being the record of a 'conversion', from one philosophy of writing to another, and as such itself partaking of both philosophies. It is a 'literary' work of pragmatic intent. As literature it proved extremely successful, being, in contrast to so much of Sartre's abundant oeuvre, short, fairly concrete and carefully written; it has economy and a certain 'style', and for all its savage anti-bourgeois moral was the book more than any other which caused Sartre to be awarded the very bourgeois Nobel Prize for literature, an award which he refused, later called 'monstrous' yet admitted had been brought about by the publication of *Words*.[13] This book belongs self-evidently to the 'literary' phase of Sartre's life but is intended to be read as a valediction, it is his well-written farewell to the world of what he sardonically called the *bel écrit* of 'fine writing'.

Words was published in 1964, when Sartre was already fifty-nine years old. But he had begun to write an autobiography some ten years before, at the moment when he thought he had been suddenly cured of the 'neurosis' of believing in the bourgeois religion of literature and had become a fellow-traveller of the French Communist Party. In Sartrian terms *Words* was thus the product of a particular historical 'situation', a topical polemic against the ideal of timelessness as enshrined in the *bel écrit*. Its original title was the curious one of 'Jean sans terre' or 'John Lackland', after the English king of that sobriquet, a title very obviously ironic in presenting the hero of the book as someone whose pretence to sovereignty is belied by the absence of real dominions over which to rule.[14] *Words* as we have it is thus that rarity for Sartre, a text which he had revised. His principal aim in recasting the draft of a decade earlier had been, he

---

[13] See his remarks in the published scenario of *Sartre: Un film réalisé par Alexandre Astruc et Michel Contat* (Paris, 1977), pp. 110–13.

[14] I am not the first reader of Sartre to wonder whether the title of 'Jean sans terre' might not equally well have been 'Jean sans père' or 'John Lackfather', since the lack of a father – Jean-Baptiste Sartre having died very soon after his son was born – functions in *Words* as a long-term determinant of Sartre's life. It is this early removal of an oppressive paternal presence which has instituted his 'freedom' and even if it has taken Sartre many years to recognize and take up residence in this heady if exacting realm, he presumably might never have been free to do so had his father lived. (His father's death meant that he grew up without a super-ego, according to Sartre, who was little better disposed towards Freudian theory than was Nabokov, and for the same reason, that it places humiliating limitations on the authority of the conscious mind.)

said, to remove 'the somewhat ironical tone', although the final text may well strike some as still too ironical, as the reformed bourgeois rounds vindictively on the family in which he was raised and on his own pretentious young self. For Sartre as he now is, irony is a device better done without because it is ambiguous and the recourse of the non-committal 'literary' writer, who shows himself complacent towards all those things in the world and in himself of which he disapproves. The ironist sits ill with the moral reformer, which is the autobiographical role adopted by Sartre in *Words*. This is the newly convinced fellow-traveller's *mea culpa* and his confession of his political blindness in the past is also a promise of his political lucidity in the future. Secularist or no, Sartre accords to autobiography a doctrinally instrumental function such as Augustine might have claimed for the *Confessions* had he written them immediately after his baptism.

Like Augustine, Sartre has been trapped from boyhood within a false theory and practice of language. He has been taught first and foremost to overvalue words, as the unreal means by which human beings take illusory possession of the real. He has come to 'confuse things with their names' and to suppose that by his ready disposition of names he was simultaneously disposing of things: 'since I had discovered the world through language, for a long time I mistook language for the world. To exist was to have a guaranteed tradename somewhere on the infinite Tables of the Word; writing meant engraving new beings on them or – this was my most persistent illusion – catching things, alive, in the trap of sentences' (125).[15] For Sartre the philosopher, words are essences which fail in their apparent fixity to register the mutability of existences. They are on the side of Being and against Becoming, and it is incumbent on the existentialist thinker to recognize their constitutional incapacity to capture reality alive, even if that recognition seems to undermine the very arguments he might advance in support of it. In *Words* Sartre can but use authoritative words to deny the authority wrongly accorded to words.

There is a concept familiar from political science which describes the linguistic situation in which Sartre has found himself: that of alienation. Alienated man is the victim of circumstances which he has been taught to believe are natural but which have in truth been

---

[15] The English translation I have quoted from is that of Irene Clephane (London, 1964), though I have made silent alterations to it in places where it seemed to me to miss a Sartrian nuance useful for the purposes of my exposition.

imposed on him by others, and the cure for his alienation is to enlighten him about how those circumstances have come to obtain. The task is one of demystification by means of a narrative, and that is the task which Sartre undertakes in his own regard in *Words*. He has been alienated more than just linguistically by the circumstances of his bourgeois upbringing, the early life which he is now narrating having imposed on him a false role of which only now is he divesting himself publicly. That is the role of idealist in both the philosophical and the psychological senses of the word; he has been brought to live too much in the head and not enough in the real world. And for the Romantic Sartre as for the Romantic Rousseau, alienation is a process damnable for working against Nature, so that to demystify it is to recover the 'natural order', the crippling impostures of society (for Rousseau) or of middle-class domesticity (for Sartre) having been finally exposed.

Sartre restages his life *en famille* as a black joke that has been perpetrated on him, in obedience perhaps to Marx's dictum concerning the repetitions of history, whereby what occurs first as tragedy returns as farce. In the early pages of *Words*, the twin ancestral lines of the Sartres and the Schweizers converge on himself in a parodic family history of malevolence, humbug and joyless procreation, the next generation having been conceived in silence among the Sartres and by surprise among the Schweizers. The object of this caustic prelude is to establish the contingent nature of his own birth; Sartre has, in the phrase used by one of his masters in philosophy, Heidegger, been not so much born as 'thrown into' the world. As existentialist neonate, he is a gratuitous arrival born to a life of free self-creation. But that is not the life which he has been allowed to lead: existential freedom is for those fortunate enough to be born without a nuclear bourgeois family to oppress them. In answering to the emotional needs and class expectations of others, the young Sartre has become a role-player, following a script prepared for him by the other actors. His father has died very soon after his own birth and has the role in *Words* of a *deus absconditus*, a momentous, freedom-bestowing absentee; but freedom for the son has entailed captivity for the mother, Anne-Marie, who as a young widow has reverted to the role of passive, virginal daughter to her father, Charles Schweitzer, the self-deceiving patriarch who has played the determining role in perverting the course of his grandson's life. Sartre has played with great talent his allotted role of prodigious only child, the heir and futurity of a smug, elitist menage. Strutting theatrically about in a home where 'everything was for show' he was, he now claims, an actor who knew he was an actor, able even as a very small child to 'feel my actions changing into gestures'(54). He is the alienated victim of the gaze of the Other, who watches himself being watched and is robbed in the process of his 'authenticity'. Sartre empowers his boyhood self again and again with these precocious insights into his own condition, as if the perspective of the present demanded no less of an autobiographer as repentant or aggrieved as he is about his failure to understand that condition long before. But one might also observe that the greater the claims he makes for the virtuosity of his childhood 'clowning' the more the other members of the household stand incriminated for their de-naturing of him.

As juvenile lead in a family cast of histrions, Sartre is, however, merely a victim typical of his class, of that posturing bourgeoisie which he now looks upon as the nursery of all 'bad faith'. His alienation takes a more particular form only when it comes to language. Charles Schweizer is the archetypal bourgeois for whom language is no longer a 'natural' medium practicable equally and indifferently by all, but a hierarchical one, some uses of which are more valuable than others. He has a cult of Great Literature and of the Great Authors who have written it. But in this as in all his other beliefs he is a sham, because his real concern with literature is mundane, having to do with his profession. Charles Schweitzer, born in Alsace, is a teacher of German and the author of a successful textbook; what the canonical works of French literature on his library shelves provide him with is examples for translation into German: 'In his heart of hearts, the author of the *Deutsches Lesebuch* regarded world literature as his raw material. He supposedly classified authors in order of merit, but this hierarchy was a facade barely concealing his utilitarian preferences'(46). As the teacher of a foreign language, Charles Schweizer is peculiarly well fitted to direct his grandson's linguistic alienation and to bestow on him his own quasi-sacerdotal belief in the mission of the intelligentsia to educate others. This is not a responsibility from which Sartre can secede even now, in the hour of his political awakening, for *Words* too has been conceived and written in didactic terms, for the enlightenment of others. Its author remains the creation of Charles Schweizer.

Sartre does not concern himself with that fundamental experience of alienation we all of us suffer when obliged to enter what Jacques

Lacan calls the Symbolic Order, which is language as such, an impersonal system of signs in which, according to Lacan, we can never be at home, because in resorting to words we have to give up the ineffable gratifications of the ego. Sartre restricts himself to that secondary experience of alienation that we may undergo when we change from the spoken to the written forms of language. Here once again he stands with Rousseau, in seeing spoken language as our 'natural' order. His own written 'style' he claims to be the opposite of natural: 'It is true that I have no gift for writing: I have been told so, and I have been treated as a school swot: I am; my books reek of sweat and effort, and I grant that, in the nose of our aristocrats, they stink'(113). But then, as he concludes, 'You talk in your own language, but you write in a foreign one.'

His own induction into this alien medium of writing has two stages, reflected in the division of *Words* into two more or less equal halves, the first subtitled 'Reading', the second 'Writing'. The great, the truly formative moment for him is the learning to read, but this too Sartre divides into two, into an experience of being read to and an imitative one of reading for himself. First he is read to: 'Anne-Marie made me sit down in front of her, on my little chair; she leant over, lowered her eyelids and went to sleep. From the face of this statue there issued a plaster voice. I grew bewildered: who was talking? about what? and to whom? My mother had absented herself: not a smile or sign of complicity. I was an exile. And then I did not recognize the language. Where did she get her confidence? After a moment, I realized: it was the book that was talking'(33). The scene is characteristic of *Words* in being so shamelessly allegorical. As a moment in Sartre's story the experience is one of trauma, fixing the boy in a state of 'exile' and the mother in the dormant, if not petrified condition of a statue, inauthentic because she has lost her own language and has become the mere conduit of another, written language. She has no entitlement to the 'confidence' she has all of a sudden gained, which conflicts with her 'natural' unconfident state and screens her from the angst which for Sartre is the one authentic response to our cosmic dereliction as human beings. There is in short nothing to be said in favour of poor Anne-Marie's performance as reader, which her son has now observed twice, once as a mystified small boy, and a second time in *Words* in his judgmental role of demystified and demystifying autobiographer.

The second stage of his alienation from the togetherness of speech into the frigid mediacy of writing is his acquisition of the power of reading for himself:

> Then I became jealous of my mother and I decided to usurp her role. I seized upon a work called *Tribulations d'un Chinois en Chine* and took it away to a box-room; there, perched on a folding bedstead, I pretended to read: my eyes followed the black lines without skipping a single one and I told myself a story out loud, taking care to pronounce every syllable. I was discovered – or I let myself be discovered – there were cries of admiration and it was decided it was time I was taught the alphabet. I was as zealous as any catechumen; I even gave myself private lessons: I climbed on to my folding bedstead with Hector Malot's *Sans famille*, which I knew by heart, and half-reciting, half-deciphering it, I went though every page, one after another: when the last was turned I knew how to read. (34–5)

There is something here of the supernal facility of Cardano learning Latin in a single night. But Sartre's experience has not been instantaneous, it has again been split into two – this series of duplications has the effect of a narrative tic in *Words*, to whose significance I shall come back. First he mimics the act of reading out loud as he has seen his mother perform it, but to a script of his own making or choosing; he has paused midway between the written and spoken languages. There follows his full initiation, as 'catechumen', into the sacred rite of reading silently, from signs which betray their exclusive, inegalitarian nature by calling for a decipherment, whereas the spoken sign must be presumed totally transparent, or as a cryptographer might say, 'in clear'. The title of the book from which Sartre has so dramatically mastered the skill of reading is well-found, to say the least, his purpose in *Words*, after all, being to make of himself a voluntary orphan, by portraying his family as that hateful bourgeois matrix from whose influence he has at last fought free, so that he may rejoin the human community at large. To be family-less is an entirely desirable state, and if that inauspicious first reading of *Sans famille* has wrongly enthralled Sartre to the printed word, *Words* is the book by which he will mark the end of that thraldom, by a re-reading or else 'decipherment' of his childhood.[16]

His initiation into reading is also an initiation into fiction, which marks the feminine side of his literary formation. In the Schweizer

---

[16] It is intriguing that this same children's story should recently have been invoked by another literary autobiographer in France, the novelist Nathalie Sarraute, who in her delectable and very artful *Enfance* cites the hero of *Sans famille* as one of the fictional characters with whom she most liked to identify in childhood. See *Enfance* (Paris, 1983), p. 77.

house as before in Rousseau's, there were two sorts of books: the permanent books belonging to his grandfather, which were kept in the 'tiny sanctuary' of his library, and the transient novels borrowed one or two at a time from the *cabinet de lecture* by his mother and grandmother. These were 'trash' in Sartre's description of them, inferior stuff despised by the grandfather but a source of genuine, conspiratorial pleasure for the two women. The boy has browsed randomly and excitedly among the encyclopaedias and other serious volumes, but it is stories which have shaped – that is, mis-shaped – him and helped to persuade him that words were invented in order to replace reality with something more satisfying. He has become the brave protagonist of stories of his own making, and has identified with the brave protagonists of stories made by others. He has wept with joy at the courage and humanity of Jules Verne's Michel Strogoff in the adventure novel of that name, which he has read, inevitably, not once but twice and the second time with the insight he had failed to get the first time. It was not the person of the hero that had so appealed to him, he now understands, but the triumphalist nature of narrative itself: 'Yet I did not like Michel, I found him too good: it was his destiny that I envied [...] Michel, entrusted, like all creatures, with a unique and vital mission, passed through our vale of tears, avoiding temptations and surmounting obstacles, savouring martyrdom, and enjoying supernatural aid, glorifying his Creator and then, his task complete, entering into immortality' (90). Michel Strogoff is a hero by appointment from God, enviably predestined to suffer and to overcome, and if Sartre now stresses how taken he was with this extravagant story it is in order to accentuate by contrast his own *true* gratuitousness, as a 'traveller without a ticket', born as we all are to no destiny at all beyond that which we finalize for ourselves. The fictional hero is a particularly corrupting model for an existentialist philosopher because the course of his life has been directed by an outside agency, the novelist, so robbing him of that freedom of action which is for Sartre the noble if also harrowing lot of humankind.

But the existentialist philosopher who writes an autobiography must cast himself in the role of *unfree* hero, the outcome of whose actions is already known. Like any narrative hero, the autobiographical subject is the captive of a script, or of what Sartre refers to as the 'retrospective illusion'. As the old saying has it: we live our lives forwards and recount them backwards. The narration of a life appears to absolve it from time altogether, by rendering it simultaneous, the true open-endedness of our movement through time having been displaced by a mortifying logic. In autobiography as in fiction, the narrator's existence can never unfold – or Sartre would say, be 'projected' – into an unknown future but only accord with a known sequence. The 'retrospective illusion' is that of 'a future more real than the present. It is not surprising: in a completed life, the end is taken as the truth of the beginning. The dead man stands halfway between being and value, between the brute fact and its reconstruction: his history becomes a kind of circular essence which is summed up in each of his moments'(137).

The existentialist ideal is that of Gertrude Stein, of a life recorded from day to day, rather than integrated into the consecutiveness of narrative. Diaries and journals may be read teleologically, by readers who already know what the diarist has become, but they are written by authors genuinely ignorant of the future and come closer therefore to instantiating the impossible degree of freedom of action demanded by Sartre. But *Words* is a narrative work, if sparing in the chronological markers that would enable us to tell how old its narrator was at this moment or that; it makes good allowance for the illusion of simultaneity. As narrative it might seem to be in obvious bad faith, for subscribing to literary conventions which its author adjudges to be dishonest. Sartre, however, believes that he can subscribe to them in good faith since he is in the act of shedding them: *Words* has the self-contradictory form of an existentialist fable, because it exemplifies Sartre's freedom as a living subject to surpass the dead objectifications of himself contained in his narrative. If we are to talk of the 'autobiographical act', then *Words* is an autobiographical act indeed, the gesture by which Sartre will reorient himself in the world. It is the idealist's last fling.

With Sartre we revert unusually clearly to the Vichian model of autobiography, as a narrative means of raising the factually 'certain' into the intelligible, or in the Sartrian terms quoted above, 'being' into a 'value'. Hegel is the link here between Vico and Sartre: the process of 'raising' facts by an act of reflection is the Hegelian process of 'taking up', by which facts are maintained but also transformed by being seen in a more lucid perspective. From the autobiographer's point of view, there are two moments to the process, of the identification of the 'fact' followed by its transformation. This is the twofold movement contained in Sartre's account of how he learnt to

read and again in how he learnt to 'read' *Michel Strogoff* at its true
value. It recurs most powerfully of all in his account of another
boyhood experience of reading, when he comes upon a volume
entitled *L'Enfance des hommes illustres* – a title whose relevance to
Sartre's autobiographical task only the sleepiest reader of *Words*
could fail to notice. Sartre has encountered this book twice, a first
time accidentally, in the course of his aleatory sampling of his
grandfather's library (his 'eccentric travels') and a second time after
he has set out purposely to retrieve it:

I had discovered it, at the time of my eccentric travels, turned over the
leaves, and then flung it away in annoyance: these young elect bore no
resemblance to infant prodigies; they were like me only in the insipidity of
their virtues, and I wondered why they were talked about. In the end the
book disappeared: I had decided to punish it by hiding it. A year later I
turned all the shelves upside down to find it again: I had changed and the
infant prodigy had become a great man victimized by childhood. What a
surprise: the book had changed, too. They were the same words but they
were telling me about myself. I had a presentiment that this work was going
to ruin me; I hated it and I was afraid of it. Each day, before opening it, I
would go and sit by the window: in case of danger, I would let the true light
of day into my eyes. (138)

Can this really be Sartre at the age of ten or eleven, compulsively
seeking confirmation of his own prodigious gifts and future glory in a
volume of didactic life-stories? It can not; it is Sartre in crisis forty
years later, dramatizing in a single scene both the baleful will to
idealization with which he had been indoctrinated and the means of
its eventual defeat. Like any good young idealist, he has identified
with the predestined children of whom he was reading, who would
grow up to be Bach, Rousseau or Molière; but as an autobiographer,
he will emphatically not identify with that delinquent young self,
because he is now out of danger and able to re-read his life in 'the true
light of day'. But the proleptic hint which he drops, in his description
of this primal scene, as to the form that the future cure for his idealism
must take, is Sartre's way of at once exploiting and exposing the
subterfuges of narrative, since we can only interpret the salutary shaft
of natural light as having been cast by the future upon the present. In
thus acknowledging the devious effects of the 'retrospective illusion'
we may identify for ourselves with the prescient young idealist of
Words, in his conclusion concerning *L'Enfance des hommes illustres*, that
'These children lived in error: they thought they were acting and

speaking fortuitously whereas the true goal of their most trivial remarks was to proclaim their destiny. The author and I exchanged moving smiles above their heads; I read the lives of these false mediocrities as God had envisaged them: beginning at the end'(139–40).

God for Sartre is that ideal onlooker for whom an individual life is meaningful even as it is being lived and who, were he to exist, would reduce the existentialist autobiographer to a supernumary, Augustinian role, of someone recovering instead of creating the sense of his existence. So God must go, and he goes for Sartre in *Words* with an impressive suddenness, one morning in La Rochelle, at the age of twelve, when he is waiting for some friends to walk with him to the *lycée*. To while away the time, he has decided to 'think about the Almighty' only to have the Almighty vanish 'without giving any explanation: he does not exist, I said to myself in polite astonishment, and I thought the matter was settled'(170). And so in one way it was settled, inasmuch as Sartre remained robustly atheistic throughout his life. But what had not been settled by this theological absconsion was the deception practised by those who play God in the making-up of stories, nor the thoroughness with which the 'religion' of literature imbibed from his grandfather came to occupy the God-shaped hole left by the loss of religious belief. Sartre the atheistic young writer – held at one further remove here, in the third person – was 'an *ersatz* of the Christian I could not be: his only concern was salvation, the one aim of his stay here below was to earn for himself posthumous bliss through trials endured worthily. Death was reduced to a rite of passage and earthly immortality presented itself as a substitute for eternal life'(169).

But against this heroic and salvationist conception of the writer's role, there has to be set another, and this time one which has indicated to Sartre the direction in which his real salvation lies. Charles Schweizer has been the false friend who must take the blame for having turned him into an idealist; Sartre has nothing good to say about him. But with his mother it is different, because she, for all her timidity towards her father, has been party to his extra-curricular reading of cheap comics and to clandestine visits to the cinema. Where Charles Schweizer stands in *Words* for classicism, authority, and all the hollow slogans of the bourgeois order, Anne-Marie represents a small seed of revolt and of proletarianism. The author of *Words* owes it to his grandfather that he is irrevocably a writer, but to his mother perhaps that he is no longer a bourgeois writer, subscribing to the ersatz religion of literature.

Words fulfils very exactly that specification of autobiography to which I have repeatedly come back: it is a work directed at the rehabilitation of its author as a member of the community, in Sartre's case of the desirable community of the proletariat. It is symptomatic that at the moment in la Rochelle when he lost his faith in God, Sartre should have been alone, but on the point of absorption into a group of schoolfellows: the loss of faith acts as his qualification for being reunited with others. The episode occurs very near the end of *Words* and it is symmetrical with another, which occurs at the end of the first half of the book, where Sartre recalls himself, again as a schoolboy only this time in Paris, unavailingly longing to be invited to take part in the games of other boys in the Luxembourg Gardens. His exclusion from their community is a moment of truth for the deluded idealist: 'Even a non-speaking part would have overwhelmed me; I would gladly have agreed to be a wounded man on a stretcher, or a corpse. I was not given the opportunity; I had met my true judges: my contemporaries, my equals; and their indifference condemned me. I never got over being unmasked by them: neither a wonder nor a jelly-fish, but a wimp who interested no-one'(92).

Words ends with Sartre's ringing – and implausible – renunciation of his singularity: 'If I put away Salvation among the stage properties as impossible, what is left? A whole man, made of all men, worth all of them, and any one of them worth him'(173). Where Descartes began by stepping forward from the crowd, Sartre ends by feigning to step back into it, always bearing in mind that his is the crowd of the Politically Correct. Such a renunciation can cut no ice coming as it does as the conclusion to an autobiography, whose specific ambition as Sartre knew is to present its subject as an admirably singular being. In Sartre's case, his singularity is compounded, not annulled by his wish to relegate it to the now transcended realm of the imaginary. The author of *Words* would like us to agree that by his savage stripping away of his past insincerities he is finally standing before us in glorious transparency, but read alas in 'the true light of day' this autobiography, like every other, can show us only the actor, strutting the boards to the very last moment.

CHAPTER 10

Leiris

The rule is for autobiographers to serve as their own biographer and to write their lives as a narrative, starting as far back in time as they care to go and advancing chronologically towards the present. They have followed biographers without serious question in presuming that a life lived in time is best projected on to the page orthogonally, the order in which events are told repeating in the main that in which they occurred. The Memory that the autobiographer makes to Speak invariably does so with its eye on the calendar, and the biographer/autobiographer who is too excitable or distracted to be bound by the linearity of public time will be adjudged a failure, or to have succeeded at something other than (auto)biography. Maverick representations of a life in which chronology would have little or no say are perfectly conceivable but they strike us more as whimsies than as workable projects: Jorge Luis Borges, to whom no literary possibility was ever closed, once envisaged 'biographies' of such compellingly strange kinds as the history of someone's dreams, or of their bodily organs, or of all the separate occasions in their life when they had imagined the pyramids. In so speculating, he was hoping surely to broaden the minds of those who write and read and to criticize the alienated state in which we most of us live, slaves as we are to formal conventions that are the imposition of culture, not prescribed by Nature, and which might be interestingly transgressed.

The fantastic forms of biography proposed by Borges would involve not the abolition of chronology but its privatization. A Life consisting entirely of its subject's dreams would contain not one master narrative but many narratives, of successive dreams arranged either in the chronological order of their dreaming or according to the perceived affinities of their subject-matter, and given unity by their ascription to a single dreamer. At the very least, time would have to be represented within each dream, since even the narratives that come to us in sleep – or more accurately, the autobiographical narratives into which we turn our dreams once we are awake again – require their sequence of before and after. As would the narrative of someone's relations with his bodily organs, or imaginings of the pyramids, neither of which is feasible except in the form of a cumulative 'history' – the model for which might be Borges's own paradoxically entitled 'History of Eternity', an essay in which he summarizes the succession of ideas held about time by philosophers since Antiquity.

As forms of biography those postulated by Borges are fantastic only because no biographer could have first-hand access to the raw material he would need in order to write them; as possible forms of autobiography, on the other hand, they are not fantastic at all, because they would exploit the right specifically vested in the autobiographer to invite us within the privacy of his consciousness and, by extension, to disclose its contents in whatever format might seem the most pertinent. As an unimpeachable authority, whose every word is autobiographical, the autobiographer can tell us things about himself which a biographer can only guess at and *auto*-biographies might easily be written by dreamers, Egyptophils or hypochondriacs which would meet Borges's apparently freakish specifications.

Borges was himself a rationalist, with no greater sympathy than Nabokov for the under-cover operations of the unconscious mind, but his speculations point the way to a vertiginous yet practicable expansion of the subject-matter of both biography and autobio-graphy, into that disturbed mental and emotional territory whose exploration by psychoanalysis has been one of the great literary innovations of the twentieth century. In recent years, some bio-graphers have tried to bring the unconscious into their narratives, by speculating about their subjects' 'real' motives for behaving as they did and about how their public and private activities may have been directed by latent psychological forces of which they were unaware. These exercises in 'psychography' have seldom been well received, for the same reason that theoretical works on autobiography such as this one may not be well received: that they seem to deny the uniqueness of their subjects' life by forcing it to exemplify a predetermined pattern, according to the Freudian or other allegiance of the biographer. 'Psychography' may indeed in practice be coarse and dictatorial, because it conducts its analyses on a patient unable by the nature of things to collaborate with it. But what of the *auto*biographer who conducts a similar analysis on his living self? What of, to coin a term, 'autopsychography'? Freudianism has long been the passion of some and a pastime of many among the literary classes in the West; it is curious that it has not so far led to any noticeable revisionism among autobiographers, who have more than anyone to gain by it.

To play psychoanalyst to oneself is an autobiographical method which should surely tempt anyone who, like the subject of the present chapter, Michel Leiris, wishes not exactly to narrate his life but, as he would say, to 'grasp' it. Leiris starts out from a very different position from that of other autobiographers: where they assume that the contours of their past are already sufficiently definite simply to be transcribed in the form of a life-story, he assumes the opposite, that there is as yet no sort of story to tell, nor contours to reproduce, self-knowledge being the end of autobiography and not its source. His is a heuristic notion of the genre, and the promise which he makes to himself on entering it is that of the self-portraitist, as neatly summarized by a recent theorist: 'I shall not tell you what I have done, but I am going to tell you *who I am.*'[1] Not that doing and being are to be too strictly opposed: it is by the exhaustive analysis of certain doings (or failures to do) that Leiris will in fact seek to determine the sort of person that he is, because no autobiographer can tell us who he is without telling us something of what he has done, nor what he has done without something of who he is. We have known since Aristotle that character and action are not to be separated, and in any autobiography narrative and self-description must coexist. We would be intolerant of examples which were all narrative – not even Cellini's *Life* is that – or all self-description.[2]

It would defeat the purpose of the 'autopsychographer' to narrate his life from beginning to end strictly by the calendar, when the

---

[1] Michel Beaujour, *Miroirs d'encre* (Paris, 1980), p. 9.
[2] The French writer Roger Laporte has gone as far as it seems possible to go in treating reflection *as* action, having published a series of autobiographical volumes whose only narrative element is the process of autobiographical narration itself, and the only role which the narrator is enabled to play that of the autobiographer sitting at his desk writing his autobiography. These remarkably subtle and resourceful volumes are of much theoretical if necessarily rather little human interest. They have appeared in a collective volume entitled *Une vie* (Paris, 1986), and been given there the generic subtitle by Laporte of 'biography', in order to show that in hard fact the autobiographer can never be more than a biographer of himself because there can be no full coincidence between the 'I' that is writing and the 'I' of the text, as this recedes word by word into the past.

psychoanalytical method demands that if it is to be successfully interpreted the past must be retrieved piece by enigmatic piece, and each piece related to the present moment rather than to whatever may have preceded or succeeded it in historical time. Psychoanalysis is a technique intended to work by retroaction, as psychic knots originally tied many years before are dissolved in the course of the analytical dialogue and the patient's past 'rewritten', to his advantage, in the present. In the professional setting of the consulting-room, that past is in truth not rewritten but re-spoken, and not by the patient alone, who if he is to keep going needs the informed promptings of the analyst. In vocal partnership, analysand and doctor between them construct autobiographemes, or the constituent elements from which an autobiography might be made. But if it is right to say that psychoanalysis delves back into the past, it does so on the specific understanding that the past is all too damagingly present, in the unconscious of the patient, whose symptoms effectively elide the time which has intervened between precipitating trauma and neurotic fixation. Patient and analyst are especially drawn to the 'folds' in time (to adapt – and how disloyally, given his declared contempt for Freudianism – Nabokov's term) created by the tendency to repetition that characterizes our psychic lives – and which we tacitly acknowledge when we say of some fresh episode of unsuccess or frustration that 'that is the story of my life'.

Taking his cue from this, the 'autopsychographer' too will pick on the situations or experiences whose recurrence seems most strikingly to have punctuated his life and try to correlate them, on the sensible assumption that there is more to be learnt from tracing the intimate connections between these than there ever could be from merely chronicling his past. Leiris is an autobiographer in pursuit of his obsessions, those dark complexes which come to the surface when we act in identical or assimilable ways at widely different times: it is repetition which gives them away. But repetition seldom gets its due in a chronological narrative because the intervals between one obsessional moment and the next are too long. In which perspective, chronology may come to look more like the writer's alibi than his compass, since the 'autopsychographer' who is embroiled in an anxious hermeneutics of his own past may revert to it for protection against the pangs and bewilderments of intense self-scrutiny. The chronological autobiographer's excuse would then be that with straight narrative you always know where you are.

There are hints of the form that 'autopsychography' might take in the perfunctory *Life* of David Hume, which is told chronologically but in such a way as to establish a pattern of repetition, the sanguine temper which he believes himself to possess having been proved in his repeated overcoming of his professional disappointments. And that Hume's autobiographical method should have been underpinned by his scepticism as to the existence of a continuous self is a further strong reason for taking his *Life* as a prototype of Leirisian, or one might now say, post-modern autobiography. For autobiographical attempts at self-analysis of Leiris's kind aim to *construct* a self where narrative autobiography aims to affirm one, in the form of an immutable essence which the writer confidently parades through the conventional time-span of the text. Orthodox narrative serves the cause of what is sometimes known as 'ego-psychology' and is founded on the presupposition, common to both its writers and readers, that the 'I' who is now writing is identical with the 'I' that is being written about – that the writing subject may take itself for its object without injury to its presumed identity. But this narrative identity, axiomatic in the *Discourse* of Descartes and later cast into doubt by Hume, appears to suffer disintegration in the meta-psychology of Freud. In a Freudian perspective, the textual 'I' is no more than the itinerant representative of an 'ego' which is itself unstable, being party to a famously dynamic psychic economy. We may most of us continue to hope that whenever we use the first-person 'I' we are asserting our identity, that each successive use of 'I' implicates the self-same person, but the Freudian theorist is trained to look askance at beliefs as brazenly flattering to our amour-propre as this. In *The Interpretation of Dreams* Freud defends the conclusion he has come to there that in a dream the dreamer distributes his or her ego among a multiplicity of dream-figures by pointing to the same multiplicity which may be masked but not altogether hidden in a simple autobiographical sentence such as 'When I think of what a healthy child I was.'[3] Is the subject 'I' that is now doing the thinking *identical* with the object 'I' who was once, years ago, a healthy child? Or may 'I' now not be attempting to reassure myself of my integrity by a dubious act of *identification* with that other 'I'? If we deny identity to these two first-person pronouns – known, suggestively, to grammarians as 'shifters' – then it follows that each 'I' holds good only in the moment of its

[3] Sigmund Freud, *The Interpretation of Dreams*, translated by James Strachey (London, 1961), p. 323.

utterance, and that the large sum of ' I's to be found in autobiography constitutes nothing more than the graph of an individual's passage through time, not the proof of his identity.

The true 'autopsychographer' is uncertain therefore on setting out whether he has a 'story' to tell or a coherent 'self' of which to paint the portrait. It is a prospect from which a writer might well draw back in fright. One autobiographer who may be suspected of having done so is the English poet, Stephen Spender. In the preface to his *World Within World*, Spender writes: 'I have let the main part of the narrative develop forwards from 1928 until the outbreak of the war. I say "I have let it" do so because this was not my original intention. I meant first to write a book discussing my themes and illustrating them with narrative taken up at any point in time that I chose. However, after two or three trials, I saw the advantage of having an objective framework of events through which I could knock the holes of my subjective experience.'[4] Spender does not say what the 'themes' are which he had anticipated would provide him with the armature of his book, but one can only suppose them to have been those especially insistent psychological motifs or recurrences that would best have marked out his private space but whose exploration he might accordingly have found the most painful. Spender settled in the event for the 'objective framework' of chronology, reclaimed for orthodoxy from a more ambitious scheme in which the autobiographer's freedom in respect of past time might have been put to more revealing use.

THE WRITING CURE

To Spender's conformism I shall – no doubt unfairly – appose the boldest, most intelligent and most comprehensive effort so far made in the direction of 'autopsychography': the autobiographical *oeuvre* of Michel Leiris. Like Spender, Leiris (born in 1901) was of an intellectual generation both excited and gratified by its discovery of the teachings of Freud, which in France and England alike found quicker and fiercer favour among writers and artists than they did among the medical community for whom they were intended. Leiris was a child of the Paris bourgeoisie who early took against the ignorant bad taste and *bien-pensant* morality of his class, embodied for him, as he tells us, in the unadmired figure of his stockbroker father.

---

[4] Stephen Spender, *World Within World* (London, 1951), p. vii.

In late adolescence he took to the arts, writing a hermetic kind of poetry and consorting eventually with the Surrealists, who were the most truculent if not necessarily the best-informed Freudians in France. The writings of Freud they believed lent an impeccably scientific authority to their cult of irrational, uncensored thought processes, as having more to teach us about ourselves and the cosmos than the cautious syllogisms of rationality.

Leiris was one of the relatively few of these Freudian fellow-travellers who actually underwent analysis. He did so late in 1929, after a number of episodes of sexual impotence, debauchery and masochism, including a half-hearted attempt to castrate himself, had persuaded him that he was not simply unhappy, but 'sick'. The fashionable 'talking cure', however, did not work for him and he turned instead, in 1930, to autobiography, intending to practise that in a novel form which would make of it a 'writing cure'. Whereas as a formal analysand he had had to submit to the interpretations of a doctor constrained by the methods and dogmas in which he had been trained, as an autobiographer Leiris could take over both parts in the therapeutic dialogue, that of traumatized patient and of probing physician, now implicated as equals in the elucidation of psychic difficulties which both haunted and inhibited him.

It was a 'cure' which, once begun, Leiris pursued for more than fifty years – did Freud himself not warn of the potential addictiveness of the analytical situation? He pursued it well past such time as he could still believe in a happy outcome, the recognition of his failure being itself recuperated easily enough as an autobiographical motif, which he uses in confirmation of the pessimistic view he had always taken of his own powers and at the same time to ensure that the writing must go on, the sense of failure being made bearable (or even honourable) by being constantly brought to public notice. Over half a century, Leiris published, volume by dense volume, an auto-biographical *oeuvre* unique both for what it had originally aspired to do for the bruised psyche of the autobiographer and for the wonderful running commentary which it contains on the virtualities of the autobiographical genre.[5]

---

[5] Although Leiris published seven volumes between 1946 and 1988 which must be classed as autobiographical, I shall draw here only on five of them: on *L'Age d'homme* (*Manhood*), written before the 1939–45 war but not published until after it; and on the four volumes of the sequence entitled *La règle du jeu*, made up of *Biffures* (1948), *Fourbis* (1955), *Fibrilles* (1966) and *Frêle bruit* (1976). The two volumes I am disregarding are *Le Ruban au cou d'Olympia* (1981) and *A cor et à cri* (1988), which are fragmentary where the earlier books are

Leiris challenges any naive belief we might hold that whoever writes an autobiography does so out of exuberance or, to revert to the language of the counting-house, in order to declare a vital surplus. He contradicts any theory that would see the autobiographical act in terms of a psychic overflow. He writes instead out of a harrowing sense of insufficiency, of a lack which a certain practice of auto-biography can alone make good. What Leiris lacks as a man is the ordinary fortitude that would enable him to live without constantly shrinking back into himself: he is not, as we say, self-possessed. Above all he is terrified by the thought of death, that irrevocable cessation of the ego whose prospect darkens his life and makes him incapable of acting positively. Where other autobiographers take their own measure in order to demonstrate their excellence, Leiris takes his in order to reveal how miserably, seen from inside, he falls short of the manly ideal – except in his willingness to make public his cowardice.

There is irony, therefore, in the title which he gave to his first volume of autobiography, *L'Age d'homme*, or in its English translation, *Manhood*.[6] For manhood is precisely that state which he means to show he has been unable to reach. Leiris begins by remarking that although officially he reached the 'climacteric' of his legal majority in 1922, when he became twenty-one, he has had from that moment on 'few illusions as to the reality of the link that, theoretically, united an actual maturity with his legal majority'(9). In terms of Stephen Spender's 'world within world', the world within has for Leiris failed humiliatingly to be synchronized with the world without; the singularity to which he lays claim as an autobiographer is one that he would sooner be without. By the time the words in question came to be published, Leiris was forty-four years old, but he found no reason to retract them; 'manhood' is a hypothetical state of maturity which not only has he failed to attain but which it is by now questionable whether he still wants to attain, since its attainment would put an end to the literary activity that has become by his own admission the chief *raison d'être* of his life. Returning yet once more, some twenty years later, to the theme of that vital insufficiency in which his auto-biography had originated, Leiris reflects that at certain moments 'this writing, which for me is fundamentally an answer to a lack,

continuous and more by way of an annotation than a serious development of the themes he had introduced earlier.

[6] References are to *Manhood*, translated by Richard Howard (London, 1968), though I have in places changed the translation where it seemed to me improvable.

reaches the point at which to express the lack is as good as possessing that which is lacking...'(*Frêle bruit*, p. 224). An autobiographical endeavour as sustained as that of Leiris alters the balance in autobiography between writing and living, life for him having become mainly endurable as what takes place in the intervals of writing.

In the same year that he began writing *Manhood*, Leiris was invited to join an ethnographical expedition to black Africa. It lasted two years and turned him into a professional ethnographer, in so far as he worked for many years afterwards at the Musée de l'homme in Paris. It led also to a book, *L'Afrique fantôme*, which consists of the *carnets de route* which he kept as he travelled and is as remarkable for what it contains of his observations of himself in his role of ethnographic observer as for its descriptions of the arts, landscapes and customs of Africa.[7] For Leiris this long and uncomfortable journey was both an escape and a test: by it he might escape from the prison of his egotism, which the practice of literature threatened to make even more secure, and encounter in reality African peoples whom he had already admired at a distance for their exoticism. He could also hope to prove his courage, by travelling in a climate and in circumstances that might involve danger to him. In both respects, the expedition failed. In a brief preamble written for a new edition of *L'Afrique fantôme* in 1981, forty-seven years after the book had first appeared, Leiris mocks at the hopes he had had in setting out that the African experience would 'make of him another man, more open and cured of his obsessions'. He had proved as anxious and self-obsessed as an apprentice ethnographer as previously he had as a young man about Paris. The cycle of setting out on a journey in hope and returning in disappointment is one that was to be repeated in his volumes of autobiography proper, notably on a visit to Maoist China made in 1955, in the long account of which Leiris again laments his constitutional inability to fraternize as he would have liked with a people whose revolutionary politics he admires but whose physical presence daunts him and reconfines him in his extreme self-consciousness. In the case of Africa it was his failure to immerse himself fully in what he saw there that had led him to call his book

---

[7] *L'Afrique fantôme* is now cited as a pioneering volume in the new mode of ethnographical writing, in which the writer includes him or herself as a presence within the text, rather than pretending to an old-fashioned objectivity, as if the customs and rituals under observation were being seen by the eye of God and not of an observer subject to the biases and blindnesses inherent in his or her own culture.

L'Afrique fantôme, so denying 'the plenitude of existence to that Africa in which I had found much but not deliverance'.[8]

The 'plenitude of existence' thus denied to Africa was the same plenitude that Leiris had failed to find in himself and whose want is the explicit inspiration of *Manhood*. He began writing this before going to Africa and finished it after he returned (though it was not published until 1946). The title betrays Leiris's new if fragile status of ethnographer. Ethnographically speaking, manhood is a condition to which the male adolescents of a given society are admitted following a rite of initiation in which they are subjected to certain hardships. A display of manhood is required before its condition can be publicly assumed. But in our own societies, no such formal test or display is normally required: male adolescents turn into men automatically, merely by reaching the appropriate age. Unless, that is, history intervenes, as it did in Europe in 1914–18, and subjects adolescent males to a ferocious *rite de passage* such as trench warfare, which many were forced to endure and in which many died. This was a test which Leiris only just missed. He was a year or two too young to have to fight and experienced the war as a boy in Paris, irresponsibly, in the form of 'a long holiday' (and by the time *Manhood* came to be published he had passed unscathed through a second war, having had this time to serve but without any serious danger to himself). He had narrowly missed undergoing a solemn, probably lethal ordeal.

The quality which is tested in war is that of courage, the quality which Leiris believes himself to be without. Reminders of his physical cowardice are given regularly in his volumes of autobiography. But wholly uncourageous as he is in the conduct of his daily life, he knows a way to be courageous in writing: by confessing boldly to his lack of manliness, he can turn the act of autobiography into a voluntary *rite de passage*, to replace that which history had so nearly forced upon him. The premiss from which he starts is that he lacks a virtue which is simply and universally admired, so that the weakness he will confess to is bound to be adjudged despicable. Leiris leaves us no room to find excuses for him; he is cowardly and that is that. Excuses would weaken the case against him, and he wishes the case to be irrefutable. His position in writing is that of the masochist: he is demanding to be punished, if only in the painless form of disapproval, and the act of confession may be assimilated to the various attacks

---

[8] *L'Afrique fantôme* (Paris, 1981), p. 3.

that Leiris has made at different times on his own person, and which have culminated in an attempt at suicide.

That confession may be an erogenous experience we know from our own occasional experiences of being driven to it. With Leiris it is an equivocal habit born of the anxiety that he suffers in company, and the company especially of women. In *Manhood* he recalls a characteristically brief and futile erotic adventure that has occurred recently, during the writing of the book, and was of so drab a nature as to make him want to stop writing, it seeming unredeemable by art. But he has recovered his nerve and made literature from it, the episode having taught him, he now finds, that he is 'a specialist in confession; yet what impels me – especially with women – to such confidences is timidity. When I am alone with a person whose sex is enough to render her so different from me, my sense of isolation and misery becomes so great that, despairing of finding something to say to my interlocutress that might support a conversation, and incapable too of courting her if I should happen to desire her, I begin – lacking any other subject – to speak of myself'(144). This for sure is the 'primal scene' of Leirisian autobiography, akin structurally to those episodes of embarrassment in female company from which Rousseau too derived an autobiographical vocation, except that Leiris differs from Rousseau in succumbing not to awkwardness but to a fluent and defensive solipsism.

And what begins as confidences rises to become literature. As Leiris soliloquizes, the 'tension' grows, and a 'strange dramatic current' begins to flow between himself and his 'partner'; and 'the more my present disturbance agonizes me, the more I speak of myself in an agonized manner, emphasizing my sense of solitude and of separation from the world, until I am ultimately uncertain whether this tragedy I am describing corresponds to the permanent reality of my being or is only the figurative expression of the momentary anguish which I suffer as soon as I come in contact with another person and am somehow called upon to speak'(144). Out of an apparently botched encounter Leiris has contrived to fashion the myth of his own creation as a mythographer, compulsively expatiating on his own life and character and, as the 'tension' builds up, establishing a dramatic if not erotic rapport with the person listening to him. The process once begun continues as if on rails, the speaker himself no longer in control of it as he assumes his central role in a 'tragedy' which is quite out of proportion with the embarrassment that had started him off. In this seemingly involuntary ascent from confusion and the fear of wordlessness into the grandiloquence of the tragic actor there is inscribed the ambivalence of Leiris's anxious venture into auto-biography, the provisional inspiration for which is soon enough transformed by submersion within a spectacularly wordy text and the writer himself brought to see that rather than sincerely confessing to his human inadequacies he is capitalizing on them, by displaying them as bait with which to hook an audience.

Autobiography is that form of literature which can make the writer's otherwise unlovable concern with himself into a source of admiration. But like all forms of literature it is gratuitous, the autobiographer being under no compulsion to write: there is for Leiris the writer no longer the intimidating physical presence of a woman to impel him into fluency, he can only *act* the role of a too easily abashed man whose one sufficient recourse is to words if he is to maintain some kind of equilibrium in his life. And Leiris's autobiographical performance is theatrical from the start. One of the main headings under which he correlates his memories of his early life in *Manhood* is that of 'Tragiques' or 'Tragic themes', a section of the book in which he questions the strong attraction that the stage has always had for him, as far back as he can remember. He has been taken to the theatre by his parents and been moved by what he saw there. It was his first, formative exposure to a world other than the real. As a small boy at the opera he could already distinguish between events on the stage and events in real life, but conceived of the theatre in terms of 'magic', as 'a world apart, distinct from reality of course, but where all things [...] are transposed on to the level of the sublime and occur in a realm so superior to that of ordinary reality that the drama developed and unravelled there must be regarded as a sort of oracle or model'(43) – a form of description we shall shortly meet with again, connected this time with his writing. And it was the theatrical members of his family – an uncle who had gone from being a straight actor to a tumbler in a circus, an honorary 'aunt' who sang in opera – whom he instinctively took to for having broken ranks with the bourgeoisie and pursued 'scandalous' careers. In their lives, they had effected that *écart* or deviation from the norm which he has not been man enough to achieve; Leiris repeatedly complains throughout his autobiography that whatever he may do, or write, and whatever view other people may hold of him, he remains at heart the timid bourgeois who has never broken away.

Of all dramas those which have drawn him the most are the ones which end badly: his particular taste is for the tragic and for what ends, as his own life must one day end, in a death. Hence the cathartic spectacle which he adopted at the outset for his model as an autobiographical writer: the bullfight. The text of *Manhood* is preceded by an extraordinary essay, written ten years after the rest of the book, in which Leiris explains what his intentions had been in writing it. It is entitled 'De la littérature considérée comme une tauromachie' (or in the English translation, 'The autobiographer as torero'). In it he draws an extended and unlikely comparison between his own confessional practice of autobiography and the ritualized movements of the matador in the bullring, both confessional autobiographer and bullfighter being implicated in the risk business. Leiris at that time admired the bullfight for its association of the balletic with the cruel, or of artistry with the physically dangerous. It is a spectacle during which the matador is at greatest risk of injury or death in the so-called 'moment of truth', when he leans over the horns in order to kill the bull, and this perilous action is the hinge by which Leiris contrives to articulate the risks he means to take in confessing to his shameful failings with the risks of a quite different order taken by the matador: 'To expose certain obsessions of an emotional or sexual nature, to admit publicly to his most shameful deficiencies or cowardices, that for the author was the means [...] of introducing even the shadow of a bull's horn into a literary work'(10). These words may have been written post hoc and in the past tense, and refer to himself in the third person, but he is not disowning them for all their excess. Lurid and unacceptable though his analogy be, it brings out with a happy clarity the tension of which I wrote at the start of this book: between autobiography as vital act and as literary document. By assimilating the dangers faced by the wilfully self-revealing autobiographer to those that the matador faces, Leiris is attempting to preserve what he writes from being indifferently canonized as literature, when it had been conceived and written as the desperate adventure in self-discovery of a unique and unhappy individual.

THE WRITING GAME

As time passes, and as his autobiography grows from volume to volume, the taurine analogy fades from view, and the element of risk entailed in confessional writing of Leiris's kind is relocated, with a far greater degree of plausibility. The 'risk' entailed in confiding one's most humiliating secrets – and Leiris never even pretends that he is ready to confide them all, self-censorship being one weakness he admits to that he can only exhibit by giving way to it and thus keeping it hidden from us – is now replaced by the rather different risk of finding in the process of writing that he is not up to it, that such are the demands made on him by his chosen method that they force him to stop, to abandon what had been designed as the literary means of his salvation. The medium in which these new risks must be taken is that of language, into which he will plunge more or less ignorant of the direction he will be led in, since unlike the orthodox narrator of an autobiography, who depends on the chronology of his past life to settle the sequence of what he writes, Leiris entrusts himself to a mode of writing in which it is the already written which largely determines the direction in which the text will be continued.

The method is associative and deliberately chancy. To employ a chiasmus first coined to describe the procedures characteristic of the French New Novel, Leiris substitutes 'l'aventure d'une écriture' for 'l'écriture d'une aventure', or 'the adventure of writing' for 'the writing of an adventure'. The distinction was drawn in order to point up the shift characteristic of the New Novelists whereby narrative was to be stripped of its mask of innocence and shown as no more than the questionable outcome of an act of narration. The 'adventure of writing' is designed to bring into the picture the chances, upsets and inspirations of the process of composition. Writing of the unplotted Leirisian kind displays what Jacques Derrida terms the 'inaugural' condition of all writing: 'It is because it is inaugural, in the young sense of the word, that writing is dangerous and upsetting. It does not know where it is going, no wisdom protects it from that essential precipitation towards the meaning that it constitutes and which at the outset is its future [...] Writing is for the writer, even if he is not an atheist, but if he is a writer, a primary navigation and without grace.'[9] It is hard, perhaps impossible, for us as readers to share in the

[9] Jacques Derrida, *L'Ecriture et la différence* (Paris, 1967), p. 22.

adventure of any 'primary navigation', because we are relegated to a state of what Derrida calls 'secondariness', the meanings in what we read reaching us in the guise of the already constituted, and as if the primary navigator himself had possessed them before starting rather than having to set out in search of them.

But Leiris's autobiographical navigation is not altogether primary, because he depends to some extent for direction on a considerable archive of *fiches* or notes which he has written down and saved over many years. He gives no indication of how full these memoranda might be, but describes them as being like 'the minutes of observations or experiences'. This fragmentary record is thus intermediate between the continuous autobiographical text and the pre-textual 'life' that the text will summon into existence; they are broken but trustworthy shards which this fanatical archaeologist of self will arrange discursively into a reassuring artefact. Without their support Leiris it seems might not have been able to write at all. At one point during the Second World War he evacuates them from Paris to the country for safe keeping, but quickly brings them back again, having found that their absence, 'by taking away the possibility of my handling them daily, prevented that sort of hypnosis thanks to which I can become one with my task, and without which I am as helpless before it as before a French dissertation set me by a pedant'(*Fibrilles*, p. 222).

These *fiches* are the means by which Leiris passes at need from the profane realm to the sacred, or from the real world to the 'world apart' in which reality finds its sublimation. They are the admission tickets to his private theatre, where the contemptible author can become a glorious protagonist. But even at the age of ten, Leiris had been too lucid to confuse what happens on the stage with what happens in real life, and as an autobiographer he is all too acutely aware that the 'world apart' into which he has passed in order to write is a distraction. No matter what he achieves by writing, it can not in the end deliver him from mortality. Autobiography then is in essence a game, a form of that ludic activity which Leiris's former associate among the Surrealists, Raymond Queneau, once summarized in a grimly comical triplet as 'Un jeu simple/ Que j'invimple/ Dans la nuimple', or in plain English, 'A simple game/ Which I invented/ In the dark'. The dark for Queneau, as for Leiris, is the adumbration cast in our lives by the prospect of our ultimate extinction, from which we can at best hope to be distracted, as we are when we write.

The sequence of four autobiographical volumes which Leiris published following *Manhood* has the overall title of *La Règle du jeu*, or 'The Rule of the Game', and something of the nature of the game he is playing in it can be learnt from the (untranslatable) titles of the individual volumes, *Biffures* (1948), *Fourbis* (1955), *Fibrilles* (1966) and *Frêle bruit* (1976). In their punning closeness to one another, these are an economical illustration of Leiris's theory of language as an *ars combinatoria*, a few phonemes having in this instance sufficed to form in different arrangements four widely different yet for him associable French terms. And by much the same token, the French word *jeu* in the larger title (like English 'play') should be read as having more senses than one, all of them applicable to what he is set on doing. There is *jeu* as game or sport, *jeu* as technique, used in discussing the performance of an actor or musician, *jeu* as the collective noun for gambling games as well as the term for a gambler's stake, *jeu* as the action of a piece of machinery, and last but far from least, *jeu* as the 'play' there may be in a mechanism which works less than perfectly. This one word contains a semantic constellation and the *jeu* of Leiris's autobiographical sequence covers all of these different senses, of game, of technique, of risk, of automatism and of that small margin of freedom sometimes allowed to us by the slight malfunctioning of a machine.

It is 'play' in this last sense which may be taken as enabling 'play' in all the other senses, it being interpretable in the context of *La Règle du jeu* as the freedom allowed to us by the cosmic machine itself to seek distraction from the iron law that has decreed our eventual abolition as human individuals. Leiris is a man playing under sentence of death. He has, as I have said, a horror of the *néant*, which seems not to have left him even in his eighties, though by that stage it reads when invoked more like a writer's tic than a freshly experienced dread. For all the doubts that he admits to, Leiris is secure throughout in his atheism and in his assumption that personal immortality is out of the question. These are negative beliefs not to be questioned, and represent a characteristically fearful yet at the same time voluptuous submission to what he takes to be 'the order of things' – his atheism might fairly be seen as deriving from his masochism and the presumption of his inescapable annihilation as reflecting his desire for punishment. Nevertheless, this is the prospect which he declares has unmanned him: 'So far as I am concerned, my persistent inability to master the obsession with death prevents me from being altogether a man and even, somehow, from existing: nothing, as I see it, can be worth my dying since for me everything is devalued by the fact that, at the end of everything, there is my death'(*Fourbis*, p. 61). The four volumes of *La Règle du jeu* leave no one in any doubt that their author is a 'chronophobe' every bit as passionate as Nabokov, but unable or unwilling to contemplate any metaphysical means of escape from the sentence of death under which he lives and writes.

Manhood had opened morbidly enough, with the words: 'I have just reached the age of thirty-four, life's midpoint' (in the end Leiris lived to be ninety), and had continued with a description of his physical appearance aimed less at objectivity à la Cardano than at emphasizing the process of degeneration on which he had by now fully entered. And when he next sets out to reassemble certain 'vestiges' of 'the metaphysic of my childhood'(27), the first heading under which he does so is that of 'Old Age and Death'. By this calculated incongruity or short-circuiting of the chronology of his life, Leiris is enabled to include as his first memory in *Manhood* a visit to the Père Lachaise cemetery with his mother, and to follow it with recollections of an engraving of a man struck by lightning and another of the suicide of an Indian rajah, from which it is above all the word 'suicide' that has lodged in his mind as a graphic image and whose implications he proceeds to draw out, in an early demonstration of that cathexis of the public signs of a language by private emotions the experience of which is a principal source of guidance to Leiris in *La Règle du jeu*. He recalls also the jacket illustration on a book in which the successive stages of a human life from birth to old age had been portrayed in different colours, and measures how far he has by now declined through this downward sequence. For degeneration starts early, once the blessed condition of infancy has been left behind, 'that irreplaceable state when, as in mythical times, all things are still undifferentiated, when the rupture between microcosm and macrocosm is not as yet entirely consummated, and one bathes in a sort of fluid universe as at the heart of the absolute'(31). This imaginary account of the infant state may or may not correspond with the way things are for the infant; but for Leiris it describes the beatific state of oneness to which he aspires, in which the inner world would be reunited with the outer and all conflict within him healed.

As it is, he is in the unhappy state of a microcosm which finds itself at odds with a coldly inhospitable macrocosm. The 'rupture' between himself and the world around him has been 'consummated' with a traumatizing completeness. In a particularly intense sequence in *Fourbis*, Leiris analyses the significance for him of a sound he had heard one evening out walking as a very small boy on a country road. He was four or five years old, it was getting dark and he had heard a faint noise – the 'frêle bruit' he was later to use as the title for the fourth volume of the series – which he found oddly frightening. His belief now is that it was made by an insect, but his father had for some reason told him that it came from a horse and cart somewhere in the distance, and this, as he supposes, false explanation frightened him even more. Leiris pursues this tiny but portentous memory over several pages, in a relentless gloss which ends by setting the unexceptional sound he had heard into the troubling category of everything in the world that is *separate* from himself. The explanation found by his father – the father for whom Leiris expresses mainly contempt all through his autobiography – is worse in its effects than the 'natural' explanation, that the sound was that of an insect, because it has impressed once and for all on the boy that 'out there' there is a human world which is utterly impervious to him. He has had the terrible experience of his fatal separateness, and the promise of his own eventual exclusion from a world which can and one day will continue without him, unmoved by his sudden absence from it. The *frêle bruit* has been converted by his deliberate analysis of it into a death-knell, its independence having expressed 'an imperturbable permanence which is that of the order of things itself, or one of the aspects of death we find it least easy to contemplate without a shudder, to wit that our own end has every likelihood of not being the end of the world but only an end limited – unjustly, it will always seem – to ourselves'(*Fourbis*, p. 31). The devastating experience to which the boy Leiris has been introduced is of death not as total extinction but as an imaginary spectacle, the posthumous state of the dead individual being now become one of everlasting solitude as the disembodied spectator of a world from which he has been excluded.

THE LINGUISTIC TURN

To describe the pages of *Fourbis* in which Leiris ruminates so productively on his *frêle bruit* as a 'sequence' would be deceptive were that description to imply that it somehow stands detachably out from its context; it does not, it fits seamlessly within the seventy-odd pages of the first section of this volume, whose heading is the one word *mors*, the French term for a horse's bit, as well as, it turns out, the name of an early make of electric motor-car. But *mors* is also the Latin word for 'death' and indistinguishable in sound from its French derivative, *mort*, so that its connections with Leiris's speculations as to what noise it was that he had long ago heard have their own phonetic logic. That harmless yet to him ominous roadside sound has been overlaid as he writes by the unequivocally ominous sound, *mors/mort*, as if Leiris were keeping an ear open to what he writes and allowing the aural associations of certain words to determine the direction of both his thoughts and his pen. *Mors/mort* is a semantic reference-point in a text so formidably digressive by its nature as to place its author under constant threat of a final disorientation.

It is apt that Leiris should have been walking along a road when he heard the *frêle bruit*, because the road, like the railway-line to which I shall come in a moment, offers itself as a familiar metaphor for the narrative progression through time to which this dissident autobiographer refuses to accede. He has stepped aside from the ordinary autobiographical road which leads so forbiddingly straight from birth to that death-like moment when the writer has to stop writing, his story being now complete. Leiris travels in *La Règle du jeu* not by the public highway but by private paths of his own. But before I go further into these, what of the *Rule* in his title? What sort of Rule is it and how does it relate to the game he is playing? It is Rule in the singular, not Rules in the plural, which at once brings to mind some such analogy as the Rule of a monastic order, or that code by which the lives of a body of religious are regulated. And that connotation is an appropriate one for Leiris, who for all his atheism has entered autobiography as on a regime of mortification and to a tran-scendental end, since having moved through the cycle of confession and correction he believes he may find reconciliation, not with God, but with himself, in the reuniting of his real and ideal selves. But there is more to Leiris's Rule than that: as well as the code which he will observe in writing, it is also the object of his literary quest, the saving discovery to which the ascesis of autobiography is intended to lead him. It is also his Golden Rule, that tonic formula which, once found, will make a man of him.

There had been an orthodox bourgeois piety in Leiris's family, and therefore no such thing in himself; he has given up God and exchanged Catholicism for a quasi-mystical devotion to language. In his notion of the Golden Rule, there is to be discerned the Surrealist faith in 'the Alchemy of the Word', or that power that the Surrealists accorded to language to transmute the base metal of life into the precious stuff of art, and above all to release that element of the 'marvellous' that lay concealed within the everyday, awaiting its release by the inspired wordplay of the artist in language.

In *La Règle du jeu* autobiography takes very luxuriantly the 'linguistic turn' that has transformed Western philosophy in the past half-century or more. Such a turn had been inscribed in the genre from the start, in Augustine's distinction between the temporal and transcendental orders of language and in his acknowledgment that what we call the 'past' is in fact the sum of what we find ourselves able to say or write of it; and in Leiris the turn is completed, completed in the sense that because his is an immanent philosophy of language where Augustine's was transcendental, there is now to be no escape upwards towards God from the horizontal regime of the human word.

La Règle du jeu contains its own, secular version of the book of Genesis: it opens with the account of a Fall. The episode comes from earliest childhood, when one of Leiris's toy soldiers had fallen from a table on to the floor. Pleased to find that it had not been damaged in dropping, he had exclaimed ' ... Reusement!' (or as he might have exclaimed had he been an anglophone small boy, ' ... tunately'), to be told by some other member of his family who was present that what he should have said was 'heureusement'. It would not do to class his ' ... Reusement' as belonging to a so-called 'private' language, when it is merely the incomplete version of the full word into which it has now been turned by adult intervention; the exchange of one term for the other represents only the *fulfilment* of the boy's insertion into the Symbolic Order of language, not an abrupt and brutal expulsion from the infant state. As Falls go, this is quite a gentle one. In the Lacanian view, insertion into the Symbolic Order is a baleful experience, in which an infant previously contentedly resident in its own imagination becomes subject to the mortal embrace of an impersonal system of signs.[10] In the context of *La Règle du jeu*, it is an experience premonitory for Leiris of that of the *frêle*

---

[10] For a very clever and often illuminating Lacanian interpretation of Leiris, see Jeffrey Mehlman's *A Structural Study of Autobiography: Proust, Leiris, Sartre, Levi-Strauss* (Ithaca and London, 1974), pp. 65–150.

bruit, the alien sounds of language being consonant with that sinister intrusion as evidence that henceforth he must submit to an order of things not of his own willing nor organized for his satisfaction.

Leiris's originary Fall is equally as ambivalent as that of Vico, the boy who was both injured and inspired by falling from a ladder. The episode of the toy soldier in *Biffures* has three moments: an error made by himself leads to a correction which leads in turn to a sudden illumination. The error is twofold: the toy soldier has fallen because of the boy's maladroitness, it 'having escaped from my unskilful hands, as yet unfitted for tracing common pothooks on an exercise-book'. His physical clumsiness Leiris had drawn attention to in *Manhood*, as a part of the very unflattering description that he gives there of his body; but the implication now is that his body – or at least one small part of it, to wit his hands – will come into its own once he has learnt how to form his letters and so begun his apprenticeship in the art of writing. The error made by his as yet 'unskilful' hands has been compounded by that made by his tongue, in using an insufficient French word by way of an exclamation. It might be stretching things a little to say of the correction of this verbal error that it has constituted a *punishment*, but it certainly functions as such, since the substitution of 'heureusement' for his stunted '…Reusement' is the means of setting the boy straight and opening up for him the channels of communication with those around him. Submission to the rules of French is a release from the near-autism of infancy.

Leiris has been brought suddenly to grasp the true nature of language, which is the great gain bestowed on him in the very moment of his loss, because in the exercise of language he will find such assuagement as exists for his alienated state as an individual exiled once and for all from the blissfully undifferentiated state of babyhood. And the same sequence of three narrative moments which makes up the episode of the falling toy soldier is writ large in the genesis of *La Règle du jeu* as a whole. First there was the 'error', or that lack of physical presence and address which is to be made good by writing; then the 'correction' which the making public of his more contemptible weaknesses will invite from those who read him; and finally the enlightenment that is to be gained by the way of autobiography, as he pursues the Golden Rule secreted somewhere in language that will finally make everything well for him.

The fall of *Biffures* is a fall into the realm of play, where, unlike in real life (or in bull-rings), falls no longer do physical damage to the faller. In this symbolic realm, Leiris can be the valiant soldier that he had narrowly missed having to be in adolescence – ' ... Reusement'. In reflecting on the tiny but creative accident of the fallen toy, he finds no significance in the fact that it was a soldier which fell as opposed to some other toy, and that is surprising; but on the other hand his reflections concerning the 'metaphysics' of toys are so couched as to make these particular toys seem remarkably apt precursors of the playthings of the grown man, of words:

The essential thing was that something belonging to me had fallen and that the thing belonging to me was a toy: that the fallen object was one belonging to the closed world of toys – which you shut away in boxes when you have finished playing – , to that separate and marvellous world the component parts of which stand out by their shape and colour against the real world at the same time as representing it, perhaps, at its sharpest [*dans ce qu'il a de plus aigu*]. A world apart, superadded to the everyday world as engraved initials are superadded to a metal drinking-mug or charms to a watch-chain; an intense world, analogous to everything that in nature gives an impression of being *there for display*. (*Biffures*, p. 11. Leiris's italics)

Quite how we should take the notion of 'sharpness' here is unclear; but given that the toys Leiris has been writing about are soldiers, one is inclined to find in it a reminder of the 'shadow of the bull's horn' of the preface to *Manhood*, as a lethally pointed object with which the writer need only play, having gained admission to the ludic 'world apart' of literature. Toys, like words, fulfil their symbolizing function most reassuringly when they represent those very things which in real life threaten our physical wellbeing.

The enforced move from ' ... Reusement' to 'heureusement' very literally supplies an original lack in Leiris, his infantile version of the correct word having been too short by a syllable. At the same time, he has been inducted into that shared linguistic order by the resolute practice of which his greater lack may be made good. The sudden illumination he has had is that words *connect up* with one another; his fall is one into articulation or, as Jeffrey Mehlman has it, into syntax.[11] His ' ... Reusement' had been, he now suggests, 'pure interjection', a sum of phonemes without semantic value. But its connection with the word *heureux* having been revealed it can be suitably completed and take its allotted place within the vast system of signs by which one French person communicates with another:

---

[11] *A Structural Study of Autobiography*, p. 103.

'To suddenly apprehend in its wholeness the word that previously I had always *murdered* [écorché] took on the aspect of a discovery, like the abrupt rending of a veil or revelation of some truth. This vague vocable – which up until then had been entirely personal to myself and remained as if closed – had been promoted by a chance to the role of link in a whole semantic chain'(*Biffures*, p. 11).

This discovery of the articulatory Rule of language is of a kind to mitigate but not to cancel out the tragic discovery of his separateness as an individual. As an initiate of language, Leiris can at least confide in others how intolerable the sense of separateness is, as when embarrassedly orating before his female companion in *Manhood*. In the *rapprochement* of '...Reusement' with *heureux* there dwells a 'magic virtue', and the 'magic' is no throwaway term, for this revelatory conjunction of what had before been two independent atoms of language is the key to his whole autobiographical method and to the great hope which had once informed it. Leiris had come to have the same 'magical' belief in the power of words over things as that to which Sartre confesses so guiltily in *Words*; but where Sartre attempts self-deludingly to divest himself of that elitist belief, Leiris plays a deeper game, for although he declares again and again in the four volumes of *La Règle du jeu* that he has long lost any faith in the 'magic' of words, he continues to write as if it were still efficacious and able to promise him the ultimate revelation he had once childishly sought.

Even in *Manhood*, he writes in the past tense of the verbal techniques acquired in his years as a believing Surrealist, by whose means he had formerly anticipated forcing language to give up its secrets to him. Essentially, they involved by-passing the instrumentality of words and treating them as ends, not means, as the manipulable and decomposable objects which they are, for example, to the writers of cryptic crossword clues, who detach words provisionally from their daily contexts in order to 'play' with them. But the ambitions of crossword-setters are terribly pedestrian compared with those of Leiris and his kabbalistic friends, who thought that a saving wisdom was to be extracted from such ideally 'poetic' procedures. Leiris writes of 'Breaking down the words of the vocabulary and reconstituting them into poetical puns which seemed to me to bring out their most profound significance', a technique which went hand in hand for him at the time with the recording of his dreams, those too being even in their recorded form verbal constructs seemingly independent of the conscious mind and thus, like the supraconscious forms of language, a source of arcane knowledge, whether of oneself or of the human mind in general.[12]

For an example of the 'poetical puns' which have determined the form of Leiris's autobiography, I shall take *Biffures*, the title of the first volume in the series. This is a word with only the one meaning in French, of an 'erasure' or 'crossing-out'; that is its public sense, open to all. But for Leiris *biffures* is the homophone of *bifur*, or the abbreviated version of the word *bifurcation* as he had once seen it displayed on a board beside a railway-track, to give train-drivers warning of a junction up ahead. A private recollection has thus been punningly introduced into the public term *biffures* in the volume's title, of which we would have suspected nothing had Leiris not told us about it. The railway-track has provided him with a second metaphorical location by which to mark his departure from the prosaic into a poetic domain. By that departure the word *biffure* has itself been caused to bifurcate, according to whether one takes it in the sense of erasure or, heard as *bifur*, of a branching off. Or to seem to bifurcate because in the event these two not obviously overlapping senses are shown by Leiris as he construes them to converge: they refer to the same constituent 'movement' of his text, whose involuntary branchings-off, as determined by the various phonetic accidents and associations of the French language, he describes as so many 'slips of the tongue' calling for 'erasure', or that retrospective gesture of self-correction which far from erasing the 'slip' in fact constitutes it as such. Loyal Freudian that he remains – without ever once, I suspect, invoking Freud's name – Leiris knows that the tongue which slips (which *forks* in the equivalent French expression: 'la langue m'a fourché') may have more interesting things to tell us than the tongue which travels unambiguously onwards.

He has adapted the word *bifur*, met with by chance in the best Surrealist tradition of the *hasard objectif*, for his private use, to describe the moments of mental excitement that would serve as direction markers in his autobiographical wanderings:

[12] Leiris published two collections of such exercises in 'word-magic', one, *Glossaire j'y serre mes gloses*, in his Surrealist youth, and a second, *Langage tangage ou Ce que les mots me disent*, in 1985, as if to show what he was still capable of in this direction even though he no longer believed in it as other than a pastime. For an example of what was involved, I take a single entry from *Langage tangage*, which for the headword 'Hamlet' offers the definition 'dont l'âme halète', or literally in English, 'whose soul pants' – an apt enough meaning to have been derived phonetically from the name of Hamlet as pronounced by a French-speaker.

... I had recourse to the expression *bifurs*, seeing in it at first nothing more than a seductive word, to designate in my personal jargon the raw materials that were hard to label but which I wanted to collect and to shuffle together: the mental jolts, stumblings or slippages that occur when a fault or a flash of light (such as the sun's reflection that dazzles you when a malicious hand tilts the small pocket mirror in the right way) or some jagged or fleeting singularity manifests itself in one's discourse – a loss of footing or sudden change of level thanks to which the individual who experiences it feels himself cast into a state of peculiar acuity which, by seeming to crack open the frame, unblocks the horizon for him – eddies, ripples, foam or other alteration of the (ordinarily tranquil) surface of the tongue, which are the generators of a very special poetry and my datable experiences of which I was anxious to record in order to isolate the drop of truth they seemed to me to contain and to prevent the seam from running out. (*Biffures*, pp. 256–7)

From this one deduces that the *bifurs* are those generative flashes of insight that he has recorded at the time when they occurred to him on his *fiches*, and which, once articulated in the continuous prose of autobiography, will generate further insights and form themselves into a coherent textual design. That design will be the alchemical sublimation of the writer's mundane self to which all autobiography aspires and not just one written to Leiris's uncommon specification. The difference is that where other autobiographers happily travel the public thoroughfare of chronology in order to be sure of finding their way in the past, he will risk following the ramifications into which his mind is led while writing, in the remarkable hope that these may finally be 'woven into a sort of network similar to those which establish communication among all the different regions making up a country'(*Biffures*, p. 259). His is as it were a structuralist's dream, of constructing a synchronic working model of his self, in which the past has been gratifyingly incorporated into the present.

BETWEEN I AND ME

The practice of Poetry was the means by which Leiris when young had hoped to possess the Absolute – an oddly sanguine programme for so pessimistic a man ever to have worked to. He writes of it years later without irony but observing a certain distance between his mature scepticism and his youthful credulity as to what Poetry might achieve for him. His faith in it survives in the early part of *La Règle du jeu* in the reduced form of a belief that in autobiography the Absolute which he might come to possess is himself. However ingenuous – and vague – such a belief might seem to others, Leiris defends it as the expression of a 'natural' desire for a 'plenitude of existence' which he takes to be the source of all religion and of the worship of gods. Since he has no god and no religion, he is thrown back on himself, to achieve a plenitude of existence by means of writing. More poignantly than for other writers, his is autobiography as act. But the quest for plenitude is self-contradictory, because the means he has chosen for its prosecution are of such a kind as to ensure it can not succeed. In *Manhood*, Leiris writes of his desire in writing 'to gather my life into a single solid block (an object that I would be able to touch as though to assure myself against death, even when, paradoxically, I was claiming to risk everything)'(19); which is a graphic trope by which to express the desire that all autobiographers feel for wholeness, and to abstract an enduring essence from their lives by means of narrative.

The autobiographer is a statuarist, a Pygmalion working to produce a fascinatingly lifelike facsimile – of himself. Leiris is fond of presenting himself in terms of a worker in stone and of emphasizing the mineral hardness of the self-image which he would like to project as an autobiographer compared with the limp plasticity of the living man. Even before he began writing autobiographically, he had envisaged it as a kind of writing by which a living being might achieve the status of a monument. In *Biffures* he describes a drawing which he had made as long ago as 1928 and then pasted into one of his surviving notebooks. It is entitled 'My life by myself' and shows him in profile, gazing at a pyramid, and being observed in turn by a woman's eye, which is looking obliquely up at him. It would be nice to take over this rough schema – this 'autobiogram' if I may so call it – to stand for the triangular relationship involved in any auto-biographical act, between writer, text and imaginary recipient, but two features of it at least are open to question. What has seemed especially significant to Leiris when he re-examined it was the 'radical separation' which it displayed between first, the image of himself and the 'imposing but cold geometrical form' of the pyramid, and again, between his image and the woman's eye drawn gazing up at it, 'as if in vain quest of an impossible union'(*Biffures*, p. 169). All is clearly not contentment in this drawing, when the solid into which his life has been successfully shaped is now 'inaccessible' to the shaper, and when the woman onlooker seems to be yearning for a union she can never achieve. Leiris offers no interpretation of this female presence: why is it a woman, why is she described as having been 'exiled', and why should she desire union with the writer's own self-image? Obviously, she is no simple Other, or third party to the autobiographical act. Rather, the woman's eye is interpretable only as belonging also to the autobiographer, distributed now among all three roles, as the writer able to observe himself at his work and suffering from the knowledge that in it there can be no final integration of writing subject with textual object, the second becoming external or 'inaccessible' to the first in the very act of its making. Elsewhere, Leiris compares the 'global apprehension' of his life which he had hoped to achieve by a 'poetic' means to that instantaneous autobiography which is reputed to pass through the mind of the drowning man; but the comparison is not a very encouraging one, because the drowning man may be said to achieve a rapid and conclusive integration with his newly created 'text' by thereupon drowning, and suffering that loss of subject-hood which Leiris is anxious to defer for as long as he can.

The division between subject and object is to be healed only in death; for Leiris the writer it is an epistemic variant of the division which he has come to know can never be healed between his real and imaginary selves. He may restate this hope in *La Règle du jeu*, but nostalgically. The 'impossible union' that he had craved between what he at one point distinguishes as 'the *here and now* and the *there*' was made impossible from the start by the discursive means by which he had thought to accomplish it. Works of statuary are not to be made from words; no more than any other autobiographer can Leiris escape the awful linearity of his text, which may not proceed chronologically but which proceeds none the less, word after fatal word, towards its end. Only by assuming a meretricious polarity between Poetry and all other uses of language, had he once been able to conceive of words as capable of standing in a vertical relation to time, as Augustine had conceived the language of God as standing: 'From an artisanal point of view, poetry may be looked on as nothing more than a genre, immediately defined by a certain mode of writing. "Non discursive" (in other words, giving precedence to a global apprehension [*une saisie globale*] or creation over analysis), it stands well apart from common utilities and this separation [*écart*] is marked from the start by the fact that in poetry, instead of playing the role of a simple means of transcription, language appears strangely *distanced*'(*Fibrilles*, p. 250).

But having once stepped off the road, Leiris could only have allowed himself back on to it either by declaring that his Golden Rule had been suddenly disclosed to him, thereby rendering his auto-biography redundant to him as a practical endeavour, or by abandoning the attempt and thus exposing himself as a failure in the aesthetic as well as the physical and moral dimension. But as he knows and admits, his vanity as an author is more than sufficient to keep him writing. Once safely ensconced in the world of play he will continue to perform, confident in the enduring support of the medium into which he had fallen as a very small child. That was in fact a fall out of Poetry and into prose, because in his exclamatory ' … Reusement' language had indeed been *distanced*, paroled from its humdrum task of transcription and foregrounded, as the Formalists would say, for our particular attention.

Leiris's grand *écart*, or secession from the real to an imaginary world, is that move which all autobiographers make, in the turn from living to writing and from society to solitariness. And the rec-onciliation with the world at which their writing aims is reflected in the desire for reunion with himself of Leiris, who has begun by internalizing the 'world' as that alter ego which makes demands on him he can not directly meet. For this autobiographer, an agonizing singularity is to be transcended only inwardly: 'it is only when things or my thoughts yield themselves to a certain articulation in which logic counts for nothing that I feel myself carried beyond my singularity, in communion with the outside and close to a state that might be called *total*' (*Fourbis*, p. 219). These are the words of an autobiographer trapped within a medium to which he had looked for salvation and found only the confirmation of his loneliness. The one courageous thing that Leiris admits to having done in *La Règle du jeu* is to have tried at one time to kill himself; that was an action which would have rejoined the 'two sides' of him, the real and the 'mythological', on the physical plane, where he would have succeeded in actually living out his 'tragedy' after all his tragic posturings as a writer. But the failed poet is also a failed suicide, whose overdose of barbiturates was not enough to kill him and whose potentially last words, as he lapsed into unconsciousness, had been 'Tout ça, c'est de la littérature', meaning that even in this supreme, sacrificial moment the writer had remained a writer, unable to re-enter the unitary state of being from which he had been so painfully exiled. Nevertheless, the scar which Leiris bears on his throat, from the tracheotomy which saved his life, is for him the proud sign that just this once he has risked everything and approached, if not quite attained the desired plane of Poetry.

The volumes of *La Règle du jeu* did not deliver to their author the solid image of himself they had been charged with delivering; in the steady, obsessive accumulation of their vagrant prose, analysis wins over creation and in its unforgiving discursiveness withholds from him the *saisie globale* that was to have been his talisman against death. *La Règle du jeu* is failed Poetry. But then the intention in which Leiris had conceived it was surely flawed for being utilitarian, his uniquely mundane *raison d'être* as an autobiographer having been to improve the conduct of his daily life. Yet we have only his own auto-biographical word for it that in this it failed and we might always choose to distrust that word as coming from a man who, in the course of all these many hundreds of pages, has missed no chance of presenting himself as someone whose practical endeavours habitually fall short of their mark. But unlike his contemporary Sartre, Leiris was wise to the bad faith inherent in what he had undertaken; he settled for being the autobiographer, on stage alone, and playing to a house which he presumed was the readier to applaud him for daring to confess his lack of heroism.

Conclusion

Michel Leiris is the author of the most significant and arresting work of autobiography to have been written in the twentieth century. In the opinion of the theorist, that is, who knows how many durable insights he has had into a slippery genre from reading *Manhood* and the four volumes of *La Règle du jeu*. The Common Reader is not so likely to agree; he or she may well decide, on the contrary, that Leiris is wordy, shapeless and chillingly narcissistic, and wonder why anyone who appears to have lived so unsatisfactory a life should have wanted to write about it at such finicking length. Leiris's autobiographical sequence seems designed to separate those who come upon it into the two sorts of reader distinguished in my Introduction, the excitement of the theorist on encountering a virtuoso of introspection such as Leiris being matched by the impatience of the Common Reader, who can not accept that even an autobiographer is entitled to put self so brazenly before story.

This polarization of response bears out in a sense the conclusion of Philippe Lejeune, the foremost French analyst of the genre, that autobiography 'is as much a way of reading as a type of writing'.[1] Lejeune argues pragmatically that if autobiography is to be defined it should be in terms of the relationship created between the autobiographical text and its readers, rather than that between the text and the 'life' of which it stands as the – unverifiable – account. Under this dispensation the genre of autobiography would begin and end where, at some appointed historical juncture, its readers determine that it should, and since the 'contractual effect', as Lejeune calls it, between text and reader will vary over time, as the literary culture in which those readers have been raised evolves, autobiography will find itself being defined by consensus and

---

[1] Philippe Lejeune, *Le Pacte autobiographique* (Paris, 1975), p. 45.

differently from age to age. The argument is historicist, if it assumes that there can be no timeless definition of autobiography, nothing that is which might hold works as distant from one another in historical time as the *Confessions* of Augustine and *La Règle du jeu* together, as evidently belonging to the same literary genre by virtue of the way they intrinsically are. It is to use the term 'definition' in its narrowest sense, and to seek only to fix the limits of autobiography as a genre vis-à-vis other, neighbouring genres, principally that of fiction, with which it patently shares much common ground, both in its subject matter and in the manner of its composition.

As a kind of writing, autobiography of course belongs within a literary 'system', and that system is in constant flux, so that the bounds of the 'autobiographical' will be measured differently from age to age; but it should also be definable in psychological and thematic terms, and more from the point of view of those who write rather than those who read autobiography. It may be that in many cultures autobiography is unknown, which is to say that it is a kind of writing that has never been practised there. But this absence is a contingency of cultural history. The fact that it has been practised as widely as it has implies that autobiography represents a virtuality of our individual existence, whose realization depends on the cultural conditions under which we happen to exist. Even in a culture which knows and honours autobiography only an elite few can practise it at the refined, literary level I have been concerned with here; but they do so with the approval and understanding of their contemporaries. We are entitled to suppose that there is something like an urge to autobiography within any individual, seeking expression at every level from the loosely and ephemerally conversational to the enduringly artistic. And following on from that, we may suppose that there are drives and thematic configurations whose combination in a text is specific to autobiography and which it is the business of the theorist to identify. In short, that autobiography has its own distinctive language, or rhetoric.

The advent of theory in the reading of autobiography has produced a new variation on the 'contractual effect', inasmuch as the theoretical reader is less preoccupied than other readers with the question of the autobiographer's truthfulness, and hence with finding definitions which would mark autobiography 'proper' categorically off from autobiographical fiction on the one hand, and from sub-literary genres such as memoirs or diaries on the other. The theorist capitalizes indeed on the unverifiability of the autobiographical text. By departing from the old 'contract' that bound autobiographer and reader, and refusing to wear the writer's implied claim that what he has written is God's truth, the theorist enjoys a new licence, to interpret various instances in the text as inventions, or as corrections of the historical record, introduced by the autobiographer for rhetorical effect. It is no longer necessary to decide whether this episode or that in autobiography is perfectly factual when the factual and the fictive alike are *intentional* – a word I use here in its perhaps less familiar philosophical sense, as describing that which is not given by the world but 'intended' by the mind. That is, whatever an autobiography contains it contains not simply because such has been the writer's experience and he therefore had no option but to include it, but because this is his past as he has chosen to project it. As theorists set on interpreting the contents of the text we can take comfort from knowing that the autobiographer was there before us, that what we are reading is *already* an interpretation and the writer an active, not a passive force.

Over the past twenty years, autobiography has been cordoned off as an inviting new subject for academic study, and specialists have gone into business to interpret it from various literary, sociological, historical and psychoanalytical perspectives. It would be good to think that in doing so they have also recognized that this is an uncommonly congenial kind of writing in which to specialize, the life-stories of others invariably having something to say to our ignoble curiosity as human beings as well as to our elevated interests as literary theorists. But new styles of theoretical reading have produced new styles of theoretical writing, and there is a real risk that the peculiar attractions of literary autobiography will go to waste as its noblest and most rewarding examples are summoned to the seminar-room to be put to the question.

That is why a compromise is in order: the theorist of autobiography should tread softly in taking for his examples the masterworks of the genre. These are the works from which the theorist has the most to learn and in which the Common Reader finds most to admire and enjoy. I hope that in the present volume I have kept the Common Reader in mind and not allowed textual analysis to turn into an autopsy. The individual studies of which the book is made are theoretical in what by the standards of the day is only a mild way:

they attempt to generalize from the evidence of particular autobiographies in order to demonstrate a certain convergence of both
means and matter among authors convened from different epochs
and languages. The first and final subjects, Augustine and Leiris, are
divided from one another by some sixteen hundred years, a huge
elapse of time which I have mainly ignored. My perspective has been
synchronic, as if all of these autobiographers were contemporaries of
one another: which is to say, contemporaries of myself, their living
reader.

It might be asked why, in that case, they should have been made
to appear in chronological order, and frequently grouped together in
threes and fours according to when they lived; as Abelard, Dante and
Petrarch form a late medieval group, and Mill, Newman and Darwin
a High Victorian one. They are arranged in this conventional
sequence, first because even if I have paid scant attention to their
historical context I have no wish to remove them from it, which
would be to imply foolishly that their dates were of no importance;
and second, more positively, because it is clear that the forms which
autobiography takes have been conditioned by the norms of the
culture in which it was produced, so that the autobiographers of late
medieval France and Italy, or of Victorian England, have more to
teach us if they are heard as a chorus than as soloists. But if the themes
I have identified as linking them – the forensic or apologetic theme in
the case of Abelard, Dante and Petrarch; the 'focal' theme in that of
Mill, Newman and Darwin, as minds representative of the age – are
topical, they are not only topical, because they can I suggest be found
in varying dosages in literary autobiography in general. They
contribute in complementary ways both to the autobiographer's
abnormally large sense of self and to the need which he feels to justify
himself for the enterprise on which he has embarked.

The out-and-out synchronist might of course go further, he might
dismember his chosen authors rather than study them as integers,
selecting what he believes to be the invariables of autobiographical
writing and illustrating these piecemeal, first from one author and
then from another, so that the autobiographers themselves would be
found scattered through the book, to be reassembled only in the
perfunctory form of an entry in the index. In the case of autobiography, dissemination of this kind would be a particular outrage,
for reasons that I have gone into in the Introduction. The
autobiographer writes in order to be received whole by those who

read him; and the Common Reader at least reads autobiography in order to grasp the author as a whole – as if the reader's own integrity were being played back at him by the text. This wholeness may very well be fantasmal, and those theorists be right who argue that by its very nature a text denies rather than authenticates any notion of the writer as an integral being; but it is a fantasm shared by auto-biographers and readers alike and a crucial if unstated clause in the hypothetical 'contract' that binds them. To behave as if it were of no account is to ignore the real conditions under which autobiography has always so far been written and received. The fortunes of autobiography are tied to the fortunes of the philosophies and ideologies of individualism that first helped it into existence and which have long sustained it in the West, and these show no signs of weakening; to approach autobiography in a spirit of deconstructive bile, out of dislike for the political, social and religious belief systems which can be invoked to explain it, is a sterile act of ill-will.

If it is the case, then, that the twenty-five or so canonical autobiographies studied here in extenso reveal a certain convergence, in what does that certain convergence lie? Above all, in the determination with which every one of these writers marks him or herself off from other people, as an individual who has come to distinction in life by his or her own efforts and by the exercise of an essentially natural endowment. The autobiographical hero rises and in order to do so breaks ranks with the stage army of the anonymous, or that undifferentiated human mass whose members may be assumed to have no story to tell. A notion I have found myself coming back to time and again in these pages is that of the 'turn', to refer to some dramatic reorientation of the life being narrated. As a narrative device such 'turns' are commonplace, and for the autobiographer they are the rhetorical means by which, in Stephen A. Shapiro's elegant phrase, 'Life's long arcs become the sharp angles of literature.'[2] They serve to enhance and accelerate the tempo of the life-process. But in autobiography turning-points are more than simply dramatic, for whoever turns turns first away from and then towards, in a movement of dissociation followed – or accompanied – by one of reassociation. This movement reflects that entailed in the

[2] Stephen A. Shapiro, 'The dark continent of literature', in *Comparative Literary Studies*, Vol.5, No.4, December 1968, p. 439.

autobiographical act itself, to perform which the writer must first turn away from society, in a protracted if necessarily intermittent withdrawal into the self, subsequently to turn back towards society qua autobiographer, who offers to the world, or it may be to posterity, a text that will be the means of his recuperation by the community. Augustine's 'turn' from paganism to Christianity, or Newman's from Anglicanism to Roman Catholicism, or the 'turn' effected by Alfieri from the thoughtless life of a gallant to the thoughtful life of a tragedian, are less narrative 'events' than the itineraries of individuals who have broken with one milieu and entered another and in so doing have affirmed their extreme individuality. The specific autobiographical 'turn' is into independence, or even autarky: it is the gesture of Descartes, employing his brief period of seclusion in the *poêle* to repudiate his intellectual heritage and accept in future no authority bar that of his own mind.

Not every autobiographer is prepared to assert this will to independence fortissimo, as Nietzsche does in *Ecce Homo*, or Rousseau in his preamble to the *Confessions*, yet all write conscious throughout of the need to individuate themselves. They use their conspicuousness as the subject of their narrative constantly to differentiate themselves from others, revelling like Freud, or Nabokov, or Vico in the fissiparous process by which they have avoided lasting identification with any group or party; or else failing absurdly like Sartre to persuade us that he is no different from any one else at the end of a book in writing which he has proved just the opposite. No two human individuals, we are told, are genetically identical, so perhaps we have been sanctioned by Nature to pursue our sublunary individuation, in order to fulfil by the manner in which we live the scientific axiom that ontogeny recapitulates phylogeny. In which case, the autobiographer may be taken as that exemplary figure who shows us how individuation is achieved.

He does so, let us not forget, on paper, the most momentous 'turn' of all which the autobiographer takes being that from life to language. The singularization of which he is the glorious subject is an effect of narrative or of writing, it takes place in front of us. In his perverse attempt to divest himself of the glory and singularity attaching to the writer, Sartre is giving the autobiographical game away, since were he absolutely serious in his wish to merge anonymously into the proletarian crowd he could but take the road of silence, instead of further distinguishing himself as someone whose desire for political correctness is so extreme as to lead him to abjure his distinctiveness. Autobiographers are not reporting on the process of their singularization, they are performing it. But this is not a process about which they can be altogether easy because it involves them in what in any society in which autobiography has been practised would be looked upon as deviancy were it not sanctioned by its status as literature: they are engaged on an exhibition of self which if it took other than a literary form would be adjudged anti-social. The autobiographer is guilty of having stepped out of line. The inaugural movement characteristic of the genre is the *écart* of which Leiris writes, or that deviation from the prosaic which marks him out as a singular being and consequently as a perilously isolated one.

I propose that the autobiographer be seen, therefore, as both the transgressor of certain norms of society and as the licensed apologist for his transgression: in the final resort, as a contentedly guilty egotist. This view finds strong support from the fascinating research currently being done into the place which narrative has in our everyday lives by the American psychologist Jerome Bruner and his associates.[3] Bruner is interested not in the elite product of literary autobiography but in 'autobiography' in its plainest, usually oral form, of the partial accounts that people give of their lives to others, whether anecdotal, as in a conversational exchange, or more formal, as when interviewed by a sociologist or oral historian.[4] His theory, much simplified, is that narrative is a prime means of cultural bonding, which we use both to integrate ourselves with our culture and also to make sense of what is going on around us. As we grow up and are socialized we become steeped in narrative. It is through narrative that cultural norms are inculcated in the young and preserved through time; but, Bruner argues, it is by means of narrative also that 'breaches' or departures from the norm are resolved. A part of the purpose of his research is thus to

show how human beings, in interacting with one another, form a sense of the canonical and ordinary as a background against which to interpret and give narrative meaning to breaches in and deviations from 'normal' states of the

---

[3] This research is summarized in short and attractive compass in Jerome Bruner, *Acts of Meaning* (Cambridge, Mass., and London, 1990).

[4] Bruner is also interested, as I know from a conversation with him, in the ways in which 'autobiography' of this kind may be used in courts of law, when people are asked to account for their indictable actions. This is a remarkable and instructive throwback to the contention of Georg Misch, that autobiography originated as a written form in fifth-century Athens, with the 'defence' of Isocrates (see p. 49).

human condition. Such narrative explications have the effect of framing the idiosyncratic in a 'lifelike' fashion that can promote negotiation and avoid confrontational disruption and strife.[5]

It is excellent to be reminded from outside of literature as narrowly conceived that autobiography is an act rooted in daily life, in the broad, social-psychological sense that the 'autobiographical' is a mode of discourse into which we all of us continually enter and for the ambivalent reason to which Bruner points, in order simultaneously to flaunt and exonerate our idiosyncrasies. As a psychological phenomenon, literary autobiography is no different in kind from these mundane, spontaneous and formally crude resorts to the mode of the autobiographical; it performs the same duplicitous function of normalizing the singular. It does so, on the other hand, in a manner so elaborate as greatly to enhance the impression of singularity at the expense of that of a recovered normality, because by the prestige and perdurability of his narrative the literary autobiographer may seem to be removing himself even further from our midst.

[5] Bruner, *Acts of Meaning*, p. 67.

Index